WOMEN AND MUSICAL SALONS IN THE ENLIGHTENMENT

Women and Musical Salons in the Enlightenment

REBECCA CYPESS

The University of Chicago Press Chicago & London

The University of Chicago Press, Chicago 60637
The University of Chicago Press, Ltd., London

Published 2022
Printed in the United States of America

31 30 29 28 27 26 25 24 23 22   1 2 3 4 5

ISBN-13: 978-0-226-81791-0 (cloth)
ISBN-13: 978-0-226-81792-7 (e-book)
DOI: https://doi.org/10.7208/chicago/9780226817927.001.0001

This book has been supported by the Margarita M. Hanson Fund and the General Publications Fund of the American Musicological Society, funded in part by the National Endowment for the Humanities and the Andrew W. Mellon Foundation.

Library of Congress Cataloging-in-Publication Data

Names: Cypess, Rebecca, author.
Title: Women and musical salons in the Enlightenment / Rebecca Cypess.
Description: Chicago : University of Chicago Press, 2022. | Includes bibliographical references and index.
Identifiers: LCCN 2021046151 | ISBN 9780226817910 (cloth) | ISBN 9780226817927 (e-book)
Subjects: LCSH: Women musicians—Europe—History—18th century. | Women composers—Europe—History—18th century. | Women music patrons—Europe—History—18th century. | Women music patrons—United States—History—18th century. | Salons—Europe—History—18th century. | Salons—United States—History—18th century. | Music—Europe—18th century—History and criticism. | Music—United States—18th century—History and criticism.
Classification: LCC ML82.C96 2022 | DDC 780.82/09033—dc23
LC record available at https://lccn.loc.gov/2021046151

♾ This paper meets the requirements of ANSI/NISO Z39.48-1992 (Permanence of Paper).

To Ellen Rosand,
who cultivates and encourages her students as if she were the salonnière and we her habitués

*

Contents

*

*

Figures, Musical Examples, and Audio Examples

Figures

Musical Examples

Audio Examples

Audio examples are indicated in the text by the symbol ♫ and may be accessed at http://press.uchicago.edu/sites/cypess.

*

Acknowledgments

I am indebted to the many colleagues, collaborators, friends, and family members who inspired and enabled me to write this book. My work on women and musical salons began in 2014 with a very fruitful collaboration with Nancy Sinkoff, with whom I organized a conference on Sara Levy that included my first concert on this theme and that led to the publication of a collection of essays, *Sara Levy's World: Gender, Judaism, and the Bach Tradition in Enlightenment Berlin*, as well as the recording *In Sara Levy's Salon*. Nancy's initial encouragement and faith in my ability to contribute something to this field was invaluable. From 2018 to 2021 I had the privilege of collaborating with Jennifer Jones as co-conveners of the working group "Experiencing the Salon," supported by the Center for Cultural Analysis at Rutgers and its directors—first Henry Turner and then Colin Jager. This working group, which culminated in the conference "The Salon and the Senses in the Long Eighteenth Century," shaped my understanding of Enlightenment-era salons and *salonnières* significantly; I have benefited more than I can say from Jennifer's expertise, insight, and generosity, as well as from that of Christopher Cartmill, Lorraine Piroux, Jennifer Tamas, and the other participants. To all the members of this small but enthusiastic intellectual community, I am deeply grateful.

Equally important in shaping my thinking about the subject of this book have been my collaborators in performance—especially Dongmyung Ahn, Sonya Headlam, Eve Miller, Yi-heng Yang, and Steven Zohn. I am thankful that these remarkable musicians have been willing to test salon repertoire and performance practices with me; the results of this experimentation can be heard in the audio examples throughout this book and in the three recordings that we have produced to this point. I also wish to thank Erin Banholzer, Loren Stata, and Geoffrey Silver for lending their expertise in the release of those recordings. I am grateful to Malcolm Bilson, whose teachings have continued to resonate as I have worked through the questions of performance practice that this book has raised. I am very fortunate to count him as my teacher.

The concerts and recordings that went into this book have been supported by the American Musicological Society, the American Philosophical Society's lecture series and its library, Chamber Music America, the Hadassah-Brandeis Institute, the Robert M. Hauser Family Foundation, the Mason Gross School of the Arts at Rutgers University, and the Rutgers Research Council. Additional funding to support portions of the research that went into this book was provided by a Franklin Research Grant from the American Philosophical Society and a grant from the Music and Letters Trust.

I have received helpful feedback on various portions of this book from numerous colleagues. I am thankful to Chiara Cillerai, Yoel Greenberg, Bruce Gustafson, Matthew Head, Edward Klorman, Annette Richards, Paolo Scartoni, Susan Wollenberg, Neal Zaslaw, and the anonymous reviewers of this manuscript for their very helpful comments and advice on matters small and large. Steven Zohn may not remember this, but it was in conversation with him that I first floated the idea of a complete book dedicated to the subject of musical salons; his encouragement set me on this path. The influence of my teachers can be discerned throughout this book; these include Rebecca Harris-Warrick, James Hepokoski, Robert Holzer, Donald Irving, and James Webster. I have also benefited from the discussions generated by presentations of material from the book at conferences of the American Musicological Society and the Association for Jewish Studies as well as lectures and lecture-recitals at Case Western Reserve University, Catholic University of America, Duke University, the Historical Performance Program of the Juilliard School, and Temple University. I am grateful to Robin Leaver, who edited the volume of *Bach Perspectives* in which an earlier version of chapter 5 appeared, and whose suggestions improved that material dramatically. It goes without saying that any remaining flaws in the book are entirely my own.

I have been very fortunate to have colleagues at Rutgers who have been willing to talk through research questions with me; in particular, I thank Nicholas Chong, Eduardo Herrera, Douglas Johnson, Steven Kemper, and

Nancy Rao for sharing their time and ideas so generously. I am also grateful to Peggy Barbarite, William Berz, Chris Delgado, Ximena Dilizia, Robert Grohman, Ellen Leibowitz, Patty Mancuso, Dave Miller, Mark Piotrowski, and Kevin Viscariello, with whom I had the good fortune to work intensively between 2018 and 2020, and whose unfailing good humor kept me sane as I sought to balance my research and teaching with administration. I also wish to thank Jason Geary, Dean of the Mason Gross School of the Arts, for entrusting me with a new leadership position and enabling me to continue my research as a complement to it. My students, past and present, have likewise been a source of inspiration and ideas; I am especially indebted to Albert Bellefeuille, Ko On Chan, Joshua Druckenmiller, Michael Goetjen, Rachael Lansang, Angelique Mouyis, MyungJin Oh, Dena Orkin, Rachel Horner, and Schuyler Thornton. Lynette Bowring deserves special mention, as always, for her brilliance and generosity, as well as for the meticulous care that she took in helping edit this volume and for the beautiful typesetting of its musical examples.

This book could not have been completed without the assistance of the many librarians and archivists who helped me gain access to sources or who answered questions about them. Jonathan Sauceda, former performing arts librarian at Rutgers University, has been of immeasurable help in this respect, as have the many librarians and staff members at Mabel Smith Douglass Library. I am very grateful to Patrick Spero (Library of the American Philosophical Society), James Green (Library Company of Philadelphia), Sarah Heim (Historical Society of Pennsylvania), and Roland Schmidt-Hensel (Staatsbibliothek zu Berlin), who have helped me with specific requests related to manuscripts and primary documentation. I am also indebted to the many libraries that have made materials freely available online, foremost among these the Bibliothèque Nationale of France. Especially during the Covid-19 pandemic, access to documents through websites such as gallica.fr, imslp.org, archive.org, and Google Books has been essential. I offer particular thanks to Cristina Ghirardini for sharing images and information about the Nicolini manuscript discussed in chapter 6. Special thanks are due to Marta Tonegutti of the University of Chicago Press for her encouragement and advice, to Marianne Tatom for her expert copyediting, and to Dylan Montanari, Caterina MacLean, and the entire team at the press for their assistance with all the logistical matters that go into making a book.

The greatest debt I owe is to my family. I thank my parents, Dr. Roberta Rubel Schaefer and Dr. David Lewis Schaefer, who endowed me with a love of learning, gave me the best education I could imagine, and continue to shower me with the unconditional love that has allowed me to thrive both personally and intellectually. For eighteen years, my parents-in-law, Dr. Sandra Messinger Cypess and Dr. Raymond Cypess, have treated me as their own daughter; I am grateful for their love, intellectual stimulation, and logistical support. My husband, Rabbi Dr. Joshua Cypess, has been my fiercest advocate and the most wonderful companion I could ask for. That he is also an ardent feminist has helped propel this book project forward. In our three children, Ben, Joey, and Sally, I see the brilliance, generosity, kindness, and love that the next generation is going to need, and I am endlessly grateful that I have the privilege of watching them grow up.

It is impossible for me to think about women and musical salons without connecting them to my advisor, Ellen Rosand, who has taught all her graduate students as if she were the *salonnière* and we her *habitués*. She has cultivated each of us according to our individual talents and tastes, and our successes are the result of her guiding hand. Often since leaving graduate school, I have called Ellen in frustration because I felt unable to answer a question, choose a direction, or organize my ideas. She always knows how to ask just the right question to make the problem solve itself. In addition, she has been an unfailing source of encouragement as I have, since graduate school, sought to do my work while raising a family. For these and countless other reasons, I am grateful for Ellen's guidance and support, and I dedicate this book to her with my deep admiration and thanks.

Rebecca Cypess
June 2021
Highland Park, New Jersey

*

Introduction

Wolfgang Amadeus Mozart's first tour of Europe, organized by his father and undertaken when the boy was only seven years old, incorporated not one, but two stops in Paris—the first toward the beginning of their journey (November 1763–April 1764) and the second toward the end (May–July 1766). Paris was among the most progressive and fashionable cities in Europe, a destination for travelers interested in art, music, literature, philosophy, science, clothing, food, and more. For the prodigious Mozart, to be seen, heard, and lauded in Paris was to be vaulted to a new level of fame and achievement. The tour was a success and established for the family a network of connections that would prove fruitful later on. Madame Geoffrin, who, as Dena Goodman has argued, helped define the Enlightenment salon as an institution, hosted the traveling Mozarts in her salon and heard them perform there.[1] Two years later, she wrote a letter of recommendation on their behalf to Prince Wenzel Kaunitz, a diplomat who became a driving force behind the spread of salon culture in Vienna: "I have learned that someone named the little Mozart, called the little prodigy in music, was in Vienna with his father . . . The father and all his family, being very *honnêtes* people, were generally well-regarded in Paris, and in particular by several people of my acquaintance, who thought very highly of the virtues of the

1. On Geoffrin's role in the creation of eighteenth-century salon culture, see Dena Goodman, *The Republic of Letters: A Cultural History of the French Enlightenment* (Ithaca, NY, and London: Cornell University Press, 1994).

father and the talent of the children. Deign, my prince, to place this *honnête* family in the shade of your wings."[2]

Madame Geoffrin's letter demonstrates the impact that a salon performance could have on the life of a professional musician. Although she was apparently not trained in music herself,[3] musical education had become *de rigueur* for the aristocratic and middle classes of eighteenth-century Europe. Nevertheless, for women of her social position, public musical displays were socially problematic, and even true "practice" or exhibitions of effort in music could be perceived as incongruous with their standing as members of the leisured elite. However, hosting professional musicians such as the Mozarts was expected of influential women: Geoffrin was an arbiter of taste, a patroness whose opinion could make or break the career of such aspiring professionals. Musical style, too, was at stake. Musicians performing in the Geoffrin salon would have geared their music-making to the tastes of the *salonnière* and her audience, perhaps also introducing musical innovations that their hostess might enjoy. Geoffrin's assessment of the family as "*honnêtes gens*" implies more than mere "honesty": *honnêteté* also encompassed a sense of grace, taste, and nobility of character. While that characteristic had, in the seventeenth century, been thought of as largely reserved for individuals of noble birth,[4] by the late eighteenth century it

2. "J'ai appris qu'un nommé le petit Mozart, dit le *petit prodige* en musique, était à Vienna avec son père . . . Le père étant, et toute sa famille, de fort honnêtes gens, ils ont été généralement considérés à Paris, et en particulier de plusieurs personnes de ma connaissance, qui faisaient un très grand cas des vertus du père et des talents des enfants. Daignez, mon prince, mettre cette honnête famille à l'ombre de vos ailes." Letter quoted in Pierre Marie Maurice Henri, Marquis de Ségur, *Le royaume de la rue Saint-Honoré: Madame Geoffrin et sa fille* (Paris: Calmann Lévy, 1897), 61. Translations are mine unless otherwise indicated. On Kaunitz's role in spreading the institution of the salon along the French model in Vienna, see John Van Horn Melton, "School, Stage, Salon: Musical Cultures in Haydn's Vienna," *Journal of Modern History* 76, no. 2 (June 2004): 274.

3. Henri, *Le royaume de la rue Saint-Honoré*, 8.

4. On seventeenth-century French salons, see Elizabeth C. Goldsmith, *Exclusive Conversations: The Art of Interaction in Seventeenth-Century France* (Philadelphia: University of Pennsylvania Press, 1988); Goldsmith argues that while seventeenth-century salons sought to project an image of erasing hierarchies, they were highly exclusive. See also Benedetta Craveri, *The Age of Conversation*, trans. Teresa Waugh (New York: New York Review Books, 2005), which traces the development of French salons from the seventeenth through the eighteenth centuries. On music in these salons, see, for example, Catherine Gordon-Seifert, *Music and the Language of Love: Seventeenth-Century French Airs*

Figure 0.1 Michel Barthelemy Ollivier (or Olivier), *Tea at the house of the Princesse de Conti, Palais du Temple* (1766). Château de Versailles, France / Bridgeman Images.

was understood to be accessible even to the professional classes through the cultivation of a noble mind.

That Geoffrin's friends—other noblemen and -women—likewise approved of the Mozarts added support to her recommendation that the recipient of her letter help the family establish itself within the musical circles of Vienna. A painting of the young Mozart in another Parisian salon—that of Marie-Charlotte Hippolyte de Campet de Saujon, mistress of the Prince de Conti—confirms his status among the aristocracy (fig. 0.1). Here the diminutive Wolfgang appears seated on the harpsichord bench next to the famed singer Pierre Jélyotte, preparing to entertain his hosts and their guests.

While Geoffrin's salon featured musical entertainments, music was not

(Bloomington and Indianapolis: Indiana University Press, 2011), ch. 7, "Salon Culture and the Mid-Seventeenth-Century French Air."

its primary focus. However, since the hostess of each salon set the agenda for her gatherings, determining what was done and what was discussed, *salonnières* with a particular talent or taste for music had the discretion to place music at the center of their activities. In these cases, music might alternate in the salon with conversation, reading aloud, theatricals, dining, dancing, games, and other activities. Moreover, within the salon, women themselves were free to display their own musical talents. Hostesses of musical salons participated in a range of musical activities, including patronage of composers; listening and informed criticism; collection of scores and instruments; performance on keyboards, harps, guitars, and in some exceptional cases, violins, cellos, flutes, clarinets, and other wind instruments, largely within the salon but in some cases outside it as well; composition; and even publication of original works.[5] The extent to which each salon hostess engaged in these activities—and the ways in which she exceeded the normal boundaries of her salon, allowing her musical activities to enter the more clearly public sphere—says a great deal about her social situation and aesthetic values.

Salons in the second half of the eighteenth century as a whole are a problematic category, if, indeed, they can be conceived of as a category at all. Social and cultural historians have long grappled with complex historical and historiographical issues surrounding salons, attempting to define and understand them. In fact, salons' resistance to definition is part of what gave them their allure during the eighteenth century: despite their regularity and formulaic conventions of behavior and discourse, most salons projected an air of the "natural"—that key Enlightenment concept—which, like *honnêteté*, encompassed grace, ease, and fluidity even as it attended to social mores and conventions of behavior.[6] Contemporary records are scarce and

5. On the conventions that dictated which types of instruments had "feminine" associations, see Richard Leppert, *Music and Image: Domesticity, Ideology, and Socio-Cultural Formation in Eighteenth-Century England* (Cambridge: Cambridge University Press, 1988). An example of a salon hostess who, unusually, played and composed for wind instruments is the Duchess Anna Amalia of Braunschweig-Wolfenbüttel.

6. Denis Diderot folded all these concepts together in his combined definitions of "Bien, (*homme de*) *homme d'honneur, honnête homme*." As he wrote, "It seems to me that an *homme de bien* is he who precisely satisfies the precepts of his religion; the *homme d'honneur*, he who follows rigorously the laws and usages of society; and the *honnête homme*, he who never loses sight, in any of his actions, of the principles of natural equity. The *homme de bien* acts charitably; the *homme d'honneur* never defaults on his promise; the *honnête homme* renders justice, even to his enemy." ("Il me semble que l'*homme de bien* est celui qui satisfait

fragmentary; recollections composed after the fact must be viewed with a skeptical eye. Moreover, the specific proceedings of eighteenth-century salons, as well as their role in a broader social and cultural landscape, were highly variable. While the institution apparently grew out of Parisian practices of the seventeenth century, as they spread across Europe and into America, their agendas and constitutions changed as they merged with local customs and circumstances, as well as the tastes and interests of individual *salonnières*.

Despite all these complexities in the study of salons as a whole, the category of musical salons in particular is worthy of consideration, and indeed, it offers a new perspective on Enlightenment musical culture as a whole. By thinking about musical salons both as an international phenomenon and through individual case studies that attend to the specific circumstances and interests of each *salonnière*, I demonstrate that musical salons played a crucial role in shaping the musical landscape of the late eighteenth century.

This book is about musical salons between roughly 1760 and 1800, and the women who hosted, governed, and made music in them. Recognizing that there were no clearly drawn lines separating "musical salons" from "salons" as a whole, I define the phenomenon broadly as salons in which the hostess displayed a strong interest in music and in which music figured prominently in the proceedings. I draw on the work of historians who have treated the Enlightenment salon as a general institution—its history, gender and social dynamics, and its role in the thought and experience of the Enlightenment—as well as studies by musicologists who have addressed salons among many other aspects of musical life during this period, to develop a new understanding of the role of salons in contributing to and defining musical culture. As I will argue, musical salons in the Enlightenment represented a crucial component in the fabric of musical life, yet one that is little understood today. In an age when musical culture was in flux, musical salons served as a mediating force, bringing together professional

---

exactement aux préceptes de sa religion; l'*homme d'honneur*, celui qui suit rigoureusement les lois & les usages de la société; & l'*honnête homme*, celui qui ne perd de vûe dans aucune de ses actions les principes de l'équité naturelle : l'*homme de bien* fait des aumônes; l'*homme d'honneur* ne manque point à sa promesse; l'*honnête homme* rend la justice, même à son ennemi.") Denis Diderot, "Bien, (*homme de*) *homme d'honneur, honnête homme*," in *Encyclopédie, ou dictionnaire raisonné des sciences, des arts et des métiers, etc.*, ed. Denis Diderot and Jean le Rond d'Alembert (University of Chicago: ARTFL Encyclopédie Project, Autumn 2017 ed.), ed. Robert Morrissey and Glenn Roe, http://encyclopedie.uchicago.edu (accessed August 5, 2019), 2:244.

musicians and their audiences of patrons, listeners, and performers.[7] Salons constituted a testing ground for new musical styles, genres, and aesthetic ideals. They represented a site of musical experimentation, innovation, retrospection, introspection, and, perhaps most importantly, musical sociability.

Developments in broader musical culture during this period found expression in the musical salon, and the musical salon played a crucial role in effecting those changes in the public sphere. Among these developments were the rise of new genres and styles of composition, the idea of musical education as an enlightening and educative force, the practice of music criticism and the cultivation of "taste," and the rise of musical historicism. As systems of patronage associated with courtly life and the church began to dissolve, musical salons provided a fruitful new meeting ground for professional musicians and potential patrons, in which musical practices and compositions could be worked out through live discussion and experimentation and in conjunction with novel instruments and personalized taste and performance practices. With a cosmopolitan nature fostered by travel and epistolary exchange that traversed the interior spaces of salons, many musical salons encouraged the spread of ideas, works, and technologies from city to city and from home to home. Local differences prompted discussion and the exchange of ideas.

At the center of this story is the *salonnière* herself. Associated with music-making among their many other avenues of "accomplishment," women used the musical salon as a site of cultural agency. Because of their situation within the home, salons formed an appropriate site for the exercising of female agency. Yet the proceedings of the musical salon invariably spilled out into the public sphere in one way or another. In some cases, women's ideas about music or their particular performance practices found their way into the published works of the professional composers in their circle; in others, women's patronage or their tastes shaped the course of the

7. Throughout this study, I will use the word "performers" to denote players of music. While that word was used in the eighteenth century to refer to the kind of sociable music-making that went on in salons, as other writers have amply demonstrated, it accumulated problematic associations in subsequent years. Today, the term connotes a "frontal" mode of presentation, in which players appear formally onstage while listeners sit silently and passively in the dark. As I will discuss in subsequent chapters, music-making in salons was far more informal, with the lines between composer, performer, and listener not yet clearly defined. I use the terms "performer" and "performance" out of linguistic necessity and not to call these later connotations to mind.

musical careers of people and institutions around them; in still others, salon hostesses stepped out into the public sphere themselves.

The historiography of salons as a whole, including musical salons, is fraught. One issue lies in its definition: in eighteenth-century usage, the term "salon" most often referred to a space—a living room or parlor where social gatherings occurred. It was only in the nineteenth century that the regular gatherings that took place within domestic parlors came to be referred to widely as "salons"; this was as true in France as it was throughout the rest of Europe and its colonies. (A precedent for the usage of the term to denote an artistic assembly, albeit one with a very different set of social connotations, lies in the French Academy's artistic exhibitions known as *Salons*, which took place starting in the mid-eighteenth century.) In English a salon gathering could be called a "conversation," "conversazione," or "rout"; in French an *assemblée* or *cercle*; in Italian a *conversazione*; in Spanish a *tertulia*; in German they might be called a *Teetisch* (tea table) or *Akademie*; they might also simply be thought of—and referred to—as social visits with friends. The variety of words used to describe salon gatherings reflects the myriad purposes and characters that such gatherings took on. Given the inconsistency of the historical terminology, using the single term "salon" is problematic. However, I adopt it here for two reasons: first, it has been applied by historians and musicologists throughout much of the secondary literature; and second, it has the advantage of highlighting the continuities among these institutions across multiple geographical regions, which might otherwise go undetected.[8] While the terminology might be flexible, the institution itself, in all its flexible forms, was real and significant.

Another reason for the historiographical problems around salons was their exclusivity. Guests generally needed a personal connection to the *salonnière* or an introduction through a credible connection to and invitation via one of the salon's *habitués*. In addition, salon proceedings were necessarily informal and ephemeral. In contrast to male-dominated academies, which often kept formal records of discussions and activities, salons rarely included such record-keeping. Moreover, many of the experiences of salons were sensual in nature, and thus resisted verbal or written description. This is certainly true of musical salons, where the act of listening assumed primary importance.

8. On the problems with the salon terminology, see, for example, Antoine Lilti, *The World of the Salons: Sociability and Worldliness in Eighteenth-Century Paris*, trans. Lydia G. Cochrane (Oxford: Oxford University Press, 2015), 1–91.

Long the subject of romantic fantasy, salons were, in the nineteenth century and much of the twentieth, viewed through the lenses of the individual historians writing about them. (This is doubtless still true to some extent, since the persona and perspective of the historian—the present writer included—can never be separated from her subject.[9]) Salons were made to represent the agenda of the historian: thus, at the beginning of salon historiography, the brothers Edmond and Jules de Goncourt, reflecting late nineteenth-century anxieties about French dominance and masculinity, condemned eighteenth-century salons, along with eighteenth-century women as a whole, for the outsized influence that they wielded through their uncontrolled sensuality and selfishness.[10] More recent writers have viewed salons from the perspectives of the intellectual life that they fostered, their social continuity with other institutions of the public sphere, and the principles of religious tolerance that they (sometimes exaggeratedly) were thought to embody.[11]

The study of musical salons in the eighteenth century has been more haphazard and, I think, incomplete. While musical salons of the eighteenth century have been considered in the context of the careers of the (predominantly male) composers who attended them, only in a handful of cases have these musical salons been considered at any length on their own terms, and from the perspective of the *salonnières* who hosted them. Among the models that I follow are Elisabeth Le Guin's brilliant essay "A Visit to the Salon de Parnasse," which offers a script based on primary sources that enacts

9. An explication of subjectivity, especially of moral and political values, in historical writing is in Frank R. Ankersmit, *Meaning, Truth, and Reference in Historical Representation* (Ithaca, NY: Cornell University Press, 2012), 220–44.

10. See Edmond de Goncourt and Jules de Goncourt, *The Woman of the Eighteenth Century: Her Life, from Birth to Death, Her Love and Her Philosophy in the Worlds of Salon, Shop and Street*, trans. Jacques Le Clercq and Ralph Roeder (New York: Routledge, 2013 [reprint]). On the context of the Goncourt brothers' writings, see Karen Offen, *The Woman Question in France, 1400–1870* (Cambridge and New York: Cambridge University Press, 2017), 28–31.

11. See, for example, Goodman, *The Republic of Letters*; Deborah Hertz, *Jewish High Society in Old Regime Berlin* (New Haven, CT: Yale University Press, 1988); Steven Kale, *French Salons: High Society and Political Sociability from the Old Regime to the Revolution of 1848* (Baltimore: Johns Hopkins University Press, 2004); Verena von der Heyden-Rynsch, *Europäische Salons: Höhepunkte einer versunkenen weiblichen Kultur* (Munich: Artemis & Winkler, 1992); and Ulrike Weckel, "A Lost Paradise of Female Culture? Some Critical Questions Regarding the Scholarship on Late Eighteenth- and Early Nineteenth-Century German Salons," *German History* 18, no. 3 (2000): 310–36.

a musical evening in a French salon; and Sarah Day-O'Connell's equally masterful interpretation of the convergence of musical, poetic, and anatomical considerations in the salon of Anne Home Hunter, wife of the surgeon John Hunter.[12] As Le Guin and Day-O'Connell show, situating musical salons within the eighteenth-century cultural and intellectual landscape is no simple matter, in part because *salonnières* did not observe clearly defined boundaries between disciplines of the arts and sciences; such boundaries, indeed, were blurry until the nineteenth century. Thus, capturing the full character and import of musical salons requires that we think across these disciplinary boundaries. While music lies at the center of this study, then, I also engage, by necessity, with other arts, sciences, and cultural practices.

Acknowledging this need for interdisciplinary engagement, my study of musical salons builds on the approach taken by recent scholars in literature and art history as well as social history.[13] I have also been involved in past publications in interdisciplinary salon history, serving as co-editor of a volume on Sara Levy, a Jewish *salonnière* in Berlin with close connections to the Bach family, who warrants treatment from the complementary perspectives of musicology and Jewish studies, among other disciplines.[14] In some respects, the study of musical salons in the nineteenth century provides a model for my work, although salon culture changed dramatically in the nineteenth century; for example, a recent volume titled *Musical Salon Culture in the Long Nineteenth Century* presents fascinating case studies of musical salons that attend to the experiences, priorities, and musicianship of individual *salonnières*.[15] This and other recent work points to the great

12. Elisabeth Le Guin, "A Visit to the Salon de Parnasse," in *Haydn and the Performance of Rhetoric*, ed. Tom Beghin and Sander M. Goldberg (Chicago and London: University of Chicago Press, 2007, 14–35); Sarah Day-O'Connell, "The Composer, the Surgeon, His Wife and Her Poems: Haydn and the Anatomy of the English Canzonetta," *Eighteenth-Century Music* 6, no. 1 (2009): 77–112.

13. Specific references will be given in individual chapters; one example is Gillen D'Arcy Wood, "The Female Penseroso: Anna Seward, Sociable Poetry, and the Handelian Consensus," *Modern Language Quarterly* 67, no. 4 (December 2006): 451–77.

14. Rebecca Cypess and Nancy Sinkoff, eds., *Sara Levy's World: Gender, Judaism, and the Bach Tradition in Enlightenment Berlin* (Rochester, NY: University of Rochester Press, 2018).

15. See Anja Bunzel and Natasha Loges, eds., *Musical Salon Culture in the Long Nineteenth Century* (Woodbridge, UK: Boydell Press, 2019). The editors' introduction suggests that the major sea change that led to the ascendency and influence of musical salon life took place as a result of the French Revolution (2). But musical salons reflecting an enlightened,

potential of this field for interpreting little-understood aspects of musical life outside of the public eye.

When scholars of eighteenth-century musical practice and culture have discussed salons in any depth, such discussions have most often considered the role of salons in cultivating the careers of the professional composers who attended them, most of whom were men. This is certainly true in the case of Anne-Louise Boyvin d'Hardancourt Brillon de Jouy (1744–1824), cited frequently in histories of music because of her connections to the likes of Benjamin Franklin, Charles Burney, Luigi Boccherini, and others, but whose compositions have lain, known but neglected, in the archive of the American Philosophical Society; they have received only a small amount of scholarly attention, few performances, and even fewer commercial recordings.[16] Alternatively, *salonnières* who composed music have sometimes been cast solely as "women composers"—a category that seems to set them in competition with professional male musicians—although the situation of the salon was their primary locus of musical activity, and one in which they were able to present themselves without fear of social stigma. Thus Marianna Martines is referred to as a "woman composer in the Vienna of Mozart and Haydn," rather than a *salonnière* at the center of an elite musical institution in (her own) Vienna.[17] In many other cases, the women at

republican agenda existed not only in France, but in other locations across Europe and America, from at least the 1760s.

16. Since the initial work of cataloguing and assessing Brillon's work was done by Bruce Gustafson in the late 1980s, musicologists have seldom engaged with it at all; I will suggest some reasons for this in chapter 3. See Bruce Gustafson, "The Music of Madame Brillon: A Unified Manuscript Collection from Benjamin Franklin's Circle," *Notes* 43, no. 3 (March 1987): 522–43; and Bruce Gustafson, "Madame Brillon et son salon," *Revue de musicologie* 2 (1999): 297–332. A biography of Brillon written from the perspective of a cultural historian and not a musicologist is Christine de Pas, *Madame Brillon de Jouy et son salon: une musicienne des Lumières, intime de Benjamin Franklin* (Pantin: Petit page, 2014). See also Claude-Anne Lopez, *Mon cher papa: Franklin and the Ladies of Paris* (New Haven, CT: Yale University Press, 1990). A documentary film exploring Benjamin Franklin's life in Paris and his relationship with Madame Brillon is *Benjamin Franklin: Citizen of Two Worlds* (New York: Phoenix/BFA Films & Video, 1979), written and directed by Meredith Martindale and Toby Molenaar, and produced by Stanley Cohen and Olivier Frapier. Excerpts from the recording that I made with the Raritan Players titled *In the Salon of Madame Brillon* (Acis Productions, 2021) will serve as the audio examples for chapter 3; it includes multiple world premiere recordings of compositions by Brillon.

17. Irving Godt, *Marianna Martines: A Woman Composer in the Vienna of Mozart and Haydn*, ed. John A. Rice (Rochester, NY: University of Rochester Press, 2010).

the center of salons appear as flattened caricatures. If such characterizations seem to echo aspects of the writing of eighteenth-century men such as Charles Burney, who wrote of women in unfailingly glowing, and perhaps, as a result, two-dimensional terms, they also fail to treat the more specific evidence that men such as Burney did provide as important historical documents. Yet accounts such as Burney's must be handled with care, not only because their hyperbolic writing renders them suspect, but also because the perspective of male critics, by definition, presents only part of the story.[18] A more emic approach to musical salons necessitates engagement with first-person accounts by *salonnières*; such documents survive in some cases but have often been overlooked. In other cases, these first-person narratives are incomplete or non-existent, such that evidence must be gleaned from unconventional sources, including collections or inventories of scores and evidence of engagement with musical instruments.

The role of women at the center of musical salons of the Enlightenment was not incidental, but crucial. While it is true that some salons were hosted by men (the musical gatherings of the Baron van Swieten and other men in Vienna are notable examples[19]), the vast majority of musical salons were organized and, to use Dena Goodman's term, "governed" by women.[20] As I argue in chapter 1, this foregrounding of women in the context of the musical salon was predicated upon the salon's liminal status, situated between the nascent public and private spheres. The understanding of salons in relation to the public sphere began with Jürgen Habermas, who argued that, during the *ancien régime*, "public" status was identified with royal courts. With the rise of commercialization and the bourgeoisie, the central role of courtly life for the establishment of cultural norms was overtaken by pub-

18. See Matthew Head, *Sovereign Feminine: Music and Gender in Eighteenth-Century Germany* (Berkeley, Los Angeles, and London: University of California Press, 2013), ch. 1, "Europe's Living Muses: Women, Music, and Modernity in Burney's *History* and *Tours*."

19. For a discussion of the musical practices in van Swieten's salon, see Wiebke Thormählen, "Playing with Art: Musical Arrangements as Educational Tools in van Swieten's Vienna," *Journal of Musicology* 27, no. 3 (Summer 2010): 243–76. Accounts of musical salons in Vienna in the late eighteenth century are in Mary Sue Morrow, *Concert Life in Haydn's Vienna: Aspects of a Developing Musical and Social Institution* (Stuyvesant, NY: Pendragon Press, 1989), 1–34. See also Dorothea Link, "Vienna's Private Theatrical and Musical Life, 1783–92, as Reported by Count Karl Zinzendorf," *Journal of the Royal Musical Association* 122, no. 2 (1997): 205–57.

20. See Goodman, *The Republic of Letters*, especially ch. 3, "Governing the Republic of Letters: Salonnières and the Rule(s) of Polite Conversation."

lic institutions such as mass media, coffee houses, and public concert life. For Habermas, the salon was one of these public institutions; together with coffee houses, salons "were centers of criticism—literary at first, then also political—in which began to emerge, between aristocracy and bourgeois intellectuals, a certain parity of the educated."[21] Joan Landes, however, noted that Habermas's work did not account for the experience of women in the public sphere; she argued that, from its inception, "the bourgeois public is essentially, not just contingently, masculinist, and that this characteristic serves to determine both its self-representation and its subsequent 'structural transformation.'"[22] Revolutionizing notions of the public sphere through a gendered reading, Dena Goodman's foundational account of the Republic of Letters in eighteenth-century France built upon Habermas's association of the salon with the public sphere but centered the narrative squarely within the domain of women—especially that of the salon. As Goodman demonstrates, the Republic of Letters in the eighteenth century was the heart of the project of Enlightenment; it was also "the very center of the public sphere."[23] The salon was the Republic's primary locus of discourse, a space where the aristocracy and the literate intelligentsia met to lay out a new agenda of education and reason. Crucially, these meetings were governed by women, who imposed the social order of *politesse* cultivated during the Old Regime onto the discourse of the *philosophes*. As Goodman writes, "The salon gave the Republic of Letters a social base, but even more important, it provided the republic with a source of political order in the person of the salonnière . . . The salonnière had always been crucial to the functioning of the salon; now she became crucial to the project of Enlightenment carried out in and through it."[24]

Subsequently, Antoine Lilti questioned the understanding of salons as situated within the public sphere, arguing that they "functioned according

21. Jürgen Habermas, *The Structural Transformation of the Public Sphere: An Inquiry into a Category of Bourgeois Society*, trans. Thomas Burger with the assistance of Frederick Lawrence (Cambridge, MA: MIT Press, 1991 [reprint]), 32.

22. Joan B. Landes, *Women and the Public Sphere in the Age of the French Revolution* (Ithaca, NY, and London: Cornell University Press, 1988), 7. A more recent statement of Landes's perspectives on these issues is in Joan B. Landes, "Public and Private: Public and Private Lives in Eighteenth-Century France," in *A Cultural History of Women in the Age of Enlightenment*, ed. Ellen Pollak, vol. 4 of *A Cultural History of Women*, general ed. Linda Kalof (London and New York: Bloomsbury Academic, 2013), 121–41.

23. Goodman, *The Republic of Letters*, 14.

24. Goodman, *The Republic of Letters*, 99.

to a dialectic of openness . . . and closure. As a privileged space for female action, the salon differed from the public sphere, without being reduced to the realm of domesticity and family space."[25] This understanding of the salon as a liminal space, bridging the public and private, is, I argue, essential to the study of salons with a distinctively musical agenda because of the strong association between women and domestic music-making in eighteenth-century Europe and America. Generally denied access to systematic education, women encountered obstacles to engagement with the intellectual movements of the Enlightenment; even the *salonnières* whose guests included the luminaries of the philosophical and moral movements of the Enlightenment gained access to knowledge through unsystematic means, including conversation and popular publications. However, women's cultivation of musical talent was socially sanctioned as a practice denoting "accomplishment"—one suitable for the feminine, domestic realm.[26] (Despite this aura of domesticity and the sensual nature of many salon experiences, I will argue in chapter 2 that their salons and their musicianship should indeed be understood within the context of the Enlightenment, which is sometimes figured as a purely intellectual, male-dominated movement.) In music-making in particular, then, women were distinctively poised to mediate between the private and the public realms. This is not to say that their status as authoritative figures in music—or as *authors*—went unchallenged, and indeed, some musical *salonnières* adhered consciously to social norms that discouraged them from seeking overt public recognition. Nevertheless, musical *salonnières* often pressed at the limits of these social norms, consciously entering the public sphere through public performance, published composition, or another authoritative status.

Past trends in music historiography have prevented serious engagement with eighteenth-century salons. Two interrelated aspects of past music historiography—both of which have become outmoded in recent years—stand out as particularly problematic in this context: one is text-centeredness, and the other (an outgrowth of the first) is the nearly exclusive focus on composers who fall easily within the category, developed by and for nineteenth-century critics, of the Romantic genius. Recent work in the

25. Lilti, *The World of the Salons*, 39. A recent study that treats the categories of public and private with respect to music is Edward Klorman, *Mozart's Music of Friends: Social Interplay in the Chamber Works* (Cambridge: Cambridge University Press, 2016), 73–108.

26. The problematics of music as a domestic activity suitable for women of the eighteenth century are explicated in Leppert, *Music and Image*.

cultural history of music has unsettled the primacy of these categories. A foundational study in this respect is Christopher Small's *Musicking*, which encourages engagement with music not as *object*, but as *act*; as Small aptly notes, "even within a literate musical culture such as the Western classical tradition the exclusive concentration on musical works and the relegation of the act of performance to subordinate status has resulted in a severe misunderstanding of what actually takes place during a performance."[27] Building on Small's ideas and the work that he has inspired, one of the aims of this volume is to consider salon experiences as an entirety—including both musical performance and the discussions and other activities that surrounded them—to understand their role in the formation of the musical cultures, practices, and aesthetics of the Enlightenment. This requires engagement not only with notated repertoire, but also with instruments, instrumental sounds and timbres, performance practices, systems of patronage, modes of listening, patterns of discourse, ideas of play, and the other sensual and intellectual experiences that surrounded music-making in eighteenth-century salons. The study of this constellation of topics requires a similarly diverse—and unconventional—constellation of approaches, only some of which hinge on musical texts.

The other problematic aspect of music historiography up to this point has been the near exclusive focus on composers reported to have achieved the status of "genius." Nineteenth-century German critics, seeking the origins and inspirations for the mythical figure of Beethoven, identified Viennese classicism, embodied in the work of Joseph Haydn and Wolfgang Amadeus Mozart, as the most important school of composition in the late eighteenth century. E. T. A. Hoffmann's review of Beethoven's fifth symphony is a *locus classicus* for this argument, as Mark Evan Bonds has noted: "Hoffmann's review was one of the earliest published commentaries to link Haydn, Mozart, and Beethoven in a single breath."[28] However, this narrative, which came to dominate musicological discourse for much of the nineteenth and twentieth centuries, did not reflect the realities of eighteenth-century musical life, as ably demonstrated by writers such as Daniel Heartz and Vanessa Agnew.[29] Vienna was, in many ways, considered a musical backwater in the

27. Christopher Small, *Musicking: The Meanings of Performance and Listening* (Middletown, CT: Wesleyan University Press, 1988), 8.

28. Mark Evan Bonds, *Music as Thought: Listening to the Symphony in the Age of Beethoven* (Princeton, NJ, and Oxford: Princeton University Press, 2006), 34.

29. Daniel Heartz, *Music in European Capitals: The Galant Style, 1720–1780* (New York

eighteenth century, and it is no coincidence that both Mozart and Haydn were associated with cosmopolitan musical salons at various points of their lives. Even the male composers who were superstars of their generation—Johann Adolf Hasse, for example—remain, at best, secondary figures in most narratives of this period. Therefore, in the present historical moment, in which the inequities between men and women that have stubbornly persisted for centuries continue to hold sway, it should come as no surprise that the famed women of eighteenth-century musical life, including the leading *salonnières* of the generation, remain shrouded in obscurity.

How ironic, then, that so many musical *salonnières* were described in their own lifetimes as geniuses. Matthew Head, drawing on the work of historian Sylvana Tomaselli, has cautioned modern readers to be wary of the hyperbolic descriptions of female musicians penned by writers such as Charles Burney. Head argues that such descriptions formed a disingenuous but essential means of validation of European civilization on the part of male critics, who viewed the status of women as an index of the advancement of a society. In this view, "primitive" societies relegated women to inferior status, while "advanced" societies allowed women to flourish in their intellectual and artistic pursuits and placed the most accomplished of their sex on the pedestal of genius. To be sure, writing about women was, like most other forms of writing, formulaic in nature, and it often featured florid exaggeration that downplayed the structural obstacles that women faced in, for example, attaining an education or advancing their careers. In addition, writing about women's achievements often took gender into account; thus Anne-Louise Brillon, the subject of chapter 3, was not simply "one of the greatest players of the harpsichord in Europe," but "one of the greatest *lady-players* of the harpsichord in Europe."[30]

Yet I contend that these formulaic modes of writing should not obscure the more substantive contents of descriptions by Burney and the many other eighteenth-century writers who encountered and praised musical *salonnières*. To be sure, like all historical documents, such descriptions should be read with a critical eye. But if we choose to dismiss them entirely, we run the risk of denying women's achievements and agency altogether. Indeed,

---

and London: W. W. Norton, 2003); Vanessa Agnew, *Enlightenment Orpheus: The Power of Music in Other Worlds* (Oxford: Oxford University Press, 2008), 11–72.

30. Charles Burney, *The Present State of Music in France and Italy: Or, the Journal of a Tour through those Countries, Undertaken to Collect Materials for A General History of Music*, 2nd ed. (London: T. Becket and Co., J. Robson, and G. Robinson, 1773), 43. Italics added.

as Elizabeth Eger has argued, eighteenth-century depictions of real women as "muses" "can be seen as a metonym for women's involvement in the cultural world of their time, conveying at once the centrality and diversity of their public role."[31] Far from negating women's achievement or forcing passivity on them, the conflation of real women with mythical muses in the eighteenth century "belong[s] to a tradition that celebrated the feminine icon as a powerful example of what women might be and do."[32] This is a topic that I will take up more extensively in chapter 6, since the women who are the subjects of that chapter cast themselves as muses. This seems to have been a conscious choice, as it offered them a socially sanctioned avenue for creative expression.

In recent years, scholars writing about eighteenth-century music have moved away from text-centered methodologies. Work by scholars such as Emily I. Dolan on timbre; Deirdre Loughridge on technology, media, and sensory reception; Vanessa Agnew on music as a driving force in the formation of Enlightenment society; and David R. M. Irving on intercultural exchange and the myth of "Western" music has shown the potential of cultural, sensory, and affective histories to illuminate understandings of music in eighteenth-century Europe.[33] Following these examples, I place the cultural institution of the salon at the center of this study. While I draw on musical texts as one body of evidence (including some musical texts that have not yet received serious attention), I engage with a wider array of methods and tools for understanding musical salons on their own terms. In the cases of *salonnières* who were also composers, I attend to their compositions as manifestations of their aesthetic ideals and as evidence of the practices of their salon environments. But I consider musical authorship as a broader

31. Elizabeth Eger, "Representing Culture: 'The Nine Living Muses of Great Britain' (1779)," in *Women, Writing, and the Public Sphere, 1700–1830*, ed. Elizabeth Eger, Charlotte Grant, Clíona Ó Gallchoir, and Penny Warburton (Cambridge: Cambridge University Press, 2001), 126.

32. Eger, "Representing Culture," 111.

33. Emily I. Dolan, *The Orchestral Revolution: Haydn and the Technologies of Timbre* (Cambridge: Cambridge University Press, 2013); Deirdre Loughridge, *Haydn's Sunrise, Beethoven's Shadow: Audiovisual Culture and the Emergence of Musical Romanticism* (Chicago and London: University of Chicago Press, 2016); Agnew, *Enlightenment Orpheus*; and, among others, David R. M. Irving, "Ancient Greeks, World Music, and Early Modern Constructions of Western European Identity," in *Studies on a Global History of Music: A Balzan Musicology Project, 2013–2015*, ed. Reinhard Strohm (Abingdon: Routledge, 2018), 21–41.

category than composition on its own. I rethink the notion of *salonnières* as patrons, arguing that the salon experience—especially its conversations and discourses—invited collaboration and, to use Emily H. Green's term, "multiple authorship."[34] I address the act of collecting musical scores as evidence of still another kind of authorship, and think about the performance practices and ideals of connoisseurship, cosmopolitanism, and canonicity that such collections reflect. I address music criticism, habits of reading, the acts of poetic recitation and improvisation, modes of conversation, and musical salon games as evidence of the multisensory environment that *salonnières* cultivated. Viewing salons as sites of female governance that simulated the domestic sphere without adhering to the intellectual limitations of domesticity, I argue that musical salons played a role in the aesthetic and technical education of both women and men. And I attend to the gender dynamics of salons, considering female subjectivity and the specific situation of each musical *salonnière* as a driving force behind her salon.

Finally, an engine that drives my thinking about musical salons is my experience as a performer. Wherever possible, I engage with the musical instruments, repertoire, and sounds of musical salons to inform my interpretations. It is certainly the case that the experiences of performance are necessarily subjective, dependent on contemporary habits of playing and listening, as well as the specific training and bodily experiences of each performer. As Tom Beghin has shown, the understanding of a single musical work can vary dramatically depending upon the perspective of reader, performer, or listener. If this was true, as Beghin demonstrates, of a composer such as Franz Joseph Haydn, a woman to whom he dedicated a keyboard sonata, and a modern-day music analyst, it is equally true of Beghin himself, as with any scholar-performer. Reflecting on his project of reconstructing the acoustics of spaces in which Haydn's keyboard music was heard during his lifetime, Beghin acknowledges the risks of reenactment: "none of this happens in spite of 'me.'" For Beghin, the "performance-anchored paradigm of 'Haydn, the rhetorical man'" offers a bridge from past to present, a means of rethinking the study of music with the problems, constraints, and subjectivities of the performer(s) front and center.[35] Beghin's project does not attempt to erase the distinctions between himself and Haydn's fe-

34. Emily H. Green, *Dedicating Music, 1785–1850* (Rochester, NY: University of Rochester Press, 2019), 148–66.

35. Tom Beghin, *The Virtual Haydn: Paradox of a Twenty-First-Century Keyboardist* (Chicago and London: University of Chicago Press, 2015), xxvii–xxviii.

male dedicatees; rather, these distinctions throw into relief the choices that go into modern-day performance—distinctions that might otherwise be elided or ignored. Beghin's foregrounding of his subjective experience in performance helps problematize the project of "reenactment," which has recently come under scrutiny in the work of Vanessa Agnew, among others. Agnew, citing Walter Benjamin, questions the tendency for modern reenactors of any historical event or practice to "collapse temporalities" and assume that "affect can indeed be considered evidentiary."[36]

Despite these pitfalls, musical performance is increasingly recognized as a vital research tool for the study of historical practices. This is true not only in the realm of "historical performance practice"—a loosely configured "movement" to whose overall philosophies, vaguely defined as they are, I adhere[37]—but also in the area of musicological inquiry more broadly. A quarter century ago, Richard Taruskin noted that "composing concerns are different from performing concerns"[38]—that is, thinking about music and realizing it in sound are separate activities that operate in different registers but also offer the rewards of complementary perspectives. Taruskin continued, "Music has to be imaginatively re-created in order to be retrieved, and here is where conflicts are likely to arise between the performer's imagination and the scholar's conscience, even (or especially) when the two are housed in a single mind."[39] It is in the working out of these conflicts that new understandings may emerge. More recently, work by scholars such as Laurie Stras has demonstrated the great extent to which performance can enhance and, in some cases, dramatically alter our understanding of musical texts and practices from the past. Stras's notion of "adaptive performance practices" finds ready application in the musical world of eighteenth-century salons, in which informal, unwritten, sometimes spur-of-the-moment alteration of notated scores was normal and expected.[40]

36. Vanessa Agnew, "History's Affective Turn: Historical Reenactment and Its Work in the Present," *Rethinking History* 11, no. 3 (2007): 309.

37. See, among the many statements of purpose for the historical performance movement, Barthold Kuijken, *The Notation Is Not the Music: Reflections on Early Music Practice and Performance* (Bloomington and Indianapolis: Indiana University Press, 2013); and John Butt, *Playing With History: The Historical Approach to Musical Performance* (Cambridge and New York: Cambridge University Press, 2002).

38. Richard Taruskin, "On Letting the Music Speak for Itself," in *Text and Act: Essays on Music and Performance* (New York and Oxford: Oxford University Press, 1995), 56.

39. Taruskin, "On Letting the Music Speak for Itself," 56.

40. Laurie Stras, *Women and Music in Sixteenth-Century Ferrara* (Cambridge: Cam-

Working through the problems that arise from realizing the sounds of musical salons—problems of instrumentation, instrumental technique, chordal realization, ensemble balance, and arrangement practices—has led me to ideas that have already been published elsewhere, as well as to a series of concerts, lecture-recitals, and (at present) three recordings, created with a remarkable group of open-minded and brilliant collaborators, to which I will make reference at various points in this volume, excerpts of which are included in its companion website (http://press.uchicago.edu/sites/cypess), as indicated in the text of the book by the symbol ♫. The hypotheses laid out in these essays and recordings are just that—hypotheses—and I do not put them forward as the only solutions to the problems I have encountered. Yet they present the best possible solutions that I have been able to discover. Perhaps most importantly, through these recordings and the accompanying essays on salon performance practices, I insist on trying to *hear* the *salonnières* discussed in this book as well as, simply, thinking about them in the abstract. Recognition of the intractable ontological gaps between my situation and theirs helps elucidate the problems and questions of their experiences.

*

I begin this book with a broad view of musical salons between 1760 and 1800, synthesizing evidence from an array of sources to draw out significant overarching themes. In chapter 1, "Musical Salons as Liminal Spaces: *Salonnières* as Agents of Musical Culture," I build on recent work that locates salons in a liminal space between the public and private spheres. With respect to musical salons in particular, this liminality was essential for enabling women to act as agents of musical culture. As Antoine Lilti has argued, the salon's situation as part of the home rendered it an acceptable site of female agency. The domestic associations of women's music-making enhanced this ethos, giving rise to what Gillian Russell and Clara Tuite call "romantic sociability."[41] Musical *salonnières* navigated the line between the salon and the public sphere in a variety of ways. Through patronage of

---

bridge University Press, 2018), 11; see also ch. 7 of that volume, "Musical Practices of the 1580s *Concerto*."

41. Gillian Russell and Clara Tuite, "Introducing Romantic Sociability," in *Romantic Sociability: Social Networks and Literary Culture in Britain, 1770–1840*, ed. Russell and Tuite (Cambridge: Cambridge University Press, 2002), 1–23.

professional performers and composers, networks of travel and epistolary exchange, collecting of scores and instruments, and activities as performers, composers, and sometimes publishers of their work, musical *salonnières* played a key role in the shaping of a modern musical culture.

In chapter 2, "Sensuality, Sociability, and Sympathy: Musical Salon Practices as Enactments of Enlightenment," I offer a reconsideration of salon music based both on historical evidence and on my experience as a performer who has engaged with the performance practices used in eighteenth-century salons. Rather than thinking about salon music in terms of compositional style, as some writers have fruitfully done in the past, I ask what may be learned by placing performance at the center of the story. This approach indeed offers new perspectives: I link the reciprocity and ludic qualities of salon performance to the sociability of games that were played there, and I show how both music and salon games were meant, simultaneously, to entertain salon participants and, equally important, to foster a sense of sympathy (what today would be called "empathy") in them. Sympathy was understood during the late eighteenth century as the key to the formation of "moral sentiment," itself the basis of moral societies. Thus, far from being divorced from the intellectual projects of the Enlightenment, the sensual experiences of music and other salon practices helped lay the groundwork for the cultivation of an enlightened self.

Subsequent chapters in this volume address individual case studies that show how musical salons reflected the particular interests, tastes, and agendas of the *salonnières* who led them. Chapter 3, "Ephemerae and Authorship in the Salon of Madame Brillon," is set in the Parisian salon of Anne-Louise Boyvin d'Hardancourt Brillon de Jouy (1744–1824), a salon hostess, amateur keyboardist, and composer whose network of musical connections extended across Europe and to North America. A composer as well as a dedicatee of published music by professional musicians, Brillon nevertheless valued the lived experiences of music in her salon above all, and I seek to understand these experiences through the medium of a square piano nearly identical to the one that she owned. Still, what I call Brillon's "poetics of the ephemeral" found their way into the public sphere through her interactions with professional composers such as Luigi Boccherini. I consider Brillon's interest in ephemeral qualities of music such as timbre and texture alongside some of the music dedicated to her—in particular, Boccherini's opus 5 sonatas for violin and keyboard. This juxtaposition opens the way to a reconsideration of women's authorship in eighteenth-century salons.

In chapter 4, "Composition, Collaboration, and the Cultivation of Skill in the Salon of Marianna Martines," I show how the Viennese *salonnière*, keyboardist, singer, and composer Marianna Martines (1744–1812) fashioned her image as an internationally recognized composer, while mitigating her presence in the public sphere through the institution of the salon. While Brillon cultivated a "natural" aesthetic, adopting a consciously unstudied approach and avoiding any semblance of effort in her self-presentation, Martines, like others in Vienna, did not hesitate to cast herself as hardworking and devoted to serious study. While other women composers drew public criticism, Martines largely succeeded in avoiding such attacks by staying out of the fully public eye. Examining some of her Italian cantatas in light of contemporary descriptions of what made her style of composition and performance distinctive, I argue that her salon was defined by her collaboration with her mentor, Pietro Metastasio, who lived with the Martines family for decades, who guided Martines's education and career, and whose poetry she set. This collaborative approach continued to define her salon after Metastasio's death.

Long dominated by the musical King Frederick the Great, the city of Berlin after the Seven Years' War saw the rise of a network of salons hosted by elite Jewish women. In chapter 5, "The Cultural Work of Collecting and Performing in the Salon of Sara Levy," I turn to one of these salons with a distinctively musical character.[42] Sara Levy (1761–1854) was a virtuosic keyboardist closely linked to the Bach family who hosted a salon starting in the 1780s. Her collection of scores of music by the Bach family as well as local Prussian composers from previous generations reflects her strong interest in the musical past, while her patronage of contemporary composers shows how she shaped musical culture in her own day. Levy was also an active patron of the Jewish Enlightenment (*Haskalah*), and she would have been aware of the debates—conducted both in German and in Hebrew—about whether Jews had the ability to be musical at all.[43] Here I offer a new interpretation of Levy's music-historicist inclinations: I argue that, in col-

42. An earlier version of this chapter was published as Rebecca Cypess, "Music Historicism: Sara Levy and the Jewish Enlightenment," in *Bach Perspectives* 12, *Bach and the Counterpoint of Religion*, ed. Robin A. Leaver (Springfield: University of Illinois Press, 2018), 129–51.

43. See Ruth HaCohen, *The Music Libel against the Jews* (New Haven, CT: Yale University Press, 2011).

lecting these scores, stamping them with her name, and, most importantly, playing them in her salon in the company of both Jews and Christians, Levy asserted the place of enlightened Jews in German musical history.

In chapter 6, "Musical Improvisation and Poetic Painting in the Salon of Angelica Kauffman," I consider the artistic salon that the famous painter Angelica Kauffman (1741–1807) held in her home in Rome in the 1780s, following her extended sojourn in London. Although Kauffman specialized in painting (with a special emphasis on history painting, unusual for a woman), music was her other talent and love from an early age. Many of her paintings feature music—a self-portrait depicting her struggle over the choice of these two arts is especially revealing—and she used music to create what Angela Rosenthal has called a "sensible studio."[44] Besides singing and playing instruments herself, Kauffman also hosted musical performances by two of the leading improvisers of sung poetry in Rome: Teresa Bandettini and Fortunata Sulgher Fantastici. Drawing on accounts of these singers as well as their model, Corilla Olimpica, and weaving that evidence together with a little-known manuscript of musical accompaniments for improvised poetry, I offer new reconstructions of the art of sung improvisations in late eighteenth-century Rome. Both Kauffman and the *improvvisatrici* consciously adopted the personae of muses and of classical poets, since these personae presented a means of framing women's creative expression. Ultimately, I argue that Kauffman fashioned her salon as a place where the fleeting sounds of women's sung poetry gained a permanent presence through painted art.

In the final chapter, "Reading Musically in the Salon of Elizabeth Graeme," I consider both music and poetry in the salon of Elizabeth Graeme (1737–1801) in Philadelphia. Influenced by the so-called Lichfield group of writers in England, whose work she encountered during her visit to England and Scotland in 1765–1766, and drawing on their neoclassical inspiration, John Milton, Graeme developed a poetic style that was modeled on musical imagery and musical sociability. But for Graeme, I argue, music was more than just a poetic symbol—it was a living art in which she was trained and participated. Her salon likely featured performances by the amateur musician, inventor, writer, and statesman Francis Hopkinson, and his musical mentor, the professional Scottish violinist James Brem-

44. Angela Rosenthal, *Angelica Kauffman: Art and Sensibility* (New Haven, CT, and London: Published for the Paul Mellon Centre for Studies in British Art by Yale University Press, 2006), 90–99.

ner. Graeme participated in the practice of writing new poetry for popular Scottish airs, and it was through such an air that Hopkinson and others in Graeme's circle memorialized Bremner after his death in 1780. Moreover, I reveal new evidence about Graeme's understanding of music as a spiritual practice through a close reading of the contents of one of her manuscripts containing her original paraphrases of the biblical book of Psalms. In this manuscript, she copied essays, letters, and sermons that attest to her deep interest in the power of music to bind together a community of faith.

Despite the wide array of intentions and motivations that led them to host musical salons, the five women at the center of these case studies were bound by their interest in the musical salon as a site of creative expression and sociability. Viewing these women within the context provided by the first two chapters of this book, I seek to bring them out of the shadows and restore them to their position as agents of musical culture.

CHAPTER ONE

Musical Salons as Liminal Spaces

Salonnières as Agents of Musical Culture

Cultural practices and institutions changed dramatically in eighteenth-century Europe. As historians have long noted, the centrality of courtly life in the *ancien régime* diminished in the eighteenth century. Spaces such as public concert halls and public gardens, accessible to individuals from a wide array of social and economic strata, assumed some of the role of cultural innovation, as well as the formation of group identity, that had formerly been centered at court. In addition, the rise of the middle or merchant class coincided with an increased social fluidity, as members of elite intellectual circles known, informally, as the "Republic of Letters" now mixed more freely with men and women of aristocratic birth. Individuals of lower means could use education and success in the mercantile economy to achieve entry into seemingly more prestigious and refined society. High-ranking family origin was no longer the only signifier of virtue; education, refined behavior, and cultural accomplishment could stand in its stead.

These widespread social changes led to—and, in some cases, were enabled by—new developments in musical life. With the rise of the bourgeoisie and increasing cultural self-consciousness, practices such as amateur music lessons became widespread.[1] Public concerts such as the "Concerts of Antient Music," as well as subscription concerts and events such as the centenary commemoration of the birth of George Frideric Handel, meant

1. Among the many sources on amateur music lessons during this period, see Richard Leppert, *Music and Image*, 51–70.

that music assumed substantial social and political significance.[2] Critics and encyclopedists published popular periodicals claiming to disseminate "true taste," as well as weighty tomes that purported to encompass all musical knowledge, thus shaping musical aesthetics and ideals in the literate public sphere. In all these institutions—music lessons, public concert life, music scholarship, and music criticism—the twenty-first-century observer may discern manifestations of a recognizably modern musical culture. They all persist today.

Some institutions of eighteenth-century musical life have, however, not survived, or survive only in a highly modified, reified form, and their roles in eighteenth-century society and musical culture are little understood. One among these is the musical salon—a regular, usually weekly gathering of professional musicians, elite amateurs, artists, and intellectuals, generally presided over by a female hostess or *salonnière*. Salons of all sorts—musical and otherwise—were instrumental in the formation and dissemination of knowledge and social practices in the second half of the eighteenth century.[3] They formed a testing ground for ideas about politics, human relationships, literature, philosophy, science, and the arts. Salons were multimedia and multisensory, often featuring good food and drink; refined visual pleasures such as artworks, furniture, and fashionable clothing; and the sounds of music. Salons constituted a venue for the expression of sentiment and, perhaps above all, the cultivation of polite conversation—an essential element in the formation of an enlightened self.

Many salons involved music to some extent, and there is no clear line separating the "musical salon" from salons more broadly. I define the institution loosely, then, as one in which the *salonnière* had a primary or strong interest in music and was, in most cases, highly involved in "musicking" herself.[4] More than simply setting the agenda for her salon gatherings, hostesses of musical salons would often play or sing with their guests and with the professional musicians in their circle; engage in spoken, conversational musical criticism; and provide the aesthetic stimulus for the salon by expressing their tastes and aesthetic values through patronage, the collecting of scores and instruments, and the coordination of the musical event.

2. See Simon McVeigh, *Concert Life in London from Mozart to Haydn* (Cambridge: Cambridge University Press, 1993), 1–72.

3. Some of the extensive literature on salons is cited in the introduction to this volume.

4. On the term "musicking," see the introduction to this volume; the reference is to Christopher Small, *Musicking: The Meanings of Performance and Listening*.

Cultivating connections with the professional composers in their regular salon circles or who visited salons while traveling, *salonnières* frequently became patrons to such musicians. While the financial aspects of this patronage—manifested, for example, in the underwriting of costs of new publications—have long been recognized, I argue that this patronage sometimes went deeper. Nor did salon women simply act as "muses"—as vague inspirations for creative art.[5] More, the women at the center of musical salons provided a time, place, and impetus for elite amateurs and professional musicians to come together to work out musical issues through conversation and collaboration. The salon offered fertile ground for the germination of ideas, styles, and practices that might eventually enter the public sphere through composition or performance. Salon hostesses also sometimes amassed collections of scores, wrote and read about music, played or sang outside the walls of their homes, and engaged in the composition and publication of their own works. The musical salon often served as a stimulus to these more public activities, thus allowing the quasi-domestic situation of the salon to spill out into the public sphere. Through their own musicianship, their cultivation of relationships with other performers, composers, and listeners, and their connections with one another, *salonnières* and their salons formed a bedrock of Enlightenment musical culture.

The purpose of this book is to consider musical salons between roughly 1760 and 1800 as sites of female cultural agency. I attempt to meet the women at their center, as much as possible, on their own terms. While the historical record on these institutions is fragmentary, I consider a variety of sources of evidence to present new interpretations of eighteenth-century musical salons that excavate the interests and musical personae of *salonnières* and their circles. I show that, while they were constrained by social conventions that viewed women's participation in the public sphere as questionable, they often used the institution of the salon and its related outgrowths, such as epistolary exchanges, diaries, and in some cases, public performance and publication, to exert agency and shape their musical environments.

In the present chapter I explore the institution of the musical salon as a liminal space that mediated between the public and private spheres—categories that were still very much in formation during the eighteenth cen-

5. On the positioning of eighteenth-century women as muses, see the divergent interpretations in Head, *Sovereign Feminine*, ch. 1, "Europe's Living Muses: Women, Music, and Modernity in Burney's *History* and *Tours*"; and Eger, "Representing Culture."

tury.[6] In contrast to writers such as Jürgen Habermas and Dena Goodman, who understand the salon as an institution of the bourgeois public, I adopt the understanding of Antoine Lilti that salons were neither fully public nor fully private—and indeed, that musical *salonnières* in particular used musical practice as a marker of domesticity to further complicate the status of the institution. Within this ambiguity lay the potential for these women to exert cultural agency. In Lilti's words, the salon formed a "privileged space for female action"—one in which they could exercise their taste, influence, and talents in order to shape their musical environments. In this chapter I discuss a wide array of musical salons and *salonnières* to show how they navigated the complexities of the private–public divide. Their networks of contacts and collaborators included both professional and elite amateur musicians, friends, mentors, and protégées. These networks, which sometimes extended across Europe and into America, enabled musical *salonnières* to act as agents of musical culture.

Musical Salons as Liminal Spaces: From Private Practice to Public Influence

The debate over women's participation in the public sphere was extensive, and salons held a prominent place in it. Jean-Jacques Rousseau's critique of women in theater, written in response to Jean le Rond d'Alembert's essay on Geneva in the *Encyclopédie*, figured women in the public eye as equivalent to actresses who inappropriately command public attention. Just as actresses have the power "to make women and girls the preceptors of the public," the salon placed women at the center of public attention and gave them power over public taste and sentiment. As Rousseau wrote,

> The ancients had, in general, a very great respect for women, but they showed this respect by refraining from exposing them to public judgment, and thought to honor their modesty by keeping quiet about their other virtues. . . . With us, on the contrary, the most esteemed woman

6. James Van Horn Melton uses the phrase "liminal space" in relation to the salons hosted by Jewish women in Enlightenment Berlin, one of which is discussed in this volume in chapter 5; he employs the term to describe the dissolution of social hierarchies in that particular environment. My usage here is a more general one. See James Van Horn Melton, *The Rise of the Public in Enlightenment Europe* (Cambridge: Cambridge University Press, 2001), 223.

> is the one who has the greatest renown, about whom the most is said, who is the most often seen in society, at whose home one dines the most, who most imperiously sets the tone, who judges, resolves, decides, pronounces, assigns talents, merit, and virtues their degrees and places, and whose favor is most ignominiously begged for by humble, learned men.[7]

Rousseau's objections to the presumption of women who would become arbiters of the intellectual agenda of the Enlightenment centered around the institution of the salon, in which women exercised such a role freely. Yet, as Dena Goodman argues, most of the *philosophes* viewed *salonnières* "as the legitimate governors of a potentially unruly discourse."[8] That the salon assumed such a role in the public discourse of the Republic of Letters contributed to Jürgen Habermas's understanding of the salon as a feature of public life: as courtly culture assumed decreased significance in the determination of artistic taste and intellectual value, and as systems of royal patronage diminished, the salon assumed some of those roles.

Goodman's understanding of French salons as an important feature of the public discourse of the Republic of Letters did much to rehabilitate the *salonnières* after a long history of condemnation that accepted Rousseau's negative judgments at face value. Yet Goodman's insistence on the intellectual agenda of salons downplayed other aspects of the institution that were rooted in sensory experience. These have been emphasized in subsequent work by scholars focused on the history of the arts, fashion, furniture, and music, among others.[9] Habermas's notion of the "public" as a body that

7. "Les anciens avoient en général un très-grand respect pour les femmes; mail ils marquoient ce respect en s'abstenant de les exposer au jugement du public, & croyoient honorer leur modestie, en se taisant sur leurs autres vertus. . . . Chez nous, au contraire, la femme estimée est celle qui fait le plus de bruit; de qui l'on parle le plus; qu'on voit le plus dans le monde; chez qui l'on dîne le plus souvent; qui donne le plus impérieusement le ton; qui juge, tranche, décide, prononce, assigne aux talens, au mérite, aux vertus, leur degrés & leur places; & dont les humbles savans mendient le plus bassement la faveur." Jean-Jacques Rousseau, "Lettre à M. d'Alembert," in *Collection complète des oeuvres* (Geneva, 1780), 6:482–84, transcribed at https://www.rousseauonline.ch/pdf/rousseauonline-0029.pdf (accessed August 3, 2020). Translated in Jean-Jacques Rousseau, *Politics and the Arts: Letter to M. D'Alembert on the Theatre*, trans. with notes and intro. by Allan Bloom (Ithaca, NY: Cornell University Press, 1960), 47, 48–49.

8. Goodman, *The Republic of Letters*, 53.

9. An example of a study that inflects the public/private dichotomy is Jennifer M. Jones, "Repackaging Rousseau: Femininity and Fashion in Old Regime France," *French Historical Studies* 18, no. 4 (Autumn 1994): 939–67.

comes together to exercise its reason and intellect—alongside or in opposition to the state—has thus been inflected by a more nuanced understanding that does not require eighteenth-century cultural and social institutions to fit clearly into the "public" or "private" spheres. Antoine Lilti has argued that the salon was one institution that "[resists] being categorized according to the binary division public/private." For Lilti, "cafés, salons, clubs, conversation circles [and] Masonic lodges. . . . define an in-between space, much more broadly open than domestic and family life, yet based on assimilation. This space, which in the eighteenth century was called 'society,' is based on an ideal type of codified exchanges, both intellectual and social, that nurtures conversations in all its various forms."[10]

Within Lilti's "in-between space," salons occupy a special position. Unlike cafés, Masonic lodges, and town squares, salon gatherings took place in the home (though often in a specially designated room), and they were usually presided over by a woman. In this respect, they filled a gap in the social landscape, enabling women to remain (or pretend to remain) out of the public eye while interacting with a broad range of individuals from across the elite and professional classes. Generally restricted from systematic education and from full participation in public discourse, women's behavior was subject to mores and conventions that circumscribed their participation in the public sphere. Salons formed one outlet in which women could exercise their intellectual curiosity and talents, continuing to receive an informal education even as they sought to edify their guests. Salons were liminal spaces, mediating between the public and private spheres.

If this point was true of salons in general, it is crucial to understanding salons with a strongly musical agenda. The domestic ethos of the salon was intensified by the musical practices enacted there, since many of the women who played music in salons would not have done so in public for fear of appearing indecorous or subjecting themselves to inappropriate scrutiny, as Rousseau accused actresses of doing in his "Lettre à M. d'Alembert." Thus, while Goodman has noted that the role of the *salonnière* frequently required women to engage in a measure of self-effacement, silencing their own perspectives in order to facilitate the conversation of their guests, the role assumed by musical *salonnières* was somewhat different.[11] Women who

10. Antoine Lilti, "Private Lives, Public Space: A New Social History of the Enlightenment," in *The Cambridge Companion to the French Enlightenment*, ed. Daniel Brewer (Cambridge: Cambridge University Press, 2014), 18.

11. As Goodman writes, "the salonnière's attentiveness to others, her silence even, was

played instruments and sang alongside their guests put forth their skills, their tastes, and their selves.

The liminal nature of the musical salon can be discerned in the various ways that *salonnières* navigated the complexities of the public and private spheres. Perhaps no case illustrates these complexities more effectively than that of Ann Ford: when Ford hosted musical parties in her London home, they were the toast of high society, but when she stepped out into the public sphere by staging paid concerts, her own father as well as other critics deemed them inappropriate. Ford was the daughter of a solicitor who had received a thorough and costly education in music, dance, visual art, and languages, likely through the engagement of private tutors. A biographical sketch in the journal *Public Characters* discovered by Peter Holman demonstrates that, as early as 1759, Ford was hosting and playing in a weekly series of musical concerts in her home that "attracted the notice of all the gay and fashionable world."[12] Her guests included members of the upper class, including the noted Bluestocking intellectual and patron Lady Montagu and her husband.

While the report on these salon concerts in *Public Characters* is a retrospective one, published in the early nineteenth century, Holman notes that it contains evidence acquired through firsthand accounts, including from Ford herself. The details that it provides are specific and offer a window onto the exclusive world of Ford's salon. As in most musical salons, Ford herself played in these gatherings together with a series of guests, whom the article in *Public Characters* divides into "amateurs" (including Ford and her future husband, Governor Thicknesse) and "professors"—that is, professional musicians. The article also lists the instruments that they played: the amateurs used the violin, viola da gamba, German (i.e., transverse) flute, voice, theorbo and lute, and pianoforte, while the "professors" sang and played the harpsichord, violin, Spanish guitar, and viola d'amore. In this listing, the Earl of Kelly—a Scottish nobleman who later played a central role in the formation and proceedings of the Edinburgh Music Society—is reported to have played first violin, with the second violin being covered

---

as much a conscious action as was the loquacity of her male guests. . . . Attention to others implied a denial of the self." Goodman, *The Republic of Letters*, 104.

12. Peter Holman, "Ann Ford Revisited," *Eighteenth-Century Music* 1, no. 2 (2004): 157–81. An examination of Ford's musical career in the context of her later literary production is in Gillen D'Arcy Wood, "'Have You Met Miss Ford?' or, Accomplishment Revisited," *European Romantic Review* 23, no. 3 (2012): 283–91.

by one of the "professors."[13] In other words, although the categories of amateur and professional musicians were distinguished from one another in *Public Characters*, within the musical salon, their roles overlapped.

Holman has noted the unusual nature of some of these instruments, including the viola d'amore and the viola da gamba, the latter of which had all but passed out of usage by the time of Ford's salon.[14] He interprets this collection of instruments as representing Ford's self-presentation within the cult of sensibility. I posit, moreover, that the situation of the salon enabled this expression of sensibility; through its environment and ethos it seemed to offer a private situation in which such expression could be appropriately shared.

The issue of Ford's social standing came to the fore when she attempted to perform publicly. While many who attended her performances, including those in the uppermost reaches of society, were brought to tears by the "exquisite sensibility" that she displayed there,[15] her father disapproved and sought to end these performances by calling on a magistrate to intervene. According to the essay in *Public Characters*, Ford's father "abhorred the idea that his daughter should appear on the stage for any period, however short, or under any circumstances however favourable."[16] The scandal of public appearance and image was also at issue in reactions to one of Ford's portraits, painted by her intimate friend Thomas Gainsborough (see fig. 1.1). With her legs crossed in what was seen as an unladylike pose, surrounded by instruments with suggestive, curved shapes, Ford's likeness provoked Mary Delany to write, "I should be sorry to have any one I loved set forth in such a manner."[17] While her salon in itself does not seem to have raised

13. On the Earl of Kelly and his position in the Edinburgh Musical Society, see Jennifer MacLeod, "The Edinburgh Musical Society: Its Membership and Repertoire, 1728–1797" (PhD diss., University of Edinburgh, 2001); and Anne McClenny Krauss, "James Bremner, Alexander Reinagle and the Influence of the Edinburgh Musical Society on Philadelphia," in *Scotland and America in the Age of the Enlightenment*, ed. Richard B. Sher and Jeffrey R. Smitten (Edinburgh: Edinburgh University Press, 1990), 259–74.

14. See also Holman's larger study of this topic: Peter Holman, *Life after Death: The Viola da Gamba in Britain from Purcell to Dolmetsch* (Woodbridge, UK: Boydell Press, 2010).

15. Holman, "Ann Ford Revisited," 171.

16. *Public Characters* (London: Richard Phillips, 1806), 95; quoted in Holman, "Ann Ford Revisited," 171.

17. Mary Delany, *The Autobiography and Correspondence of Mary Granville, Mrs Delany*, ed. Augusta Hall, Baroness Llanover (London: Richard Bentley, 1861), 1:605. Quoted in Holman, "Ann Ford Revisited," 157. Further on this portrait, see Leppert, *Music and Image*, 40–42.

Figure 1.1 Thomas Gainsborough, *Portrait of Miss Ann Ford later Mrs. Philip Thicknesse*. Cincinnati, Cincinnati Art Museum, Ohio, USA. Bequest of Mary M. Emery / Bridgeman Images.

any eyebrows, being considered a suitable venue for a woman of middle-class standing whose family sought a higher social rank, it was when Ford's musicianship exceeded the limits of the salon and spilled out into the more clearly public sphere that problems arose. Indeed, in other salons, she seems to have been satirized, as Gainsborough himself noted. In a private letter that touched on his own daughters' acquisition of female accomplishment, Gainsborough wrote, "I don't mean to make them only Miss Fords in the Art, to be partly admired & partly laugh'd at at every Tea Table."[18] Ford's case, which features a family member concerned with a woman's musical appearances outside the walls of her parlor, is echoed in that of the famous professional singer Elizabeth Linley, later Sheridan. Linley's father had never been reluctant to put his daughter on stage, but when she married, her husband restricted her activities as a performer, deeming them unsuitable for a married woman of her social standing.[19]

In addition to providing a socially sanctioned context for the expression of interior sentiment, Ann Ford's musical salons also possessed an air of exclusivity, such that the author of the essay in *Public Characters* was "at great pains" to report on them to an eager readership.[20] This exclusive nature was a common—indeed, essential—feature of musical salons, and it forms another aspect of their liminal status between the private and public spheres. Another case in which exclusivity played a key role was in the musical salon of Mrs. Fox Lane. Reporting on the weekly "academia" that she hosted, which featured the professional singers Regina Mingotti and Felice Giardini, Charles Burney wrote,

> As Giardini was seldom to be heard in public after his first arrival, she [Mrs. Fox Lane] invited very select parties of the first people in the kingdom to hear him at her house, for which happiness she did not suffer them to be ungrateful at his benefit. When Mingotti arrived in this kingdom, having united her interests with those of Giardini in the conduct and management of the opera, Mrs. Lane espoused *her* cause with zeal. . . . With two such performers, the concerts she gave to her choice

18. Quoted in Holman, "Ann Ford Revisited," 178.

19. See Leslie Ritchie, *Women Writing Music in Late Eighteenth-Century England: Social Harmony in Literature and Performance* (Aldershot, UK, and Burlington, VT: Ashgate, 2008), 67–71.

20. Holman, "Ann Ford Revisited," 164.

friends were subjects of envy and obloquy to all those who were unable to obtain admission.[21]

As in the case of Ann Ford, Mrs. Fox Lane and her upper-class friends joined these professional musicians in making music: "At these concerts Mrs. Lane frequently played the harpsichord herself; as did Lady Edgcumbe and the late Lady Milbanke, both admirable performers on that instrument. Lady Rockingham, the Dowager Lady Carlisle, and Miss Pelham, scholars of Giardini, and Mingotti, used to sing." As Burney makes clear, it was not just the allure of hearing the professional singers that drew London's high society to Mrs. Fox Lane's home. Instead, "the difficulty, or rather impossibility, of hearing these professors and illustrious dilettanti any where else, stimulated curiosity so much, that there was no sacrifice or mortification to which fashionable people would not submit, in order to obtain admission." In restricting their appearances to such exclusive situations, both the "professors" and the "illustrious dilettanti" elevated their reputations in music. The "mortification" to which Burney referred resulted from Mrs. Fox Lane's habit of soliciting donations from her friends to benefit Giardini and Mingotti—a breach of decorum endured for the sake of the musicians' welfare and the opportunity to hear them sing.[22]

The novelist Fanny Burney, daughter of Charles Burney, was not highly skilled as a musician herself, but her association with her father meant that she was—and was widely regarded as—an authority on musical subjects. It may have been her authoritative status that led her to be invited, on April 30, 1780, to hear a private performance by the professional keyboardist Jane Mary Guest in Bath, which took place at Guest's home, and not in public. Writing in her diary, Burney explained that Guest was "come hither to give Lessons to Miss Thrale [i.e., the daughter of Hester Lynch Thrale, later Piozzi], to help keep up her singing." Burney compared Guest's abilities (not all favorably) with those of her own sister; one of the pieces Guest played in that session, a sonata by Ernst Eichner, was a work that Burney's sister played frequently, so the comparison was inevitable. Simon McVeigh has posited that the domestic setting in which Burney heard Guest was a sign that "Guest was evidently able to present herself as a young lady of

21. Charles Burney, *A General History of Music from the Earliest Ages to the Present Period*, vol. 4 (London: Printed for the author and sold by Payne and Son, 1789), 671.

22. See Michael Burden, *Regina Mingotti: Diva and Impresario at the King's Theatre, London* (London and New York: Routledge, 2017), 55–57.

quality."[23] The private situation in which Guest entertained Burney simulated the environment of the home or the salon, rather than that of the public sphere, where Guest also made frequent appearances.[24]

The tricky negotiation of the professional–amateur divide is evident, too, from the case of Hester Thrale Piozzi herself. An elite woman of letters in the Bluestocking salons of Britain and a close protégée of Dr. Samuel Johnson, the widowed Thrale had been expected to marry someone at her social station and with a fortune to match her own. Instead, in 1784, after two years of agonizing, she embarked on a second marriage to the tenor Gabriel Mario Piozzi—a move that sent shock waves through her circle of friends and alienated her from Dr. Johnson. She justified her decision in her diary, noting that because her fortune was already established, "to marry for *love* would therefore be rational in me."[25] The newly married couple left for a tour of Europe, perhaps in part to escape the gossipmongers at home, who had been scandalized by her husband's inferior fortune and social position. Her own daughters were among those who refused to accept the marriage, and, writing from Florence, their mother complained to one of them,

> Why do you my sweetest Girl, write so coldly and so queerly? & why do you hinder your Sisters from writing at all? is it because I am married to Mr Piozzi? . . . When *every* body then is thus goodnatured to me, when *every* body expresses a just sense of Mr Piozzi's Merit, and seeing his Value pays him a proper Respect—why should you be the only Per-

23. McVeigh, *Concert Life in London from Mozart to Haydn*, 185. Fanny Burney's account of the meeting appears in Frances Burney, *Early Journals and Letters of Fanny Burney, Volume IV: The Streatham Years: Part II, 1780–1781*, ed. Betty Rizzo (Montreal and Kingston: McGill-Queen's University Press, 2003), 92–93. Further on Jane Mary Guest, see Nicholas Salwey, "Women Pianists in Late Eighteenth-Century London," in *Concert Life in Eighteenth-Century Britain*, ed. Susan Wollenberg and Simon McVeigh (Aldershot: Ashgate, 2004), 282–84.

24. As the daughter of a professional musician and a published author herself, Fanny Burney well knew about the complexities of female presence in the public sphere. See Cassandra Ulph, "Frances Burney's Private Professionalism," *Journal for Eighteenth-Century Studies* 38, no. 3 (2015): 377–93. Charles Burney's acceptance into the so-called Streatham Circle is discussed in Valerie Rumbold, "Music Aspires to Letters: Charles Burney, Queeney Thrale and the Streatham Circle," *Music & Letters* 74, no. 1 (February 1993): 24–38.

25. Quoted in William McCarthy, *Hester Thrale Piozzi: Portrait of a Literary Woman* (Chapel Hill and London: University of North Carolina Press, 1985), 35; see also the larger discussion especially on 34–39.

> son to stand out? the only Person not pleased to see your Mother happy, and well treated.[26]

Piozzi's salon circle was ambivalent about music, as I will discuss further below. However, consideration of her salon life in juxtaposition with her marriage to a professional musician is highly revealing for the social fault lines that it indicates.

Significantly, Piozzi's travels with her new husband following their marriage included a visit to the salon of Marianna Martines, a Viennese *salonnière* whom I will address more fully in chapter 4, whom she described in her diary. Piozzi's primary interest was in literature, so it is perhaps not surprising that she described Martines through reference to the latter's mentor, Pietro Metastasio, who had shared an apartment with Martines's family and trained her in aesthetics and the arts from her birth. Piozzi viewed this connection as central to the proceedings in Martines's salon, noting that Martines and her sister "set [Metastasio's] poetry and sing it very finely, appearing to recollect his conversation with infinite tenderness and delight."[27] While in Martines's salon, Piozzi also met professional musicians of great stature. The colorful if not entirely trustworthy memoir attributed to the Irish tenor Michael Kelly, who was resident in Vienna from 1783 to 1787 and sang in the premiere of Mozart's *Marriage of Figaro*, reports on the convergence of talented individuals at the musical parties that Martines held:

> At one of [Martines's] parties I had the pleasure to be introduced to Mrs. Piozzi, who, with her husband, was travelling on the Continent; there appeared to me a great similarity in the manners of these two gifted women, who conversed with all around them without pedantry or affectation. It was certainly an epoch, not to be forgotten, to have had the good fortune, on the same evening, to be in the company with the favourites of Metastasio and Dr. Johnson; and last, not least, with Mozart himself.[28]

26. Hester Lynch Piozzi [formerly Mrs. Thrale; née Salusbury] to Hester Maria Elphinstone, Viscountess Keith [née Thrale], Tuesday, 26 July 1785. *Electronic Enlightenment*, http://www.e-enlightenment.com/item/piozheUD0010156b1c/?letters=corr&s=piozzheste005720&r=58 (accessed August 14, 2018).

27. Quoted in Godt, *Marianna Martines*, 196.

28. Michael Kelly [and Theodore Hook], *Reminiscences of Michael Kelly of the King's Theatre, and Theatre Royal, Drury Lane, Including a Period of Nearly Half a Century; with*

The observation that Martines and Piozzi behaved similarly to one another, "conversing with all around them without pedantry or affection," is a testament to the role of the salon—musical and otherwise—in training women in the art of sociable behavior. The presence of two such "gifted women" served to enhance the experience of the evening, leading Kelly (or his ghostwriter) to reflect on his "good fortune" at being in their presence—another testimony to the value of musical salons as exclusive experiences.

Another way in which musical *salonnières* both reflected and influenced public musical life was in their demonstration of interest in music historicism. The vogue for "ancient music" has long been identified as a component of public concert life in the second half of the eighteenth century.[29] Yet music-historicist tendencies also permeated musical salons, reinforcing, supporting, and perhaps contributing to the public interest in such approaches. Sara Levy's collection of scores reflects an interest in music from earlier decades of the eighteenth century; her music historicism is a topic that I will take up at length in chapter 5. Accounts of Marianna Martines suggest that, in the 1780s, she fashioned herself as a point of access to a musical past—especially to a lost poetic tradition embodied by Metastasio. Elizabeth Graeme, a poet and salon hostess in Philadelphia, modeled her salon after those of the Lichfield group in Britain. Like Anna Seward and other Lichfield writers, Graeme sought to emulate the poetry of John Milton and his neoclassical style, evoking a poetic form that achieved its truest realization in music; neoclassicism itself was an attempt to revive an aspect of the past. As I will discuss in chapter 7, Graeme's commonplace book containing her translations of the book of Psalms suggests that she understood her poetic work as a means of reviving the art of biblical poetry. In addition, she composed new poetry to be sung to the Scottish airs so much in vogue in the eighteenth century—"folk" songs thought to encompass a mythical and ancient musical past. Each of these cases suggests that notions of historicism were current in musical salons in various guises. Sociable expressions of sentimentalism merged with this music-historical aesthetic, rendering salons a locus for the exploration of ancient art in modern guise.

Original Anecdotes of Many Distinguished Persons, Political, Literary, and Musical (London: Henry Colburn, 1826), 1:252–53; see also the discussion in Godt, *Marianna Martines*, 196–97. Kelly's *Reminiscences* were partly or mostly written by Theodore Hook, who apparently altered considerable aspects of what Kelly told him.

29. McVeigh, *Concert Life in London from Mozart to Haydn*, 11–27.

Musical Salons and the Complexities of Composition

Definitions and modes of women's authorship are notoriously problematic in the study of eighteenth-century musical culture. On one hand, some women did act as composers, creating original works and sometimes publishing them under their own names. However, as Matthew Head has noted, the long-standing "equation of writing and agency," which grew, in musicology, out of the identification of the written work as the primary or exclusive locus of meaning, is highly problematic with respect to women.[30] Whether through limitations placed on their education, through social conventions that discouraged women from subjecting themselves to public scrutiny through publication, or through other means, women were often restricted from composition, such that "discussions of women's music [tend] to dwell on and celebrate the fact of its existence."[31] Women of the eighteenth century were certainly aware of the issues surrounding authorship. Hester Thrale Piozzi, when asked in 1789 to comment on the playing of a female violinist, addressed the common belief that women should be neither violinists nor authors: "a Violin is not an Instrument for *Ladies* to manage, very likely! I remember when they said the same Thing of a *Pen*."[32]

In subsequent chapters of this study, I follow Head and others in problematizing the equation of musical authorship with musical composition. While Stephen Rose is right to point out that there was a clear distinction between the role of performer and professional composer in the seventeenth and eighteenth centuries, *salonnières* did not often seek out recognition within the category of professional composer, and they pursued creative authorship in a variety of ways that brushed up against composition.[33] The musical salon constituted a space in which the boundaries separating composer, performer, and listener easily blurred or broke down. The collaboration of professionals and amateurs enacted and enabled by the *salonnières* means that multiple people might be responsible for the creation of a com-

30. Matthew Head, "Rethinking Authorship through Women Composers: *Women Writing Opera: Creativity and Controversy in the Age of the French Revolution*, by Jacqueline Letzter and Robert Adelson," *Women and Music: A Journal of Gender and Culture* 6 (2002): 36–50.

31. Head, "Rethinking Authorship through Women Composers," 36.

32. Quoted in McCarthy, *Hester Thrale Piozzi*, 42.

33. Stephen Rose, *Musical Authorship from Schütz to Bach* (Cambridge: Cambridge University Press, 2019).

position. The collection of musical scores, undertaken by many *salonnières*, may also be understood as an act of authorship, in that it has the potential to endow music with new meaning. The same is true of performance.

While these broader questions of authorship will be addressed later in this book, for the moment I discuss a handful of cases of women's composition narrowly construed, to understand how networks of mentorship, patronage, and sociability affected women's participation in the public sphere. For Anne-Louise Boyvin d'Hardancourt Brillon de Jouy, the norms that limited public female authorship were apparently right and proper. Brillon related to Benjamin Franklin that she was fully accepting of the conventions of modesty that circumscribed her experience; as she wrote, "I am a woman, and my lot and my taste are modesty; I have a lively mind, and nothing prevents me from using it, but [only] for myself and for my most intimate friends."[34] Yet Brillon did not view her adherence to these norms as incompatible with her roles as a *salonnière*, keyboardist, or chamber musician alongside professional players, nor as a composer of music for private usage. As I will argue in chapter 3, her collaboration with professional male composers within the context of her salon offered an opportunity for her ideas to enter the public sphere under their name—and, in some cases, with her name featured prominently as dedicatee.

The salon hostess and keyboardist Sara Levy, a member of the elite Jewish community in Berlin, seems to have adhered to some of the same standards of modesty that Brillon espoused. Trained in music by Wilhelm Friedemann Bach during the last decade of his life, Levy must have learned aspects of counterpoint, thoroughbass, and perhaps also composition that were so integral to the Bach family's pedagogy.[35] Yet she never signed her name to any compositions, raising the possibility that she viewed composition as inappropriate for a woman of her social standing. Nevertheless, her

34. "Je suis fémme, mon lot et mon gout sont la modéstie; j'ai la teste vive, rien ne me déffend de l'occupér; mais pour moi, et pour mes amis les plus intimes." Anne-Louise Boyvin d'Hardancourt Brillon de Jouy to Benjamin Franklin, after November 14, 1780. French text at https://franklinpapers.org (accessed July 14, 2019). Further discussion of Brillon, including references to literature on her life, her salon, and her compositions, appears in chapter 3.

35. As Richard D. P. Jones notes of Wilhelm Friedemann Bach's education under his father, "composition and performance are united through the medium of the keyboard." See Richard D. P. Jones, "The Keyboard Works: Bach as Teacher and Virtuoso," in *The Cambridge Companion to Bach*, ed. John Butt (Cambridge: Cambridge University Press, 1997), 143.

reputation as a keyboardist attracted international visitors even before her marriage, when she was still living in her parents' home, with one visitor reporting, "The banker [Daniel] Itzig [Levy's father] has sixteen children, of whom some already have situations in their own right, and others are just at the age when beauty begins to unfold. The charm of the daughters' beauty is heightened by their talents, particularly for music, and by a finely developed intellect."[36]

After her marriage in 1783, Levy began hosting a musical salon in her home, attracting members of the Jewish and non-Jewish families of Berlin as well as visitors to the city. After her teacher's death in 1784, she commissioned works from Carl Philipp Emanuel Bach and Johann Christoph Friedrich Bach.[37] While Levy either never composed or never chose to acknowledge her position as composer, the influence of her salon extended into the public sphere in other ways. She amassed an enormous collection of scores, including music from the Bach family as well as other composers in the orbit of Berlin, such as the Graun brothers, Johann Gottlieb Janitsch, and Johann Joachim Quantz, among many others. Starting in the early nineteenth century, she donated hundreds of these scores to the bourgeois musical society known as the Sing-Akademie zu Berlin, then directed by Carl Friedrich Zelter. As a component of this venerable institution, Levy's collection came to form part of the Prussian national patrimony; her great-nephew, Felix Mendelssohn-Bartholdy, probably encountered the materials that she had collected at the Sing-Akademie while he was studying under Zelter. Following the death of her husband in 1806, Levy began to play concertos with the Ripienschule of the Sing-Akademie, thus stepping into the public eye as a performer. Moreover, Levy took an interest throughout her life in the welfare of professional musicians, seeking to help them establish connections and attain opportunities that would benefit their careers. This can be seen clearly, for example, in the letters that she exchanged with Elise Reimarus, a prominent intellectual in Hamburg. While Levy's half of the correspondence is now lost, Reimarus's responses show that the two discussed the career of the

36. Account by August Hennings, quoted in Hilde Spiel, *Fanny von Arnstein: Daughter of the Enlightenment*, trans. Christine Shuttleworth, intro. Michael Z. Wise (New York: New Vessel Press, 2013), 17.

37. Christoph Wolff, "Sara Levy's Musical Salon and Her Bach Collection," in *Sara Levy's World: Gender, Judaism, and the Bach Tradition in Enlightenment Berlin*, 48. Further discussion of Levy, including references to literature on her life and her salon, appears in chapter 5.

Jewish composer (who would later convert to Christianity) Carl Bernhard Wessely at great length, noting his successes and discussing opportunities for his professional advancement.[38]

Other *salonnières* navigated the complexities of authorship and publication, exceeding the boundaries of their salon to enter the public sphere through the permanent—albeit disembodied—medium of print. Ann Ford published two short treatises: one on playing the guitar and another on playing the musical glasses.[39] While these diminutive works may seem insignificant compared to some of the didactic tomes on performance published by male writers of the eighteenth century, they extended the exclusive domain of the musical salon to the public sphere. In this respect, it is significant that Ford's subjects are instruments that she played and that were strongly associated with women. Her treatise on musical glasses, which discussed the disposition and use of glasses filled with water to varying proportions in an arrangement apparently designed by the Irish musician Richard Pockridge, appeared in print in the same year that Benjamin Franklin first wrote of his glass armonica, which was meant to improve upon Pockridge's configuration.[40] Ford associated the musical glasses especially with women, suggesting that "every lady, who can play or sing . . . will be furnished with" a set.[41] This same feminine association attached itself to Franklin's invention. By the end of the eighteenth century, this link would generate anxieties about

38. These letters are preserved in the Staatsbibliothek zu Berlin (D-B) under the shelfmark Nachlass 434 (Familie Cauer), case 3.

39. Ann Ford, *Lessons and Instructions for Playing on the Guitar* ([London]: Author, [1761]); Ann Ford, *Instructions for Playing on the Musical Glasses: So That Any Person, Who Has the Least Knowledge of Music, or a Good Ear, May Be Able to Perform in a Few Days, If Not in a Few Hours: With Clear and Proper Directions How to Provide a Compleat Set of Well-Tuned Glasses at a Very Moderate Expense* ([London]: s.n., [1761]).

40. The attribution of the configuration of glasses is from Benjamin Franklin's letter to Giambattista Beccaria, in which Franklin describes his motivation for inventing the glass armonica. The letter was printed in Benjamin Franklin, *Experiments and Observations on Electricity, Made at Philadelphia in America: To Which Are Added, Letters and Papers on Philosophical Subjects* (London: David Henry, 1769), 427–33. However, musical glasses of varying configurations had been used for playing music since at least the turn of the eighteenth century, as attested in Richard Neve, *Arts Improvement: Or, Choice Experiments and Observations in Building, Husbandry, Gardening, Mechanicks, Chimistry, Painting, Japaning, Varnishing, Guilding, Inlaying, Embossing, Carving, Preserving Several Things in Their Natural Shape and Colour and in Other Arts and Sciences Profitable and Pleasant* (London: D. Brown, 1703), 220–21. Neve advocates using musical glasses for playing Psalm tunes.

41. Ford, *Instructions for Playing on the Musical Glasses*, 1.

the propriety of the instrument for women, who were seen as susceptible to its haunting sounds.[42] Ford's treatise on the guitar was also oriented toward women, claiming that it sets the body into a "line of beauty" like the one that William Hogarth had described in his *Analysis of Beauty*: "the Attitude this Instrument almost naturally throws the Performer in, is very graceful . . . I will venture to affirm, a graceful Person cannot, sitting down, be placed in a more becoming Attitude."[43] For Ann Ford, the treatise on playing the musical glasses and the guitar helped her extend her reputation for sentimental musicianship and reach a broader female audience through the medium of print.

Marianna Martines was highly trained and admired as a composer, and her skill in that domain earned her the distinction of being the first woman to gain entry into the Accademia filarmonica of Bologna, one of the most prestigious musical academies in Europe.[44] Most of her compositions survive only in manuscript, with the largest collection, a set of 24 concert arias titled *Scelta d'arie composte per suo diletto*, having been given by Martines to Maria Carolina of Austria, daughter of the Empress Maria Theresa and Queen of Naples.[45] If the queen had not preserved the manuscript, these compositions would be lost, and indeed, it is quite likely that many of Martines's compositions did not survive. Curiously, two of her keyboard sonatas appeared in print during her lifetime, in an anthology titled *Raccolta musicale contenente . . . sonate per il cembalo solo d'altretanti celebri compositori italiani*. Within this collection, Martines's sonatas stand out as exceptional for several reasons. She is the only woman represented in the anthology. Moreover, while the other composers are listed *co' loro nomi e titoli* (with their names and titles), indicating their high degree of professional prestige, Martines is called "Signora Maria Anna Martines, dilettante a Vienna." (She was not alone among the composers represented in the anthology who was not, in fact, Italian.) The word "dilettante"—one who delights in music, rather than one who is paid to do music—is an indicator of Martines's

42. Heather Hadlock, "Sonorous Bodies: Women and the Glass Harmonica," *Journal of the American Musicological Society* 53, no. 3 (Autumn 2000): 507–42; Annette Richards, "Ghost Music, or the Otherworldly Voice of the Glass Armonica," *Keyboard Perspectives* 8 (2015): 1–42.

43. Ford, *Lessons and Instructions for Playing on the Guitar*, 3–4.

44. See the discussion in Godt, *Marianna Martines*, 133–54, and in chapter 4 of this volume.

45. This manuscript is now housed in the library of the Conservatorio di musica San Pietro a Majella (I-Nc), shelfmark 33–327/8.

attempt to navigate the social strictures around composition and publication, and their attending implications of class status. The same is true of her collection of concert arias; while these were not published during her lifetime, when she gave them to the queen, she included a title page calling them *Arie composte per suo diletto*. In addition, the dedication of the keyboard anthology resonates with Martines's epithet, "dilettante." The volume as a whole is dedicated to "Amatori della musica"—"lovers of music," or perhaps "amateurs of music"—so the inclusion of Martines's name and amateur status may have seemed significant, in that she constituted a musical role model for purchasers of the volume.

As I will discuss in chapter 4, the dissemination of Martines's compositions was facilitated by the professional-class men who supported her work. After all, while it is easy for contemporary scholars to categorize her as a "woman composer," the primary venue for her musicianship was her musical salon, which she held in her home throughout her adult life, and which attracted the notice of musicians and members of high society, both within Vienna and abroad. The publication of her sonatas may have been facilitated by Padre Giovanni Battista Martini, who presided over the Accademia filarmonica.[46] Clearly the most influential connection for Martines, though, was Pietro Metastasio. As imperial poet, Metastasio helped Martines's brothers gain access to professional positions at court, and it was probably through Metastasio that Martines attained the distinction of performing for Empress Maria Theresa.

A similar circumstance may explain how Martines's music came to be included in the collection of the *salonnière* Maria Josefa Pimentel, Countess-Duchess of Osuna y Benavente in Madrid, whose inventory of scores includes a "Miserere a quatro de Doña Mariana Martínez" and a "Salmo . . . por Martínez."[47] An avid collector of Viennese music, the countess had commissioned Franz Joseph Haydn to send her copies of as many as a dozen

46. Metastasio's collaborative relationship with Martines will be discussed in this volume in chapter 4. On her connection to Padre Martini, see Godt, *Marianna Martines*, especially ch. 6, "Padre Martini and the *Dixit Dominus*."

47. This inventory, taken in 1824, includes music from the early nineteenth century as well as a large collection amassed during the eighteenth. It is transcribed in Juan Pablo Fernández-Cortés, *La música en las casas de Osuna y Benavente (1733–1882): Un studio sobre el mecenazgo musical de la alta nobleza española* (Madrid: Sociedad Española de Musicología, 2007), 444–62. The references to Martines are on 455 and 458. Other inventories from the same family are also included in that volume.

compositions per year between 1783 and 1787.[48] Haydn had been a teacher to Marianna Martines in the 1750s, and he, too, had lived in an apartment in the same multistory house where her family lived.[49] It seems possible that Haydn sent a copy of Martines's work to the Madrid *salonnière*, perhaps thinking that their mutual identities as accomplished female musicians would be of interest to the countess.

Although Martines largely avoided criticism for composing, Burney reported Johann Adolf Hasse's judgment that Martines's activities in composition adversely affected her voice. Burney concurred: "I had observed, indeed, the same morning, that she took the high notes with difficulty. It is an axiom among all good masters of singing, that stooping to write, and even sitting much at the harpsichord, hurts the chest, and greatly affects the voice."[50]

Musical Salons as Sites of Mentorship and Education

The spread of Martines's music—whether in manuscript to the Queen of Naples, to Padre Martini and the other members of the Accademia filarmonica in Bologna, or to the home of Maria Josefa Pimentel in Madrid—exemplifies the wide reach of work by musical *salonnières*. Indeed, whether through their hostesses' ingenuity, through epistolary networks, through travel and social relationships, or through publication, the influence of musical salons was felt across Europe and as far away as America. The salon in its ideal form was a locus of friendship—one in which relationships among men and women proved influential and creatively fruitful. Again Madame Brillon serves as a powerful example: her musical salon was a gathering place for her friends and select professional musicians who had long been resident in Paris, such as the violinist Noël Pagin, who had retired from a career that included performance at the Concert spirituel. In addition, prominent musicians and composers who resided or traveled through Paris, including Burney, Johann Schobert, and Luigi Boccherini, visited her salon

48. Judith Ortega, "Repertorio musical en la casa de Benavente-Osuna: El *Yndice* de música de la condesa-duquesa de Benavente de 1824," *Revista de musicologia* 28, no. 1 (2005): 373.

49. Godt, *Marianna Martines*, 17–21.

50. Burney, *The Present State of Music in Germany, the Netherlands, and United Provinces* (London: T. Becket, 1773), 1:348.

and helped promote her stature in the public sphere. That she acquired an English piano through Johann Christian Bach, as Burney reports, attests to her strong network of professional connections. Boccherini's appearance decades later as music director for the orchestra in the salon of the Countess-Duchess of Osuna y Benavente is a signal of how musical styles, practices, compositions, aesthetics, and personnel spread across Europe through salons.[51] As seen in her collection of music by Haydn and other central European composers, as well as music by local Spanish composers, the countess sought to cultivate a cosmopolitan taste through her lavish musical establishment. The inclination toward cosmopolitanism was a central feature of the Spanish Enlightenment—especially among women who sought to update conventions of Spanish cultural and political life to accommodate women's agency.

More than establishing social, professional, and cultural networks, salons also served as sites of education. This education could be reciprocal, benefiting men and women alike, as Daniel Gordon writes: "Because French secondary education offered little besides theology and classics, it is plausible to think of institutions of sociability as centers of adult education in which people of different backgrounds acquired whatever was necessary to supplement their knowledge."[52] In the salon, Gordon explains, women could compensate for their lack of formal education, while men gained knowledge of the niceties of language and behavior that would enable them to succeed in high society.

A prime example of this educative salon sociability lies in the relationship between Brillon and Benjamin Franklin, who was her neighbor in the village of Passy between 1777 and 1785. As I discuss in chapter 3, Franklin himself was adept at navigating the public and private domains; his role as a statesman and educator existed along a continuum with his private friendships. Indeed, in addition to the satisfaction and pleasure that he derived from these friendships, they also contributed to his success in the public realm. Franklin's close relationship with Brillon is attested in over 100 surviving letters between the two, as well as in Franklin's correspondence with other men and women in Europe and America, and in accounts by

51. On Boccherini's connection to the Countess-Duchess of Osuna y Benavente, see Fernández-Cortés, *La música en las casas de Osuna y Benavente*, 369–75.

52. Daniel Gordon, *Citizens Without Sovereignty: Equality and Sociability in French Thought, 1670–1789* (Princeton, NJ: Princeton University Press, 2017), 39.

other observers. The artist Élisabeth Vigée Le Brun left one such account, noting that "No man in Paris was more *à la mode*, more sought after than Doctor Franklin. . . . I saw him frequently at the home of Madame Brillon, who lived all along in Passy. Franklin passed all his evenings there. Madame Brillon and her two daughters made music that he seemed to have heard with pleasure."[53] That Vigée Le Brun attended Brillon's gatherings is a sign of her influence in the realm of professional visual arts as well as music; indeed, Burney relates that Brillon was skilled in this area as well.[54]

As Susan Stabile has noted, Franklin was committed to the institution of the female-led salon, viewing it as an important site of women's education.[55] Moreover, she suggests, Franklin learned as much from his salon hostesses as they did from him; she notes that women "could influence and improve men's manners, thereby securing their own place in sociable institutions of polite society in their parlors."[56] In addition, both Stabile and Claude-Anne Lopez point out that Brillon provided Franklin with an education in the French language, editing and commenting on his letters to her. They note Franklin's admiration for women's knowledge, although such knowledge might be acquired through experience or intuition; Franklin, for his part, viewed reason as an attribute of both men and women, but such intuitive knowledge only as accessible to women. In a letter to Brillon, Franklin pointed out the limitations of reason, playfully calling it a "very uncertain thing, since two sensible persons, like you and me, can draw diametrically opposed conclusions from the same point. . . . That is why, as long as I was fortunate enough to have a wife, I had adopted the habit of letting myself be guided by her opinion on difficult matters, for women, I believe, have a certain feel, which is more reliable than our reasonings."[57] Brillon's response—again in a playful tone—claimed that not only was her instinct

53. "Nul homme à Paris n'était plus à la mode, plus recherché que le docteur Franklin . . . Je l'ai beaucoup vu chez madame Brion [*sic*], qui habitait constamment Passy; Franklin passait là toutes ses soirées. Madame Brion et ses deux filles faisaient de la musique qu'il semblait écouter avec plaisir." Louise-Élisabeth Vigée Le Brun, *Souvenirs: notes et portraits 1755–1789* (Paris: Arthème Fayard, [1909]), 118. See also Melissa Percival, "Sentimental Poses in the *Souvenirs* of Élisabeth Vigée Le Brun," *French Studies* 57, no. 2 (2003): 149–65.

54. Burney, *The Present State of Music in France and Italy*, 43.

55. Susan Stabile, "Salons and Power in the Era of Revolution: From Literary Coteries to Epistolary Enlightenment," in *Benjamin Franklin and Women*, ed. Larry E. Tise (University Park: Pennsylvania State University Press, 2000), 129–48.

56. Stabile, "Salons and Power in the Era of Revolution," 138.

57. Quoted and translated in Lopez, *Mon cher papa*, 82.

superior to that of men, but her reason was on par with that of the most elite *philosophes*:

> I am a female guided by instinct. . . . I might build long dissertations on the basis of my instinct, yet my reasonings might not be more unreasonable than those of your admirable, illustrious Encyclopedists—economists—moralists—journalists—theologians—atheists—materialists—and all imaginable sorts of –ists![58]

The convergence of reason and sentiment was on display in another salon that featured music—one in which Franklin was also involved: that of Antoine-Laurent and Marie-Anne-Pierrette Paulze Lavoisier, who, until the French Revolution, hosted a salon in their home at the Arsenal in Paris. Their salon reflected their many interests and talents: they both studied and practiced chemistry, with Antoine-Laurent running their laboratory and attaining most of the public recognition for their work. Marie-Anne-Pierrette was present during her husband's laboratory work, collaborated with him in his scientific writing, and employed her skills as an artist, attained through study with no less a painter than Jacques-Louis David, to create the illustrations for her husband's *Traité élémentaire de chimie* of 1789.[59] That she was highly knowledgeable in chemistry herself is demonstrated by her transla-

58. "animal fémmélle que l'instinct du sentiment guide . . . je pourrois peut estre, avéc mon instinct faire de longues dissértations pour appuyér mon opinion et peut estre mes raisonnements, ne seroient pas plus dé-raisonnables que ceux de la pluparts de nos admirables, illustres;—Encyclopédistes—Economistes—moralistes—journalistes—théologiens—athées—matérialistes et sçavants en tous les istes possibles!" Anne-Louise Boyvin d'Hardancourt Brillon de Jouy to Benjamin Franklin, [November] 26, [1780]. French text at https://franklinpapers.org (accessed November 17, 2021). Translated in Lopez, *Mon cher papa*, 81.

59. Antoine-Laurent Lavoisier, *Traité élémentaire de chimie, présenté dans un ordre nouveau et d'après les découvertes modernes par M. Lavoisier . . . avec figures & tableaux* (Paris: chez Cuchet, 1789). On David's portrait of the Lavoisiers and the couple's participation in artistic life of Enlightenment Paris, see Mary Vidal, "David Among the Moderns: Art, Science, and the Lavoisiers," *Journal of the History of Ideas* 56, no. 4 (October 1995): 595–623. On the role that Madame Lavoisier played as a collaborator in the laboratory, see, for example, Ruelland Jacques, "Marie-Anne Pierrette Paulze-Lavoisier, comtesse de Rumford (1758–1836): Lumière surgie de l'ombre," *Dix-huitième siècle* 36, no. 1 (2004): 99–112; and Adriane P. Borgias, "Marie Anne Pierrette Paulze Lavoisier (1758–1836)," in *Women in Chemistry and Physics: A Biobibliographic Sourcebook*, ed. Louise S. Grinstein, Rose K. Rose, and Miriam H. Rafailovich (Westport, CT: Greenwood Press, 1993), 14–35.

tion of Richard Kirwan's *Essay on Phlogiston and the Constitution of Acids*, which she could not have made without understanding it, as well as other collaborative projects undertaken with her husband.[60] Indeed, as the English economist Arthur Young observed after a visit to the Lavoisier salon in 1787,

> Madame Lavoisier, a lively, sensible, scientific lady, had prepared a *déjeuné Anglois* of tea and coffee, but her conversation on Mr. Kirwan's Essay on Phlogiston, which she is translating from the English, and on other subjects, which a woman of understanding, that works with her husband in his laboratory, knows how to adorn, was the best repast.[61]

On January 24, 1783, the couple sent a note to Franklin, who had recently been engaged in negotiations leading to the Treaty of Paris. While the final treaty between Britain and the United States was not finally signed until September 1783, on January 20, a preliminary peace agreement had been reached between Britain and France. They wrote of their pleasure at having "spent Wednesday evening *chez* M. Francklin [*sic*] to congratulate him on the great revolution that his genius had prepared and which has just been affirmed by the signing of the Peace."[62] And they sought to extend the festivities by reciprocating the invitation: "They propose to engage [Franklin] to come dine with them next Monday the 27th at the Arsenal. They will have a little music after dinner, and they would be flattered to be able to amuse M. Franklin for a few moments."[63]

While the Lavoisiers' note mentions only "a little music after dinner," it

---

A recent biography of Madame Lavoisier is Jean-Pierre Poirier, *La science et l'amour: Madame Lavoisier* (Paris: Pygmalion, 2004).

60. The Lavoisiers form an example of the ideal of companionate marriage, emerging in the second half of the eighteenth century, in Meghan K. Roberts, *Sentimental Savants: Philosophical Families in Enlightenment France* (Chicago: University of Chicago Press, 2016).

61. Arthur Young, *Travels During the Years 1787, 1788, and 1789* (London: W. Richardson, 1792), 64, quoted in Denis I. Duveen, "Madame Lavoisier 1758–1836," *Chymia* 4 (1953): 17.

62. "Mr. et Mde. Lavoisier sont passés mercredy au soir chez M. francklin [*sic*] pour le feliciter sur la grande revolution que son genie avoit preparée et qui vient d'etre affermie par la signature de la Paix." Antoine-Laurent Lavoisier and Marie-Anne-Pierrette Paulze Lavoisier to Benjamin Franklin, January 24, 1783. Transcribed at https://franklinpapers.org (accessed July 14, 2019).

63. "Ils se proposoient de l'engager a venir diner avec eux lundi prochain 27 a l'arsenal. Ils auront un peu de musique apres diner et ils seroient bien flattés quelle put amuser M. francklin quelques instans."

seems that music was in fact an integral component of their salon gatherings, alongside conversations about the arts and scientific demonstrations. Any instruments and scores that Madame Lavoisier collected were likely confiscated or destroyed when her home was stormed by the Terror. (To the shock of Franklin and other participants in the European Enlightenment, Antoine-Laurent Lavoisier fell victim to the guillotine in 1794.) However, after her second, failed marriage to the American Benjamin Thomson, Count of Rumford, when Marie-Anne-Pierrette rebuilt her life, she amassed a collection of scores gathered in binders' volumes that suggest that she was a formidable keyboardist with an impressive and sustained interest in music.[64]

Indications of the Lavoisiers' musical practice before the Revolution emerge from the two manuscript catalogues created of Madame Lavoisier's private library in the nineteenth century. One of these, the *Catalogue de la musique de Madame la Comtesse de Rumford*, records the contents of her music collection, which was made up of vocal and instrumental chamber music and operatic arrangements published in the early nineteenth century, and which holds no scores from the eighteenth. By contrast, the *Catalogue des livres de la bibliothèque de Madame La Comtesse de Rumford* records a vast collection of books on wide-ranging topics, consistent with the encyclopedic interests of a scientist-philosopher of the late eighteenth century, and it includes a short list of seventeenth- and eighteenth-century music scores and theoretical treatises on music; these include works by Francesco Cavalli, Louis-Nicolas Clérambault, François Couperin, Francesco Geminiani, and a handful of others.[65]

This latter catalogue records not only the titles but also the location of the books in Madame Lavoisier's home, and the architectural plan of her home (fig. 1.2) helps illustrate this distribution of volumes. The *Catalogue*

64. I discuss this collection and Madame Lavoisier's collecting habits in Rebecca Cypess, "Madame Lavoisier's Music Collection: Lessons from a Private Library of the Nineteenth Century," *Notes: The Quarterly Journal of the Music Library Association* 77, no. 2 (2020): 224–52.

65. See the *Catalogue de la musique de Madame la Comtesse de Rumford* (Lavoisier 4712 Bd. Ms.11, Division of Rare and Manuscript Collections, Kroch Library, Cornell University) and the *Catalogue des livres de la bibliothèque de Madame la Comtesse de Rumford* (Lavoisier 4712 Bd. Ms. 44++, Division of Rare and Manuscript Collections, Kroch Library, Cornell University). A printed catalogue prepared after Madame Lavoisier's death also includes some of the eighteenth-century scores and treatises; see Constant Potelet, *Catalogue de livres faisant partie de la bibliothèque de feu Madame Lavoisier, Comtesse de Rumford* (Paris: Galliot, 1836).

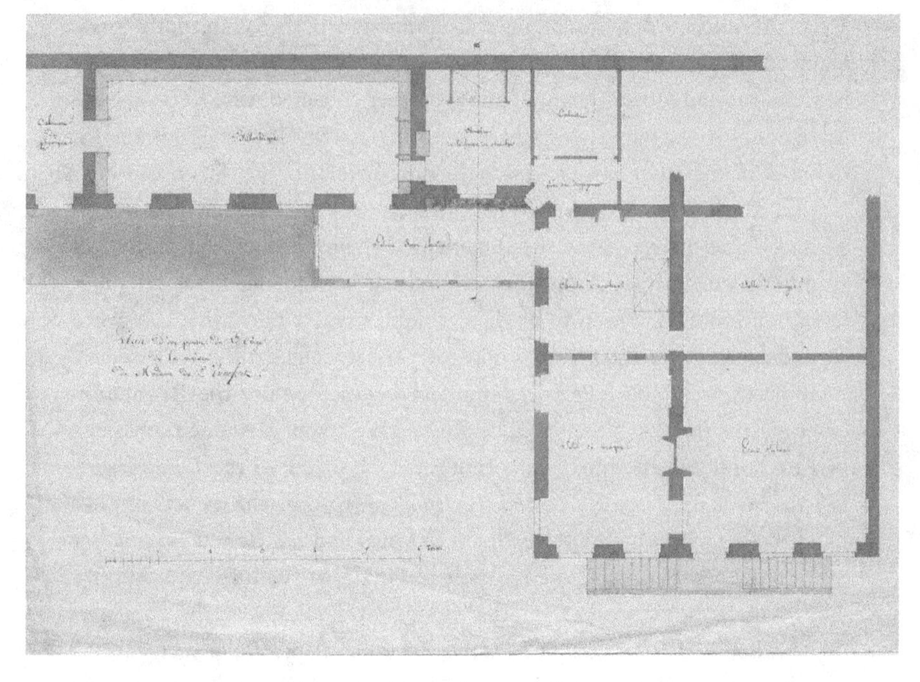

Figure 1.2 Excerpt from "Plans and architectural drawings of the exterior and interior, and landscaping of the residence erected by Madame Lavoisier (Countess Rumford) in Paris, [18—]." Lavoisier Manuscript Collection, Box 27h, Division of Rare and Manuscript Collections, Kroch Library, Cornell University Library, USA.

des livres indicates that the eighteenth-century music scores and treatises were kept with the rest of the general book collection, which occupied the large *bibliothèque* and spilled out into some hallways. The music collection described in the *Catalogue de la musique* must have been kept separately, perhaps in the *salon de musique*, where she held her musical soirées. This collection was the one in active use. The seventeenth- and eighteenth-century scores, by contrast, must have stayed on the shelves in the *bibliothèque*, serving as a reminder of her musical life with her first husband prior to the Revolution.

Before his arrival in Paris, Franklin had experienced literary salons in England, and he extended his encounters in salons through epistolary exchange, as shown by his extensive correspondence with Brillon as well as numerous other women.[66] Franklin encouraged Elizabeth Graeme (who had, at one point, been engaged to marry his son William Franklin) in the

66. On the importance of letter-writing for women of the Enlightenment, see Dena

hosting of her own salon on Saturday evenings in Philadelphia, after she, too, had visited London and attended salons there.[67] Although Graeme was primarily a poet, she also owned a harpsichord, had studied music, and was connected to the amateur musician Francis Hopkinson and his professional teacher and friend the violinist James Bremner.

A final anecdote underscores the extent to which Franklin served as a link among musical salons. In 1788, Francis Hopkinson published a collection of songs, and in his dedication to George Washington he called himself "the first Native of the United States who has produced a Musical Composition."[68] Franklin sent a copy of the publication to Madame Brillon's neighbor, Louis-Guillaume Le Veillard, asking him to "translate one of them, the Vth. and give a Copy to our ever-amiable Madame Brilon [*sic*], to be play'd & Sung; when I hope they may do some honour to the American Muse."[69] On February 21, 1789, Le Veillard responded that he would bring the songs to Brillon and attempt to translate them in verse; "it is very right," he wrote, "that she should play the first productions of America in this genre."[70] On March 6, Brillon wrote to Franklin herself, expressing admiration for the engraving but complaining that the paper was too thin. "There are one or two songs that I would have played for my good papa [i.e., Franklin] who likes them . . . This is a cause of both regrets and sweet memories!"[71]

Another strong mentoring relationship existed between Marianna Mar-

---

Goodman, *Becoming a Woman in the Age of Letters* (Ithaca, NY, and London: Cornell University Press, 2009).

67. On Elizabeth Graeme and her salon, see Anne M. Ousterhout, *The Most Learned Woman in America: A Life of Elizabeth Graeme Fergusson*, intro. by Susan Stabile (University Park: Pennsylvania State University Press, 2004). Further references appear in chapter 7.

68. Francis Hopkinson, *Seven [Eight] Songs for the Harpsichord or Forte Piano* (Philadelphia: Laitken, 1788), unnumbered dedication page.

69. Benjamin Franklin to Louis-Guillaume Le Veillard, December 10, 1788. https://franklinpapers.org (accessed July 31, 2019).

70. "il est bien juste qu'elle jouisse des pre[mières] productions de l'amerique en ce genre." Le Veillard to Franklin, February 21, 1789. https://franklinpapers.org (accessed July 31, 2019). In addition to Brillon's general interest in Franklin's welfare and the ongoing political situation in America, Le Veillard may have been thinking of the composition that she had written, apparently, on the occasion of the American victory over the British Army at Saratoga in 1777. The "Marche des insurgents" survives in the collection of the American Philosophical Society (US-PHps).

71. "il y a un ou deux airs que j'aurois joués pour mon bon papa qui les aime. . . . Cela cause et des regréts et des souvenirs bien doux!" Anne-Louise Boyvin d'Hardancourt Bril-

tines and Pietro Metastasio. When Burney visited them in Vienna, it was Metastasio who "propose[d] her sitting down to the harpsichord, which she immediately did, in a graceful manner, without the parade of diffidence, or the trouble of importunity."[72] Burney later asked Martines's brother "of whom his sister learned music, and where she had acquired her expressive manner of singing; he said, she had had several masters to teach her the grammar and mechanism of music; but that it was Metastasio who had done the rest."[73]

Musical salons were not only places where men and women educated one another, but also where women educated each other alone. This is evident in Brillon's education of her daughters, who frequently played and sang with her. Her duos and trios scored for the various keyboard instruments that she collected—a French harpsichord, an English square piano, and a German piano—were apparently written so that she could play with her two daughters. Indeed, as I discuss in chapter 2, keyboard duos were frequently used to fulfill a didactic role within the families of professional musicians, as well as between teacher and student, and members of a single family of amateur players.[74] Keyboard duos constituted a method of instruction by demonstration while also offering the players a satisfying musical experience that served to heighten their awareness of the other—to build their sympathetic responses to one another through physical and sonic interplay.

The memoirs of Stéphanie Félicité Ducrest de Saint-Aubin, the Comtesse de Genlis, published in 1825, reflect on the musical salon that she held during the winter of 1767. At these events, like the other musical *salonnières* discussed here, she made music alongside a mixed group of professionals and amateurs; she herself "played the harp, the guitar, and the *musette*." Her daughters would later benefit from their mother's expertise on the harp; Genlis reported that one of them had achieved success at the harp

lon de Jouy to Benjamin Franklin, March 6, 1789. https://franklinpapers.org (accessed July 31, 2019).

72. Burney, *The Present State of Music in Germany, the Netherlands, and United Provinces*, 1:307.

73. Burney, *The Present State of Music in Germany, the Netherlands, and United Provinces*, 1:317.

74. See chapter 2 as well as Rebecca Cypess, "Keyboard-Duo Arrangements in Eighteenth-Century Musical Life," *Eighteenth-Century Music* 14, no. 2 (September 2017): 183–214.

using "the method that I invented of exercising the two hands separately in passages containing, successively, all difficulties."[75]

Within Genlis's salon of 1767, apparently her closest collaborator was the professional composer Marie-Emanuelle Bayon, who composed the music for the comic opera that they performed for their friends. While these soirées included such virtuosos as violinist Wilhelm Cramer and cellist Jean-Louis Duport, it was Bayon who received Genlis's extended description and special praise as "a charming young person, pretty, sweet, modest, wise, spiritual, a pianist of the highest order, a marvelous composer, with astonishing facility."[76] If Bayon imparted some of her musical knowledge to Genlis during these gatherings, Bayon may have learned from her hostess the art of being a *salonnière*. When Bayon married and moved with her husband, the architect Victor Louis, to the city of Bordeaux in 1776, she began hosting a salon herself. According to her husband's biographer, she "knew how to do the honors [of the salon] with an attractive charm and an amiability that made the most distinguished people of the city seek ardently to attend it."[77] The notion that Bayon had learned the art of the *salonnière* from Genlis resonates with Dena Goodman's characterization of hosting salons as "a career based on a long apprenticeship and careful study, resulting in

75. "la méthode que j'ai inventée d'exercer séparément les deux mains, par des passages contenant successivement toutes les difficultés." Stéphanie Félicité Ducrest de Saint-Aubin, Comtesse de Genlis, *Mémoires inédits . . . sur le dix-huitième siècle et la Révolution francoise, depuis 1756 jusqu'à nos jours* (Paris: Chez Ladvocat, 1825), 3:129. Genlis's skills as a singer and harpist were important in her early life, as she made frequent appearances in salons and private concerts from the age of twelve; see Antoine Lilti, *Le monde des salons: sociabilité et mondanité à Paris au XVIIIe siècle* (Paris: Fayard, 2005), 259. Her method of playing the harp was published as Stéphanie Félicité Ducrest de Saint-Aubin, Comtesse de Genlis, *Nouvelle méthode pour apprendre à jouer de la harpe en moins de six mois de leçons* (Paris: Chez Mme. Duhan et compagnie, [1800]).

76. "Mademoiselle Baillon étoit une charmante jeune personne, jolie, douce, modeste, sage, spirituelle, jouant du piano de la première force, composant à merveille, et avec une étonnante facilité." Genlis, *Mémoires inédits*, 1:388.

77. "savait en faire les honneurs avec un charme attractif et une amabilité qui en faisaient rechercher avec empressement la fréquentation par tout ce que la ville offrait de distingué." Louis-Eusébe-Henri Gaullieur L'Hardy, *Porte-feuille ichnographique précédé d'une notice architectonographique sur le grand-théâtre de Bordeaux, rédigée d'après des documens authentiques* (Paris: Chez Carilian-Goery, 1828), 32. See also Deborah Hayes, "Marie-Emanuelle Bayon, Later Madame Louis, and Music in Late Eighteenth-Century France," *College Music Symposium* 30, no. 1 (Spring 1990): 14–33.

the independence of mastership. . . . The women who became *salonnières* always apprenticed in an established salon before breaking out on their own."[78] An educational agenda shared among women was also clearly behind the publication of Ann Ford's treatise on musical glasses, as discussed above, which served to extend the reach of her performances to the homes and practices of other musical salons.

Critiques of Musical Salons

The wide array of cases that I have discussed thus far demonstrates how musical *salonnières* came to exert agency on musical culture during the Enlightenment. While it is true that they had limited access to formal education, their status as women often enabled them to attain a high degree of training in music—enough to keep pace with the professional musicians with whom they collaborated. Through those collaborations with professionals, their ideas entered the public sphere in a socially sanctioned way. Indeed, in some cases, professional-class women, viewing the advantages of hosting a salon, succeeding in doing so themselves, thus placing themselves at the center of an elite musical circle. Even the elite *salonnières*, often more restricted in their public activities than professional female musicians, found various ways to step into the public sphere. Through connections between professional and amateur musicians formed in salons, and through links to men of letters such as Burney and Franklin, musical *salonnières* saw their ideas and even their music spread across the European continent and to America.

This is not to say that musical salons always met with approval. In a letter to the Dutch diplomat Pieter van Bleiswyck dated April 10, 1778, John Adams expressed shock at the libertine behavior displayed *chez* Brillon. After describing Madame Brillon as "one of the most beautifull Women in France, a great Mistress of Musick, as were her two little Daughters,"[79] Adams recounted meeting, over dinner, the little girls' governess (a "woman in company"). He continued,

78. Goodman, *The Republic of Letters*, 76. Goodman does not view Genlis as a true *salonnière* (75), but the regular, exclusive gatherings that she hosted suggested that she should be understood within that category, and Lilti treats her as such (Lilti, *The World of the Salons*, 169–70).

79. John Adams to Pieter van Bleiswyck, April 10, 1778. Transcribed at http://www.masshist.org/publications/adams-papers/index.php/view/DJA04p48 (accessed May 31, 2021).

> When I afterwards learned both from Dr. Franklin and his Grandson, and from many other Persons, that this Woman was the Amie of Mr. Brillion and that Madam Brillion consoled herself by the Amitie of Mr. Le Vailliant, I was astonished that these People could live together in such apparent Friendship and indeed without cutting each others throats. But I did not know the World. I soon saw and heard so much of these Things in other Families and among allmost all the great People of the Kingdom that I found it was a thing of course. It was universally understood and Nobody lost any reputation by it. Yet I must say that I never knew an Instance of it, without perceiving that all their Complaisancy was external and ostensible only: a mere conformity to the fashion: and that internally there was so far from being any real friendship or conjugal Affection that their minds and hearts were full of Jealousy, Envy, revenge and rancour. In short that it was deadly poison to all the calm felicity of Life. There were none of the delightful Enjoyments of conscious Innocence and mutual Confidence. It was mere brutal pleasure.

It was perhaps this experience that led John and Abigail Adams to be wary of salons, viewing them, from their Puritan perspective, as sites of debauchery and excess. Thus, when Abigail the Younger, daughter of John and Abigail, wrote to John Quincy Adams from London in 1785, she expressed some dismay at not being allowed to attend the musical salon held weekly by Miss Paradise, daughter of the Americans John and Lucy Paradise. Abigail the Younger first describes salons of a more general sort, centered on card games:

> There are a kind of assemblys here called routs, were the name changed I should not dislike them. A Lady sets apart a particular day in a week when She is to be found at home and her acquaintance who wish to see her, call upon her that Evening, or She sends invitations to whatever Gentlemen or Ladies She pleases. Cards are usualy introduced after tea and those Play who choose. Others who do not, let it alone. And at ten or Eleven the company Leaves her. The Lady of the House never Plays herself, and it is a kind of rule that if you Play at one House, you must at every one, at which you visit in this Way.

The other category of salon that Abigail the Younger describes to her father is of a distinctly musical nature:

> This Mrs. Paradise has a Musical [Party?] every sunday Eve. Miss P—— Plays, and she has a Number of Gentlemen and Ladies of her acquaintance who sing and Play, who visit her that Evening. She has no Cards. She has often told Mamma and myself that she is allways at home of a sunday Eve, but we have not yet ever visitted her, nor I dont suppos ever Shall.[80]

Nor were the Adamses alone in early America in viewing the institution of the salon with suspicion. Thomas Jefferson was equivocal about the French salons and the loose mores that they encompassed, but, in Paris in 1786, he began an intimate relationship with the *salonnière* Maria Cosway. An artist as well as a musician with published compositions to her name, Cosway had been born into the professional class and had achieved some success as an artist in London, supported especially by the Swiss-born painter Angelica Kauffman. Cosway and her husband, with whom she had a difficult marriage, left London for Paris, where she met Jefferson. In the words of historian William Howard Adams, in her relationship with Jefferson, Cosway "downplayed her artistic and musical abilities, treating them as amateur social accomplishments useful in promoting her husband's career."[81] In fact, as can be discerned from the other cases outlined here, it was in treating her accomplishments as amateur in nature that she promoted her own social success.

Nevertheless, although Jefferson frequented salons of Cosway and other, more elite women such as Suzanne Necker, he was skeptical of the suitability of salons—musical or otherwise—in America. As Brian Steele has observed, "throughout his correspondence ran an implicit disgust about a national culture that prized politeness and wit in the salon over the industrious labor and manly democracy of American political culture."[82] Jefferson's reticence about salons did not prevent him from insisting on a thorough and systematic education in music for his own daughters in

80. Abigail Adams the Younger to John Quincy Adams, August 26, 1785, *Founders Online*, National Archives, last modified June 13, 2018, http://founders.archives.gov/documents/Adams/04-06-02-0096. Original source: *The Adams Papers*, Adams Family Correspondence, vol. 6, *December 1784–December 1785*, ed. Richard Alan Ryerson (Cambridge, MA: Harvard University Press, 1993), 299–312.

81. William Howard Adams, *The Paris Years of Thomas Jefferson* (New Haven, CT, and London: Yale University Press, 1997), 225.

82. Brian Steele, *Thomas Jefferson and American Nationhood* (Cambridge: Cambridge University Press, 2012), 80.

Virginia.[83] In addition, he ensured that his wife and daughters learned to be generous and sociable hostesses, adopting some of the spirit of the *salonnière*; they frequently entertained dignitaries from Europe and America in their home.[84]

The responses of the Americans Jefferson and Adams to the social customs of the French salon seem to have been heavily influenced by the salons of Britain. While the musical salons such as that of Ann Ford existed in England by 1760, members of the most prominent salon circle there—that of the Bluestockings—tended to be skeptical of the French-style salon as an institution, and they were ambivalent about women's musical education more broadly. As Susan Staves and others have demonstrated, the Bluestockings viewed the sensuous art of music as a threat to their agenda of promoting women's education, exercise of reason, and publication as authors of literary works. Staves cites Catharine Macaulay's *Letters on Education* (1790), which acknowledges that ancient philosophers had viewed music as having a positive effect on the human constitution. However, Macaulay refers to modern authorities in music who claim that "those kinds of [music] which are excellent as pieces of art, seldom penetrate farther than the ear; and that though elegant in a high degree as pleasures of sense, they contribute to encrease imbecility; nor are they able to produce those lively emotions of the mind, which are the genuine effects of music."[85]

The Bluestocking writer Hannah More viewed music as a distraction employed to keep women away from more rational activities, and she reckoned that the time wasted on musical practice by young ladies between the ages of six and eighteen amounted to an astonishing 14,400 hours. More cites one mother who took pains to ensure that her daughter would acquire the skill of music so as to attract a husband; yet, she notes, the young lady in question "is now married to a man who *dislikes music!*"[86] Mary Wollstonecraft concurred that "girls learn something of music, drawing, and geography; but they do

83. See Cynthia A. Kierner, *Martha Jefferson Randolph, Daughter of Monticello: Her Life and Times* (Chapel Hill: University of North Carolina Press, 2012), 45 and passim.

84. Kierner, *Martha Jefferson Randolph*, 27.

85. Catharine Macaulay, *Letters on Education; with Observations on Religious and Metaphysical Subjects* (Dublin: H. Chamberlaine et al., 1790), 63. See Susan Staves, "The Learned Female Soprano," in *Bluestockings Displayed: Portraiture, Performance and Patronage, 1730–1830*, ed. Elizabeth Eger (Cambridge: Cambridge University Press, 2013), 145–46.

86. Hannah More, *Strictures on the Modern System of Female Education*, vol. 1 (London: Printed for T. Cadell Jr. and W. Davies, 1799), 80–81.

not know enough to engage their attention, and render it an employment of the mind." However, Wollstonecraft notes that "when a girl has a fondness for the art, and a desire of excellence," it can carry her beyond her sensual experiences. "Whatever tends to make a person in some measure independent of the senses, is a prop to virtue."[87] Thus members of the Bluestocking salons generally rejected music as a component of their project of women's advancement in more rational areas. Nevertheless, as Staves notes, they viewed certain kinds of music, including Handel's oratorios, as edifying.

A passion for Handel dominated the salon of the poet Anna Seward, who hosted gatherings that encompassed both music and literature in her home in Lichfield, England. The library in Seward's home included extensive holdings in music criticism, and Seward's salons featured performances by her close friend, the professional singer John Saville.[88] Another British poet connected to the Bluestockings, Anne Home Hunter, likewise held salons that encompassed both music and literature. As Sarah Day-O'Connell has shown, Hunter's salon should be understood as entwined with the gatherings that her husband, the surgeon John Hunter, held in an adjacent room. While John Hunter's surgical demonstrations and his publications in the field of anatomy might seem quite distant from the sentimental experiences of his wife's salon, Day-O'Connell argues that sentiment was understood as a function of women's bodily compositions. She shows how the English canzonettas of Franz Joseph Haydn, composed to poetry by Hunter and tested in her salon, reflect this fascination with the continuum of women's bodies and their emotional interiors.[89]

The American writer and politician Doctor Benjamin Rush threaded the needle between salon sociability and the conservative views of these English writers. Rush was part of the salon circles of Elizabeth Graeme and Annis Stockton, both members of the mid-Atlantic school of poets.[90]

87. Mary Wollstonecraft, *Thoughts on the Education of Daughters, with Reflections on Female Conduct in the More Important Duties of Life* (London: J. Johnson, 1787), 25–27.

88. An account of Anna Seward's salons, including their musical aspect, is in Amy Prendergast, *Literary Salons across Britain and Ireland in the Long Eighteenth Century* (London: Palgrave Macmillan, 2015), 147–52. On Seward's taste for Handel, see Wood, "The Female Penseroso."

89. Day-O'Connell, "The Composer, the Surgeon, His Wife and Her Poems."

90. Biographical information on Annis Stockton and an edition of a manuscript of her poetry are in Annis Boudinot Stockton, *Only for the Eye of a Friend: The Poems of Annis Boudinot Stockton*, ed. Carla Mulford (Charlottesville and London: University Press of Virginia, 1995).

Figure 1.3 Charles Willson Peale, *Portrait of Julia Stockton Rush (Mrs. Benjamin Rush)*, Philadelphia, Pennsylvania, United States (1776), 1960.0392 A. Gift of Mrs. Julia B. Henry. Courtesy of Winterthur Museum, Winterthur, Delaware, USA.

Stockton followed Graeme in hosting a literary salon in her home. Rush became so intimate with the Stockton family that he married Annis and Richard Stockton's daughter Julia. While it is unclear whether Annis Stockton played instruments or sang herself, her daughter Julia was invested enough in music to have had her wedding portrait painted with a guitar (see fig. 1.3). Rush argued in his treatise on women's education that, for most women, instrumental music was wasteful: "to perform well, upon a musical instrument, requires much time and long practice," which time was "an immense deduction from that short period of time which is allowed by the peculiar circumstances of our country for the acquisition of the useful branches of literature . . . How many useful ideas might be picked up in these hours from history, philosophy, poetry, and the numerous moral essays with which our language abounds, and how much more would the knowledge acquired upon these subjects add to the consequence of a lady, with her husband and with society, than the best performed pieces of music upon a harpsichord or a guittar!"[91]

Like Hannah More, Rush lamented the time that ladies spent learning music when they would simply abandon the practice upon their marriage, relegating their harpsichords to the status of "side-boards for their parlours." Perhaps it was the fact that Annis Stockton's and Elizabeth Graeme's salons centered on "useful" literature that made Rush feel justified in attending their salons. And yet, his treatise included a caveat about women's cultivation of instrumental music that makes allowances for his wife's musical practice. In Rush's words,

> Let it not be supposed from these observations that I am insensible of the charms of instrumental music, or that I wish to exclude it from the education of a lady where a musical ear irresistibly disposes to it, and affluence at the same time affords a prospect of such an exemption from the usual cares and duties of the mistress of a family, as will enable her to practice it. These circumstances form an exception to the general conduct that should arise upon this subject, from the present state of society and manners in America.[92]

In Rush's view, an "irresistible" (natural?) inclination toward music must be combined with sufficient wealth to exempt a woman "from the usual cares and duties of the mistress of a family" to justify an education in instrumental music. Certainly, Julia Stockton and Elizabeth Graeme—at least in her youth—met the latter qualification. Rush's disapproval of instrumental music as a pastime for other girls and women, he explains, was a function of the specific situation in colonial America and the early United States, but his explanation echoes the discourse of English writers in its re-

91. Benjamin Rush, *Essays, Literary, Moral, and Philosophical*, 2nd ed. (Philadelphia: Thomas and William Bradford, 1806), 85.

92. Rush, *Essays, Literary, Moral, and Philosophical*, 86.

strictive approach. While the study of literature, history, moral instruction, and philosophy might prove "useful" among women in the new nation, and some forms of vocal music aided in piety and discipline, instrumental music should be reserved for the wealthy elite.

Conclusion

As Antoine Lilti has argued, salons were neither entirely public nor entirely private spaces, and this liminal status is key to understanding the phenomenon of musical salons in particular. Situated within the walls of the home, musical salons held an aura of domesticity even as they opened their doors to intellectuals, artists, and professional musicians, elite amateurs, and listeners from the outside. As a liminal space that mediated between the public and private spheres, musical salons offered *salonnières* a platform for exercising cultural agency. Salons allowed them to play and sing with other highly skilled musicians, sharing their tastes and talents with their *habitués* and with guests from abroad. Because salons generally featured conversation as a central component of their proceedings, musical *salonnières* were often able to share their ideas and shape the ideas of their interlocutors. These ideas spread through the networks of sociability that linked salons across Europe and in America. Men of letters such as Pietro Metastasio, Charles Burney, and Benjamin Franklin met women, mentored them, learned from them, and reported on them to a wider audience. In addition, women such as Hester Thrale Piozzi and Fanny Burney—both well-traveled authors—shared knowledge about and across salons. And women who did not travel as widely, such as Madame Brillon, Sara Levy, and the Countess de Genlis, mentored other girls and women in the practices of musical salons through personal contact and epistolary exchange. Musical salons and the women at their center sometimes met with disapproval, whether for their engagement with the public sphere or because of accusations that they were wasting time on a sensual art and engaged in libertine behavior more generally. However, this did not stop musical *salonnières* from using the institution of the salon as a site of cultural agency.

CHAPTER TWO

Sensuality, Sociability, and Sympathy

Musical Salon Practices as Enactments of Enlightenment

The status of music within the Enlightenment is a contentious issue; equally fraught is the status of women. The Enlightenment has often been figured as a purely intellectual movement, divorced from both sensuality and sentiment. Thus, while music theory and acoustics have been treated as components of the Enlightenment, musical practice seems to occupy a separate discursive and experiential space. Daniel Heartz, in his monumental study of the galant style, rejects the term "Enlightenment" to describe the music-historical period 1720–1780, instead defining the Enlightenment as a "philosophical movement" and asserting that the "Enlightenment is best understood in its literal etymological sense as a movement spreading light to the intellect."[1] Such a narrow definition raises a related question: Did women experience the Enlightenment, and if so, how? Since, with few exceptions, women were restricted from receiving a formal education equivalent to that of men, and were generally characterized during the eighteenth century as sentimental, sensual beings rather than rational ones, is it possible that they experienced the Enlightenment at all? In the words of historian Ruth Dawson, "Could women have an Enlightenment movement corresponding to the movement of scientific, philosophical, literary, and civil discourse and activity that educated middle-class and aristocratic men enjoyed throughout most of the eighteenth century?"[2] For Dawson, the

1. Heartz, *Music in European Capitals*, 3–4.

2. Ruth Dawson, "'Lights Out! Lights Out!' Women and the Enlightenment," in *Gender in Transition: Discourse and Practice in German-Speaking Europe, 1750–1830*, ed. Ulrike Gleixner and Marion W. Gray (Ann Arbor: University of Michigan Press, 2009), 219.

Enlightenment was "only one thread of intellectual and cultural discourse occurring in the eighteenth century," with the movement of *Empfindsamkeit* (sensibility) representing a competing thread that was more often gendered female.[3]

The questions of whether either women or music belong in discussions of the Enlightenment become heightened in consideration of musical salons. Although *salonnières* were sometimes more educated than ordinary women, in part as a result of their frequent conversations and exchanges with the male intellectuals who visited them, salons as a whole were often attacked—both by the eighteenth-century critics and by scholars of salon culture since then—for their sensual and emotional excess, for the ways in which they distracted from rational activities. In musical salons, the sensual aspects of salon practice were intensified through musical practice. Since music itself was seen by many as a trifling accomplishment with no rational substance, the extensive focus on music within salons compounded their problems. Eighteenth-century *salonnières* and their musical salons are easily dismissed as representative of little more than trivial entertainment, far removed from the serious intellectual work of the Enlightenment.

My contention is that these assumptions and arguments are misleading. First, in the eighteenth century, the Enlightenment was not understood universally as a purely intellectual phenomenon; and second, while music was surely entertaining and amusing, it also had a role to play in moral education. As recent work by Jessica Riskin, Andelheid Voskuhl, and others has demonstrated, sentimental expression in response to sensual stimuli was an integral component of the formation of an enlightened and moral society—a central concern of Enlightenment thinkers, both male and female.[4] Antoine Lilti's study of salons as a component of the French obsession with the taste and judgment of fashionable society—known collectively as *le monde*—brought discussion of sensuality back into the conversation. More recently, Peter Clark has identified (predominantly homosocial) clubs and societies as a site of a "fashionable form of public sociability" that encompassed music among other activities,[5] and Gillian Russell and Clara Tuite

3. Dawson, "'Lights Out! Lights Out!,'" 220.

4. See Jessica Riskin, *Science in the Age of Sensibility: The Sentimental Empiricists of the French Enlightenment* (Chicago and London: University of Chicago Press, 2002); Adelheid Voskuhl, *Androids in the Enlightenment: Mechanics, Artisans, and Cultures of the Self* (Chicago and London: University of Chicago Press, 2013).

5. Peter Clark, *British Clubs and Societies 1580–1800: The Origins of an Associational World* (Oxford: Oxford University Press, 2000), 26.

have advocated for the consideration of women's experiences—including sensual activities such as music and dance—within a "romantic sociability" that arose around 1770.[6] These studies present a strong case for understanding sensual experiences, including those prompted by music, within the story of the Enlightenment.

Writers such as Adam Smith and David Hume affirmed that the cultivation of moral sentiment required the exercise and experience of emotions. The sensual arts such as painting and music offered opportunities for such emotional engagement. In addition, the arts allowed individuals to experience situations outside of their own, fostering a sense of "sympathy" (what we would now call "empathy") with other people. It is that sympathy, they suggest, that allows people to act morally. Moses Mendelssohn and Gotthold Ephraim Lessing articulated these ideas in their own theories of the arts and politics. Perhaps most notably, the French *salonnière* Sophie de Grouchy Condorcet, who translated and commented on Smith's *Theory of Moral Sentiments* during the Reign of Terror, advocated an understanding of sympathy based on the balance of sentiment and reason. In this, her ideas reflect the milieu of the salon, where sensual and emotional experiences were interspersed with conversation. Such conversation—even about seemingly trivial matters such as music—fostered moral sentiment.

How did music-making in salons contribute to this cultivation of sympathy? In order to answer this, I consider what Edward Klorman calls "music in the present tense"[7]—music's lived experience, created by and for the players and listeners in the room. Moving away from composition as the primary locus of meaning in the study of eighteenth-century music, I place performance practices in the center of my discussion. I base my observations on my experience as a historical keyboardist who has sought to replicate the musical practices of eighteenth-century salons. While my perspective is surely different from that of eighteenth-century women, many of the practical considerations and challenges that I have encountered in playing this music with willing (and good-humored) colleagues would have been encountered by the women I am studying as well. The act of playing reveals considerations that cannot be discerned through silent score study. Motivated by an overall project of giving voice to these

6. Russell and Tuite, "Introducing Romantic Sociability." I am indebted to the discussion in Wood, "The Female Penseroso."

7. Klorman, *Mozart's Music of Friends*, 73–108.

women, I use performance as a tool for investigating their musical customs and priorities.

Interpreting those customs and priorities is another matter. Thus, following my explication of musical salon practices, I will turn to Smith and Hume, Mendelssohn and Lessing, and the *salonnières* Sophie Condorcet and Suzanne Necker, whose writings open pathways to understanding the role of performance in salons within the agenda of the Enlightenment. I show that, through the lived experiences of both music and conversation, musical salons constituted sites with the potential for the cultivation of sympathy and fostering of moral sentiment.

Flexible Instrumentation and Salon Practice

Compositional styles of eighteenth-century Europe have long been understood as analogous to modes of sociability, and in some cases these styles have been linked to musical salons. W. Dean Sutcliffe has argued that, as a whole, instrumental music in the age of Enlightenment assumed an aspect of "human comportment."[8] Edward Klorman has expanded upon this analogy by locating a conversational style in the chamber music of Mozart.[9] Barbara Russano Hanning has addressed a musical style that developed in French salons, the so-called *style dialogué*, which, she shows, manifests the principles of *politesse* and reciprocity,[10] both in the music's own mode of conversational expression and in consideration of the listeners' ability to hear and comprehend with ease and grace.[11] For Daniel Heartz, the Italian concertos from the 1750s onward display "concertante dialogue and [a] dramatic yet intimate tone, sometimes approaching that of conversation."[12] Steven Zohn has pointed to the quartets of Carl Philipp Emanuel Bach, commissioned by the Berlin *salonnière* Sara Levy, as examples of salon sociability made manifest in compositional style.[13] And, examining a slightly

8. W. Dean Sutcliffe, "The Shapes of Sociability in the Instrumental Music of the Later Eighteenth Century," *Journal of the Royal Musical Association* 138, no. 1 (2013): 2.

9. Klorman, *Mozart's Music of Friends*, 3–72.

10. Barbara Russano Hanning, "Conversation and Musical Style in the Late Eighteenth-Century Parisian Salon," *Eighteenth-Century Studies* 22, no. 4 (1989): 512–28.

11. On listening in the eighteenth century, see Matthew Riley, *Musical Listening in the German Enlightenment: Attention, Wonder and Astonishment* (Aldershot: Ashgate, 2004).

12. Heartz, *Music in European Capitals*, 284.

13. Steven Zohn, "The Sociability of Salon Culture and Carl Philipp Emanuel Bach's Quartets," in *Sara Levy's World*, 205–42.

later repertoire, Nancy November has considered salon sociability in the string quartets of Beethoven's Vienna.[14]

And yet, Sutcliffe and Klorman, among others, have pointed out the limits of the "conversational" analogy in compositional style. For Sutcliffe, "linguistic analogies such as conversation and dialogue are susceptible to other rationales—they could be as much a justification as an explanation for the modern instrumental manner that could, after all, cause such a commotion."[15] In this view, the comparison between elements of composition such as the presence of melody in a given instrumental line and elements of linguistic conversation between people may have served to orient listeners without functioning as the impetus for composition. Klorman's theory of "multiple agency" helps address this problem, as it "[constructs] a framework for analyzing chamber music as play, expressing in prose the kind of dynamic social intercourse that musicians experience while playing this repertoire."[16]

Without denying the links between certain features of eighteenth-century composition and salon sociability—indeed, I agree that they reflect important aspects of salon practice—I propose to refocus the discussion away from composition and around the lived experience of music-making within salons. With Klorman, I view the lived experience of music-making—especially its ludic qualities—as the primary locus of musical salon sociability; my study complements his in focusing on performance practices rather than compositions. The distinction that I am making here is a subtle one. After all, in the eighteenth century, performance and composition existed along a continuum. Conventions of composition meant that notation during this period was "thin,"[17] leaving space for performers to shape lines as they wished through articulation and dynamic shading, and to elaborate on the text through the addition of ornaments or variations and the realization of a basso continuo line. Performances frequently included improvised

14. Nancy November, *Cultivating String Quartets in Beethoven's Vienna* (Woodbridge, UK: Boydell Press, 2017), especially ch. 4, "Locating String Quartets in Beethoven's Vienna."

15. W. Dean Sutcliffe, *Instrumental Music in an Age of Sociability: Haydn, Mozart, and Friends* (Cambridge: Cambridge University Press, 2020), 146.

16. Klorman, *Mozart's Music of Friends*, 111.

17. On the concept of "thin notation," see Bruce Haynes, *The End of Early Music: A Period Performer's History of Music for the Twenty-First Century* (Oxford and New York: Oxford University Press, 2007), 4 and passim.

material in the form of cadenzas, preludes, or fantasies, and, as Klorman has shown, composition could easily morph into improvisation in music-making of the eighteenth century.[18]

Nevertheless, thinking about salon sociability through the act of performance can be highly revealing. In facing the specific realities of performance, we may come to terms with the meanings of musical salons in new ways. Key to this approach is the recognition that salons encompassed an array of experiences that cannot be easily encapsulated within a single, overarching framework. Indeed, the performance practices of musical salons were, by definition, dependent upon the circle of friends who gathered to enact them. Musical styles used in salons across Europe ranged widely, as local interests and the tastes of *salonnières* and their guests determined what music was played, and how. I do not propose to define a distinct category of musical salon practices that were used exclusively in salons but excluded from other domestic settings. While there were certain practices that were especially well suited to musical salons, those practices may be discerned in other aspects of eighteenth-century musical life. Any compositional style could be rendered in the sociable terms of musical salons: these institutions had the power to transform, in effect, any compositional style into one that reflected salon sociability. Sociability, a key concept of the eighteenth century, involved norms of behavior such as politeness, reciprocity, and sympathy, all of which are predicated on an awareness of other people.[19] Music-making within the salon was a participatory act that required individuals to temper their needs in pursuit of social harmony; this musical metaphor was enacted through the music itself. Merely by making music within a salon, *salonnières* and their *habitués* rendered it sociable.

It is a truism that, before the age of recorded sound, musical experiences depended on the players who participated and the instruments that they used. Within salons, where music-making could be either well planned or a spur-of-the-moment activity, much depended on who was present on any given evening. Burney makes this point clear in describing his visit to the salon of Madame Brillon in 1770. Brillon first played some of her own pieces; she then sight-read some of Burney's: "she played the second of my

18. Klorman, *Mozart's Music of Friends*, 86–108.

19. Sutcliffe, *Instrumental Music in an Age of Sociability*, 1–24. On the history of the term "sociability" (*sociabilité*), coined in the eighteenth century, see Gordon, *Citizens Without Sovereignty*.

sonatas very well at sight on the pianoforte accompanied by M. Pagin—and for want of a violoncello I played that part on the harpsichord."[20] Similarly, when Marianna Martines performed a pair of her arias for Burney, she did so without the aid of other instruments, but merely accompanying herself on the harpsichord. None of her compositions survive in such a configuration, suggesting that, in Burney's company, she may have reduced the score at sight.[21] The unique collection of instruments used in the salon of Ann Ford suggests that the adaptation of music to suit those instruments must have been *de rigueur.*[22] Moreover, the fact that Benjamin Franklin gave Madame Brillon a glass armonica and, in his fanciful depiction of heaven, described playing it with her there, indicates that it was used in her salon.[23] Yet no works calling for the armonica survive in her collection, which makes it highly likely that the instrument was added to other works in unnotated and perhaps spontaneous ways.[24]

From one side these reconfigurations of instrumentation were simply a matter of practical necessity, brought about by the absence of the "correct" instrumentation among the party. Seen from another angle, however, the fluid nature of salons meant that personnel was constantly shifting, and therefore realization of music in salons was highly variable. This, in turn, underscores aspects of the "work concept" in the eighteenth century. In an age when instrumentation and timbre were in constant flux from one social situation to another, these parameters of performance were necessarily unstable.[25] As Wiebke Thormählen has explained, "the

20. Charles Burney, *Music, Men, and Manners in France and Italy*, ed. H. Edmund Poole (London: Folio Society, 1969), 20.

21. Burney, *The Present State of Music in Germany, the Netherlands, and United Provinces*, 1:307.

22. See the discussions in Holman, "Ann Ford Revisited," and in chapter 1 of this volume.

23. Franklin's vision of playing music in Paradise with Madame Brillon is preserved in a letter: Benjamin Franklin to Anne-Louise Brillon de Jouy, after December 10, 1778? https://franklinpapers.org (accessed August 4, 2019). The glass armonica that Franklin gave to Brillon survives at the Bakken Museum in Minneapolis, Minnesota; a photo and description have been archived from the Bakken Museum's website and can now be found at https://web.archive.org/web/20070405115543/http://www.thebakken.org/exhibits/mesmer/glass-armonica.htm (accessed August 1, 2019).

24. Brillon's collection of surviving scores, now in private hands, is catalogued in Gustafson, "Madame Brillon et son salon"; since this publication, Gustafson has produced an expanded "Catalogue du fonds Brillon," which he was kind enough to share with me.

25. Opposing notions of the "work concept" are in Lydia Goehr, *The Imaginary Mu-*

salon became a forum for individuals to repeat and experience music frequently in guises other than those associated with public performance."[26] Music that was composed, originally, for the church, the theater, or the public concert hall could be adapted by salon participants so that it assumed a personalized form. While Thormählen primarily addresses notated arrangements that were published during the eighteenth century, the fluidity of eighteenth-century performance conventions means that her observations can be fruitfully applied to unnotated chamber music. Adaptation of notated music was intrinsic to music-making, and within the salon, this immediate adaptation was a function of sociability. Adaptive performance practices such as changes in instrumentation meant that each musical experience was unique—and uniquely tied to the salon from which it emerged.

In some cases, variations in instrumentation were notated, with part books copied out for distribution to the various players. Although such realizations could be repeated from one performance to the next, they were nevertheless tied to the specific circumstances and instrumentation available within the salon. It is likely that the performances of Marie-Emanuelle Bayon's *Fleur d'Épine* at the soirées of the Comtesse de Genlis, with the composer as a participant, were executed in arrangements, a number of which are preserved in manuscript or published versions.[27] Sara Levy's collection of manuscript part books used in her salon includes numerous arrangements, including a unique version of the sonata in E-flat major attributed to Johann Sebastian Bach, BWV 1031.[28] Generally known in the scoring for flute and obbligato keyboard, the arrangement in Levy's collection takes the obbligato right-hand part away from the keyboardist and assigns it to a violinist instead; the keyboardist's right hand is therefore free to realize a chordal thoroughbass accompaniment or a more complex

seum of Musical Works: An Essay in the Philosophy of Music (Oxford: Oxford University Press, 1992); and Harry White, "If It's Baroque, Don't Fix It: Reflections on Lydia Goehr's 'Work Concept' and the Historical Integrity of Musical Composition," *Acta Musicologica* 69, no. 1 (1997): 94–104.

26. Thormählen, "Playing with Art," 368.

27. A catalogue of arrangements of works from this opera is in Barbara Garvey Jackson, *"Say You Can Deny Me": A Guide to Surviving Music by Women from the 16th Through the 18th Centuries* (Fayetteville: University of Arkansas Press, 1994).

28. The manuscript is in the Staatsbibliothek zu Berlin, shelfmark D-Bsa SA 3587. On the attribution of the piece to Bach, see Jeanne Swack, "Quantz and the Sonata in E-flat Major for Flute and Cembalo, BWV 1031," *Early Music* 23, no. 1 (1995): 31–53.

Example 2.1A Johann Sebastian Bach (?), Sonata BWV 1031 in E-flat major, movement 2, Siciliano, mm. 1–8, in the arrangement for flute, violin, and basso continuo. The elaborated keyboard right-hand part, shown in small notes, is my suggestion.

Example 2.1B

contrapuntal line.[29] In example 2.1 and audio example 2.1, I propose an arpeggiated thoroughbass realization that complements and punctuates the two treble lines. ♫

This practice is consistent with the description of Bach's own performance practices as reported by Carl Philipp Emanuel Bach to Johann Nikolaus Forkel in 1774:

> Thanks to his greatness in harmony, he accompanied trios on more than one occasion on the spur of the moment and, being in a good humor and knowing that the composer would not take it amiss, and on the basis of a sparsely figured continuo part just set before him, converted them into complete quartets, astounding the composer of the trio.[30]

The spontaneity and fluidity captured in this description speaks to the flexibility of chamber music in performance. In addition, this description

29. I am grateful to Steven Zohn for calling this arrangement to my attention.

30. "Vermöge seiner Größe in der Harmonie, hat er mehr als einmahl *Trios accompagnirt*, und, weil er aufgeräumt war, u. wuste, daß der Componist dieser *Trios* es nicht übel nehmen würde, aus dem Stegereif u. aus einer elend beziferten ihm vorgelegten Baßstimme ein vollkommenes *Quatuor* daraus gemacht; worüber der Componist dieser *Trios* erstaunte." Transcribed in *Bach-Dokumente* (Leipzig: VEB Deutscher Verlag für Musik and Kassel: Bärenreiter, 1963–present), vol. 3, no. 801. Translated in *The New Bach Reader: A Life of Johann Sebastian Bach in Letters and Documents*, ed. Hans T. David and Arthur Mendel, rev. and enlarged by Christoph Wolff (New York: W. W. Norton, 1999), 397. I have discussed the implications of this description for the realization of trios in Rebecca Cypess, "How Thorough Was Bach's Thoroughbass? A Reconsideration of the Trio Texture," *Early Music* 47, no. 1 (2019): 83–97.

of Bach's "playful humor" and his confidence that the composer of the trio "would not take it amiss" points to the sociability that permeated the performance. This sociability found a ready home in the salon, where musicianship, friendship, play, competition, and sympathy were intertwined.

Another notated arrangement associated with Levy which, however, opens the way to a discussion of *unnotated* arrangement practices, is the set of six organ trios, BWV 525–530, by Johann Sebastian Bach, arranged for two (non-organ) keyboard instruments (fig. 2.1 and audio ex. 2.2 ♫). When played on the organ, each of these two treble lines is executed by one of the organist's hands, while the bass line is played by the feet on a set of pedals. In the arrangement for keyboard duo, the two treble lines are taken by the right hands of the two keyboardists, and the bass line is played by both keyboardists' left hands. While this type of arrangement can be executed on any two keyboard instruments, the fortepiano–harpsichord combination, known to have been used in Levy's salon, offers a means of simulating the distinctive voices available on the organ in an instrumentation that reflects the context of Levy's salon, where there was no organ, but there were multiple stringed keyboard instruments.

While this manuscript survives in the collection of Levy's sister Fanny von Arnstein, its date and the inscription of Fanny's maiden name on the title page demonstrate that it reflects a performance practice in use in her childhood home in Berlin. Levy herself owned a copy of the organ trios in full score, suggesting that she read from that version and extracted the relevant treble line from that score. This practice was described by François Couperin as early as the 1720s in the introduction to his *Apothéose de Lully*:

> This trio, as well as the *Apothéose de Corelli*, and the complete book of trios that I hope to publish next July, may be executed on two harpsichords, as well as all other types of instruments. I play them [on two harpsichords] with my family and with my students, with a very good result, by playing the first soprano line and the bass line on one of the harpsichords, and the second [soprano line], with the same bass line, on another at the unison. The truth is that this requires having two copies [of the score] instead of one, and two harpsichords as well. But I find that it is often easier to assemble these two instruments than four separate professional musicians.[31]

31. "Ce trio, ainsi que l'Apothéose de Corelli; & le livre complet de trios que j'espere donner au mois de Juillet prochain, peuvent s'exécuter à deux clavecins, ainsi que sur tous

What Couperin describes here is precisely the sort of *ex tempore* realization that would have been at home in the playful environment of the salon. In the absence of notated part books such as those owned by Arnstein, the musicians would have adapted the notated music on the spur of the moment, accommodating the score to the medium of performance as they went. When used for the first time, such a process might well have led to confusion or embarrassment—experiences that, as Klorman explains, were part of the process of sight-reading in the late eighteenth century.[32] And yet, in explaining that he played keyboard duos with his family members and his students, Couperin suggests that such arrangements served a didactic purpose, fusing technical demonstration with the expression of familial bonds.[33] These two purposes would also have underpinned the realization of keyboard duos in salons. As discussed in chapter 1, salons served as sites of education, including musical education; and they promoted the articulation of relationships between the *salonnière*, her family members, and her guests, whether women or men.

As I have shown elsewhere, the keyboard-duo arrangement process that Couperin described is widely attested in late eighteenth-century manuscript sources; given his advice that such arrangements need not be notated, these sources should be seen as vestiges of a primarily unnotated tradition.[34] While it is clear that this process was used outside of the salon as well as within it, I contend that it held special significance within the salon. Aside from the voice, keyboard instruments were perhaps the main musical medium for elite women, since they allowed for the player to occupy herself self-sufficiently if she found herself alone; in company, the

autres instrumens. Je les exécute dans ma famille; & avec mes éléves, avec une réüssite tres heureuse, sçavoir, en joüant le premier dessus, & la basse sur un des clavecins: & le second, avec le même basse sur un autre à l'unisson: la verité est que cela engage à avoir deux exemplaires, au lieu d'un; & deux clavecins aussi. Mais, je trouve d'ailleurs qu'il est souvent plus aisé de rassembler ces deux instrumens, que quatre personnes, faisant leur profession de la musique." François Couperin, "Avis," in *Concert instrumental sous le titre d'Apothéose composé à la mémoire immortelle de l'incomparable Monsieur de Lully* (Paris: L'auteur and Le Sieur Boivin, 1725), unpaginated.

32. Klorman cites descriptions of embarrassing episodes of sight-reading; see Klorman, *Mozart's Music of Friends*, 91–94 and passim.

33. Keyboard performance and keyboard compositions often doubled as didactic tools; see Jones, "The Keyboard Works."

34. Cypess, "Keyboard-Duo Arrangements in Eighteenth-Century Musical Life."

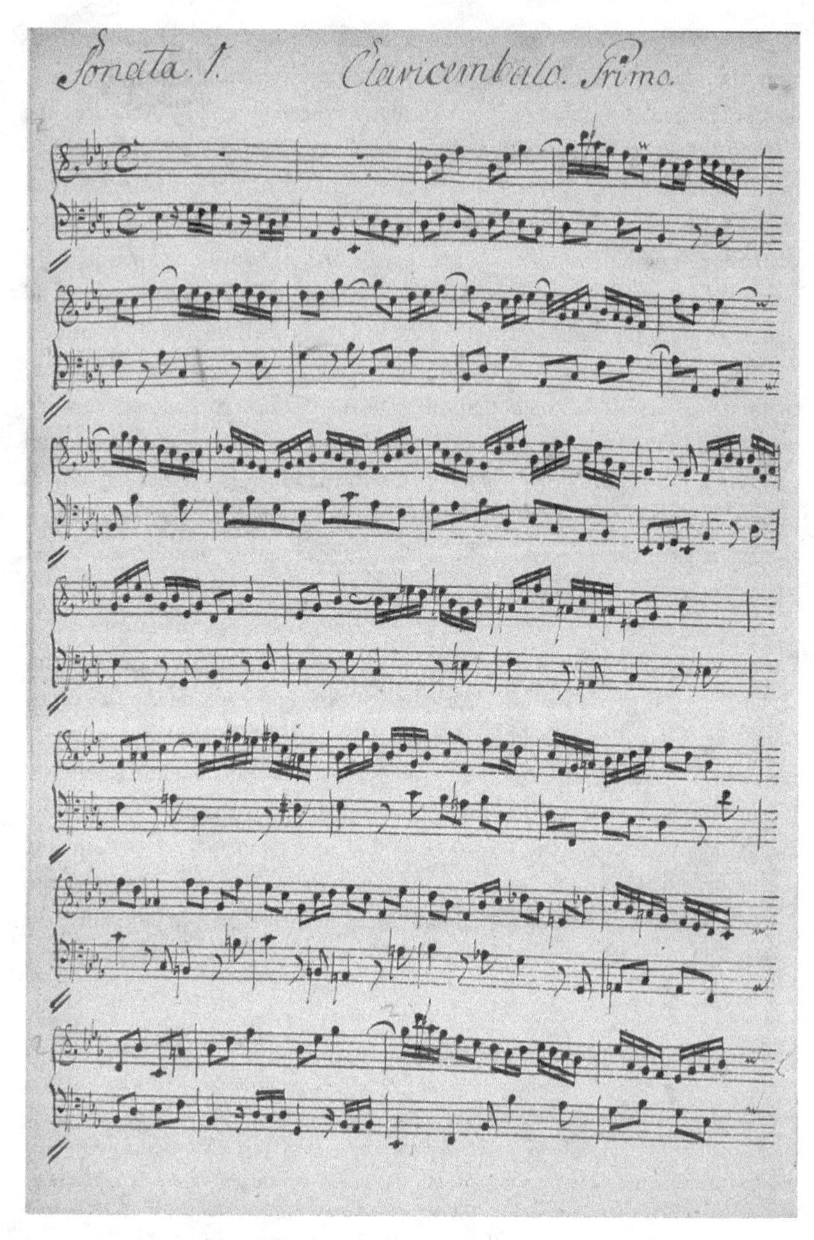

Figure 2.1A Johann Sebastian Bach, Organ trio BWV 526 in C minor in the arrangement for two keyboards, Österreichische Nationalbibliothek, Mus.Hs.5008. First opening of the two part books, side by side. Reproduced by permission of the Österreichische Nationalbibliothek, Austria.

Sonata. 1. Clavicembalo. Secondo

Figure 2.1B

keyboard accommodated women's bodies in a seemly manner.[35] Moreover, the method of adaptation that Couperin describes was oriented toward the cultivation of mutual understanding and shared experience. The players execute identical bass lines in unison and must, therefore, be highly attuned to one another; their distinct right-hand parts, however, demonstrate how two voices may respond differently to the same bass line, which serves as a physical, sonic, and emotional stimulus.

Within musical salons, where professional and amateur musicians mixed and collaborated, familial and gender dynamics could play out through the medium of keyboard duets. For much of the eighteenth century, this meant having two keyboards together in the same room. If this seems like an extravagance that would hinder the practice of keyboard duets, some salons indeed possessed multiple keyboard instruments. This is certainly true of Madame Brillon, who owned a French harpsichord, an English square piano, and a German piano, and wrote compositions for two or all three of these instruments together, designating specifically the parts for each. In France, two other male composers published works in this configuration. Brillon owned copies of the *Symphonies concertantes* for pianoforte, harpsichord, and orchestra by Jean-François Tapray.[36] While it cannot be demonstrated definitively that she owned copies of the duets for harpsichord and fortepiano by Henri-Joseph Rigel,[37] it is highly likely that she did; Rigel dedicated another set of sonatas to Brillon and wrote in his dedication of having been among the listeners in her salon (see chapter 3).

However, in publishing his duos, Rigel recognized that not every potential purchaser would own a piano and a harpsichord, and it was presumably for this reason that he offered the possibility of an alternate instrumentation: "one may play these duos in quartet on the pianoforte with two violins and cello, which are engraved separately and sold in place of the harpsichord

35. See Leppert, *Music and Image*, ch. 7, "The Female at Music: Praxis, Representation, and the Problematic of Identity."

36. Tapray's four compositions in this configuration are in Jean-François Tapray, *Four* Symphonies concertantes *for Harpsichord and Piano with Orchestra* Ad libitum, ed. Bruce Gustafson (Madison, WI: A-R Editions, 1995).

37. Henri-Joseph Rigel, *Trois duo pour le forte-piano et clavecin . . . oeuvre XIV. On peut exécuter ces duo en quatuor sur le piano-forté avec deux violons et violoncelle qui sont gravés séparément* (Paris: L'auteur, 1778). Modern editions of these three duets are in Henri-Joseph Rigel, *Duo pour piano-forte et clavecin, op. 14 no. 1 [2, and 3]* (Versailles: Éditions du Centre de Musique Baroque de Versailles, 2008).

[part] for the same price."[38] The flexibility of instrumentation suggested by the medium of the keyboard duo is manifested, too, in a 1785 publication by Maria Cosway.[39] The title page of the volume indicates that the two pieces have been "arrangées pour deux. Harpe et clavecin, piano-forté ou l'orgue" by Philippe-Jacques Meyer, a harpist, composer, and arranger active in both London and Paris. Cosway's simple melodies and idiomatic accompaniments could be easily executed on keyboard instruments or harp; the implication, perhaps, is that timbral contrast would render the sonatas even more interesting. Additional timbral contrast could be provided by the optional violin part, which, more often than not, doubles a melody or accompanimental figure in one of the two keyboard parts. In a keyboard culture in which timbres could be readily altered through the application of devices operated by pedals and hand-stops, the violin accompaniment serves as yet another means of altering timbre.[40] Its incorporation into the performance was a matter of both taste and practical factors: Was a violinist available to play?

The cultivation of keyboard duos within salons coincided with a flurry of activity by instrument builders to create combination keyboard instruments in which two people could play keyboard duos at a single instrument. The sketch in figure 2.2 does not represent a salon gathering *per se*, but rather, a music lesson in which two women play together at a combination keyboard instrument. Their high social rank is indicated by their clothing, their decorative headwear, the portraits on the wall, the large size of the room and the tall window, the sideboard with its fringed cloth cover, and the open door which offers a glimpse of another spacious room adjoining. Moreover, the instrument itself would have been costly; the *vis-à-vis* combination instrument was a curiosity, and its decorated lid, propped against the wall, demonstrates the interest in the fusion of sensual experiences. The scene depicted in this illustration is a music lesson: the two young ladies

38. This advertisement is included on the title page of the volume; see Henri-Joseph Rigel, *Trois duo pour le forte-piano et clavecin*. See also Bruce Gustafson, Introduction to Jean-François Tapray, *Four* Symphonies concertantes.

39. Maria Cosway, *Deux sonates pour le clavecin, avec un violon . . . arrangées pour deux. Harpe et clavecin, piano-forté, ou l'orgue par P. J. Meyer* (London: Chez Messrs. Birchall & Andrews, [1785]).

40. Deirdre Loughridge, "Timbre Before Timbre: Listening to the Effects of Organ Stops, Violin Mutes, and Piano Pedals, ca. 1650–1800," in *The Oxford Handbook of Timbre*, ed. Emily Dolan and Alexander Rehding (New York: Oxford University Press, 2021), 269–90.

Figure 2.2 Two women at a *vis-à-vis* keyboard instrument. Drawing from Recueil. Musique et musiciens, vol. 9, Instruments à cordes, Bibliothèque Nationale de France, Kd-3 (9)-Fol. Image courtesy of the Bibliothèque nationale de France.

are under the instruction of a male music teacher who directs them using a rolled-up scroll in his left hand and holds a score in his right. The single listener, who doubles as a chaperone to ensure the propriety of the lesson, seems to shadow the music master's motions with her right hand. The high social standing of the women in the sketch suggests that they could easily have applied their practice in this lesson to a salon performance.

Perhaps the most important aspect of this drawing is the sociability that it implies. Like other (but not all) combination keyboard instruments, it sets the players face-to-face with one another. The same setup is attested in other instruments such as the 1777 *vis-à-vis* combination fortepiano–harpsichord by Johann Andreas Stein, now housed in the Accademia filarmonica of Verona (on loan from the Museo di Castelvecchio in Verona).[41]

41. A description of the instrument is at http://www.accademiafilarmonica.org/visavis.pdf (accessed August 5, 2020); it has been discussed in numerous scholarly sources, including Michael Latcham, "The Combination of the Piano and the Harpsichord Throughout the Eighteenth Century," in *Instruments à claviers—expressivité et flexibilité sonore / Keyboard Instruments—Flexibility of Sound and Expression: Actes des Rencontres In-*

In conditioning salon hostesses and their guests to engage in musical sociability, these artifacts, and the practices associated with them, fostered a sense of sympathy for others, educating them in moral sentiment even as it provided an amusing pastime. As I will show, some sources attest to musical salon practices as an enactment of sympathy. In attempting to understand the implications of this enactment, however, a richer perspective is offered through the act of recreating salon practices in performance.

Salon Performance as Sympathetic Play

In 1777 Burney published a volume of sonatas for two keyboardists to play on a single instrument. In this collection—certainly among the first of its kind—he appended an introduction acknowledging the virtues of two-keyboard performances but justifying his more practical configuration:

> That great and varied effects may be produced by *Duets upon Two keyed-Instruments*, has been proved by several ingenious compositions, some of which have been published in Germany; but the inconvenience of having two Harpsichords, or two Piano-Fortes, in the same room, and the short time they remain exactly in tune together, have prevented frequent trials, and even the cultivation of this species of music, notwithstanding all the advantages which, in other respects, it offers to musical students. The played Duets by *two persons* upon *One instrument*, is, however, attended with nearly as many advantages, without the inconvenience of crowding a room, or of frequent or double tuning.[42]

In referring to the keyboard duos published in Germany, Burney may have been thinking of the *Duetto* in E-flat for two keyboards by Johann Gottfried Müthel, printed in 1771 and performed in Burney's own musical soirées in 1775.[43] Burney must also have been familiar with the double concertos and duets for two keyboards by Carl Philipp Emanuel Bach, Wilhelm Friedemann Bach, and perhaps also Johann Sebastian Bach, manuscripts of

---

ternationales harmoniques / Proceedings of the Harmoniques International Congress, Lausanne 2002, ed. Thomas Steiner (Bern: Peter Lang, 2004), 113–52.

42. See Charles Burney, preface to *Four Sonatas or Duets for Two Performers on One Piano-forte or Harpsichord* (London: Printed for the Author, 1777), unpaginated.

43. See David Yearsley, "'Nothing More to Conquer: Müthel's *Duetto* in the Burney Drawing Room and Beyond," *Keyboard Perspectives* 9 (2016): 1–31.

which continued to circulate in northern Germany during the second half of the eighteenth century. Sara Levy collected and played many of these with her teacher, Wilhelm Friedemann Bach, until his death in 1784, and she perpetuated the tradition, apparently, by commissioning double concertos from Carl Philipp Emanuel Bach and Johann Christoph Friedrich Bach, as noted in chapter 1. She played these duos and double concertos with her sisters and perhaps others in her salon. Such duo compositions were as much at home in the salon as the duo arrangements discussed above. And, while Burney's published four-hand compositions opened the door to amateur performances in homes that lacked a second keyboard instrument, four-hand playing on one keyboard would also become an important performance practice of salons.[44] This point is clear from an account in the memoir attributed to the *salonnière* Caroline Pichler:

> when I was sitting at the pianoforte playing "Non più andrai" from *Figaro* . . . [Mozart] suddenly moved a chair up, sat down, told me to carry on playing the bass, and began to improvise such wonderfully beautiful variations that everyone listened to the tones of the German Orpheus with bated breath.[45]

Likewise, the memoirs attributed to the Irish tenor Michael Kelly relate that, during his years in Vienna in the 1780s, he heard Mozart play four-hand compositions with Marianna Martines:

> When I was admitted to [Martines's] conversaziones, and musical parties, she was in the vale of years, yet still possessed the gaiety and vivacity of a girl, and was polite and affable to all. Mozart was an almost constant attendant at her parties, and I have heard him play duets on the piano-forte with her, of his own composition. She was a great favourite of his.[46]

In explaining his motivation for publishing four-hand keyboard music, Burney links this medium, as well as that of duets for two keyboards, to

44. On the widespread use of this practice in salons of the nineteenth century, see Thomas Christensen, "Four-Hand Piano Transcription and the Geographies of Nineteenth-Century Musical Reception," *Journal of the American Musicological Society* 52, no. 2 (Summer 1999): 255–98.

45. Quoted and translated in Klorman, *Mozart's Music of Friends*, 108.

46. Kelly [and Hook], *Reminiscences of Michael Kelly of the King's Theatre*, 1:252.

both education and sociability. These factors explain why keyboard-duo performance was so central to salons. In a household in which two keyboardists each need to practice, but in which only one keyboard resides, the two keyboardists run the risk of conflict—a risk that keyboard duos help mitigate:

> Indeed, it frequently happens, that when there are two students upon the same keyed-instrument, in one house, they are in each other's way; however, by compositions of the following kind, they become reciprocally useful, and necessary companions in their musical exercises.[47]

In addition, Burney argues, keyboard duos help the players listen to each other well, assist one another in correcting errors, and improve each other's technique. If either of the two players speeds up or slows down, the other will catch the mistake.

Of course, Burney's mention of two players "in each other's way" raises the dimension of physical encounters of a more romantic or potentially awkward nature. He admits that the first attempts at playing four-hand music can be "aukward [*sic*] and embarrassing" because of the "near approach of the hands of the different performers." In writing keyboard parts in which the two players are required to cross hands and arms, Burney choreographed such encounters, providing both an impetus and an excuse for physical intertwining. The usage of keyboard duos by a man and a woman together is attested in the illustration on the cover of Franz Seydelmann's publication of four-hand compositions of 1781, and this type of usage would certainly have been possible in the heterosocial environment of the salon.[48] Whether for edification, for sensual intimacy, or both, four-hand keyboard performance sets the *salonnière* and members of her circle of whatever gender into sociable interaction. That this music prompted true sociability, rather than functioning simply as a metaphor, is apparent from Burney's equation of four-hand musicianship with conversation:

> And with respect to the *Pianos* and *Fortes*, each Performer should try to discover when he has the *Principal Melody* given to him, or when he is only to *accompany* that Melody; in order, either to make it more con-

47. Burney, preface to *Four Sonatas or Duets*, unpaginated.

48. Franz Seydelmann, *Sechs Sonaten für zwo Personen auf einem Clavier* (Leipzig: Gottlob Immanuel Breitkopf, 1781). See also Christensen, "Four-Hand Piano Transcription."

> spicuous, or merely to enrich its harmony. There is no fault in accompanying, so destructive of good melody, taste, and expression, as the vanity with which young and ignorant Performers are too frequently possessed, of becoming *Principals*, when they are only *Subalterns*; and of being heard, when they have nothing to say that merits particular attention. If the part which would afford the greatest pleasure to the hearer be suffocated, and rendered inaudible, by too full, and too loud an accompaniment, it is like throwing the capital figure of a piece into the back-ground, or degrading the master into a servant.[49]

In contrast to solo music, which leads a single player selfishly to occupy the keyboard instrument to the detriment of others in the house who also need to practice, sociable music-making involving two keyboardists bestows both literal and figurative harmony, rendering the two players "reciprocally useful, and necessary companions" to one another. If awkwardness and embarrassment arise from the close interaction necessitated by the four-hand medium, players would learn to experience such embarrassment (and its attending pleasures) in front of an audience. Keyboard duos also foster a sense of self within the context of the whole: neither player can be soloist for long, and the two must constantly accommodate each other through active listening and sensitive playing. As a tactile experience, keyboard duos instill in the body the lessons needed to become a sociable, sympathetic person.

My attempts to recreate the performance practices of salons, including keyboard-duo arrangements, have offered perspective on Burney's comments. These arrangements seemed, in fact, like a puzzle that needed solving, analogous to a salon game. In this respect, Burney's report that keyboard duos offer access to both "amusement" and "improvement" is significant, for it echoes descriptions of games that were commonly played in salons. One such game that bears much in common with the process of creating off-the-cuff arrangements is the "sonderbares musicalisches Stück" shown in figure 2.3. Here, Johann Schobert, who identifies himself as the "Musicus" of the Prince de Conti but who was also closely connected to Madame Brillon and her salon, perhaps even serving as her music teacher, offers musicians a means to fill their time through musical sociability.[50] This piece, he writes, "can be played on the clavier, the violin and

49. Burney, preface to *Four Sonatas or Duets*, unpaginated.

50. Gustafson, "The Music of Madame Brillon," 525.

Figure 2.3 Johann Schobert, *Ein sonderbares musicalisches Stuck; welches auf dem Clavier, der Violin und dem Bass, und zwar auf verschiedene Arten, kan gespielet werden* (Nürnberg: Winterschmidt, n.d.). Image courtesy of the Bibliothèque nationale de France.

the bass, in a variety of ways." The five short menuets on the page use the same basic material, but each requires experimentation on the part of the players in order to unravel the riddle of their execution. Thus Menuet 1 can be read identically upside down and right side up, meaning that players sitting across from each other at a table could read from the same page but still play in unison. In Menuet 2, the same seating yields two distinct treble parts and two distinct bass parts, but they all harmonize with each other. Reading the music in company and solving the puzzle of each menuet yields a distinctive sort of sociable experience.

This musical game, which sets players across from one another as they read from the score, serves a similar function to the *vis-à-vis* keyboard shown in figure 2.2. As a material artifact of a lived experience, it denotes visual as well as aural communication. This musical sociability is fostered by other objects such as the quartet tables of the eighteenth century, around which four musicians would arrange themselves for maximal visual inter-action. These objects resonate with the iconography of eighteenth-century

Figure 2.4 Daniel Chodowiecki, engraving of a chamber music scene, in Johann Bernhard Basedow, *Das Elementarwerk für die Jugend und ihre Freunde* (Berlin and Dessau: Basedow, 1774), table VIIIa. / G. Dagli Orti / De Agostini Picture Library / Bridgeman Images.

salons. The image in figure 2.4 shows a concert that could well take place in a salon gathering. The musicians arrange themselves around the female keyboardist, who serves to bind them together, while their listeners sit and stand just opposite.[51] In Edward Klorman's formulation, these objects "[make] a focal point of the musicians as a group and [draw] attention to the drawing room as a site for both *social* music-making and *musical* socializing."[52]

While Schobert's published musical game cannot have been restricted to play only within the setting of the salon, his close connection to the salons of Brillon and others in Paris suggest that it would have been very

51. Other images of sociable music-making are discussed in Klorman, *Mozart's Music of Friends*, 3–9 and passim; and in Zohn, "The Sociability of Salon Culture."

52. Klorman, *Mozart's Music of Friends*, 7; Klorman provides a detailed discussion of the implications of such artifacts of eighteenth-century chamber music.

much at home there. Indeed, game playing, musical and otherwise, was common in salons. The eighteenth century saw the publication and practice of a number of musical games, including dice games that enabled someone not highly trained in composition to compose through a highly constrained set of aleatoric means.[53] Sometimes framed as a system appropriate for professional composers and sometimes as a pastime for amateurs such as those in musical salons, dice games called into question the idea of expertise, placing composition within the domain of the untutored amateur. As Roger Moseley writes, "although [the pleasure of dice games] still relied on compositional labor, the source of that labor was hidden from view."[54] Through play, such creative acts became a polite enterprise, one available even to upper-class women precisely because of their apparent (and paradoxical) ease. Outside of music, too, games often figured in proceedings of musical salons. Brillon and Franklin played chess regularly, as Franklin explained to the American diplomat William Carmichael in 1780: "with her Daughters who sing prettily, and some friends who play, She kindly entertains me and my Grandson with little Concerts, a Dish of Tea and a Game of Chess. I call this my Opera; for I rarely go to the Opera at Paris."[55]

The juxtaposition of music and chess in Brillon's salon is instructive. Two years before Franklin wrote this letter to Carmichael, also during his stay in Paris, Franklin had composed an essay titled "The Morals of Chess," in which he expounded on the game's capacity to foster sociability. He begins the essay with the claim that "the game of chess is not merely an idle amusement. Several very valuable qualities of the mind, useful in the course of human life, are to be acquired or strengthened by it, so as to become habits, ready on all occasions."[56] He expounds on these qualities, which include foresight, circumspection, caution, and perseverance, offer-

53. Stephen A. Hedges, "Dice Music in the Eighteenth Century," *Music & Letters* 59, no. 2 (April 1978): 180–87.

54. Roger Moseley, *Keys to Play: Music as a Ludic Medium from Apollo to Nintendo* (Oakland: University of California Press, 2016), 159. Further discussion of dice games as a means of—and analogy for—musical creativity is in David Yearsley, *Bach and the Meanings of Counterpoint* (Cambridge: Cambridge University Press, 2002), 184–86.

55. Benjamin Franklin to William Carmichael, June 17, 1780. https://franklinpapers.org (accessed August 2, 2019).

56. Benjamin Franklin, "The Morals of Chess," written before June 28, 1779, published in *The Columbian Magazine* 1 (December 1786): 159–61. https://franklinpapers.org (accessed August 4, 2019).

ing practical advice on each that could be easily applied to life more generally. In closing, however, Franklin refers to a more sociable form of chess, in which a player's adversary becomes more a friend than a foe:

> If the game is not to be played rigorously, according to the rules above mentioned, then moderate your desire of victory over your adversary, and be pleased with one over yourself. Snatch not eagerly at every advantage offered by his unskilfulness or inattention; but point out to him kindly that by such a move he places or leaves a piece in danger and unsupported; that by another he will put his king in a dangerous situation, &c. By this generous civility (so opposite to the unfairness above forbidden) you may indeed happen to lose the game to your opponent, but you will win what is better, his esteem, his respect, and his affection; together with the silent approbation and good will of impartial spectators.[57]

Like the keyboardist in Burney's four-hand compositions, Franklin's ideal sociable chess player presents a "generous civility" that suppresses selfish inclinations in favor of the success of a friend.

Another episode in which games were juxtaposed with music was in the musical soirées of the Comtesse de Genlis during the winter of 1767. As in Franklin's account of his evenings *chez* Brillon, Genlis allows musical and non-musical games to elide in her description: "We not only played proverbs, but also [performed] a comic opera, for which my friend, Mademoiselle Bayon (later Madame Louis, wife of a famous architect), composed the music."[58] The game of proverbs could be played in numerous ways, but it involved learning witty or edifying proverbs and either acting them out silently or giving spoken hints until the other players guessed the proverb. The purpose of this in relation to Genlis's educative system becomes clear in consulting one of her other publications. A lady-in-waiting to the Duchess of Chartres, Genlis became governess to the Duke and Duchess's children in 1777, and she developed a system of education for them that reflected her interest in games as a tool of education. Her *Leçons d'une gou-*

57. Franklin, "The Morals of Chess."

58. "Je m'amusai aussi beaucoup chez moi cet hiver; mon salon étoit fort grand, nous y jouâmes non-seulement des proverbes, mais un opéra-comique, dont mon amie, mademoiselle Baillon (depuis madame Louis, femme du fameux architecte) fit la musique." Genlis, *Mémoires inédits*, 1:357–59.

vernante à ses élèves, published in French in 1791 and in English translation the following year, includes a note about the game of proverbs. Speaking in the voice of a governess, she writes, "I intend to make [the children] play Proverbs all this winter: for this purpose it is necessary to be able to compose them extempore; to give them an instructive and moral cast, and to play them with propriety." A footnote reads "This amusement is equally agreeable and instructive when it assumes a moral complexion; it teaches to speak with collectedness and propriety, and gives a considerable command of language and style."[59]

The game of proverbs, in Genlis's formulation, was both amusing and instructive. It fostered rhetorical fluency by forcing the students to speak extemporaneously. In encouraging engagement with moral proverbs, moreover, the game was equally instructive for its players' characters. In her account of her salon of 1767, music, theater, and the game of proverbs intertwined to create an experience that may be understood from the perspective of this same two-part effect, combining entertainment with edification. Indeed, musical play within salons is instructive in a similar fashion: in the act of attempting to realize a piece with the instruments and personnel present on a given evening, participants learn to listen to and accommodate one another, with the goal of solving the puzzle—that is, of creating music that enacts a pleasing harmony and reciprocity, as in Schobert's musical game.

For my duo partner, Yi-heng Yang, and me, keyboard-duo arrangements constituted a similar kind of puzzle. One aspect of this phenomenon was purely practical. In setting up our instruments in the manner shown in figure 2.2, we quickly found that it was easier to hear the other player than it was ourselves. When I practiced alone, I heard only my treble line; when I combined my part with that of my partner, the soundboard of her instrument was right beside my ear, which meant that the notes she was playing resonated more strongly than my own. As a result, on more than one occasion, both in rehearsal and (once) in performance, I found myself playing her treble part—anticipating her next musical statement.

Perhaps a more interesting result of this experimentation with keyboard-duo arrangement practices was the realization that the trio texture, executed literally in the manner recommended by Couperin, sounded and felt bare. If such trios are played by two treble instruments with basso continuo, the

59. Stéphanie Félicité Ducrest de Saint-Aubin, Comtesse de Genlis, *Lessons of a Governess to Her Pupils*, anonymous translation (Dublin: P. Wogan et al., 1792), 100.

Example 2.2A Johann Sebastian Bach, Sonata BWV 1039 in G major, movement 3, Adagio e piano.

harmonies are realized by a chordal instrument. In the configuration that Couperin describes, that layer of harmonic enrichment is absent. As a result, Yang and I began to realize the harmonies through the introduction of improvised inner voices; this became the next step in solving the arrangement puzzle, and, as I have shown elsewhere, it is one for which historical evidence exists.[60] Example 2.2 shows the score for the third movement of J. S. Bach's Sonata in G major, BWV 1039. Using the methods described by Couperin and enacted in salons, we arranged the piece for two keyboards.

60. Cypess, "How Thorough Was Bach's Thoroughbass?," 83–97.

Example 2.2B

But we also filled out the harmonies as indicated by the bass figures, using idiomatic keyboard figuration that sought to take advantage of the two-keyboard idiom. During our process of trial and error, we found that, in certain spots, only one of us was able to reach the necessary inner voices, while the other had, for example, more intricate passagework. As a result, we took turns serving the accompanimental role in a manner that resonates with Burney's description of two players accommodating each other. The result is in audio example 2.3. ♫

Aside from keyboard duos, the role of the *salonnière* in binding together other musicians, as in figure 2.4, was enacted on a musical level as well as a visual one. One repertoire that was very much at home within salons was the

Example 2.2c

accompanied sonata, in which the keyboardist assumes the central position and the other musicians play a supporting role. Elisabeth Le Guin, in her fanciful "script" recreating a conversation within a musical salon, offers an interpretation of this repertoire. While it might seem that the accompanied sonata places the keyboardist—most often a woman—in the spotlight, Le Guin shows that "these elegant 'speeches' made by the keyboardist"—her extensive thematic material, often played solo—"do not prevent the other instrumentalists from joining in, but result in their being shown to advantage in their turn. She takes this tuneful role only in order to set the 'conversation' going. Her ideas—that is to say, the tunes—may only be said to have their full meaning in being heard and confirmed—which is to say, doubled or reinforced—by the string players."[61]

In some accompanied sonatas, the idiom of the genre results in a level of simplicity, and even a literal doubling of parts, that can seem curious and uncomfortable to modern-day performers (see fig. 2.5, an accompanied sonata by Johann Christian Bach), but which, to eighteenth-century players and listeners, yielded an easy, affable experience for both players and listeners. In other pieces in this genre, however, the thematic material is shared among instruments in a more complex and thoroughgoing way. The trio in C minor by Schobert, dedicated to Madame Brillon and therefore probably played in her salon, is one such example: from the outset, the violin and keyboard have independent thematic material in which the two instruments weave around each other, and they execute quick ornamental gestures and passagework in turn (see ex. 2.3). While the cello doubles the left hand of the keyboard almost everywhere in this movement, Schobert offers the cello one modest solo cadenza (m. 59) on a dominant chord that hints at its independent voice (see ex. 2.4). In the keyboard part book, this measure appears squeezed between measures of complicated figuration; visually, therefore, this dominant moment seems unimportant (audio ex. 2.4 ♫).

Indeed, this trio by Schobert again bespeaks salon sociability, albeit through different means than the keyboard duo. While the accompanied sonata by J. C. Bach shown in figure 2.5 was published in score as well as part books, so that the keyboardist could anticipate what the violinist or flutist would play, this trio by Schobert was apparently only issued in part books. The experience of playing the Schobert trios, then, is full of surprises. The ornamental gestures exchanged by the keyboardist and the violinist are irregular and unpredictable, meaning that the two players must learn to accommodate and support one another. When the cellist finally emerges from the background and plays the cadenza in example 2.4, the keyboardist and violinist might be caught unawares, but it is their responsibility to make way for the cellist. This, indeed, was the experience I had

61. Le Guin, "A Visit to the Salon de Parnasse," 23–24. Elizabeth Morgan has argued that the accompanied sonata should be interpreted through the lens of the Bluestocking feminism of writers such as Mary Wollstonecraft in the 1790s. However, this reading does not account for the widespread composition and playing of accompanied sonatas from the 1760s onward, both in salons and in domestic settings more generally. See Elizabeth Morgan, "The Accompanied Sonata and the Domestic Novel in Britain at the Turn of the Nineteenth Century," *19th-Century Music* 36, no. 2 (Fall 2012): 88–100.

Figure 2.5 Johann Christian Bach, Sonata no. 4 in C major, movement 1, Andante, from *Six sonates pour le clavecin accompagnées d'un violon ou flute traversière et d'un violoncello*, op. 2 (London: Welcker, 1770). Image courtesy of the Bibliothèque nationale de France.

in playing this piece for the first time with violinist Dongmyung Ahn and cellist Eve Miller. Having prepared our parts separately, we figured out in the first rehearsal how the thematic material fit together, and the process of working out the ornamental figuration traded by the violin and keyboard was both engaging and confusing. When we arrived at the dominant chord

Example 2.3A Johann Schobert, Trio op. 6 no. 2, movement 1 in C minor, Andante non molto, mm. 1–13. From Johann Schobert, *Sonates en trio pour le clavecin avec accompagnement de violon et basse ad libitum dédiées à Madame Brillon de Joüy* (Paris: Vendôme, 1765).

Example 2.3B

in m. 59, I began to improvise a small cadenza of my own, thus stepping on Miller's toes. This required apology and accommodation of a sort that seems to resonate with salon games and sociability.

Of course, Schobert's trios were not the only pieces published in partbook format, and it is difficult to tell whether it was the composer or the

Example 2.4 Johann Schobert, Trio op. 6 no. 2, movement 1 in C minor, Andante non molto, mm. 53–62. Note the short cello cadenza in m. 59. From Johann Schobert, *Sonates en trio pour le clavecin avec accompagnement de violon et basse ad libitum dédiées à Madame Brillon de Joüy* (Paris: Vendôme, 1765).

printer who decided on the format in any case. Nevertheless, the complexity of musical interaction in the Schobert trio, combined with its publication format, maximizes the ludic qualities of the salon experience. Again, though, the notion of salon music as play does not mean that such music-making was merely an amusement. Just as the Comtesse de Genlis discerned the dual capacity for the game of proverbs to amuse and edify her young charges, so, too, the experience of playing music in the context of the salon served a dual purpose. Playing this Schobert trio must have been an entertaining pastime, to be sure, but it also encouraged (and continues to encourage) active listening, emotional sympathy, and the capacity to incorporate surprise into an overall air of sentimental expression.

Sociability, Music, and the Cultivation of "Moral Sentiment"

While the experiences of performance that I have described here cannot be taken to stand for an eighteenth-century perspective, the written accounts of figures such as Genlis, Franklin, and Burney help orient the modern player or listener in the attempt to uncover the aesthetics of the salon. Certainly, far more repertoire and numerous other performance practices remain to be explored in relation to the aesthetics of the eighteenth-century salon. As noted above, the music and musical practices of salons varied widely, and I will consider some of these themes in subsequent chapters. At present, however, I propose to draw some preliminary conclusions about the experience of salon performance based on the evidence that I have presented thus far.

If my discussions of performance practices within salons—and my own twenty-first-century perspective based on attempted puzzle-solving around those practices—seem far from the topic of Enlightenment theory, the theme of sympathy forms a thread that binds them together. While sociable music was a sensual experience, it was understood to have the potential to generate moral sentiments. Like Benjamin Franklin's polite chess player, who learned the habits of civility by aiding his adversary, musical *salonnières* and their guests partook of a hands-on experience that taught them to listen to and accommodate others. This notion links musical salons to the movement of the Enlightenment.

A strong defense of the heterosocial institution of the salon appeared in 1752, when the Scottish philosopher David Hume published an essay titled "Of Luxury" in his *Philosophical Discourses*. Later republished as "Of Refinement in the Arts," Hume's essay asserted, first, that sensual pleasure was in itself neither good nor bad, but that it could be used for either. While individuals who indulge overly in material goods, food, or drink are marked by "gross stupidity," the pursuit of "great refinement in the gratification of the senses," tempered with virtues such as "liberality or charity," could be of benefit to humankind.[62] Indeed, while cautioning against luxury "carry'd a degree too far," Hume asserted that "the ages of refinement and luxury are both the happiest and most virtuous," and that such refinement may have a beneficial effect "both on *private* and on *public* life."[63] In the former category, Hume counts an increase in human sociability (note that private life was not equivalent to solitude). As he explained,

> The more these refin'd arts advance, the more sociable do men become; nor is it possible, that, when enrich'd with science, and possess'd of a fund of conversation, they shou'd be contented to remain in solitude, or live without their fellow-citizens in that distant manner which is peculiar to ignorant and barbarous nations. They flock to cities; love to receive and communicate knowledge; to show their wit or their breeding; their taste in conversation or living, in cloaths or furniture. Curiosity allures the wise; vanity the foolish; and pleasure both. Particular clubs and societies are every where form'd: Both sexes meet in an easy and sociable manner; and the tempers of men, as well as their behavior, refine apace. So that, beside the improvements which they receive from knowledge and the liberal arts, 'tis impossible but they must feel an increase of humanity, from the very habit of conversing together, and contributing to each other's pleasure and entertainment. Thus *industry, knowledge*, and *humanity*, are link'd together by an indissoluble chain, and are found, from experience as well as reason, to be peculiar to the more polish'd and luxurious ages.[64]

With this passage Hume presented a defense of sensual experience as a component of the Enlightenment. Hume bestowed special praise on the "clubs and societies" that met for the enjoyment of conversation and the cultivation of taste in the arts. Including both men and women, these groups

62. David Hume, "Of Luxury," in *Essays and Treatises on Several Subjects*, vol. 4, *Political Discourses*, 3rd ed. with additions and corrections (London: A. Millard and Edinburgh: A. Kincaid and A. Donaldson, 1754), 20.

63. Hume, "Of Luxury," 21.

64. Hume, "Of Luxury," 23–24.

encourage "an increase of humanity, from the very habit of conversing together." Sensual experience brought people together, and it served the edifying purpose of stimulating sociable conversation.

Adam Smith's *Theory of Moral Sentiments* likewise gives pride of place to conversation as a sociable art form; Smith, moreover, connects it to music: "The great pleasure of conversation, and indeed of society, arises from a certain correspondence of sentiments and opinions, from a certain harmony of minds, which like so many musical instruments coincide and keep time with one another."[65] Smith takes it as a given that refinement in the arts is of benefit to humankind. In contrast to Bernard Mandeville, who had argued earlier in the eighteenth century that whatever was good for private individuals was a detriment to the public good,[66] Smith states that an interest in sensuality among the wealthy is the only way that the "arts of refinement," including music, could ever advance.[67]

For Smith, sympathy was predicated upon mutual sentiment; sentiment, in turn, could be stimulated by conversation and friendship, or by the expansion of sentimental experience through the arts, since sentiment could stimulate a sense of sympathy among their participants or observers.[68] It is within society—within the company of others—that human beings learn to put themselves in the place of others, experiencing their pain or condoling with them in moments of grief. This requires that each individual assume the role of a spectator, observing other human beings and "striv[ing] to render, as perfect as possible, that imaginary change of situation upon which his sympathy is founded."[69] Experience of the arts can aid human beings in the stimulation of sympathy; after all, no one individual will have accumulated all the experiences of another; thus, the arts serve to stretch one's experiences through imagination. Smith argues that, in Greek tragedy, it is the sentiments of the subjects—their solitude, their sadness—that

65. Adam Smith, *The Theory of Moral Sentiments*, 2nd ed. (London: Millar, 1769), 428.

66. Bernard Mandeville, *The Fable of the Bees, or, Private Vices, Publick Benefits*, 3rd ed. (London: J. Tonson, 1724).

67. Smith, *Theory of Moral Sentiments*, 382–83.

68. On the eighteenth-century notion of sympathy as a force behind human relationships, see Jonathan Lamb, *The Evolution of Sympathy in the Long Eighteenth Century* (New York: Routledge, 2016).

69. Smith, *Theory of Moral Sentiments*, 26. On the theatricality inscribed in Smith's *Theory*, see David Marshall, "Adam Smith and the Theatricality of Moral Sentiments," *Critical Inquiry* 10, no. 4 (June 1984): 592–613; and John Dwyer, *Virtuous Discourse: Sensibility and Community in Late Eighteenth-Century Scotland* (Edinburgh: John Donald, 1987).

touch the imagination.[70] Music, even in the absence of text, can elicit similar effects: "When music imitates the modulations of grief or joy, it either actually inspires us with those passions, or at least puts us in the mood which disposes us to conceive them."[71]

Within the Enlightenment salon, sensuality and sociability converged. Through experiences of visual art, poetry, music, and games, participants used their senses to stimulate conversation as well as their sympathetic imaginations. It is therefore not surprising that the diary of the *salonnière* Suzanne Necker echoes Smith's *Theory of Moral Sentiments*. Just as Smith understood sympathetic conversation as "so many musical instruments [that] coincide," Necker writes, "It seems that one of the charms of the spirit and of conversation is to be able to bend to the spirit, to proper love, and to the ideas of others, in waves, if one may use the expression, and like the accompaniment in music."[72] The "waves" in this passage refer to the sympathetic resonances of well-tuned instruments and minds. Just as, in music, it is the role of the accompanist to enter into a sympathetic relationship with her partner, so, too, in conversation, each interlocutor tempers herself to the spirit of the other. In a song, Necker further explains, "the accompaniment . . . seems to enter into dialogue with the actor who sings the words; he speaks; the accompaniment responds."[73] For Necker, then, music made by two people is equivalent to a conversation in which the two interlocutors attend closely to each other's words, reactions, and moods.[74]

There is another, more chilling link between Smith's *Theory of Moral Sentiments* and the French salons. While the *Theory* had already been trans-

70. Smith, *Theory of Moral Sentiments*.

71. Smith, *Theory of Moral Sentiments*, 58. Smith viewed tragedy as an ideal means for the stimulation of sympathy; see *Theory of Moral Sentiments*, 47–51 and passim. On Gotthold Ephraim Lessing's conception of Greek tragedy as a vehicle for the stimulation of sympathy, see Benjamin W. Redekop, *Enlightenment and Community: Lessing, Abbt, Herder, and the Quest for a German Public* (Montreal and Kingston: McGill-Queen's University Press, 2000).

72. "Il semble qu'un des charmes de l'esprit et de la conversation, est de pouvoir se plier à l'esprit, à l'amour propre et aux idées des autres, par ondulation, si l'on peut s'exprimer ainsi, et comme l'accompagnement dans la musique." Suzanne Necker, *Mélanges extraits des manuscrits de Mme. Necker* (Paris: Charles Pougens, 1798), 2:93.

73. "L'accompagnement représente la nature et semble entrer en dialogue avec l'acteur qui chante les paroles: il parle, l'accompagnement répond." Necker, *Mélanges extraits des manuscrits de Mme. Necker*, 2:75.

74. On the limitations of the analogy between music and conversation, see Zohn, "The Sociability of Salon Culture," 208–14.

lated into French in the 1760s and 1770s, another translation was made in 1793 (but not published until 1798) by the one-time *salonnière* Sophie de Grouchy Condorcet.[75] Produced at the height of the Terror, with her husband only months from death at the hands of its leaders, Condorcet's translation, together with the *Lettres sur la sympathie* that she appended to it, reads as an indictment of those who would ignore the call to sympathy.

Among the points on which Condorcet diverged from Smith was the role of reasoned reflection in the formation of sympathy. While Smith viewed sympathy as a product of sensation alone, Condorcet argued that the human capacity for reflection is what allows human beings to move beyond mere physical reflexes, interpreting sensation in order to develop a reasoned response to it. In Condorcet's words, reflection on the physical senses "conditions our sensibility by prolonging its activity and so installs humanity in our souls as an active and permanent sentiment."[76] In inserting reasoned reflection into the equation, Condorcet was perhaps drawing on her experience as a *salonnière*: the salon offered its participants the ability to experience the sensual and to assimilate it into their reasonable minds through reflective conversation.

In bringing the work of Hume, Smith, Necker, and Condorcet into this discussion, I am not suggesting a direct link between their writings and the performance practices in musical salons that I have discussed in this chapter. These writers were all familiar with various articulations of the multifaceted institution of the salon, and they used musical language as a metaphor for salon sociability; whether Necker and Condorcet played keyboard duos or accompanied sonatas is unknown. Indeed, anyone who has played chamber music understands its vague ability to foster communication and

75. An explication of Condorcet's translation and its deviations from Smith's text, as well as an affecting contextualization of this work within her personal circumstances, is in Jeanne Britton, "Translating Sympathy by the Letter: Henry Mackenzie, Sophie de Condorcet, and Adam Smith," *Eighteenth-Century Fiction* 22, no. 1 (Fall 2009): 71–98. See also Ruth Scurr, "Inequality and Political Stability from Ancien Régime to Revolution: The Reception of Adam Smith's *Theory of Moral Sentiments* in France," *History of European Ideas* 35, no. 4 (2009): 441–49; and Evelyn L. Forget, "Cultivating Sympathy: Sophie Condorcet's Letters on Sympathy," *Journal of the History of Economic Thought* 23, no. 3 (2001): 319–37. A critical edition of the translation, together with an extensive explanatory introduction, is in Sophie de Grouchy, *Letters on Sympathy (1798): A Critical Edition*, ed. Karin Brown, letters trans. James E. McClellan III (Philadelphia: American Philosophical Society, 2008).

76. de Grouchy, *Letters on Sympathy (1798)*, 115.

emotional ties; it is not my goal to rehearse such general observations here. Instead, having explored a handful of the specific performance practices that can be tied to musical salons in the age of Enlightenment, I have aimed to uncover how the act of making music in the company of the *salonnières* and their *habitués* might have attended to the very specific modes of sympathetic understanding that were so highly sought after by Enlightenment thinkers and the fashionable European public alike.

Burney's description of the effects of keyboard duos provides a means for understanding how such performance practices might reflect the desire to stimulate sympathetic experiences within musical players. In his vision, the two musicians create a mutual bond through the experience, improving both their musicianship and their sociability. Material artifacts such as the *vis-à-vis* double keyboard instrument and Schobert's printed musical game, both of which set musicians into visual as well as sonic dialogue with each other, reinforce this experience of sympathy. In keyboard-duo arrangements, played in the manner suggested by François Couperin and employed throughout eighteenth-century Europe, the sonic realization serves as a model, showing how two individual (treble) voices can respond in different but harmonious ways to the same (bass-line) stimulus. The experience of playing complex accompanied sonatas from part books means that players might be constantly surprised and need to leave room for one another's expressive moments.

Conclusion

Musical salon practices presented myriad practical puzzles. Within salons, musicians might need to sight-read, play a part that is idiomatic to another instrument, or improvise a new line to fit in with an ensemble. Arrangements could be notated, but they might also be created on the spur of the moment—that is, played in an environment in which adaptation was inherent in musical creativity—to suit the specific situation of each salon. Reading from scores and part books might produce two entirely different sets of expectations on the part of the players, with dramatically different results. In all cases, the conventions of sociable behavior necessitated that these puzzles be met with grace and good humor. Like Franklin's chess player, the salon musician must know how to downplay her own needs and accommodate another person.

For Suzanne Necker, "thought is reality, and conversation is spectacle."[77] Whatever the implications of this statement for Necker's behavior as a theatrical display, the notion of salon conversation as a spectacle captures the nature of salon experiences as essentially temporal, fleeting, and fragile. So, too, salon music: the primary experience of music was a temporal one. As a result, thinking through score study and styles of composition used in salons will only carry us so far. By attempting to recreate and reenact the performance practices used in eighteenth-century salons, we may gain a new perspective on their realities, their playful register, and the sympathetic bonds that they created. Engaging with both reason and the senses, with both verbal and musical modes of communication, musical salons enacted modes of sociability that contributed to education, self-cultivation, and the project of Enlightenment.

77. "la pensée est la réalité, et la conversation est le spectacle." Necker, *Mélanges extraits des manuscrits de Mme. Necker*, 2:66.

CHAPTER THREE

*

Ephemerae and Authorship in the Salon of Madame Brillon

In his fanciful and poignant essay "The Ephemera," Benjamin Franklin describes a species of tiny flies called *éphémères*, which he claims to have seen on a small bush on the island of Moulin Joli, situated in the middle of the Seine River of Paris. True to their name, the *éphémères* live out their entire lives in the course of a single day. Taking his cue from natural philosophers before him, some of whom had viewed the *éphémères* as a *memento mori*, Franklin presents the fragile insects of this story as an allegory for the lives of humankind. Clearly autobiographical, "The Ephemera" casts Franklin as a melancholy, regretful elder statesman coming to terms with the transience of life. He describes overhearing—and, Solomonic in his wisdom, understanding—a soliloquy of one of the elder members of this unfortunate species, who cries:

> What now avails all my Toil and Labour in amassing Honey-Dew on this Leaf, which I cannot live to enjoy! What the political Struggles I have been engag'd in for the Good of my *Compatriotes*, Inhabitants of this Bush; or my philosophical Studies for the Benefit of our Race in general! For in Politics, *what can Laws do without Morals!* Our present Race of Ephemeres will in a Course of Minutes, become corrupt like those of other and older Bushes, and consequently as wretched. And in Philosophy how small our Progress! Alas, *Art is long, and Life short!*[1]

1. Benjamin Franklin to Anne-Louise Boyvin d'Hardancourt Brillon de Jouy, "The Ephemera," September 20, 1778. Quoted from "Founders Online," https://founders

This wise old fly mocks the younger members of his species who spend too much time arguing over trivia, wasting their time on earth. Among the unimportant matters that these flies debate are the relative merits of French and Italian opera. Nevertheless, Franklin, speaking through the older *éphémère*, concludes his vignette by referring to another kind of music-making that was, in his estimation, one of life's few truly worthwhile pastimes:

> My Friends would comfort me with the Idea of a Name they say I shall leave behind me; and they tell me I have *lived long enough, to Nature and to Glory*: But what will Fame be to an *Ephemere* who no longer exists? . . . To me, after all my eager Pursuits, no solid Pleasures now remain, but the Reflection of a long Life spent in meaning well, the sensible Conversation of a few good Lady-Ephemeres, and now and then a kind Smile, and a Tune from the ever-amiable *Brillante*.

The moniker "La Brillante" refers to Franklin's friend Anne-Louise Boyvin d'Hardancourt Brillon de Jouy, his neighbor in the Parisian village of Passy during his years of diplomatic service in France.[2] Brillon was widely known as an accomplished keyboardist and composer; she also assembled a large collection of music, some of which survives in private hands today.[3] And she hosted soirées in her home, entertaining guests in one of the most glittering and highly regarded musical salons in Europe.

.archives.gov/documents/Franklin/01-27-02-0408 (accessed November 23, 2021). The various sources of Franklin's text—French and English, manuscript and print—as well as the sources on which he drew in composing "The Ephemera" are discussed in Gilbert Chinard, "Random Notes on Two 'Bagatelles,'" *Proceedings of the American Philosophical Society* 103, no. 6 (December 1959): 727–60. The poignant question "What can laws do without morals?" is taken from Horace, while the line "Art is long, and life is short" is from Hippocrates; see Chinard, "Random Notes on Two 'Bagatelles,'" 744.

2. A recent biography is Christine de Pas, *Madame Brillon de Jouy et son salon*; a valuable explication of the correspondence between Brillon and Franklin is in Lopez, *Mon cher papa*.

3. Brillon's compositions are housed in the library of the American Philosophical Society, Philadelphia (US-PHps), having been acquired by that institution in the 1950s; the compositions are catalogued in Gustafson, "The Music of Madame Brillon." For the catalogue of her collection, see Gustafson, "Madame Brillon et son salon." Until recently, Brillon's compositions have not been recorded and are scarcely performed. Selections from the recording by the Raritan Players, *In the Salon of Madame Brillon*, are presented as part of this chapter.

In addition to featuring music prominently, Madame Brillon's gatherings offered good food and drink, literary-theatrical games, and enlightened conversation. At these gatherings she hosted a variety of visitors—men and women, statesmen and philosophers, amateur and professional musicians. Written accounts of her salon, as well as the surviving scores from her collection and the published music dedicated to her, present a picture of a highly skilled musician and a woman at the center of musical culture in late eighteenth-century Paris.

It was as a letter to Brillon that Franklin's "Ephemera" first took shape: drafted in English, translated into French for Brillon's benefit and presented to her in manuscript, printed in French as a "Lettre à Madame B." on the press that Franklin operated at his home, and subsequently published in French and English in Franklin's musically titled *Bagatelles*, "The Ephemera" opens a vista onto the permeable boundary between the author's private and public lives.[4] This story formed part of Franklin's public presence as a writer, humorist, statesman, and educator of masses.[5] For Brillon, by contrast, the cultivation of a fully public persona was impossible. As a member of the French aristocracy, she had wealth and privilege, but her conduct, as for most upper-class women, was subject to the constraints of social norms. Brillon claimed to adopt these norms without complaint

4. The *Bagatelles*, first printed on the private press that Franklin kept at his home in Passy, survive in a sole copy now housed in the Beinecke Rare Book and Manuscript Library at Yale University; a facsimile was published as Benjamin Franklin, *The Bagatelles from Passy: Text and Facsimile* (New York: Eakins Press, 1967). On the purposes of Franklin's private press, especially with respect to his political objectives, see Ellen R. Cohn, "The Printer at Passy," in *Benjamin Franklin: In Search of a Better World*, ed. Page Talbott (New Haven, CT: Yale University Press, 2005), 241–45. Although the term "bagatelle" indicated a "trifling," not yet being exclusively associated with music, it had already come to be used in musical contexts. The *Dictionnaire de la langue françoise* of 1732 used it in defining the word "Chanson": "a verse that one sings, composed in a simple, easy, and natural manner . . . meaning a *bagatelle*" ("Chanson . . . Vers tournez d'une maniére simple, aisée & naturelle qu'on chante . . . On se sert de ce mot, pour dire, *bagatelle*"). See Pierre Richelet, *Dictionnaire de la langue françoise ancienne et moderne . . . nouvelle édition corrigée & augmentée d'un grand nombre d'articles* (Basel: Chez Jean Brandmuller, 1735), 1:358.

5. On the role of Franklin's friendship with Brillon in his political life, see Kelsa Pelletiere, "Friendship and Sociability: A Reexamination of Benjamin Franklin's Friendship with Madame Brillon de Jouy," *Age of Revolutions* (January 12, 2021), https://ageofrevolutions.com/2021/01/12/friendship-and-sociability-a-reexamination-of-benjamin-franklins-friendship-with-madame-brillon-de-jouy/ (accessed June 1, 2021).

(though perhaps with a touch of sarcasm) when, in November 1780, she wrote a story for Franklin, to entertain him while he was bedridden, suffering from gout. Introducing the story in a note to Franklin, she explained, "I am a woman, and my lot and my taste are modesty; I have a lively mind, and nothing prevents me from using it, but [only] for myself and for my most intimate friends."[6]

Brillon was far from alone in this understanding, and the social conventions that constrained upper-class behavior constitute one of the obstacles to gaining a clear picture of what took place in musical salons of the eighteenth century. While male-dominated institutions such as academies often kept written records of their agendas and proceedings, textual evidence of women's salons in the eighteenth century was—and remains—scarce, fragmentary, and exclusive. In this very exclusivity lay their allure. As explained in chapter 1 of this study, it was the musical salon's situation as a liminal space between the private and public spheres that enabled *salonnières* to use them as a platform for the exercising of agency. Discouraged from participation in public life, musical salon hostesses utilized the domestic ethos of the salon to shape their musical environments.

Understanding Brillon's musical priorities has, paradoxically, been hindered by aspects of her compositions. She took a purposefully unstudied approach to composition, and she apparently did not concern herself with conventions of voice leading and counterpoint. Instead, she prioritized more ephemeral aspects of music such as timbre and texture. In light of this, an approach rooted primarily in textual analysis proves inadequate to the task. Instead, Franklin's essay "The Ephemera" provides an invitation to think about Brillon from an unconventional perspective. I consider her musicianship, and her salon as a whole, in terms of the ephemeral experiences that she valued—what I call a "poetics of the ephemeral." In defining the ephemeral, I take a broad view: I understand it to encompass the fleeting, temporary experiences of her salon, in which she passed time in the company of friends, playing games and music. I locate the ephemeral in the fragility of sound that she cultivated, attested in verbal accounts, in her compositions, and in sounds of her English square piano—her favored instrument. The ephemeral also lies in Brillon's interest in qualities

6. "Je suis fémme, mon lot et mon gout sont la modéstie; j'ai la teste vive, rien ne me déffend de l'occupér; mais pour moi, et pour mes amis les plus intimes." Anne-Louise Boyvin d'Hardancourt Brillon de Jouy to Benjamin Franklin, after November 14, 1780. French text at https://franklinpapers.org (accessed July 14, 2019).

of music that cannot be captured in notation: special effects of timbre, the blurred sounds caused by damper-raising pedals. To be sure, in the age before recorded sound, all musical performance was ephemeral; yet Brillon's aesthetic values, as captured in her compositions, her instruments, her writings, and accounts of her salon, suggest that she prioritized the ephemeral above all. Her private persona—unfixed in the public medium of print and shielded from public view—enhanced each aspect of her poetics of the ephemeral.

It is ironic, then, that through Madame Brillon's salon, the poetics of the ephemeral entered the public sphere. The salon provided a space for mutual influence and collaboration between the *salonnière* and her guests, who included some of the leading male composers of eighteenth-century Europe. These musicians attended her salon and heard her play; significantly, as part of the ordinary proceedings of such evenings, they would also have conversed with her about music, among other subjects. In some cases, they dedicated music to her; in at least one case—the opus 5 sonatas for violin and keyboard by Luigi Boccherini—there is strong reason to believe that the compositions were inspired by aspects of Brillon's musicianship. This case, in turn, sheds new light on the idea of authorship: rather than being the work of one inspired individual, these sonatas, born in the collaborative context of the salon, may be understood as a case of collaborative authorship. They formed a vehicle through which Brillon could have a lasting impact on her musical environment without breaching the social conventions that circumscribed her behavior.

Brillon's Compositions as Indicators of Her Musical Values

The most famous and oft-cited account of Madame Brillon comes from the diary of that intrepid traveler, Charles Burney, who visited her within two weeks of leaving England for his tour of France and Italy in 1770. Burney's private diary and his resulting published work, *The Present State of Music in France and Italy* (1773), contain detailed descriptions of his impressions of the evening. While he did not hesitate to deride the poor playing of Brillon's companion, the professional violinist Noël Pagin, Burney gushed over Brillon as hostess and musician, calling her "one of the greatest lady-players of the harpsichord in Europe."[7] He continued,

7. Burney, *The Present State of Music in France and Italy*, 43. The diary account is in Burney, *Music, Men, and Manners in France and Italy*, 19–20.

> Madame Brillon in person is rather pretty, but in her manner charming—polite, easy, and always naturally chearful. There was a good deal of company at dinner which was excellent and *bien servi*. After coffee we went into the music room where I found an English pianoforte which Mr. [Johann Christian] Bach had sent her. She played a great deal and I found that she had not acquired her reputation in music without meriting it.

In support of his assessment, Burney noted in the published version of his account that "many of the famous composers of Italy and Germany, who have resided in France at any time, have dedicated their works; among these are Schobert and Boccherini."

It is no coincidence that this published portrait of Brillon refers to her status in relation to other publications: when revising for his reading public, Burney anchored the private, exclusive experience of Brillon's music-making within the context of names and compositions with which this public would have been familiar, all while raising his own stock by showing that he had gained access to the elite and exclusive world of Brillon's salon. Brillon's network of connections to professional musicians formed a significant component of her musical persona, allowing her to shape her musical environment both within and beyond the walls of her home. That Luigi Boccherini and Johann Schobert, along with Henri-Joseph Rigel and Ernst Eichner, had dedicated published compositions to her—and Johann Christian Bach's involvement in her acquisition of an English square piano—were among the factors that had brought Burney to her door.

Burney's description goes on to praise Brillon's skill as a composer: "She likewise composes and was so obliging as to play several of her own pieces both on the harpsichord and piano forte accompanied with the violin by M. *Pagin*, who is reckoned in France the best scholar of Tartini ever made." And, as Burney notes, her compositions grew out of her activities as a player of numerous instruments; he explains, "she plays on several instruments; knows the genius of all that are in common use, which she said it was necessary for her to do, in order to avoid composing for them such things as were either impracticable or unnatural." This point is significant, for it points to her intimate knowledge and idiomatic usage of instruments—not just keyboards and harp, but "all that are in common use." If this statement is true, it is possible that Burney declined to name them because, as an upper-class woman, Brillon might not have wished to be openly associated with instruments such as the violin or cello, for which she also composed.

In hinting at the wide range of Brillon's skills as a performer, Burney again teases his readers by showing that he had gained access to knowledge about the *salonnière* that was not available to the public. Indeed, Burney's effusive praise of Brillon extends to nearly every aspect of her musicianship. He criticizes her in only one respect, and that very mildly: "I could not persuade Madame B. to play the piano forte with the stops on—*c'est sec*, she said—but with them off unless in arpeggios, nothing is distinct—'tis like the sound of bells, continual and confident." Brillon's use (or, in Burney's estimation, overuse) of the damper-raising mechanism of her English square piano is a significant point, and one to which I will return below.

Overall, Burney's praise of Brillon crosses the line into hyperbole. Discussing Burney's approach to Brillon and the multitude of other remarkable, ingenious women whom he met during his travels and described in his diary, Matthew Head has applied the insights of historian Sylvana Tomaselli, who views descriptions of exceptional women by eighteenth-century European writers as an attempt to assert the superiority of their societies over those of primitive peoples. For writers of the French and Scottish Enlightenments, "however bad conditions were for women in civilised nations, they had been a great deal worse in primitive societies."[8] As Head explains, for writers like Burney, "the position of women in society provides an absolute measure of its degree of progress: simply put, the further a society travels from the primitive, the more freedom it accords women to develop their intellectual and artistic potential."[9] This "indexical theory of Enlightenment" encourages caution in reading sources like Burney's travel diary. His enthusiastic account of Madame Brillon—her person, her character, her musicianship—requires a contextual reading and must be understood as a subjective position with an agenda.

And yet, what interests me in Burney's account is not the general and hyperbolic terms in which he praises her, but the specific facets of her musicianship that he mentions. Three interconnected points stand out: first, her interest in multiple types of keyboard instruments; second, her extensive use of the damper-raising mechanism on her English piano beyond what Burney was used to; and third, her intimate knowledge of the various instrument technologies at her disposal, which, paradoxically, allows her to

8. Sylvana Tomaselli, "The Enlightenment Debate on Women," *History Workshop* 20 (Autumn 1985): 110.

9. Head, *Sovereign Feminine*, 30. A critique of this position is in Eger, "Representing Culture"; see also the introduction to this volume.

produce music that transcends technology to achieve the "natural." As I will show, all three of these points are borne out in her compositions, and they also provide an idea of how she interpreted the music of other composers that she collected. All three are critical components of her poetics of the ephemeral.

The compositions for which Brillon is best known are her duos for harpsichord and pianoforte, and her trios for harpsichord, English piano, and German piano; she also wrote a sonata for piano and harp together. These works are remarkable for their codification of the practice of juxtaposing different keyboard timbres and technologies within salons. (As I have argued elsewhere, this juxtaposition of instrument mechanisms was common in salons across Europe, but it was a practice most often left to the discretion of performers.[10]) In adopting and advocating for these different keyboard technologies, Brillon showed herself to be an erudite, progressive collector. Even before Burney visited her and remarked on her English square piano in 1770, this same instrument appeared in the background of the portrait of Brillon painted by Jean-Honoré Fragonard in the late 1760s (fig. 3.1).[11] While Bruce Gustafson has dated all of Brillon's compositions to ca. 1775–1785, Burney's report from 1770 indicates that she was playing her own compositions by that point, and her prized English piano was already in her home, together with, at least, her harpsichord. The keyboard duos and

10. See Cypess, "Keyboard-Duo Arrangements"; and Rebecca Cypess, "Fortepiano–Harpsichord Duos in Two Late Eighteenth-Century Salons," *Harpsichord and Fortepiano* (Spring 2018): 20–26. My understanding of fortepiano–harpsichord duos is informed in particular by the work of Michael Latcham; see, for example, Michael Latcham, "Swirling from One Level of the Affects to Another: The Expressive *Clavier* in Mozart's Time," *Early Music* 30, no. 4 (November 2002): 502–20. See also chapter 2 of this study. On the significance of technology for the Enlightenment, see Paola Bertucci, *Artisanal Enlightenment: Science and the Mechanical Arts in Old Regime France* (New Haven, CT, and London: Yale University Press, 2017).

11. This painting forms part of a series of "fantasy" portraits by Fragonard, unified in terms of framing and technique. Most of the sitters were identified only in 2012, when a page of Fragonard's sketches that included the identifications was put up for auction. See the account in Marie-Anne Dupuy-Vachey, review of Melissa Percival, *Fragonard and the Fantasy Figure: Painting the Imagination*, *The Art Tribune* (July 20, 2012), http://www.theartribune.com/Fragonard-and-the-Fantasy-Figure.html (accessed August 6, 2019). The website of the National Gallery of Art, Washington, DC, includes an application that enables viewers to superimpose images from the sketch sheet on top of images of the portraits; see https://www.nga.gov/features/fantasy-figures-identified.html (accessed August 6, 2019).

Figure 3.1 Jean-Honoré Fragonard, *L'Étude*. Portrait of Anne-Louise Boyvin d'Hardancourt Brillon de Jouy (late 1760s). Musée du Louvre, Paris, France. Scala/Art Resource.

trios may have been composed later as didactic exercises that allowed the *salonnière* to play with her two young daughters, born, respectively, in 1764 and 1768.[12] After all, the part for the German piano in the trios is simple enough for her youngest daughter to have played at quite an early age. But this dating is not definitive, and I know of no reason why some of her surviving compositions could not have been written in the 1760s.

From a musical standpoint, the effect—and perhaps the purpose—of

12. Gustafson, "The Music of Madame Brillon," 529.

juxtaposing diverse instruments in the keyboard duos and trios is a foregrounding of the issue of timbre. In a period when keyboard technologies developed and proliferated quickly, keyboard instruments came to be understood as capable of encompassing all the sounds of the orchestra, and timbre was used as an expressive device, both in composition and in unnotated performance practices.[13] While some of the most fanciful keyboard instruments were produced in Germany, with the builder Philipp Jacob Milchmeyer boasting in 1783 that he had produced a combination keyboard instrument that could produce no fewer than 250 different sounds,[14] English and French builders became equally convinced of the expressive potential of timbre in keyboard construction and performance.[15]

The precise specifications of the three keyboard instruments that Madame Brillon owned (if, indeed, there were only three) are not known. However, certain characteristics may be inferred from general principles of instrument manufacture, as well as from evidence in Brillon's compositions. Given that the French school of harpsichord building was both local and highly prized, it seems likely that Brillon's harpsichord was a French one—perhaps by Pascal Taskin, "Facteur des clavessins du Roy," the most sought-after keyboard builder of pre-Revolutionary France. By 1768 Taskin had introduced his *peau de buffle*, a rank of buffalo-leather plectra, which responded to variations in finger weight and offered the possibility of inflection of timbre and volume. A description published in the *Journal de musique* of 1773 sang the praises of this innovation:

> The effect of this leather [plectrum] on the string of the instrument is a velvety and delicious sound; these sounds can be increased at will by increasing or decreasing the pressure on the key. By this means one obtains sounds that are full, mellifluous, suave, or even voluptuous, for the most Epicurean ear. Do you desire sounds that are passionate, tender, dying? The *buffle* obeys the pressure of the finger. It no longer plucks,

13. See Dolan, *The Orchestral Revolution*.

14. Rebecca Cypess, "Timbre, Expression, and Combination Keyboard Instruments: Milchmeyer's Art of *Veränderung*," *Keyboard Perspectives* 8 (2015): 43–69; see also Latcham, "Swirling from One Level of Affects to Another," 505.

15. See Latcham, "Swirling from One Level of Affects to Another," as well as Michael Latcham, "The Apotheosis of Merlin," in *Musique ancienne: instruments et imagination. Actes de rencontres internationales "harmoniques," Lausanne 2004 / Music of the Past: Instruments and Imagination. Proceedings of the "Harmoniques" International Congress, Lausanne 2004*, ed. Michael Latcham (Bern: Peter Lang, 2006), 271–98.

but caresses the string. The touch—in sum—the touch of the harpsichordist alone suffices to operate these charming vicissitudes in alternation, without changing either the keyboard or the registration.[16]

The result of this innovation, as in the various *Veränderungen* introduced by German builders, was "greater variety on one's instrument" (plus de variété sur son instrument). This pursuit of variety in timbre, volume, and character resonates with Brillon's juxtaposition of diverse keyboard instruments; that, along with the fact that she seems to have prized music-technological novelties, raises the possibility that she owned an instrument with a *peau de buffle* rank. In any case, her indication, in the C-minor duet for harpsichord and pianoforte, that the harpsichordist should play "avec la sourdine" (fig. 3.2) refers, at least, to the "lute stop," which allows the player to mute all the strings on a given rank of the instrument. Brillon's use of the lute stop indicates her interest in timbral effects. In this case, the effect is deployed to suit the simple, harp-like accompaniment that appears in the harpsichord in this movement, which serves as a backdrop for the lyrical melody in the piano part. Naturally, the *sourdine* may be applied just as well at the discretion of the performer in music where it is not explicitly called for; this example serves as a written record of this practice and an invitation to consider its application in music where it is unnotated (ex. 3.1 and audio ex. 3.1 ♫).

In its simple ABA form, its lyrical melody, and its gentle, muted, harp-like accompaniment, this movement evokes song, and in fact, it bears much in common with Brillon's own song compositions. These pieces, contained in a manuscript volume titled *Romances*, are invariably strophic, written for a female voice (perhaps her own or one of her daughter's) with an accompanying keyboard part made up of arpeggiated figuration in one pattern or another. Many of these keyboard parts contain special performance instructions: for example, "avec la grande pédale," or "lié" (legato or con-

16. "De l'effet de cette peau sur la corde de l'instrument, il résulte des sons veloutés et délicieux; on enfle ces sons à volonté, en appuyant plus ou moins fort sur le clavier; par ce moyen on obtient des sons nourris, moëlleux, suaves, ou plutôt voluptueux, pour l'oreille la plus épicurienne. Désire-t-on des sons passionnés, tendres, mourans? Le buffle obéit à l'impression du doigt; il ne pince plus, mais il caresse la corde; le tact enfin, le tact seul du claveciniste suffit pour opérer alternativement, & sans changer ni de clavier ni de registres, ces vicissitudes charmantes." Gilbert Trouflaut, "Lettre aux auteurs de ce journal, sur les clavecins en peau de buffle, inventés par Mr. Pascal," *Journal de musique* 5, no. 2 (December 1773): 13.

Figure 3.2 Anne-Louise Boyvin d'Hardancourt Brillon de Jouy, Duet in C minor for harpsichord and pianoforte, movement 2, detail of the harpsichord part book. Image courtesy of the American Philosophical Society, Philadelphia, USA.

Example 3.1 Anne-Louise Boyvin d'Hardancourt Brillon de Jouy, Duet in C minor for harpsichord and piano, movement 2, Andante, mm. 1–12. Collection of the American Philosophical Society.

Figure 3.3 Anne-Louise Boyvin d'Hardancourt Brillon de Jouy, "Romance attribuée a Chibaut comte de Champagne, accom.[t] avec la grande pédale et le plus doux possible," from Brillon's manuscript *Romances: 1[e] et 2[d] œuvres*. Image courtesy of the American Philosophical Society, Philadelphia, USA.

nected) (see fig. 3.3). On an English square piano of the 1760s or 1770s, damper-raising pedals or hand-stops do not simply facilitate legato playing; they also affect the timbre of the instrument. Burney made this observation when he wrote that Brillon's constant use of the damper-raising pedal approximated the "sound of bells."

It is nearly certain that Brillon played these songs on her English square piano. That she favored this instrument above her German piano is suggested by Burney's special mention of the English square as part of his account of his visit to her salon. Further evidence of her preference comes from the fact that Brillon chose this instrument to be depicted in her portrait by Fragonard (shown above in fig. 3.1). Brillon sits comfortably, easily, with one of her hands extended in a gesture of invitation, while the other hand fingers a volume of music—perhaps a bound copy of her own manuscripts. Behind her is the unmistakable image of her English square, its lid propped open and resting against the wall. In this portrait, marked by Fragonard's characteristically dynamic brushstrokes, even Brillon's glance is ephemeral: she seems poised at any moment to turn her back, exchanging the visual gaze of her viewer for the sound of music from her favorite instrument.

While working on this chapter and on a recording of music from the salon of Madame Brillon, I had the rare opportunity to use a square piano built in 1780 by Johannes Zumpe, the German builder based in London whose instruments would become ubiquitous in both England and France by the end of the eighteenth century.[17] While this instrument may be different in some minor respects from the one that Madame Brillon owned, Zumpe's actions remained consistent during this period. My use of this instrument was instructive in discerning Brillon's poetics of the ephemeral. I found that the sense of intimate sociability and ephemerality she cultivated is supported by the sound of the instrument. Such instruments from the 1760s through the 1780s are certainly capable of a strong character and wide dynamic range—a fact that Brillon and other composers in her orbit knew how to exploit, as I will explain below. And yet, when used for pieces like Brillon's Romances, English squares possess an ethereal quality that resonates with the aesthetics of her songs as a whole. In comparison to the clavichord, the instrument most strongly associated with the "cult of solitude,"[18] the English square piano is a sociable instrument, with a core of sound that is more present and fuller than that of a clavichord. Yet it is capable of the same quiet intimacy, light frivolity, fantasy, and brooding depths as the clavichord. The English square orients those inward qualities toward communal, sociable musicianship.

The rich palette of colors that the instrument is capable of producing may be attributed to the technique that it seems to require. Lacking an escapement mechanism,[19] the English piano sounds best when the fingers sweep the keys and release them almost immediately in a motion that simulates Fragonard's dynamic brushstrokes; otherwise the sound becomes muted or overdetermined. (This technical feature, necessitating a certain amount

17. For use of the instrument, I am deeply indebted to Leslie Martin, who purchased it at auction in Paris in 1976, and to Willard Martin, whose expertise and commitment to this project facilitated the loan and use of the instrument for these purposes. This piano was restored by Tim Hamilton in 1993.

18. Annette Richards, *The Free Fantasia and the Musical Picturesque* (Cambridge: Cambridge University Press, 2000), ch. 5, "Sentiment Undone: Solitude and the Clavichord Cult."

19. The mechanisms and construction of English square pianos are described in Michael Cole, *The Pianoforte in the Classical Era* (Oxford: Clarendon Press, 1998), ch. 2, "John Zumpe and the English Pianoforte."

of detached finger movement, may also help explain why Brillon was so interested in the legato effect offered by the damper-raising mechanism.) In playing this instrument, form imitates content: the most fleeting technique, minimizing contact with the key, is used to create fleeting experiences, shared among intimate friends and preserved only in memory.

This wispy technique is very much at home in Brillon's Romances, including, for example, "Viens m'aider o dieu d'amour." This song is in ABA form, with the A section in E minor and the B section in E major. While the majority of the song uses the rich lower and middle registers of the piano in arpeggiated figuration, the postlude to the B section ascends to the heavenly upper reaches of the instrument, where the accompaniment takes on a touchingly simple, harp-like character. I hear this postlude as linked to a line in the second stanza of the poem: "Son parler semble une lyre"—"her speech is like a lyre" (the first two stanzas are translated below). Here the piano sings with the enchanting voice of the beloved, calling to mind the mythical music of an Orphic past (ex. 3.2 and audio ex. 3.2 ♫).

Viens m'aider o dieu d'amour,[20]
A pourtraire celle,
Celle, tant, tant belle,
Que tant aimerai toujours.
Elle a bien du gai printemps,
Gente humeur et fin sourire.
Blanches perles sont ses dents,
Roses sa bouche respire.

Son maintien est si très doux,
Son parler semble une lyre;
Si son regard luit sur vous,
Votre ame toute il attire.
Viens m'aider &c.

(Come help me, oh god of love, / to portray this one, / this one, so, so beautiful, / whom I will always love so much. / She has the gentle disposition / and fine smile of happy springtime. / White pearls are her teeth, / her mouth breathes roses. // Her bearing is so very sweet, / her

20. I adopt Brillon's text and spellings, which deviate in minor respects from the printed version that I will discuss below.

Example 3.2A Anne-Louise Boyvin d'Hardancourt Brillon de Jouy, "Viens m'aider o dieu d'amour," from *Romances: 1er et 2d œuvres*. Collection of the American Philosophical Society.

12
-mour,
A
pour
-
traire
15
cel
-
-
-
le,
Cel
-
le,
18
tant,
tant
bel
-
-
-
le,
21
Que
tant
ai
-
-
me
-
rai
tou -

Example 3.2B

Example 3.2c

36
[Fine]
Elle a bien du
39
gai prin - temps, Gen - te hu -
42
- meur et fin sou - ri - re.
45
Blan - ches per - les sont ses

Example 3.2D

Example 3.2E

speech is like a lyre. / If her countenance shines on you, / it draws in your whole soul.)

In fact, Erin Helyard has recently linked Brillon's generous use of the damper pedal, especially in passages with arpeggiated figuration, to the sounds of the Aeolian harp, an instrument to which "many were attracted . . . because the forces of nature controlled it." Helyard continues: "Although Burney refers dismissively to the sound of the square piano as an imitation of bells, it is entirely possible that Brillon was adding 'reverb' to an instrument in a small room, thus evoking for the performer and her listeners the expansiveness of a public realm—a realm that, whether in- or outdoors, was generally considered off-limits for the majority of female amateur performers."[21] I agree with Helyard's interpretation but propose that Brillon sought to imitate instruments such as the Aeolian harp or the guitar in order to evoke not just the outdoors, but the *pastoral* outdoors—an environment to which any number of musical, theatrical, poetic, and artistic tropes were linked, and one to which the genre of the Romances was certainly connected. Indeed, as is well known, the adoption and embodied performances of a pastoral aesthetic were favorite pastimes of the French aristocracy, from Queen Marie Antoinette down.[22]

In linking Brillon's Romances to the pastoral mode, I draw on the widely known associations of this genre in France, as described by Jean-Jacques Rousseau in his *Dictionnaire de musique*: for Rousseau, the Romance is a strophic song with "a simple, touching style and a taste that is a little antique," with "no ornaments, nothing mannered, and a sweet, natural melody."[23] The manner of performance, moreover, should be "naïve." Rousseau goes on to suggest that an unaccompanied voice was all that was needed for the ideal performance of a Romance: "It is a certain conclusion that any accompaniment from an instrument detracts from this impression [of a song]. To sing a romance, nothing is required but a clear, correct voice, which pronounces well and which sings simply."[24]

21. Erin Helyard, "'To Prevent the Abuse of the Open Pedal': Meticulous Pedal Markings from Madame du Brillon to Moscheles," *Keyboard Perspectives* 9 (2016): 100.

22. See, for example, Amy S. Wyngaard, *From Savage to Citizen: The Invention of the Peasant in the French Enlightenment* (Newark: University of Delaware Press, 2004), especially ch. 2, "The Sentimental Peasant."

23. "d'un style simple, touchant, & d'un gout un peu antique." Jean-Jacques Rousseau, *Dictionnaire de musique* (Paris: Veuve Duchesne, 1768), 420.

24. "C'est une expérience certaine que tout accompagnement d'instrument affoiblit

The text of "Viens m'aider o dieu d'amour" was penned by the poet "most instrumental in reviving" the poetic genre of the Romance, François Augustin Paradis de Moncrif.[25] Moncrif had been cited in the article on the Romance in the *Encyclopédie* edited by Denis Diderot and Jean le Rond d'Alembert, since his work constituted a model for the genre. This article, perhaps penned by Diderot himself, explained that Moncrif's Romances are "all of exquisite taste,"[26] but that his most famous Romance, *Les constants amours d'Alix et d'Alexis*, was so exceptional that "everyone knows [it] by heart."[27] Central to this easy recollection of his poem was its simple, unaccompanied melody, notation for which Moncrif provided at the beginning of the published version, and which could be used as a formula for recitation of the 29-stanza work. It is likely that Brillon and her aristocratic contemporaries knew this poem as well as Moncrif's later publication, the *Choix de chansons*, in which the poem "Viens m'aider o dieu d'amour" appeared; musical notation for the melody of this and other poems appears in the main body of the work and in the appendix to the collection.[28] In the following decade, the same poem appeared in both volumes 1 and 2 of the *Recueil de romances historiques, tendres, et burlesques* (1767 and 1774).[29] In volume 1, the poem is attributed to Moncrif, but it is set to a new melody composed by

---

cette impression. Il ne faut, pour le chant de la *romance*, qu'une voix juste, nette, qui prononce bien, & qui chante simplement." Rousseau, *Dictionnaire de musique*, 420.

25. The description of Moncrif is from Daniel Heartz, "The Beginnings of the Operatic Romance: Rousseau, Sedaine, and Monsigny," *Eighteenth-Century Studies* 15, no. 2 (Winter 1981–1982): 151.

26. "toutes d'un goût exquis." Denis Diderot [?], "Romance," in *Encyclopédie, ou dictionnaire raisonné des sciences, des arts et des métiers, etc.*, ed. Denis Diderot and Jean le Rond d'Alembert (University of Chicago: ARTFL Encyclopédie Project, Autumn 2017 ed.), ed. Robert Morrissey and Glenn Roe, http://encyclopedie.uchicago.edu (accessed July 18, 2019), 14:343. The provisional attribution of this article to Diderot appears in this edition of the *Encyclopédie*.

27. "Tout le monde sait par cœur la *romance* d'Alis & d'Alexis." Denis Diderot [?], "Romance." The Romance of Alix and Alexis is in François-Augustin Paradis de Moncrif, *Les constantes amours d'Alix et d'Alexis, romance* (s.l.: s.n., 1738).

28. François-Augustin Paradis de Moncrif, *Choix de chansons, à commencer de celles du Comte de Champagne* (Paris: s.n., 1755). The text of "Viens m'aider o dieu d'amour" appears in vol. 2:58–59, and the music is in an appendix to vol. 2.

29. The two volumes are M. D. L. [Charles de Lusse], *Recueil de romances historiques, tendres, et burlesques, tant anciennes que modernes, avec les airs notés* (s.l.: Par de Lusse d'après Barbier, 1767); and M. D. L. [Charles de Lusse], *Recueil de romances. Tome second* (s.l.: Par de Lusse d'après Barbier, 1774). The text of "Viens m'aider o dieu d'amour" appears in vol. 2:139–40.

Charles de Lusse, editor of the collection. In volume 2, the poet's name is given but not the composer's (fig. 3.4); it is possible that the second melody is by Moncrif himself. Throughout the *Recueils*, as in Moncrif's *Choix de chansons*, the melodies are entirely unaccompanied.[30] In keeping with the simple characteristics of the Romance as a genre, the melodies lie in a comfortable range for virtually any singer, and thus seem to eschew artifice in favor of seemingly natural simplicity.[31]

Moreover, the text of "Viens m'aider" was perhaps especially appropriate within the setting of the salon, where the creation of "literary portraits" of *habitués* was a long-standing custom. Early eighteenth-century musical portraits—especially those captured in the titles of instrumental compositions by François Couperin—demonstrate that instrumental music came to be understood as capable of capturing the character of its "sitter" in a manner analogous to painted portraits.[32] The proliferation of melodies for "Viens m'aider"—some of which circulated in publication while others, including Brillon's, did not—raises the possibility that, among the French nobility of the later eighteenth century, the creation of melodies for poetic Romances formed a kind of musical salon game.[33] Guests could occupy themselves with the creation of such melodies together or they could prepare their melodies privately and come to the salon gathering ready to sing. Publications of poetry like the *Recueil de romances historiques, tendres, et burlesques* record such games by presenting monophonic melodies composed by prominent amateurs, and they also serve as a handbook for the creation of new melodies by those who would emulate the practice.

30. Rousseau's own work *Le devin du village* (1752), set in a distinctly pastoral world, includes the Romance "Dans ma cabane obscure," which includes a figured bass line and an obbligato instrumental melody to complement the simple melody.

31. I am indebted to my former student Joshua Druckenmiller, whose master's project at Rutgers University, completed in 2018, advanced an interpretation of *Le devin du village* that associates the *haut-contre* range, occupied by the character of Colin for much of the work, with the supernatural. Druckenmiller argued that the singable quality of Colin's Romance coincided with his rejection of the artifice of the city and his embrace of the natural aesthetics of the pastoral world. Further on the Romance in the context of Rousseau's *Devin*, see Heartz, "The Beginnings of the Operatic Romance," 149–78.

32. David Fuller, "Of Portraits, 'Sapho' and Couperin: Titles and Characters in French Instrumental Music of the High Baroque," *Music and Letters* 78, no. 2 (May 1997): 149–74.

33. Benedetta Craveri has described "the portrait game" among French *salonnières* of the seventeenth century; see Craveri, *The Age of Conversation*, 159–72. The creation of literary portraits as a pastime persisted through the eighteenth century; see Craveri, *The Age of Conversation*, 316–18.

Figure 3.4 Music for Moncrif's "Viens m'aider o dieu d'amour" from M. D. L. [Charles de Lusse], *Recueil de romances. Tome second* (s.l.: Par de Lusse d'après Barbier, 1774), unpaginated appendix. Image courtesy of the Bibliothèque municipale de Lyon, France.

Andante con espressione

Pianoforte

Example 3.3A Anne-Louise Boyvin d'Hardancourt Brillon de Jouy, Sonata IV in G minor, movement 1, Andante con espressione, mm. 1–16. From *Troisieme recueil de sonates pour le piano forte avec accompag.[t] par Madame Brillon* (ad libitum violin part lost). Collection of the American Philosophical Society.

Example 3.3B

In her unpublished Romances, Brillon engaged the same aesthetic of simplicity, but her means to achieve that natural sound were quite different from those of the published settings that I have discussed here. Far from excluding accompaniment, she wrote lush keyboard parts and called for enthusiastic use of the "special effect" offered by the damper-raising pedal. The novelty of this approach cannot be overstated. Past scholars have suggested that the first fully written-out keyboard parts for French Romances did not appear until ca. 1784, when Jean-Paul-Gilles Martini published a collection of airs from his opera *Le droit du seigneur*, together with three newly composed Romances.[34] On the cover of this collection, Martini or his publisher called special attention to the innovative step of providing a fully worked-out accompaniment for the harp or pianoforte for the operatic airs, writing that "the author of the music of this work viewed himself as obliged to make accompaniments for harp or fortepiano himself."[35] The

34. [Jean-Paul-Gilles] Martini, *Airs du Droit du seigneur et trois romances nouvelles avec accompagnement de harpe ou forté piano* (Paris: Chez le portier de Mr Lenormant d'Etiolles, [ca. 1784]). This dating of the volume, based on the date of the premiere of *Le droit du seigneur*, is suggested in Maurice Cauchie, "La version authentique de la romance 'Plaisir d'amour,'" *Revue de musicologie* 18, no. 61 (1937): 13. For an assessment of Martini's Romances as the first to incorporate fully worked-out keyboard parts, see Jack Sage, Susana Friedmann, and Roger Hickman, "Romance," *Grove Music Online* (2001), https://www.oxfordmusiconline.com (accessed July 18, 2019).

35. "L'auteur de la musique de cet ouvrage s'est vû obligé de faire lui même des accompagnemens de harpe ou de forté piano à ses airs pour les réhabiliter." Martini, *Airs du Droit du seigneur*, title page.

reason, he explained, was that the performance materials for the operatic excerpts would otherwise have been available only in orchestral score; the implication is that potential purchasers of the volume would not have such forces at their disposal. His piano or harp accompaniments rendered the music suitable for the drawing room.

While Brillon's song compositions are undated, it is likely that they predate Martini's publication of ca. 1784. If so, then the idea of fully notated keyboard accompaniments occurred to her before Martini; if not, they were still highly progressive. What might have motivated her to adopt this approach in her compositions? Unlike Martini's operatic airs, which had to be adapted for performance on the harp or pianoforte, Brillon's Romances were inextricably linked to her musical salon. Her conception of musical composition is tied to the instruments that she kept there—her English square piano in particular. Her use of that instrument motivated her compositional choices, and not the other way around. Her intimate knowledge of the English square allowed her to employ its unique timbres, its rich bass sonorities, its glimmering upper range, and the lush sounds afforded by its damper-raising pedal, to evoke the "antique," pastoral world associated with the Romance.

The same pastoral register—together with evocations of the Aeolian harp—may be discerned in Brillon's sonatas, especially in the cantabile movements. The opening movement of her G-minor sonata, marked *Andante con espressione*, from a collection of works for which the *ad libitum* violin part is now lost, adopts a distinctly vocal style, again with a simple, harplike accompaniment. While the interior title page of the volume indicates that the sonatas may be played on either the pianoforte or the harpsichord, the bound cover calls the manuscript the *Troisieme recueil de sonates pour le piano forte avec accompag.t par Madame Brillon*. In any case, the spirit of this sonata is very much in keeping with that of her song accompaniments for the English piano. Brillon seems to become lost in her own melody, repeating it again and again. Harmonic differentiation is slow in coming; time becomes suspended, and the only thing that seems to matter is the sound of her instrument. Lingering in the upper registers of the piano, Brillon's sonata exploits the distinctively ethereal sound of which the English square is capable, while using the middle register of the instrument to provide a gentle bed of arpeggiation (ex. 3.3 and audio ex. 3.3 ♫).

Recall Burney's report that Brillon "plays on several instruments; knows the genius of all that are in common use, which she said it was necessary for her to do, in order to avoid composing for them such things as were either impracticable or unnatural." Certainly, in her keyboard writing, her goal seems to have been to adopt an air of the natural despite—and perhaps as a function of—the complexity of the technologies at her disposal. She uses the piano and harpsichord idiomatically, exploits the piano's pedal for expressive purposes, and becomes lost in the sonorities of her instrument. Nowhere is this approach more apt than in her Romances, a genre designed to evoke the natural above all. Paradoxically, then, she employed the technologies at her disposal in idiomatic ways in order to mask her artifice—to create the impression of an unstudied and purely natural approach to music.

I have lingered over Brillon's compositions in order to draw out aspects of her poetics of the ephemeral that would otherwise go unnoticed. The notion of writing a harp-like keyboard part for her songs would have come from her interest in the sounds of her instruments—perhaps especially her English square piano. The rich, bell-like quality of the instrument calls for a delicate yet continuous engagement, and this is what her song accompaniments provide. The instrument itself guides the player in developing the fragile, brush-like movements required to make it sound well. Irrespective of their occasional breaches of contrapuntal principles, Brillon's compositions incorporate ephemeral aspects that hover above the page.

The Poetics of the Ephemeral and the Question of Authorship

Although Brillon's compositions offer some evidence of her musical aesthetics and values, this evidence is incomplete on its own. Her compositions need to be treated as she understood them—as essentially private documents, unpolished and unfinished. In the letter that I have already cited that accompanied her story to entertain Franklin during his illness, she made excuses for her written work, which she may have been comparing to the stories that Franklin had written for her: "I have corrected certain faults in this story; there is still much to do, but I am afraid of becoming like the sculptor who, finding the nose of one of his creations a little too big, reduces it until it disappears entirely."[36] Her story was an intimate gift, to be appreciated as much for its faults as for its successes in wit or sentiment. She begged Franklin to keep the story from the eyes of others. Just as she

36. "J'ai corrigé quelques fauttes a la fable, il y auroit encore beaucoup a faire mais j'aurois peur de réssemblér a certain statuaire qui trouvant le nei d'une teste de fantaisie un peu trop gros, le diminua tant qu'il n'en résta plus." Brillon to Franklin, after November 14, 1780. French text at https://franklinpapers.org (accessed July 14, 2019).

trusted Franklin to value her story as a memento of their lived friendship, she would have expected the guests in her salon to overlook her errors as a composer and focus instead on the musical parameters of her compositions that resided in the realm of ephemerae: sound and timbre, sentimental, expressive melodies sustained through time, an aesthetic of the natural, the simple, the fragile.

Despite Brillon's imperfections as a composer and her acceptance of the conventions that kept her away from publication and out of the fully public eye, her poetics of the ephemeral made an impression on her musical environment—in particular, through the collaborative music-making that took place in her salon. The strongest evidence for this collaboration comes from Luigi Boccherini's sonatas for keyboard and violin, opus 5, published in Paris in 1768 with a dedication to Madame Brillon; the text of his dedication states explicitly that these works were inspired by Brillon's keyboard playing, and there is reason to think that this was more than a mere rhetorical trope. In fact, I suggest that these sonatas bear Brillon's imprint so strongly that they may well constitute a case of "collaborative authorship."

In order to understand how Brillon's presence may be discerned in Boccherini's opus 5 sonatas, I turn to Emily H. Green's recent explication of practices of musical dedication and her notion of "multiple authorship." A tendency has existed in past scholarship to view eighteenth-century dedications as primarily utilitarian: in this understanding, composers dedicated their works to a given patron solely to increase the prestige, and with it, the marketability of their publications. This functional, financial layer was surely at play in many cases—it was one of the ways in which composers navigated the changing European markets for music that came with the increase in musical amateurism and the disruption of earlier systems of patronage based primarily in courts and churches. However, Green's work has complicated this monolithic understanding of musical dedications. Without denying the function of dedications with respect to prestige and commercial success, Green argues that they may carry aesthetic or creative weight as well. As she writes, "the rhetorical connection between dedications and multiple authorship is implicit in the language" of dedications. "References to approval and inspiration in both dedicatory epistles and the reception of dedicated works designate the dedicatee as an authorial influence. . . . [T]he implication is that the patron heard the works before they were complete—or at least fit to print—and offered an opinion."[37] If this

37. Green, *Dedicating Music*, 154.

was true of dedications in general, it is perhaps especially apposite in the setting of salons, where offering opinions about music was *de rigueur.*

While letters of dedication to aristocrats such as Brillon are formulaic by necessity, and clearly involve a level of flattery and therefore perhaps exaggeration, the precise terms in which professional composers wrote to her are worth considering. After all, Brillon was no ordinary *salonnière*—someone who dabbled in music but had no real talent or expertise. She was a proficient keyboardist whose reputation as a musician reached across Europe. It seems possible, then, that composers engaged with her musicianship in more active ways than they might in other cases of dedication. With the art of conversation a centerpiece of salon experiences in the Enlightenment, such encounters could not have been unidirectional; Brillon—outspoken and lively in the privacy of her own parlor—would likely have shared ideas with her guests as readily as they would with her. If these experiences, exchanges, and musical encounters were fleeting and ephemeral, they nevertheless could make a lasting impression.

The role of such encounters in the creation of musical works is suggested by the letter of dedication that Henri-Joseph Rigel, a German composer who made his career in France, wrote to Brillon in his opus 7 sonatas:

> In publishing this work under your protection, I would create a monument to your rare talents as a keyboardist, to your true connoisseurship of music, to the excellence of your taste, to the justness of your discernment, and finally to your declared beneficence for all that is meritorious. . . . If there are any new or happy ideas in [these sonatas], it is you who has inspired them. I have gathered them in those moments of enthusiasm in which you have ravished your listeners.[38]

It is not Rigel's formulaic hyperbole that interests me, but rather, the specific terms in which he describes his link to Brillon. His dedication, however utilitarian, was the result of a live encounter with Brillon—one

38. "En publiant cet ouvrage sous vos auspices, je devrois faire l'éloge de vos rares talents pour le clavecin, de vos vraies connoissances en musique, de l'excellence de votre goût, de la justesse de votre discernement, et enfin de votre bienveillance déclarée pour tous ceux qui ont quelques mérites. . . . S'il s'y trouve des idées neuves et heureuses, c'est vous qui les avez inspirées. Je les ai recueillies dans ces moments d'enthousiasme où vous ravissez vos auditeurs." Letter of dedication in Henri-Joseph Rigel, *Sonates en quatuor pour le clavecin avec accompagnement de deux violons, deux cors et violoncelle ad libitum . . . Oeuvre VII* (Paris: l'Auteur, [ca. 1772]). Quoted in de Pas, *Madame Brillon de Jouy et son salon*, 37.

that took place in her salon, where he listened to her playing, and, presumably, where he played as well. If I seem to be stating the obvious, it is to emphasize that the material remnants of that encounter, Rigel's published music, are but a shadow of the salon experience. The truly remarkable facet of Brillon's salon was the "moments of enthusiasm in which [she] ravished her listeners." If we take Rigel's words seriously, his sonatas represent crystallizations of ideas formed there.

The letter of dedication of Luigi Boccherini's accompanied sonatas, opus 5, dedicated to Madame Brillon, underscores how such inspiration might have worked its way into the compositions of the professional composers in Brillon's orbit (see the title page in fig. 3.5). The letter survives in just a single printed copy of the sonatas, now housed in Cambridge, England, which may have been Boccherini's presentation copy to Brillon.[39] His dedication connects the sonatas specifically to Brillon's manner of playing the keyboard. As he wrote,

> Madame, I have never before composed for the keyboard; I heard you play on that instrument, and then I wrote these sonatas; the homage that I offer you through them is, simultaneously, a fitting tribute, and one of *reconnaissance*; you have inspired them, and you embellish them.[40]

The term that Boccherini uses here—*reconnaissance*—encompasses multiple meanings. It implies, most obviously, "re-cognition," "re-knowing," or "remembrance." Another layer of meaning is explained in the royally sanctioned French-English dictionary published in the 1760s, where *reconnaissance* is defined as a "*recognizance*, a bond to acknowledge a debt or duty." *Reconnaissance*, moreover, allows for "*an acknowledgment*, or *knowing again*."[41] While it is possible that Boccherini meant only to recall the experiences that he and Madame Brillon had shared in her salon—a statement

39. Rudolf Rasch, "Description of the Sources," in Luigi Boccherini, *Sei sonate per tastiera e violino*, ed. Rudolf Rasch (Bologna: Ut Orpheus Edizioni, 2009), xciii.

40. "Madame / Je n'avois point encore composé pour le Clavecin; je vous ai entendu jouer cet instrument, et j'ai Ecrit ces Sonates; l'hommage que je vous en fais est tout a la fois un tribut de justice et de reconnoißance; vous les avés inspirées et vous les Embellißés. / Je suis avec l'admiration la plus vraïe et le plus profond respect / Madame / Votre très humble et très obeissant Serviteur / BOCCHERINI." Transcribed in Rasch, "Description of the Sources," xciii.

41. Abel Boyer, *The Royal Dictionary, French and English, and English and French: Extracted from the Writings of the Best Authors in Both Languages* (London: T. Osborne et al., 1764).

SEI SONATE
DI
CEMBALO
E
VIOLINO OBBLIGATO
Dedicate,
A MADAMA
BRILLON DE JOUY
DA
LUIGI BOCCHERINI
Di Lucca.
Gravée par Mme. La Ve. Leclair.
OPERA V.
Prix 9tt
A PARIS
A LYON
AVEC PRIVILEGE DU ROY.

Figure 3.5 Title page of Luigi Boccherini, *Sei sonate di cembalo e violino obbligato dedicate, a Madama Brillon de Jouy . . . opera V* (Paris: Veuve Leclair, 1768). Image courtesy of the Bibliothèque nationale de France.

meaningful on its own—I think there is reason to consider the possibility of a "debt" in relation to Boccherini's sonatas. Could Brillon have inspired some particular facet of these works?

Elisabeth Le Guin has remarked on the distinctive features of Boccherini's style of composition for string instruments. Taking note of what she calls Boccherini's "textile-like writing," she explains that Boccherini's music has "an astonishing repetitiveness, an affection for extended passages with fascinating textures but virtually no melodic line, an obsession with soft dynamics, a unique ear for sonority, and an unusually rich palette of introverted and mournful affects. They gave Boccherini an unmistakable profile both to the ear and under the hand."[42] Boccherini's sound world is one of the ephemeral: time seems suspended, fragmentary motives and melodies sound again and again before disappearing like so many clouds, and instruments produce hushed whispers to create the most intimate effects.

That Boccherini, a cellist, understood how to exploit string instruments to create these effects is not surprising, though his style is surely unique, as Le Guin demonstrates. But in his opus 5 sonatas dedicated to Brillon, he found a keyboard-based language analogous to that of his string chamber music. Melodic fragments meander, calling to and answering one another, supported by a harp-like bed of arpeggiated figures that shares much in common with the harp-like figuration in Brillon's songs and sonatas. (The analogy between the keyboard and the harp is made explicit in Boccherini's statement that "many of these pieces may be executed on the harp."[43]) More than simple Alberti bass lines, these arpeggiated figures appear in all registers of the instrument, creating a woven textile familiar from Boccherini's string music. Harmonic shifts occur at times without notice, and surprising changes from major to minor mode alter both mood and timbre. In fast movements, quick figuration creates washes of sound that seem to mask their individual notes in favor of large-scale color.

Boccherini's sonata in D major, op. 5 no. 4, may serve to illustrate these points. The first movement, an Andante, is set in a pastoral landscape. Simple harmonic motion and a slow harmonic rhythm give the movement a sunny quality, while the light triplet sixteenth notes in the left hand of the keyboard create an undulating sound. The right hand of the keyboard plays a sentimental melody punctuated by arpeggios in the violin (ex. 3.4). The second theme, in the dominant key, is composed of fragments—wisps of melody that come into focus and move away again. Ornamental figuration in the right hand creates a blurry atmosphere (ex. 3.5). A minor-mode section in the development brings back the first theme, now in the guise of plaintive weeping (ex. 3.6). Throughout, the harp-like figuration in the left

42. Elisabeth Le Guin, *Boccherini's Body: An Essay in Carnal Musicology* (Berkeley, Los Angeles, and London: University of California Press, 2006), 2.

43. "Plusieurs de ces pièces peuvent s'exécuter sur la harpe."

Example 3.4 Luigi Boccherini, Sonata op. 5 no. 4 in D major, movement 1, Andante, mm. 1–9. From *Sei sonate di cembalo e violino obbligato dedicate, a Madama Brillon de Jouy . . . opera V* (Paris: Veuve Leclair, 1768). Transcription based on the critical edition in Luigi Boccherini, *6 Sonate per tastiera e violino*, ed. Rudolf Rasch (Bologna: Ut Orpheus Edizioni, 2009).

Example 3.5A Luigi Boccherini, Sonata op. 5 no. 4 in D major, movement 1, Andante, mm. 19–34. From *Sei sonate di cembalo e violino obbligato dedicate, a Madama Brillon de Jouy . . . opera V* (Paris: Veuve Leclair, 1768). Transcription based on the critical edition in Luigi Boccherini, *6 Sonate per tastiera e violino*, ed. Rudolf Rasch (Bologna: Ut Orpheus Edizioni, 2009).

Example 3.5B

Example 3.6A Luigi Boccherini, Sonata op. 5 no. 4 in D major, movement 1, Andante, mm. 59–70. From *Sei sonate di cembalo e violino obbligato dedicate, a Madama Brillon de Jouy . . . opera V* (Paris: Veuve Leclair, 1768). Transcription based on the critical edition in Luigi Boccherini, *6 Sonate per tastiera e violino*, ed. Rudolf Rasch (Bologna: Ut Orpheus Edizioni, 2009).

Example 3.6B

hand of the keyboard provides a lush bed of sound, over which the treble-range gestural melodies seem to hover. In its embrace of this harp-like writing and its sentimental melodic gestures, this movement bears much in common with Brillon's style (audio ex. 3.4 ♫).

The second movement is an extended sonata form that requires a muscular technique—far more so than Brillon's fast movements do. Here, too, Boccherini seems to paint in watercolor strokes. The keyboard rumbles, first in the left hand and then in the right, and there is no melody to speak of. In measure 11, the right-hand figuration evokes the bariolage technique used in string writing, but the intricate passagework only serves the larger gesture (ex. 3.7). In measures 71–80, this bariolage gesture is overtaken suddenly by a harmonic excursion composed of violin double-stops and triplet arpeggiation in the keyboard (ex. 3.8). There are few truly melodic moments here; instead, the movement consists of motives, gestures, glances, digressions, fragments, and above all, sound. Despite all of Boccherini's formal rigor—and this is a sonata-form movement of substantial proportions—the overarching impression is one of splashes of color (audio

Example 3.7A Luigi Boccherini, Sonata op. 5 no. 4 in D major, movement 2, Allegro assai, mm. 1–24. From *Sei sonate di cembalo e violino obbligato dedicate, a Madama Brillon de Jouy . . . opera V* (Paris: Veuve Leclair, 1768). Transcription based on the critical edition in Luigi Boccherini, *6 Sonate per tastiera e violino*, ed. Rudolf Rasch (Bologna: Ut Orpheus Edizioni, 2009).

Example 3.7B

Example 3.7c

Example 3.8A Luigi Boccherini, Sonata op. 5 no. 4 in D major, movement 2, Allegro assai, mm. 71–80. From *Sei sonate di cembalo e violino obbligato dedicate, a Madama Brillon de Jouy . . . opera V* (Paris: Veuve Leclair, 1768). Transcription based on the critical edition in Luigi Boccherini, *6 Sonate per tastiera e violino*, ed. Rudolf Rasch (Bologna: Ut Orpheus Edizioni, 2009).

Example 3.8B

ex. 3.5 ♫). And, after all this, the third movement of this sonata returns to the pastoral landscape. A menuet in ABA form, its opening and closing material involves droning octaves in the bass of the keyboard—perhaps something like a hurdy-gurdy.

Although the title page of these sonatas suggests that they are playable on any keyboard instrument—and that some can be played on the harp—the English square piano in Brillon's home would have supported Boccherini's distinctive keyboard language. In contrast to the clear articulations available on Viennese and German pianos, English square pianos, especially when played with the dampers raised, as Brillon did so insistently, paint in broad, watercolor strokes. Moments of articulate phrasing emerge from the texture only to fade away again. It is precisely these fragmentary qualities that characterize Boccherini's style. Perhaps most importantly, the arpeggiated figuration that permeates these sonatas is of a piece with Brillon's harp-like arpeggiation in her songs. It is this thoroughgoing texture—altered through Boccherini's kaleidoscope of harmonies and sentiments—that creates the fabric of the sonatas.

Rudolph Rasch, in the introduction to his edition of Boccherini's opus 5, notes that "There is no evidence suggesting that Boccherini ever was a keyboard performer himself. . . . Nevertheless, the writing of the keyboard part of the Sonatas Opus 5 is mostly quite idiomatic."[44] I happily confirm this point: the opus 5 sonatas are a joy to play. This is all the more striking given Boccherini's admission that he had never before composed for the keyboard. He would not return to keyboard composition until the 1790s,

44. Rudolf Rasch, introduction to Luigi Boccherini, *Sei sonate per tastiera e violino*, ed. Rudolf Rasch (Bologna: Ut Orpheus Edizioni, 2009), xxxiv.

when he revised these sonatas and composed his quintets for piano and strings, opus 56 and opus 57.

It is difficult to imagine that Boccherini suddenly developed this perfectly idiomatic approach to keyboard performance and composition all on his own, only to abandon it again for some thirty years. However, if we take his dedication letter to Madame Brillon seriously, then the possibility emerges that these pieces grew out of his experiences in her salon—listening to her, conversing with her, learning from her, playing alongside her. Burney's account provides evidence that informal sight-reading was a normal component of her musical gatherings, and so it requires no stretch of the imagination to think that Brillon might have tested Boccherini's sonatas, providing feedback on their playability and their idiomatic use of her instrument.

From an aesthetic standpoint as well as a technical one, Boccherini's sonatas and Brillon's have much in common. The ineffability of their melodic material, their repetitive use of fragmentary motives, the way they place these melodies atop a layer of watercolor accompaniments, their concern with the exploration of the various timbres of each register of the keyboard—all these parameters point to a nexus of their aesthetic concerns. To be sure, Brillon's compositions must be understood as amateur efforts not intended for the public eye or ear, but they provide ample evidence of these central musical values, rooted in her poetics of the ephemeral. And, even if Boccherini and Brillon employed divergent means to incorporate this poetics of the ephemeral in their music, aspects of their treatment of the keyboard overlap in suggestive ways, as I have noted. To judge from his letter of dedication, Boccherini found something valuable in Brillon's approach to music, and to the keyboard in particular, and these values are recorded in his opus 5 sonatas.

If my speculation about the origins of these sonatas in Brillon's salon is correct, then Green's notion that dedications provide evidence of "multiple authorship" is apt. In dedicating his sonatas to Brillon, Boccherini was acknowledging a *reconnaissance*: the dedication stands both as a memento of their shared experiences and as a recognition of the debt that he owed her for her role in shaping his compositions. To be sure, the example of Boccherini's sonatas is extreme; most of the composers who dedicated music to Brillon were keyboardists, and we cannot necessarily expect to find evidence that their style changed remarkably because of her influence. Nevertheless, she and her salon may still have cultivated composers' work in more than simply financial or commercial ways.

Conclusion

I return to Benjamin Franklin's "Ephemera." In its original manuscript form, the story served as a private document, shared between Franklin and Brillon as intimate friends. In its manuscript copies and in its limited publication from the private press that Franklin kept in his home at Passy, the story circulated in a wider, yet still exclusive circle. When it was finally published as part of Franklin's volume of *Bagatelles*, the story achieved a public aspect, and it came to form part of its author's public persona and his broader project in moral education. In these various manifestations, the medium of the story reflects its contents: as a manifesto on both the ephemerality of worldly joys and their true value when shared with friends, Franklin's "Ephemera" sought to transcend the ephemeral and achieve permanence.

For Brillon, such a public persona was impossible; social norms meant, as she said, that "modesty was her lot and her taste." Despite their fixity on paper, her compositions need to be understood within this context—as ephemerae. Still, they provide valuable evidence of her musical ideals, values, and concerns—especially the musical manifestations of her poetics of the ephemeral—and these found their way, I argue, into the public music that emerged from the intimate world of her salon. Brillon's ephemeral values and the ways in which she brought them to life at her keyboards contributed to Boccherini's sonatas, providing her with an indirect and socially sanctioned means of presenting her private musical persona to a public world. This influence is suggested by the title page of Boccherini's opus 5 sonatas, in which her name dominates the page, appearing in larger font than that of the composer. If such a typographical feature appeared in other publications as well, that fact does not negate the integral way in which she is bound up with this volume's contents, and it might encourage us to rethink what other such dedications might have meant as well.

Fragonard's portrait of Brillon, shown in figure 3.1 above, is suggestive. The sitter of this painting was identified based on its relationship to a surviving sketch, discovered only in 2012, with her name on it. The finished portrait, too, has something of the quality of a sketch. Like many of Fragonard's portraits, but in contrast to the well-defined lines of more formal portraits of this period, this image is composed of fragmentary strokes that come together to form the total image. Despite the lady's ornate dress, she appears informally situated, her left hand open and inviting. With her right hand, she fingers scores of music—the permanent, material evidence of her musical skill. In the shadows behind her, however, stands her English square piano. Indeed, even as she invites us into her musical scene, she is preparing to turn her back on us in order to play. Leaving behind her momentary interaction with her viewers, she is poised to return to her piano and the exclusive, ephemeral world that it opens.

CHAPTER FOUR

Composition, Collaboration, and the Cultivation of Skill in the Salon of Marianna Martines

On August 4, 1773, the *Wienerisches Diarium* reported that a resident of Vienna, Marianna Martines (fig. 4.1), had recently been inducted into the famed Accademia filarmonica of Bologna—in fact, she was the first woman granted this honor.[1] Making note of Martines's talent in general terms, the *Diarium* ultimately attributed this remarkable occasion to the beneficence and example of Empress Maria Theresa, cultivator of the arts in her city:

> A short time ago the musical Academy de' Filarmonici of Bologna admitted Mademoiselle Marianna Martines, a native of Vienna, although of Spanish ancestry, into their famous society. The official diploma, executed with the most honorable expressions, has already been sent here. It is a fact that the Academy, by their voluntary admission, has done no more than justice to the rare and special merits of Mademoiselle Martines. All the members could not express sufficiently their amazement at the combination of beauty, ingenuity, nobility of expression, and an astonishing correctness in the compositions of the new candidate. Such a unanimous judgment leads us also to reproach the Academy for waiting so long to share the honor with so worthy a member of their famous and celebrated society. How much patriots must rejoice as every day they see

1. Osvaldo Gambassi notes that the few women inducted into the Accademia filarmonica in the eighteenth century were granted only honorary membership and were not entitled to participate in the academy's proceedings. See Osvaldo Gambassi, *L'Accademia filarmonica di Bologna: Fondazione, statuti e aggregazioni* (Florence: Olschki, 1992), 122.

Figure 4.1 Anton von Maron, *Portrait of Marianna Martines* (ca. 1773). Wien Museum Inventory no. 158.809. © Wien Museum, Austria. The inscription, as transcribed by Michael Lorenz, translates to "Maria Anna Martines. Pupil of Pietro Metastasio. Born in Vienna, on the fourth day before the Nones of May 1744, member of the Philharmonic Academy." See Michael Lorenz, "Martines, Maron and a Latin Inscription" (October 12, 2012), http://michaelorenz.blogspot.com/2012/10/martines-maron-and-latin-inscription.html (accessed July 17, 2020).

ever more how the German nation takes pains to distinguish itself in all the arts with such fine progress! And what [a] rare and special honor it is to the fair sex here, to be able to count as a member for whom so many cities have reason to envy them. Thanks be to the glorious reign of our most honorable queen, under which all the sister arts have soared so high, and will soon lead us to expect a certain level of perfection.[2]

In attributing Martines's successful application to the *Filarmonici* to the vision and active patronage of Empress Maria Theresa, in linking it to the progress of the "German nation" in the arts overall, and in promoting Martines's accomplishment as the pride of the "fair sex" in Vienna, the *Diarium* held up Martines's accomplishments as an example of the potential of Viennese women in the arts. With the empress's support, other women could not fail to thrive; within an active and innovative musical environment, music must flourish. Indeed, Martines enjoyed a connection with Maria Theresa's court, performing for the empress and her daughters—a connection facilitated by her family's close relationship with the imperial court poet, Pietro Metastasio. Maria Theresa and her daughters often turned to women to create artistic representations of womanhood, as art historian Heidi A. Strobel has argued: "These relationships were fruitful because these queens felt, perhaps, an affinity for the female artists in their employ, for they were

2. "Die musikalische Akademie de' Filarmonici zu Bologna hat vor kurzer Zeit, die Mademoiselle Marianna Martines seine gebohrne Wienerinn, obgleich von Spanischer Herkunft, in ihrer berühmten Gesellschaft aufgenommen. Das authentische Diploma, so in den ehrenvollesten Ausdrücken abgefasset worden, ist derselben bereits anhero übersandt. In der That hat die Akademie durch diese freywillige Aufnahme denen besondern und seltenen Verdiensten der Mademoiselle Martines nur Gerechtigkeit wiederfahren lassen. Wie denn sämmtliche Mitglieder in denen Compositionen der neuen Kandidatinn den Zusammenfluß von Zierlichkeit, Genie, Adel des Ausdrucks und einer erstaunenswürdigen Präcision nicht genug bewundern können. Ein so eingestimmiges Urtheil verursachte auch, daß es sich die Akademie zum Vorwurfe machte, sich nicht schon lange der Ehre theilhaftig gemacht zu haben, ein so wirdiges Mitglied, in ihrer ruhmwürdigst bekannten Gesellschaft aufgenommen zu haben. Wie sehr muß es dem Patrioten freuen, wenn er täglich mehr und mehr wahrnimmt, wie sich die deutsche Nation in allen Künsten mit so gutem Fortgange hervorzuthun bemühet! Zu welcher vorzüglichen und besondern Ehre gereichet es aber auch dem schönen Geschlechte allhier, wieder ein Mitglied aufweisen zu können, um dessentwillen ihnen so manche Stadt zu beneiden Ursache hat. Dank sey es der glorwürdigen Regierung unserer verehrungswürdigen Monarchinn, unter der sich alle verschwisterten Künste so hoch empor geschwungen, und bald einen gewissen Grad der Vollkommenheit erwarten lassen." *Wienerisches Diarium*, August 4, 1773, translated in Godt, *Marianna Martines*, 140–41.

also women participating in a predominantly masculine field during a time when traditional definitions of gender were changing."[3]

Yet Martines's own account of how she rose to such heights was quite different. In a short autobiographical sketch sent to Padre Giovanni Battista Martini, the legendary historian and composer who presided over the *Filarmonici*, Martines attributed her success to her diligent study and practice of composition and performance. In her own telling, Martines built upon her natural inclination toward music through effort and artifice. In this respect, the case of Martines contrasts with that of Madame Brillon, discussed in chapter 3: whereas Brillon sought to project an aura of unstudied, "natural" musicianship, distancing herself (even if only rhetorically) from any exertion of effort in music, Martines cultivated an image as someone who combined "natural" musicianship with extensive study. This point is all the more remarkable in light of the fact that Martines was not born into the aristocracy. She and her family sought to, and succeeded in, advancing their social position over the course of her life, and she therefore had more to lose by admitting to the sort of "labor" associated with the professional classes. Yet neither Martines's acknowledgment of her diligent study and effort nor her work and reputation as a composer undermined her family's attempts to raise its social position.

How can we account for Martines's social success, when so many women of her age were derided for their forays into authorship and their search for recognition of their talents in the public sphere? This chapter will address these questions by considering the case of Marianna Martines from several perspectives. First, as Karen Painter has shown, the status of the amateur in late eighteenth-century Vienna was not incompatible with the cultivation of skill through diligent study.[4] In Vienna, the combination of work and pleasure within the figure of the "dilettante" was an accepted paradigm, and in this respect, the environment in Vienna diverged from that in Paris, as seen in the case of Madame Brillon. Even then, however, Martines clearly exceeded the accomplishments and recognition of most women. This point is clear not only from her remarkable compositional output, but also from cases of other musical women in her orbit who were maligned for seeking public acknowledgment through composition. While Martines was appar-

3. Heidi A. Strobel, "Royal 'Matronage' of Women Artists in the Late-18th Century," *Woman's Art Journal* 26, no. 2 (Autumn 2005–Winter 2006): 7.

4. Karen Painter, "Mozart at Work: Biography and a Musical Aesthetic for the Emerging German Bourgeoisie," *Musical Quarterly* 86, no. 1 (Spring 2002): 186–235.

ently the object of some gossip, this did not prevent her fortunes from rising over the course of her life, as it did in the case of some other musical women. Among these was Maria Rosa Coccia, a Roman composer and the second woman to be inducted into the Accademia filarmonica; Martines was apparently involved in defending Coccia from the attacks that she endured.

I argue that Martines was able to experience social success, despite her potentially risky status as a composer, in large measure because of her musical salon. Throughout her adult life, she hosted musical salons at which she performed her own compositions and works by other composers; the salon represented her primary venue for performance. Such private musical events occurred with increasing frequency in Vienna in the second half of the eighteenth century, and Martines came to be numbered among the most widely admired salon hostesses in the city.[5] Her relationship with Metastasio meant that she had access to a vast network of friends and contacts in the professional musical world as well as the aristocracy. Attendance at one of her *Akademien* in the 1760s and 1770s doubtless promised conversation with Martines and Metastasio as well as musical performances ranging from solo keyboard playing and solo singing to concertos, arias, cantatas, and even choral works with a substantial instrumental accompaniment. Following Metastasio's death in 1782, Martines moved to a larger home, where she hosted musical salons on Saturday evenings that continued to attract notable figures from Vienna and abroad, including Mozart, Michael Kelly, and Hester Thrale Piozzi. For Martines, the musical salon served as a creative venue and a site of artistic collaboration, while simultaneously protecting her from accusations of immodesty.

"Composta della Signora Maria Anna Martines, Dilettante a Vienna"

Anna Catherina Martines, later Marianna Martines, was born in Vienna on May 4, 1744. Her Spanish grandfather had moved to Naples, where her father, Nicolo Martines, was born; Nicolo left Naples for Vienna, where

5. An overview of musical salons and other private concerts in Vienna during Martines's lifetime is in Morrow, *Concert Life in Haydn's Vienna*, 1–34. See also Link, "Vienna's Private Theatrical and Musical Life, 1783–92"; Melton, "School, Stage, Salon," 274–78; and Ingrid Fuchs, "'. . . spielt das Fortepiano mit vieler Empfindung und Präzision': Damen im musikalischen Salon rund um Joseph Haydn," in *Phänomen Haydn 1732–1809: prachtliebend, bürgerlich, gottbefohlen, crossover*, ed. Theresia Gabriel (Eisenstadt: Schloss Esterházy, 2009), 144–53.

he worked as *maestro di camera* for the papal nuncio. It is unclear whether Nicolo met Pietro (Trapassi) Metastasio in Naples or in Vienna, but Metastasio and the Martines family resided together from 1734/1735 until the poet's death in 1782, together with Nicolo's wife, Maria Theresia, and children. In the same building—the Altes Michaelerhaus at Kohlmarkt 11—lived Nicola Porpora, who may have taught Marianna singing, and a young Franz Joseph Haydn, whom she would cite as her keyboard teacher.[6]

As Irving Godt notes, the nature of the relationship between Metastasio and the Martines family will probably never be understood clearly. After Nicolo Martines died in 1764, Metastasio "assumed the role of a second father to the Martines children, who held him in the highest regard as long as he lived and honored his memory after his death."[7] The Martines family's connection to Metastasio opened doors; it may have been he who helped Marianna's brother Joseph to secure a position as a librarian at the imperial court, and later as *Hofrath* (court councilor). These connections to the court raised the Martines family's fortunes: although they were not of aristocratic lineage, Marianna's brothers were granted knighthood in a process that started in 1774; this entitled Marianna to sign her name "von Martines."[8] Marianna herself benefited from Metastasio's mentorship and professional connections as well as his creative instruction and collaboration—a subject that I will explore below.

Relatively few documents penned by Marianna Martines survive, but the ones that do offer an opportunity to meet her on her own terms and understand her priorities from a first-person perspective. Among these is an autobiographical letter that she wrote to Padre Martini in December 1773, following her induction into the *Filarmonici*. In describing her life in music up to that point, Martines emphasized both her pedagogical lineage and her own hard work. While she admits to having a "natural" talent for music, she attributes her success to her extensive study with noted practitioners and her own efforts to surpass nature:

> I was born in the year 1744 on the 4th day of May. In my seventh year they began to introduce me to the study of music, for which they believed me

6. See A. Peter Brown, "Marianna Martines' Autobiography as a New Source for Haydn's Biography During the 1750's," *Haydn-Studien* 6, no. 1 (1986): 68–72.

7. Godt, *Marianna Martines*, 14. Biographical information is summarized from Godt, *Marianna Martines*, 1–21.

8. Godt, *Marianna Martines*, 141–42.

inclined by nature. Its rudiments were taught me by Signor Giuseppe Haydn, currently Maestro di Cappella to Prince Esterházy, and a man of much reputation in Vienna, particularly with regard to instrumental music. In counterpoint, to which they assigned me quite early, I have had no other master than Signor Giuseppe Bonno, a most elegant composer of the imperial court, who, sent by Emperor Charles VI to Naples, stayed there many years and acquired excellence in music under the celebrated masters Durante and Leo. My exercise has been, and still is, to combine the continual daily practice of composing with study and scrutiny of that which has been written by the most celebrated masters such as Hasse, Jommelli, Galluppi and the others who are famous today and who are praised for their musical labors—and without neglecting the older [masters] such as Handel, Lotti, Caldara, and others. Persuaded, then, that, in order to prevail in music, I would need still other fields of knowledge; thus, aside from my natural languages, German and Italian, I undertook to familiarize myself with French and English, in order to be able to read the great poets and prose writers that have distinguished themselves in these: and I have never left off continually exercising myself in both speaking and translating from one idiom to the other various noteworthy written works, such as the *Galateo* of Monsignor della Casa, which I have translated from Italian into French.

But in all my studies, the chief planner and director was always, and still is, Signor Abbate Metastasio who, with the paternal care he takes of me and of all my numerous family, renders an exemplary return for the incorruptible friendship and tireless support which my good father lent him up until the very last days of his life.[9]

9. "Io nacqui nell'anno 1744 nel dì 4 di Maggio. Nel settimo dell'età mia incominciarono ad introdurmi nello studio della musica alla quale mi crederono per natura inclinata. I principj di questa mi furono insinuati dal Sig.[r] Giuseppe Haiden presentemente Maestro di Cappella del Sig.[r] P[rinci]pe Estherazi, e uomo di molto credito in Vienna particolarmente riguardo alla musica instrumentale. Nel contrapunto, al quale mi applicarono molto di buon ora non ò mai avuto altro Maestro che il Sig.[r] Giuseppe Bonno, Compositore elegantissimo della Corte Imperiale, che mandato dall'Imperador Carlo VI. a Napoli vi rimase molti anni et apprese ad eccellenza la musica sotto i celebri Maestri Durante, e Leo. I miei esercizi sono stati, e tuttavia sono l'accompagnar la continua diurna prattica dello scrivere allo studio, et esame di ciò che anno scritto i più celebrati Maestri, come l'Hasse, il Jommella, il Galluppi, e gli altri de' quali sono al presente illustri, et commendati i lavori armonici: e senza trascurare i più antichi come l'Hendel, il Lotti, il Caldara, et altri. Persuasa poi che per potersi prevalere della musica bisognano ancora altre cognizioni; oltre

In this letter, then, Martines framed her musical life as one characterized by diligent study under reputable teachers, and by the exertion of effort to build upon her natural inclinations in pursuit of higher abilities. At the beginning of this passage, she describes her studies as having been prompted by the recognition by those around her that she was "inclined" to music "by nature." Later, she herself became convinced that she would need to acquire skills in multiple languages in order to succeed in music, and she therefore undertook the study of languages other than her two native tongues—her "naturali lingue." Describing her long list of teachers and influences, her study of the works of composers from previous generations, and her daily routine of practice and learning, Martines presents herself as a diligent, serious practitioner of the art of composition.[10]

This manner of self-presentation provides a fascinating contrast to the choices made by Madame Brillon, as described in chapter 3. Notwithstanding Burney's observations that Brillon had studied the properties of each instrument in order to compose for them idiomatically and "naturally," her surviving letters indicate that she presented herself to her friends as taking a deliberately unstudied approach to composition; she framed her compositions as the products of an amateur seeking little more than momentary enjoyment in private circles. Martines's autobiographical sketch, by contrast, portrays her work as a composer as a product of effort and craft.

At first blush, it seems possible that this manner of self-presentation might conflict with Martines's wish to be understood as an amateur—one

---

le mie naturali lingue tedesca, et italiana; ò procurato di rendermi familiari la francese e l'inglese, per poter leggere i buoni poeti e prosatori che si distinguono in esse: e non tralascio di continuamente esercitarmi e parlando, e traducendo dall'uno nell'altro idioma qualche scritto riguardevole, come il Galateo di Monsignor della Casa da me in francese, dall'italiano ultimamente trasportato. Ma di tutti questi miei studj, è stato sempre, et è tuttavia il principale ordinatore, e direttore il Sig[r] Abate Metastasio, il quale con la paterna cura che prende e di me, e di tutta la mia numerosa famiglia, rende un'esemplare contraccambio all'incorrotta amicizia, et alla indefessa assistenza che gli à prestata il mio buon Padre fino agli ultimi de' giorni suoi." Marianna Martines to Giovanni Battista Martini, December 16, 1773. Transcribed and partially translated in Godt, *Marianna Martines*, partial translation on 22, original text on 218.

10. This formulation echoes her initial letter of gratitude to the *Filarmonici*, in which she promised to "exert" herself in the study of music; see Godt, *Marianna Martines*, 140. On Martines's involvement with composers of preceding generations, among her other activities, see Ingeborg Harer, "Alte Musik in Wien um 1800: Neue Erkenntnisse zu Marianne Martines (1744–1812)—Ein Beitrag zur Erinnerung an den 200. Todestag der Musikerin, Sängerin und Komponistin," *Musicologica Austriaca* 30 (2011): 27–42.

who did not engage in music for money, but for pleasure, and whose social position therefore remained respectable. The salon provided Martines with a socially sanctioned venue for engagement with public musical figures such as Burney, Farinelli, Hasse, and many others. Using the salon as her primary platform, she was able to perform her own compositions, read and comment on the music of other composers, and engage in conversation about musical and aesthetic issues.

The schedule of Martines's musical *Akademien* in the 1760s and 1770s is not known for certain, and her gatherings during these years ranged from private audiences and readings of musical compositions to musical events on a larger scale. It was during these decades that Viennese women and men began to host regular musical salons.[11] While salons based on the French model apparently began later in Vienna than they did elsewhere in Europe, the line between the salon and other forms of private music-making is a blurry one. As a result, the precise moment at which Martines's private concerts became "salons" *per se* cannot be easily identified. However, eyewitness accounts indicate that Martines's gatherings during these early decades included the conversation and sociability, as well as the mixing of professional and amateur musicians, that were the hallmarks of musical salons across Europe. By the 1780s, Martines's activities were more firmly documented, allowing confirmation that she held a musical salon as a regular event each Saturday evening.

On the few occasions when Martines did attempt entry into the public sphere, she and her mentor, Metastasio, worked to curate her image carefully. This was necessary especially because she was not just a performer, but also a composer. In 1762 and 1765, Martines had two keyboard sonatas published—itself a remarkable circumstance for a non-professional woman composer. As I discussed in chapter 1, publication represented a step into the public sphere that was fraught with problems for women. This was certainly true in Martines's cultural milieu, as I will show through comparison with another noteworthy case in her orbit. Indeed, the very fact that Martines published only two compositions out of her large compositional *oeuvre*—and these early on in her adult life—suggests that she made a conscious decision subsequently to avoid this mode of public exposure.[12]

11. See the discussion in Morrow, *Concert Life in Haydn's Vienna*, 13–17; and Melton, "School, Stage, Salon," 274–75.

12. The total number of Martines's compositions is unknown, but Godt records "four masses, two litanies, a *Regina caeli* for double chorus, two Latin psalms (one accompanied

Aspects of the volumes in which her sonatas appeared may start to explain why she chose to publish, and how she sought to craft her public image. The sonatas were published in anthologies put out by the Nürnberg printer Giovanni Ulrico (Johann Ulrich) Haffner in a series titled *Raccolta musicale contenente VI. sonate per il cembalo solo d'altretanti celebri compositori italiani messi nell'ordine alfabetico co' loro nomi e titoli* ("musical anthology containing six sonatas [per volume] for solo keyboard by various celebrated Italian composers, placed in alphabetical order with their names and titles"). In fact, not all the composers were Italian; among them, for example, was "Signor Francesco Krafft, Maestro di Capella e Compositore di Musica in Brusselles." It was evidently the style of the keyboard pieces contained in the anthology—the brilliant yet technically accessible idiom associated with the Neapolitan galant school—that qualified these works and their composers as "Italian"; the names and titles were rendered in Italian to match. The professional titles of the composers must have been important to Haffner and purchasers of his publications, perhaps since those titles lent credibility to the volumes' contents. In this context, it is significant that Martines is the only composer in these volumes who did not hold a professional post. Haffner identifies her as "Signora Maria Anna Martines, Dilettante a Vienna."

How these two sonatas by Martines came to be included in Haffner's collections is not entirely clear. Haffner advertised in 1759 that he was accepting submissions of sonatas for his collections (and that he would give six free exemplars to each composer whose work was published), but this might not have been an obvious route for Martines to take if she had not had a network of connections to professional Italian composers.[13] Indeed, the

by basso continuo only, one accompanied by full orchestra), four Italian psalms for soloists, chorus, and orchestra, two Italian oratorios, seven solo motets, twenty-seven Italian arias, seven Italian cantatas, four keyboard concertos, one independent overture, and three keyboard sonatas." Yet this impressive quantity of works is dwarfed by the number that was reported by Martines's relative Anton Schmid, who worked in the Viennese court library, writing in the mid-nineteenth century. According to Schmid, she wrote "'156 arias and cantatas, 31 piano sonatas, and twelve keyboard concertos'; and his enumeration seems too precise to be a gross fabrication or a wild guess." See Anton Schmid, "Zwei musikalische Berühmtheiten Wien's aus dem schönen Geschlechte in der zweiten Hälfte des verflossenen Jahrhunderts," part 2, *Wiener allgemeine Musik-Zeitung* 6 (1846): 513–14 and 517–18, cited in Godt, *Marianna Martines*, 5–6.

13. Lothar Hoffmann-Erbrecht, "Der Nürnberger Musikverleger Johann Ulrich Haffner," *Acta musicologica* 26, no. 3–4 (August–December 1954): 126.

publication of her music in an anthology that aligns itself overtly with the Italian school of keyboard composition may have formed part of a larger strategy. As seen in her letter to Padre Martini, she identified herself with that Italian network—the Neapolitan tradition, as exemplified by Giuseppe Bonno, a native of Vienna who worked in Naples, and by Hasse and Jommelli, both of whom had studied in the Neapolitan conservatories.[14] A work by Padre Martini himself appeared in the 1765 volume of Haffner's *Raccolta* series, opening the possibility that he had served as a link between Haffner and Martines. Padre Martini had been aware of Martines and her compositions at least since 1761, when he corresponded with Metastasio about the poet's young protégée. Metastasio had apparently sent Padre Martini copies of some of Martines's compositions—two fugues that she would later incorporate into her Mass in C and the Italian cantata *L'inverno*, which I will discuss below.[15]

The term "dilettante" was one that Martines would apply to herself again later in the 1760s. A substantial two-volume manuscript of her Italian arias, dated 1767 and now held in the library of the Conservatorio di musica San Pietro a Majella in Naples, bears the title *Scelta d'arie composte per suo diletto*—"Choice Arias Composed for Her Own Delight."[16] While Godt suggests that the title gives "prominent expression to her sense of independence"—that is, her independent spirit—it seems equally likely that this title represented Martines's insistence that she be understood as an amateur who composed only for her own "delight," and not someone whose social situation required her to earn a living through music. This, indeed, was the distinction that Haffner's anthology made in its dedication: "Ai respettivi signori compositori virtuosi ed amatori della musica dedica questa raccolta raccommandandosi alla di loro benevolenza" (To the respected gentlemen, virtuous composers and lovers of music, is this anthology dedicated, recommending itself to their benevolence). Here, "virtuous composers" appears in contrast to "amatori della musica," with the former indicating members of the professional class and the latter referring to those who engage in music for pleasure and not for money. By noting Martines's social position at the start of her two sonatas, Haffner's anthology identifies Martines with the *amatori* rather than the professionals whose works surrounded hers.

In this sense, these Italian-language categories—*professori*, *composi-*

14. Godt, *Marianna Martines*, 22–23.

15. Godt, *Marianna Martines*, 135.

16. This two-volume manuscript is in I-Nc, Arie 417 A–B.

tori, *amatori*, and *dilettanti*—intersect in complex ways with the German-language categories of *Musikant*, *Kenner*, and *Liebhaber*. *Musikant* most often referred to professional musicians; *Kenner* and *Liebhaber* did not always distinguish social situation or profession, but rather referred to modes of musical engagement, understanding, and listening.[17] The term *dilettante*, by contrast, referred to social situation. And yet, some German writers equated *Liebhaber* and *Dilettanten* in a straightforward way. For example, an 1808 description of music in Vienna claimed, "Nowhere will one find this divine art [of music] pursued so extensively and practiced as enthusiastically as here; nowhere can one find *Liebhabern (Dilettanten)* as accomplished on almost all instruments, some of whom should be professors of music on the side, indeed some are even better than professors."[18]

If anyone could blur these lines, it was Martines. Such a judgment appears in Giambattista Mancini's *Riflessioni pratiche sul canto figurato* of 1777, where he wrote that Martines, "although a dilettante, can justifiably be called a great master and a rare genius in music."[19] For Mancini, the word "dilettante" does not normally align with "master" and "rare genius," but he saw Martines as someone who traversed these lines. Martines inspired a similar conflation of categories in Johann Ferdinand von Schönfeld's *Jahrbuch der Tonkunst von Wien und Prag* of 1796: "Martines, Miss Nanette [i.e. Marianna], is one of the most exquisite *Kennerinnen* among our many *Dilettantinnen*."[20]

In presenting herself as a *dilettante*, then, Martines was tapping into an array of musical meanings and social connotations that differ in marked

17. A recent work on the complex topic of *Kenner* and *Liebhaber* is Matthew Riley, *Musical Listening in the German Enlightenment*, ch. 4, "Forkel on Expert and Amateur Listening Practices."

18. "nirgends wird diese göttliche Kunst so ausgebreitet betrieben, so sehr geliebt, und so eifrig ausgeübt, wie hier; nirgends wird man unter den Liebhabern (Dilettanten) auf fast allen Instrumenten so viele vollendete Ausübende finden, deren manche sich den Professoren dieser Kunst an die Seite setzen dürfen, ja wohl einige sie sogar noch übertreffen." S.n., "Uebersicht des gegenwärtigen Zustandes der Tonkunst in Wien," *Vaterländische Blätter für den österreichischen Kaiserstaat* 6 (May 27, 1808): 39. Translated in Painter, "Mozart At Work," 196.

19. "sebbene dilettante, può a giusto titolo chiamarli gran maestra, e raro genio della musica." Giambattista Mancini, *Riflessioni pratiche sul canto figurato*, 3rd ed. (Milan: Giuseppe Galeazzi, 1777), 230.

20. "Martines, Fräulein Nanette [i.e. Marianna] von, ist eine der vorzüglichsten Kennerinnen unter unsern zahlreichen Dilettantinnen." Johann Ferdinand von Schönfeld, *Jahrbuch der Tonkunst von Wien und Prag* (s.l.: im von Schönfeldischen Verlag, 1796), 41.

ways from those of Madame Brillon. Whereas Brillon sought to distance herself from hard work and study, in Martines's world, the status of *dilettante* did not necessitate choosing between music-as-pleasure and the serious engagement and study that could lead to expertise. Instead, as Karen Painter has shown, the notion of amateurism in late eighteenth-century Vienna could encompass work as well as pleasure. Discussing the reception of Mozart in early biographies, Painter shows how he came to be understood as an embodiment of the fusion of "the older aristocratic world of pleasure and grace" and the emerging "bourgeois milieu that cherished virtuous labor and production."[21] If the ethos of "work" is generally associated with Protestant northern Germany, Painter shows how that concept merged with "an expressivity and a pursuit of pleasure favorable to artistic creation" in the Catholic Hapsburg empire.[22] Thus, in the earliest biographies, Mozart appears as a figure who is both divinely inspired and intellectually effortful.

Although Painter's study centers primarily on Mozart's reception in the years after his death, a similar combination of pleasure and work can be discerned in earlier sources, too. Years before Martines wrote her autobiographical letter to Padre Martini, Metastasio had corresponded with Martini about her compositions. Metastasio thanked Padre Martini for his praise of Martines's works, writing, "The young composer, in sending you some attempts of her studies, aspired only to advice and correction, but you have chosen to honor her with approval and with praise." In particular, Metastasio took pride in Padre Martini's comments that affirmed Martines's skill in "combin[ing], in an uncommon fashion, the rigor of profound knowledge [*rigida profondità della scienza*] with *humanità* and with *grazia*."[23] Metastasio's juxtaposition of "profound knowledge" with "humanity" and "grace" in his description of Martines's music serves to reinforce her image as possessing a natural talent and the capacity for natural expression even as it emphasizes her self-discipline in the study of music.

21. Painter, "Mozart at Work," 192.

22. Painter, "Mozart at Work," 194.

23. "La giovane compositrice non ambiva, inviandole qualche saggio degli studj suoi, che avvertimenti, e correzioni: ed ella ha voluto onorarla di approvazioni, e di lodi"; "accoppiare, con facoltà poco comune, la rigida profondità della scienza all'umanità, ed alla grazia." Metastasio to Martini, March 9, 1761, in Pietro Metastasio, *Lettere del signor Abate Pietro Metastasio* (Nizza: Presso la Società Tipografica, 1786), 3:135. Translated in Godt, *Marianna Martines*, 135.

Acceptance of the need for work in combination with pleasure even opened up the art of composition, normally associated with the craft of professional musicians, to *Dilettanten*. Johann Friedrich Daube, a north German residing and working in Vienna, explicitly addressed his compositional treatise to amateurs in naming it the *Musikalische Dilettante* (1773). Daube promised to provide knowledge that was "valuable and enjoyable, that the growth of music may be furthered thereby, and that a most agreeable relief from daily work may be provided by the purest pleasure in music."[24] While he wrote that he would "make every effort to present this knowledge in the clearest and easiest way for amateurs [*Liebhabern*]," he cautioned that such amateurs would get the most out of his volume if they "have read our treatise on thorough-bass and understand the succession of chords, together with the relationship of keys."[25] Ultimately, Daube apologized for any failures in his volume, recommending a little work as the appropriate remedy: "Even though we might not have described everything clearly, a little reflection and practice . . . will still compensate for that deficiency."[26] The "purest pleasure," in other words, still involved diligence and effort.

It is in this sense that Martines's epithet "dilettante," attached to her name in Haffner's sonata anthology, should be understood. The title of her *Scelta d'arie composte per suo diletto* may also comprise a statement about how the ideal singer would use the volume. The surviving manuscript copy of this collection was apparently compiled as a parting gift to Maria Theresa's daughter, Maria Carolina, who married King Ferdinand III of Naples

24. "Daß alles hier Vorgetragene zum Nutzen und Vergnügen gereichen: daß dadurch der Wachsthum der Musik befördert werden, und die allerangenehmste Abwechslung mit der Arbeit, durch das unschuldigste Vergnügen an der Musik, geschehen möge." Johann Friedrich Daube, *Der musikalische Dilettant: eine Abhandlung der Komposition* (Vienna: Johann Thomas Edlen von Trattnern, 1773), 333. Translated in Johann Friedrich Daube, *The Musical Dilettante: A Treatise on Composition by J. F. Daube*, trans. and ed. Susan Snook-Luther (Cambridge: Cambridge University Press, 1992), 267.

25. "alle Mühe anwenden, diese Wissenschaft den Liebhabern aufs deutlichste und leichteste vorzutragen"; "unsre Abhandlung vom Generalbasse gelesen, und die Folge der Akkorde, nebst der Anverwandschaft der Tonarten inne haben." Daube, *Der musikalische Dilettant*, [2]. Translated in Daube, *The Musical Dilettante*, 35.

26. "Sollten wir auch nicht alles deutlich beschrieben haben; so wird ein geringes Nachdenken, und eine Uebung dasjenige Abgehende noch ersetzen." Daube, *Der musikalische Dilettant*, 333. Translated in Daube, *The Musical Dilettante*, 267.

in 1768. The manuscript's contents had been composed by a *dilettante*, requiring both natural ability and skill. In giving the manuscript to the new Queen of Naples—the city to which Martines traced her family as well as her musical lineage—Martines suggested that its use required the same combination of natural talent and diligent study.

Notwithstanding Daube's affirmation that even *Dilettanten* could now participate in the craft of musical composition, the question of Martines's gender still threatened to undermine her respectability. Her exceptional status as a woman composer is underscored by the dedication of Haffner's anthology to "signori compositori virtuosi ed amatori della musica": in using the term "signori," he seemed to place Martines, the only woman whose works appeared in the anthology, in brackets.

Playing through Martines's sonata allowed any purchaser of Haffner's anthology—man or woman—to occupy the composer's bodily movements and even her emotions. As L. Poundie Burstein explains, Martines's use of galant schemata as the basis of her compositions meant that she was drawing on a gestural vocabulary that was "embedded in [her] ears, vocal cords, and fingers."[27] In this sense, Martines's presence in the volume disrupts the fiction of the ideal male reader—one of the "signori compositori virtuosi ed amatori della musica." She stands out as the only female *amatore della musica* represented in the anthology; her act of publication might be interpreted as an invitation to the reader to enter her drawing room and even inhabit her bodily motions at the keyboard.

If this suggestion sounds uncomfortable, it serves to underscore some of the tensions around women composers in the public sphere. The risks of assuming a fully public persona as a composer would have been clear to Martines, and they are exemplified in an episode in which Martines was apparently involved. In 1774, the young Roman composer Maria Rosa Coccia (fig. 4.2) became the first woman to pass the qualifying examination of the Accademia di Santa Cecilia to earn the title of *maestra di cappella* in Rome, thereby earning the right to work in churches in that city.[28] The examination

27. L. Poundie Burstein, "'Zierlichkeit und Genie': Grace and Genius in Marianna Martines's Sonata in A Major," in *Analytical Essays on Music by Women Composers: Secular & Sacred Music to 1900*, ed. Laurel Parsons and Brenda Ravenscroft (Oxford: Oxford University Press, 2018), 131.

28. See Marie Caruso, "Ten Fugues Shed Light on an Old Debate," *Il saggiatore musicale: Rivista semestrale di musicologia* 21, no. 1 (2014): 6. A life-and-works study of Coccia is in Candida Felici, *Maria Rosa Coccia: maestra compositore romana* (Rome: Colombo Duemila, 2004).

Figure 4.2 Giovanni Domenico Porta (?), *Portrait of Maria Rosa Coccia* (ca. 1800). Museo Civico Bibliografico Musicale, Bologna, Italy. The open volume bears an inscription that reads "Componimenti mus[icali] / di / Maria Rosa Coccia / Maestra di capella romana / e Accademia filarmonica / di / Bologna." Luisa Ricciarini / Bridgeman Images. The attribution to Porta is in Candida Felici, *Maria Rosa Coccia: maestra compositore romana* (s.l.: Colombo Duemila, 2004), 57.

required her to compose a fugue extemporaneously before a panel of judges. In preparation, Coccia's father had arranged for her to study counterpoint under Sante Pesci, *maestro di cappella* of the Basilica Liberiana. As Marie Caruso argues, it was "to satisfy a contemporary readership fascinated with the manifestation of female knowledge" that the fugue that Coccia had composed for her examination was published.[29] The published pamphlet, titled *Esperimento estemporaneo fatto dalla Signora Maria Rosa Coccia romana*, opens with a single page of four-voice counterpoint—Coccia's fugue on the antiphon "Hic vir despiciens mundum"—concluding with a declaration of approval by the four examiners, one of whom was her teacher, Pesci. The remainder of the slim pamphlet contains epigrams and poems written in praise of Coccia. Among these is a poem, written in English to "Miss Mary Rose Coccia," reflecting on the contest between nature and art that had resulted in Coccia's success; as in the case of Martines, mastery of counterpoint signaled the intellectual effort required to build upon a natural inclination for music. "Nature her utmost efforts us'd to shew, / How far her skill, how far her strenth [*sic*] could goe. / Art did the same: they with each other vie: / Each nice, each boldest stroke by turns they try." With the conflict unresolvable, nature and art content themselves with raising "A monument, which should to future days / Record their league immortal."[30]

Coccia's success was short-lived, however, as Caruso explains. Rumors soon began to circulate that Coccia had only succeeded in passing the examination at Santa Cecilia because she was a woman. These rumors were most likely spread by Francesco Capalti, who finally published his objections in 1781, pointing to what he considered damning evidence of Coccia's faulty counterpoint. In fact, Caruso argues that Coccia's published fugue as well as ten others that were held back from publication followed new trends in counterpoint that Capalti simply did not accept. Capalti himself was still smarting from having failed the examination at Santa Cecilia, and it is possible that he sought to undermine Coccia out of professional jealousy. After Coccia was admitted to the Accademia filarmonica of Bologna in 1779, Capalti wrote to Padre Martini to complain about improprieties in modern counterpoint; he included a copy of Coccia's published fugue in support of his argument.[31] Coccia's reputation never recovered from these public

29. Caruso, "Ten Fugues," 8. The fugue was published in Maria Rosa Coccia et al., *Esperimento estemporaneo fatto dalla Signora Maria Rosa Coccia romana nell'esame da essa sostenuto avanti i quattro sig. maestri di cappella esaminatori della congregazione de' signori musici di Santa Cecilia di Roma . . . coll'aggiunta di vari poeticii componmenti, che in quell'occasione furono al di lei merito dedicati* (Rome: nella stamperia di San Michele a Ripa, presso Paolo Giunchi, 1775).

30. Coccia et al., *Esperimento estemporaneo*, 10.

31. See Caruso, "Ten Fugues," 26–28; and Elisabetta Pasquini, *L'esemplare, o sia saggio fondamentale pratico di contrappunto: Padre Martini teorico e didatta della musica* (Florence: Olschki, 2004), 105.

humiliations. Despite having qualified to become a professional *maestra di cappella*, she never attained a professional position in church or court. As Caruso concludes, despite being an "'exceptional' female, an ideal figure for a print culture that was hungry for news of spectacular women," this exceptional status "did not benefit Coccia in advancing her career."[32]

Even before Capalti had published his attack on Coccia's counterpoint, accusing her of benefiting from special treatment because she was a woman, another volume running to some 96 pages appeared in print in praise and defense of Coccia. The *Elogio storico della signora Maria Rosa Coccia romana* contains a biographical account of Coccia, laudatory poems (some reproduced from the *Esperimento estemporaneo*), and letters written in her support. The preface from the printer addresses all "dilettanti e professori della musica," assuring them that his volume would be well received by all "lovers of virtue and truth."[33] The authors of the letters published in the *Elogio storico* in support of Coccia included some of the musical luminaries of the age, including Padre Martini and Farinelli, as well as several by Metastasio. In the first of these, Metastasio thanks Coccia for having sent her "three excellent pieces of her musical composition, which I saw, and respected." Admitting, though, that he had been "unable to judge of their worth,"[34] Metastasio explained,

> I therefore instantly called a person extremely skillful in the art [of music], who, after carefully examining them in my presence, and with great pleasure, assured me, that they were written, not only in a correct, but masterly, manner. I rejoiced at this, and was flattered to find, that my dear country produced young ladies of such uncommon abilities.[35]

32. Caruso, "Ten Fugues," 29.

33. Michele Mallio et al., *Elogio storico della signora Maria Rosa Coccia romana* (Rome: Cannetti, 1780), 3.

34. "tre eccellenti di lei musicali componimenti, ch'io vidi, ma rispettai, non essendo abile a giudicarne," Metastasio to Maria Rosa Coccia, December 29, 1777, printed in Mallio et al., *Elogio storico*, 27; translation in Charles Burney, *Memoirs of the Life and Writings of the Abate Metastasio: In Which Are Incorporated, Translations of His Principal Letters* (London: G. G. and J. Robinson, 1796), 3:70.

35. "Chiamai per altro subito persona pratica, e peritissima, che dopo averli in presenza mia attentamente con sommo piacere esaminati, mi assicurò essere questi non solo correttamente, ma magistralmente scritti, me ne rallegrai, e mi compiacqui che la cara mia patria producesse donzelle di abilità così rara." Mallio et al., *Elogio storico*, 27; translation in Burney, *Memoirs of the Life and Writings of the Abate Metastasio*, 70.

Metastasio apologized, however, for being unable to secure for Coccia the patronage of the imperial court, confessing that "here music is, at present, in the last stage of decline," with "the princes of this court having, many years since, made a rule, never to receive a present, or dedication of any book, especially of poetry, or music; to save themselves from the indiscreet torrent of such homages as they were formerly inundated with."[36] With music at court thus deteriorating, Metastasio wrote, the ability "to know the merit of such a composition as yours . . . is possessed by very few people," and potential patrons "can only appreciate musical merit by the report of professors."[37]

Irving Godt has argued that "the person extremely skillful in the art [of music]" on whom Metastasio called to evaluate Coccia's compositions was Marianna Martines. Noting similarities in their compositional output and their admittance into musical academies, Godt writes that "Coccia seems to have modeled herself, to some extent, on Martines."[38] When Metastasio called on his anonymous expert to judge Coccia's work, Godt observes, "Metastasio carefully hid his expert's identity and (using the Italian word *persona*) sex." This suggestion is entirely plausible, especially given Metastasio's claim that he had "instantly" placed Coccia's work before his expert's eye; who better to turn to than the young musician with whom he shared an apartment? Writing a letter that he knew would become public, Metastasio shielded Martines from public involvement in this debate. Naming Martines openly would have undermined her carefully cultivated social standing even as it would have opened the door to public scrutiny and potential attack on her compositions.

It was likely more than just convenience that had led Metastasio to seek Martines's approval of Coccia's work. While Godt suggests that Martines had "some reason to think of the young Roman as a potential rival," there is, in fact, no basis to assume that Martines would have taken such a combative stance against other women composers. In fact, Metastasio's descrip-

36. "Quì presentemente è nell'ultima decadenza la musica"; "Le persone di questa augustissima corte già da molti anni si sono proposte la legge di non accettare offerte, o dediche di libro alcuno, e specialmente di poesìa e di musica, per salvarsi dall'indiscreto torrente di simili omaggi che le inondavano." Mallio et al., *Elogio storico*, 28; translation in Burney, *Memoirs of the Life and Writings of the Abate Metastasio*, 71.

37. "per conoscere il merito d'una compositrice sua pari . . . che la maggior parte non hanno"; "non possono apprezzarlo, che sulla relazione de' professori." Mallio et al., *Elogio storico*, 28; translation in Burney, *Memoirs of the Life and Writings of the Abate Metastasio*, 71.

38. Godt, *Marianna Martines*, 159.

tion of the event, read in the context of his statements about the decline of patronage at the imperial court, casts his anonymous expert in the role of a patron. If he had sought out the expert opinion of one of the Viennese "professori" described in his letter, he would have named that person openly. Hiding the identity of his expert implied that she was of a higher social standing, from which perch she was capable of bestowing approval on Coccia's compositions.

This episode, then, highlights the tensions surrounding women's forays into composition. For Coccia, born into a professional class and lacking familial connections in music, a public career in music—including published compositions, spectacle surrounding her accomplishments, and the pursuit of a position as a *maestra di cappella*—appeared to offer the most promise for success. For Martines, by contrast, public acclaim by an institution such as the Accademia filarmonica apparently required attenuation through anonymity in other respects. When Martines published, she presented compositions without pretense of serious learning—galant keyboard sonatas, rather than counterpoint—and when she performed, it was in the liminal space of her musical salon, situated between the public and private spheres, rather than in full view of the public eye.[39] Just as Metastasio offered Martines the cover of anonymity in her evaluation of Coccia's compositions, the salon placed Martines's performances behind a veil of upper-class respectability.

Martines, Metastasio, and the Strategy of Collaboration

To the limited extent that Marianna Martines has been discussed from a critical perspective in recent literature, her image has been filtered through the lens of the male observers who visited her, heard her performances, and encountered her compositions. Chief—and, characteristically, most effusive—among these was Burney, who visited her, together with Metastasio, numerous times during his stay in Vienna in 1772; indeed, he became so familiar with the household that he considered himself "amico della

39. In the nineteenth century, Martines's reputation underwent some damage at the hands of the novelist and musician Caroline Pichler, who criticized Martines's compositions and implied that she was Metastasio's mistress. Schmid defended his relative's reputation through her association with Empress Maria Theresa, which he saw as proof "of the moral purity of our artist, since the strictly moral empress never consorted with any females whose reputations were not absolutely irreproachable." See Godt, *Marianna Martines*, 3 and 34.

casa."[40] Here, as in the case of Burney's description of Madame Brillon, his words must be handled with care: as Matthew Head points out, Burney was so prone to hyperbole in describing female musicians that the effect was to render them as caricatures, lacking any individuality or agency.[41] Yet, as with Burney's description of Brillon, I would argue that there are aspects of his passages on Martines that reveal important features of her persona as represented both in her own words and in her musical compositions.

For Head, the central problem of Burney's description of Martines is its apparent erasure of her agency. Rather than understanding her as an individual, Head argues, Burney sees her as nothing more than an extension or avatar of Metastasio. This interpretation of Burney's report is supported by the generalizing way in which Burney bookends his encounter with Martines. Before meeting her, he writes, "I was extremely curious to know what kind of music would best fulfil the ideas of Metastasio, when applied to his own poetry; and imagined that this young lady, with all the advantages of his instructions, counsel, and approbation, combined with her own genius, must be an *alter idem*, and that her productions would include every musical embellishment which could be superadded to his poetry, without destroying or diminishing its native beauty."[42] And, in taking his final leave of Martines at the conclusion of his stay in Vienna, Burney identifies her with no less a figure than the patron saint of music, casting her as an embodiment of St. Cecilia: "I went to Metastasio, for the last time! I found with him much company, and the St. Cecilia, Martinetz, at the harpsichord, to which she had been singing."[43] In Head's interpretation, the Martines of Burney's account recedes into a "neoclassical ideal"—a mere caricature of a musician, or the object of an aesthetic experiment in the "neutral, aesthetic laboratory of Kohlmarkt 11."[44]

Notwithstanding Burney's tendency to generalize about the women whom he encountered, I think it is possible that he was picking up on aspects of Martines's deliberate strategies in cultivating a socially sanctioned musical persona. In particular, it seems possible that Martines viewed

40. Burney, *The Present State of Music in Germany, the Netherlands, and United Kingdom*, 1:314.

41. Head, *Sovereign Feminine*, 64–69.

42. Burney, *The Present State of Music in Germany, the Netherlands, and United Kingdom*, 1:250–51.

43. Burney, *The Present State of Music in Germany, the Netherlands, and United Kingdom*, 1:362.

44. Head, *Sovereign Feminine*, 68, 66.

music-making as a collaborative undertaking. Her relationship with Metastasio was certainly distinctive and perhaps odd, given his long residence in her family's apartment, but from a creative standpoint it was apparently not unique. Metastasio's mentorship of Martines suggests an intimate creative relationship, but the imperial poet enjoyed a similarly close working relationship with other musicians as well. For example, he developed such an intimate understanding with the castrato Farinelli, who sang Metastasio's librettos countless times, that each referred to the other as his *gemello*—his "twin."[45]

In this respect, it is important to note the context in which Burney's first discussion of Martines appears. Before meeting her, Burney was introduced into the home that she shared with Metastasio by the British ambassador to Vienna, Lord Stormont. Together, Burney and Lord Stormont interviewed Metastasio about his views on both poetry and music. While Burney attests that Metastasio was fully informed about complicated aspects of music theory and history, including topics from "the musical scales of the ancient Greeks" to the "noise" that characterized the music of the eighteenth century, he notes that Metastasio denied composing music for any of his own poetry, stating that "he was not musician sufficient":

> Metastasio said, that musical composition, was now an affair of so much skill and science, in regard to counterpoint, the knowledge of instruments, the powers of a singer, and other particulars, that to know it thoroughly, in all its parts, required much more time and application, than a modern poet, or man of letters, could spare from his own studies.
>
> He said, he did not think that there was now one singer left who could sustain the voice in the manner the old singers were used to do. I endeavoured to account for this, and he agreed with me, that theatrical music was become too instrumental; and that the cantatas of the beginning of this century, which were sung with no other accompaniment than a harpsichord or violoncello, required better singing than the present

45. See, for example, the correspondence between Metastasio and Farinelli published in Burney, *Memoirs of the Life and Writings of the Abate Metastasio*, 3:89 and passim. In a letter of April 1780, Metastasio praised Farinelli's keyboard sonatas, but wrote that he relied on Martines to play them for him: "I should esteem it a sacrilege to defile them with the inexperience of my own [hand]," since it was "deprived of the necessary practice." Burney, *Memoirs of the Life and Writings of the Abate Metastasio*, 3:245.

songs, in which the noisy accompaniments can hide defects as well as beauties, and give relief to a singer.[46]

In Burney's telling, Metastasio did not deny that he had an innate musical sense. Instead, he had made a conscious choice not to compose, and he attributed that choice to the state of music in his lifetime. Composition had become an "affair of so much skill and science," a field of intense specialization that required technical knowledge of counterpoint, instruments, and idiomatic vocal writing. This circumstance contrasts with the state of composition early in the eighteenth century, when the pure human voice could be supported by nothing more than basso continuo. Taken literally, Burney's statement that "theatrical music was become too instrumental" refers to the overuse of instruments in opera orchestras—a practice that obscured the singer's voice. On a more figurative level, this statement may be understood to allude to the technologization of opera as a whole. With its excess of instruments and its treatment of the voice itself as an instrument, opera had become diminished by the noise of the modern world.

Metastasio confessed that he "had, indeed, now and then given a composer the *motive*, or subject of an air, to show how he wished it should express his words,"[47] and Burney pressed the point: he came to his interview prepared to ask about a melody that he had heard the poet himself had composed: "He likes no one of the many thousand translations and imitations of his *Grazie agl'Inganni tuoi*. I asked him, if he was author of a duo to these words, which I had procured many years ago, and sung him the two or three first bars; and he said, 'something like it.'"[48] Decades later, in his biography of Metastasio, Burney printed this duet as he remembered it; by that point this text had been set countless times in numerous guises: "as a Venetian Ballad, a Canzonet, a Duo, and a Cantata, by so many great composers, to . . . elaborate and fanciful music." Burney offered Metastasio's own setting "to [his] musical readers, as a curiosity" (fig. 4.3). In comparison to the complex compositions of other composers, "Metastasio's

46. Burney, *The Present State of Music in Germany, the Netherlands, and United Kingdom*, 1:304–5.

47. Burney, *The Present State of Music in Germany, the Netherlands, and United Kingdom*, 1:304.

48. Burney, *The Present State of Music in Germany, the Netherlands, and United Kingdom*, 1:301–2.

Figure 4.3 Pietro Metastasio (text and music), "La libertà," printed in Charles Burney, *Memoirs of the Life and Writings of the Abate Metastasio. In which are Incorporated, Translations of his Principal Letters* (London: G. G. and J. Robinson, 1796), 1:128–29.

melody, which has been composed more than fifty years, has still its merit; and, compared with airs of the same period and kind, will be found superior to most of them in elegant simplicity."[49]

Why did Burney bring up this composition in 1772, and why was he still fixated on it more than twenty years later?[50] First, this case establishes

49. Burney, *Memoirs of the Life and Writings of the Abate Metastasio*, 1:127.

50. This composition became widely known as the work of Metastasio; it is mentioned in the first edition of Ernst Ludwig Gerber's *Historisch–Biographisches Lexicon der Tonkünstler*: "Von seinem berühmten Duett: Grazie agl'Inganni tuoi, läuft auch eine

that Metastasio had the capacity to write music if he chose to. Second, his description of Metastasio's setting is laced with nostalgia for a bygone time in which composition was a matter of "elegant simplicity." This nostalgia was an important feature of Metastasio's aesthetic views in the last decades of the eighteenth century.

It is in this context that Burney's encounters with Martines should be understood. Martines appears as an antidote to the ills of which Metastasio had complained only the day before. In Martines's voice, Burney hears echoes of past generations of singers—singers whom he had never heard himself. Likewise significant is the intertwining of Martines's singing, keyboard playing, and composition. If Metastasio complained that music had become too much a specialized art for him to maintain on his own, Martines showed how a musician could be well rounded, sensitive to poetry and counterpoint, "natural" expression, and technical artifice:

> Her performance indeed surpassed all that I had been made to expect. She sung two airs of her own composition, to words of Metastasio, which she accompanied on the harpsichord, in a very judicious and masterly manner; and, in playing the ritornels, I could discover a very brilliant finger.
>
> The airs were very well written, in a modern style; but neither common, nor unnaturally new. The words were well set, the melody was simple, and great room was left for expression and embellishment; but her voice and manner of singing, both delighted and astonished me! I can readily subscribe to what Metastasio says, that it is a style of singing which no longer subsists elsewhere, as it requires too much pains and patience for modern professors. I should suppose that Postocco, Bernacchi, and the old school of singing, in the time of the cantatas, sustained, divided the voice by minute intervals, and expressed words in this manner, which is not to be described: common language cannot express uncommon effects. To say that her voice was naturally well-toned and sweet, that she had an excellent shake, a perfect intonation, a

Komposition in der Liebhaber Händen um, welche era als sein Werk anerkannt hat." Ernst Ludwig Gerber, *Historisch–Biographisches Lexicon der Tonkünstler: welches Nachrichten von dem Leben und Werken musikalischer Schriftsteller, beruhmter Compositionen, Sänger, Meister auf Instrumenten, Dilettanten, Orgel- und Instrumentenmacher, enthält* (Leipzig: Johann Gottlob Immanuel Breitkopf, 1790), 1:934.

> facility of executing the most rapid and difficult passages, and a touching expression, would be to say no more than I have already said, and with truth, of others; but here I want words that would still encrease the significance and energy of these expressions. The Italian augmentatives would, perhaps, gratify my wish, if I were writing in that language; but as that is not the case, let me only add, that in the *portamento*, and divisions of tones and semi-tones into infinitely minute parts, and yet always stopping upon the exact fundamental, Signora Martinetz was more perfect than any singer I had ever heard: her cadences too, of this kind, were very learned, and truly pathetic and pleasing.
>
> After these two songs, she played a very difficult lesson, of her own composition, on the harpsichord, with great rapidity and precision. She has composed a *Miserere*, in four parts, with several Psalms, in eight parts, and is a most excellent contrapuntist.[51]

Significantly, Burney's estimation of Martines's musical style resonates with her own: her style sought to blend old and new, offering a vehicle for Metastasio's poetry that fused the grace and clarity of earlier music with the technical skill and instrumental writing of the modern style. Reflecting on one of her Psalm compositions, set to an Italian translation by Metastasio, Burney wrote, "It was a most agreeable *Mescolanza*, as Metastasio called it, of *antico e moderno*; a mixture of the harmony, and contrivance of old times, with the melody and taste of the present."[52] This "agreeable" combination of old and new represented the ideal of composition in 1770s Vienna, as Daube's treatise confirmed: "If we combine the art of the old music with the grace and natural beauty of the present music, the two can achieve a perfection to which must be counted principally the representation of the passions. We do not need to discard the old, but rather only to strive to improve it."[53] Martines's technical skill in music represented something that

51. Burney, *The Present State of Music in Germany, the Netherlands, and United Kingdom*, 1:311–14.

52. Burney, *The Present State of Music in Germany, the Netherlands, and United Kingdom*, 1:345.

53. "Wenn wir die Kunst der alten Musik mit der Anmuth und natürlichen Schönheit der itzigen verbinden; so kann beydes zusammengezogen eine Vollkommenheit zuwege bringen, worunter hauptsächlich die Vorstellung der Leidenschaften gehöret. Wir haben nicht nöthig, das Alte hinweg zu werfen, sondern nur es zu verbessern zu trachten." Daube, *Der musikalische Dilettant*, 332. Translated in Daube, *The Musical Dilettante*, 266.

Metastasio could not achieve. Understood in this light, Burney's celebration of their creative collaboration recognized that they each possessed talent and learning that complemented that of the other.[54]

Metastasio's modest setting of his "Grazie agl'inganni tuoi" can help illuminate what he and Burney heard as so distinctive in Martines's Italian arias and cantatas. Take, as a first case study, her setting of the aria "Conservati fedele," from Metastasio's libretto for *Artaserse*:

> Conservati fedele,
> Pensa ch'io resto, e peno,
> E qualche volta almeno
> Ricordati di me.
> Che io per virtù d'amore
> Parlando col mio core
> Ragionerò con te.

> (Stay faithful, / think how I stay here, grieving, / and, at least sometimes, / remember me. // While I, by virtue of love, / talking with my own heart, / converse with you.)

One of five texts drawn from *Artaserse* included in Martines's *Scelta d'arie composte per suo diletto*, the da capo aria "Conservati fedele" is scored for soprano solo, two violins, viola, two oboes, and two bassoons. Notwithstanding this ample orchestration—not at all unusual for Martines—her setting shares certain key features with Metastasio's canzonetta. For the first statement of the first stanza, the setting is syllabic; melodic motion is predominantly by step or third, with only occasional larger leaps. When the voice enters, the instrumental accompaniment thins to strings only and is marked *piano*. The winds enter on the words "e qualche volta almeno ricordati di me," accompanied by sixteenth-note figuration in the strings, but the dynamic markings seem designed to ensure that the voice part remains clearly audible (ex. 4.1 and audio ex. 4.1 ♫).

Only after the text of the first stanza has been rendered in this clear fashion, prioritizing the comprehensibility of the text above all, does the voice part become more complex and virtuosic. At first, this new complex-

54. Ernst Ludwig Gerber cited and paraphrased some of Burney's language, but he emphasized her technical skill and learning even more; see Gerber, *Historisch–Biographisches Lexicon der Tonkünstler*, 1:888–89.

Example 4.1A Marianna Martines, "Conservati fedele," mm. 17–31, reduction for keyboard and voice (a full score is available on the companion website). From *Scelta d'arie composte per suo diletto* (San Pietro a Majella in Naples, I-Nc, Arie 417 A).

ity takes the shape of a syncopated figure with chromatic lower neighbors in the voice part on the word "pena" (grieving) (ex. 4.2, m. 35; audio ex. 4.2 ♫). While the voice line has a slur over the syncopated figure, the violins punctuate it softly with a breathless off-beat figure. This continues into a long melisma that lasts until m. 43. Melismatic figuration becomes increasingly virtuosic, with difficult coloratura leaps appearing, for example, in mm. 48–49 on the word "ricordati" (remember; see ex. 4.3 and audio ex. 4.3 ♫). The passagework in mm. 69–79, again underscoring the meaning of the word "pena," demands chromatic precision in sixteenth notes that would tax the most adept singer (ex. 4.4 and audio ex. 4.4 ♫).

Example 4.1B

The B section of "Conservati fedele" returns to the largely syllabic manner of text setting that characterizes the opening of the A section. At the da capo, Martines would surely have added improvised ornamentation to elaborate the A section, rendering it in a less straightforwardly syllabic manner. However, there would still not be room in this elaborated opening to insert the kind of virtuosic passagework that appears later in the A section. The progression from simplicity to complexity would be reenacted through the da capo form.

To summarize, in this aria Martines seems to have taken an approach that deliberately balances clear declamation with vocal virtuosity. Her initial priority is setting the text in a clear manner that attends to the Italian declamation above all. Only after the text has been established does she allow her vocal virtuosity to come through, and that with increasing complexity. Burney's observation, upon hearing Martines sing one of her compositions, that "the words were well set, the melody was simple, and great room was left for expression and embellishment," is readily understandable in light of this approach. Similarly, the more complex, chromatic passagework that she includes toward the end of the A section renders plausible Burney's amazement at hearing her "*portamento*, and divisions of tones and

Example 4.2 Marianna Martines, "Conservati fedele," mm. 34–43, reduction for keyboard and voice (a full score is available on the companion website). From *Scelta d'arie composte per suo diletto* (San Pietro a Majella in Naples, I-Nc, Arie 417 A).

Example 4.3 Marianna Martines, "Conservati fedele," mm. 47–51, reduction for keyboard and voice (a full score is available on the companion website). From *Scelta d'arie composte per suo diletto* (San Pietro a Majella in Naples, I-Nc, Arie 417 A).

Example 4.4 Marianna Martines, "Conservati fedele," mm. 69–79, reduction for keyboard and voice (a full score is available on the companion website). From *Scelta d'arie composte per suo diletto* (San Pietro a Majella in Naples, I-Nc, Arie 417 A).

semi-tones into infinitely minute parts, and yet always stopping upon the exact fundamental." In other words, I do not think that Burney was merely generalizing about Martines's vocal compositions and her vocal brilliance: rather, it seems that he was responding to the specific compositional strategies that she employed to display her sensitivity to text as well as her vocal technique.

Compare Martines's approach in "Conservati fedele" to that of Johann Adolf Hasse, whose setting of *Artaserse* Martines may have known. (Metastasio wrote to Hasse in 1773 that Martines had a "rich store" of Hasse's works "that she never tires of augmenting,"[55] and this opera had been revived in Naples as recently as 1760.) Hasse's setting, like that of Martines, is in a delicate triple meter—his is marked "Un poco moderato ma poco," while hers is "Andante affettuoso"—and the bass lines have the same simple, minuet-like profile, predominantly in quarter notes. The vocal melody, however, is somewhat different. Whereas Martines opens by rendering the text in a largely syllabic fashion with predominantly conjunct motion, Hasse's melody is ornamented with sixteenth-note figures from the beginning. And, while Martines increases the virtuosity of her vocal passagework over the course of the aria, Hasse's setting maintains a similar ornamental profile throughout (ex. 4.5 and audio ex. 4.5 ♫).[56]

Hasse enjoyed a close relationship to Metastasio; the two collaborated on numerous projects for the imperial court. Hasse knew and admired Martines as well. Given the closeness of these relationships, we should not presume that Metastasio would have objected to Hasse's setting of "Conservati fedele" at all. However, the distinctive profile of Martines's setting is worth noting in light of Metastasio's statements about the unnecessary complexities of modern music. His own modest composition offers incidental support for the notion that he preferred simpler settings of his texts. Given these preferences, it seems entirely likely that Metastasio would have mentored Martines to compose in a way that threw his texts into the light that he most preferred. It is easy to imagine them discussing the advantages of a simple, straightforward text setting while also recognizing the place of virtuosity. Especially given Martines's remarkable vocal technique, settings such as her "Conservati fedele" seem designed to prioritize text setting first, and then to reveal that technique in increasingly marvelous ways as the piece unfolds.

The dichotomy between simple declamation and virtuosic, highly elaborated vocal writing can be conceived as a distinction between nature and artifice. Within Martines's cantata writing, the procedure of moving from a straightforward, "natural" declamation to an elaborated style that cloaks the text in a layer of ornamental divisions is common. The same approach

55. "un ricco Tesoro"; "mai si stanca d'accrescerlo." Metastasio to Hasse, October 23, 1773, in Pietro Metastasio, *Tutte le opere di Pietro Metastasio: Lettere*, ed. Bruno Brunelli (Milan: A. Mondadori, 1954), 5:265; translated in Godt, *Marianna Martines*, 6.

56. Mozart's setting of this same text in K. 23 is closer to that of Martines, especially in its approach to the text. Mozart's work was composed in The Hague in 1765–1766. It is not clear that Martines would have known Mozart's setting, but it speaks to a shared interest in textual clarity.

Example 4.5A Johann Adolf Hasse, "Conservati fedele," mm. 1–27, reduction for keyboard and voice (a full score is available on the companion website). From *Artaserse*, 1760 Naples revival (Leipzig University Library, Biblioteca Albertina, D-LEu N.I.10286a).

14
- sa ch'io res-to e pe - no, pen - sa ch'io res-ta e pe - no, e
tr
18
qual che vol - ta al - me - no ri cor - da - ti di me, e
tr
poco f
22
qual-che vol-ta al - me - no ri-co - - - -
p
25
- da-ti ri - cor-da - ti di me
tr

Example 4.5B

is at work in the cantata *L'inverno*, one of the works that Metastasio sent to Padre Martini to evaluate in 1761.[57] The first aria in this cantata, in da capo form, opens with a setting of the A section that is almost entirely syllabic (ex. 4.6, mm. 1–18; audio ex. 4.6 ♫). Following this initial, complete statement of the A section, Martines doubles back to the second couplet, "Che gelato il ruscelletto / Fra le sponde è prigionier," using the word *gelato* ("freezes") as an opportunity for ornamentation that seems to represent the shivering of the singer. As the vocal line reaches higher and higher, achieving a high B in m. 29, the singer's virtuosity emerges as a natural reaction to the circumstances of nature—to the chill of winter (ex. 4.6, mm. 19–31). When the singer's voice "freezes" on a B in mm. 32 and 33, the violin shudders in response by introducing its own sixteenth-note figuration, and the singer resumes her ornamentation toward the end of the phrase (ex. 4.6, mm. 36–40).

So che il bosco, il monte, il prato
Non han più che un solo aspetto:
Che gelato il ruscelletto
Fra le sponde è prigionier.
  Dai rigor del freddo polo
  Sento anch'io qual aura spiri:
  So che agghiacciano i respiri
  Su le labbra al passaggier.

(I know that the forest, the mountain, the field, / have no more than a single aspect: / that the stream is ice, / a prisoner among the shores. // Even from the stricture of the cold pole / I feel the wind blow. / I know that breaths freeze / as they pass the lip.)

The B section shifts to the relative minor and adopts an entirely new character. Marked *piano*, this section is in 3/8 and contains an off-beat, arpeggiated figuration in the bass part. This accompaniment is amplified by off-beat sixteenth-note figuration in the violins starting in measure 122.

57. See Godt, *Marianna Martines*, 135. This cantata is preserved in the autograph manuscript I-Bc, GG 157, which also contains two fugues from her Mass no. 3 of 1761. Padre Martini wrote the text on the cover of the manuscript indicating that it was a *Saggio di composizioni della Sig^a Anna Maria Martines*. Metastasio's letter of March 9, 1761, written in response to Padre Martini's praise of Martines's work, is quoted and cited above in note 23.

Example 4.6 Marianna Martines, "So che il bosco, il monte, il prato," mm. 1–42, reduction for keyboard and voice (a full score is available on the companion website). From *L'inverno* (Civico Museo Bibliografico Musicale, Bologna, I-Bc, GG 157).

23
che ge - la - - - - - - - -
27
- - - - - - to il ru - scel-
31
let - to fra le spon - de e
35
pri - gio - nier e pri - gio -

Example 4.6B

Example 4.6c

The vocal melody, sometimes static and sometimes angular, is haunting, and it seems designed to depict the death of winter. Vocal virtuosity is abandoned in favor of clear textual declamation (ex. 4.7 and audio ex. 4.7 ♫).

This progression from natural declamation to the artifice that treats the voice as an instrument represents a prominent and distinctive feature of Martines's Italian cantatas and arias. It serves as a response, in effect, to Metastasio's view, conveyed to Burney, that vocal music had become too "instrumental." Martines's approach achieves a compromise between the older, simpler cantata style and the more ornate style epitomized by mid-century *opera seria*.

The line between nature and artifice is a focal point of many of Metastasio's texts, and Martines's musical settings explore that line in a variety of ways. Another example is in the cantata *La tempesta*, composed in 1778, set to a text by Metastasio in which pastoral characters must seek refuge from a storm, and in doing so, they discover their love. In the opening accompanied recitative, the speaker, a shepherd, recognizing that a storm is coming, arrives to help the shepherdess, Nice, to gather her flock; he promises not to renew the subject of his love for her, but only to help her. A storm begins and the two must seek shelter in a cave. In the first aria, "Ma tu tremi, o mio tesoro," the shepherd sees Nice trembling and promises to remain by her side, but not to renew his amorous advances:

Ma tu tremi, o mio tesoro,
Ma tu palpiti, cor mio,
Non temer, con te son io,
Ne d'amor ti parlerò.
Mentre folgori, e baleni
Sarò teco, amata Nice,

Example 4.7A Marianna Martines, "So che il bosco, il monte, il prato," mm. 110–135, reduction for keyboard and voice (a full score is available on the companion website). From *L'inverno* (I-Bc, GG 157).

Example 4.7B

> Quando il ciel si rassereni,
> Nice ingrata, io partirò.

(But you tremble, my treasure, / But you flutter, my heart, / Do not fear, I am with you, / I will not speak to you of love. // Amid lightning and thunder, / I will be with you, beloved Nice, / When the sky calms itself, / Nice, ungrateful one, I will leave.)

Martines's setting of this aria reflects Nice's trembling through the persistent use of eighth-note figures in its opening lines. Still, the text is clearly declaimed, and the voice part embraces an overall aesthetic of pastoral simplicity. Only at cadences does the figuration increase in complexity, but these moments pass quickly. The string arpeggios, rendered in sixteenth-note figures, provide a reminder of the raging storm outside the cave (ex. 4.8 and audio ex. 4.8 ♫).

In the second recitative, the shepherd responds as Nice moves closer to him, seeking his comfort; he recognizes that she may be motivated not by fear of the storm, but by her love for him, formerly suppressed. Rejoicing that Nice is blushing out of embarrassment due to her love for him, the shepherd sings the second aria, "Alfin, fra le tempeste," which contrasts the

Example 4.8a Marianna Martines, "Ma tu tremi, o mio Tesoro," mm. 1–21, reduction for keyboard and voice (a full score is available on the companion website). From *La tempesta* (Österreichisches Nationalbibliothek, A-Wn, Mus. Hs. 16569).

Example 4.8B

storm, which rages outside the cave, with the peace that the shepherd has found inside:

> Alfin frà le tempeste
>   La calma ritrovai;
>   Ah non ritorni mai
>   Mai più sereno il dì.
> Questo de' giorni miei
>   Questo è 'l più chiaro giorno.

Viver così vorrei,
Vorrei morir così.

(Thus, amid the storm, / have I found peace. / Ah! If only the more serene day / would never return. // This, among all my days, / This is the brightest day. / Thus do I wish to live, / Thus do I wish to die.)

It is in this second aria that Martines's setting presents a conflict between nature and art. The raging storm outside the cave represents the unleashing of nature. Parallel to this, inside the cave, Nice drops the pretense that she does not love the shepherd, yielding to her natural inclination. Thus the text of the cantata may be understood to represent the triumph of nature over artifice. Musically, however, the story is more complex: Martines's setting of "Alfin fra le tempeste" announces the triumph of love through celebratory fireworks of vocal virtuosity. Again, her initial setting of each line of text is predominantly syllabic, meaning that she prioritizes clarity of meaning; only after her initial statement of each line of text does she introduce the impressive passagework that Burney praised when he heard her singing (ex. 4.9 and audio ex. 4.9 ♫). If the text of the aria celebrates Nice's pretense and artificial behavior yielding to her love for the shepherd, Martines's musical setting suggests that this unleashing of nature—whether outside the cave or inside—leads the voice to new virtuosic heights.

Based on the evidence presented here—Burney's account of his discussions with Metastasio, his description of Martines's singing and compositional style, and, crucially, Martines's own compositions—I conclude that the relationship between Martines and Mestastasio was one of collaboration. In my reading, Burney's account illuminates this collaboration by juxtaposing Metastasio's views of contemporary opera and Martines's role in solving the problems that Metastasio identifies. Metastasio, the poet of the pastoral and classical worlds, prioritized the "natural" declamation of poetry; Martines showed, in her aria and cantata settings, how this priority could merge with the impressive virtuosity that required so much training and practice. The results of this collaboration were noted by visitors to Martines's salon who heard her sing her settings of Metastasio's poetry. Mancini, for example, reflected on the sympathy between Martines and Metastasio, in evidence in the poet's reactions to Martines's compositions: "I heard her myself, when she was still very young, sing and play the cembalo with astonishing mastery, accompanying her own compositions, sung and

Example 4.9A Marianna Martines, "Alfin fra le tempeste," mm. 1–25, reduction for keyboard and voice (a full score is available on the companion website). From *La tempesta* (A-Wn, Mus. Hs. 16569).

Example 4.9B

Example 4.9c

expressed with such force of musical emphasis that Sig. Abbate Metastasio himself felt again the emotion that he had been able to excite in the human heart with his inimitable librettos."[58]

The notion of Martines's salon as a site of collaboration does not minimize Martines's agency, but rather acknowledges and promotes it. When she presented her compositions in this context, she did so in a way that was uniquely suited to her own voice. After all, her compositional style did not only place Metastasio's texts in the foreground; it also allowed her to enact the process of "developing" or even "discovering" the capacities of her voice in each performance. As the complexity of her vocal ornamentation increases over the course of an aria, that process is dramatized over and over, with astonishing new effects in each work.

Moreover, this unfolding of complexity and virtuosity contributes to the broader narrative, described above, concerning natural talent and skill cultivated through practice and learning. In her surviving writings, Martines cast herself as a studious and diligent musician who applied herself seriously to her work, despite her amateur status. Her Italian-language arias and cantatas reflect the same trajectory. In general, they begin in a seemingly "natural" manner, allowing the singer to declaim the text in the most comprehensible and straightforward way. Only upon repetition of the text does the singer's training in ornamentation assume control of the composition. To be sure, improvised ornamentation would have been added even

58. "Io stesso l'ho sentita ne' suoi più teneri anni cantare, e sonare il cembalo con una maestria sorprendente, accompagnando le sue produzioni, cantate ed espresse con tanta forza di metro musicale, che lo stesso Sig. Abbate Metastasio ne risentiva quell'emozione, che ha saputo egli eccitare nel cuore umano colle inarrivabili sue poesie drammatiche." Mancini, *Riflessioni pratiche*, 229–30n1; translated in Godt, *Marianna Martines*, 33.

in the opening sections of her arias, but there would not be room in those opening sections to add the measures-long florid, virtuosic passagework that generally appears in later sections of her compositions. These compositions enact the very process of musical development, encapsulating the improvement of nature through art that she claimed to have undergone in her own musical training.

Collaboration and Salon Sociability

In the years following Metastasio's death in 1782, with two of her brothers, Joseph and Carl, and her sister, Antonia, Marianna Martines moved to a first-floor apartment on Vienna's Herrengasse—a far more prestigious and spacious home than the one she had lived in at Kohlmarkt 11. During this period, the culture of musical salons in Vienna became more widespread, and documentation of them increased, such that it is possible to confirm that Martines hosted a musical salon in her home each Saturday night. Johann Ferdinand von Schönfeld counts her among the numerous hostesses (and hosts), mostly from the middle class and lower nobility, whose salons featured the best performances: "Fräulein von Martines. Every Saturday there is a very grand social gathering [*Gesellschaft*] at the home of this skillful musician, at which a great deal [of music] is always sung and played on the *Flügel*. On these days, one also sometimes finds here a wind ensemble that plays through the entire evening."[59] While Schönfeld mentions Martines's "skill" in this passage, it is clear that the music-making in her home was a collaborative enterprise. This notion is supported by Schönfeld elsewhere in the *Jahrbuch*:

> She reads at sight, accompanies from the full score, and is an excellent singer. Rigorously correct in composition and execution, her taste is largely after the older Italian style. For amusement [*Unterhaltung*] and out of love for art she almost always maintains her own vocal studio, where she develops excellent singers, of whom the recently deceased

59. "Fräulein von Martines. Bei dieser geschickten Tonkünstlerinn ist alle Sonnabende sehr große Gesellschaft, bei welcher Gelegenheit immer viel gesungen und auf Flügel gespielt wird. Auch findet man zuweilen an diesen Tagen eine Harmoniebande daselbst, welche den ganzen Abend durch bläst." Schönfeld, *Jahrbuch der Tonkunst von Wien und Prag*, 71. Translated in Godt, *Marianna Martines*, 195. See also Link, "Vienna's Private Theatrical and Musical Life," 230.

> Frau von Dürfeld (née Fräulein von Hacker) stood out. She has written masses and a large number of arias, which sometimes come close to Jommelli's style, and is in every respect a great supporter of music.[60]

Schönfeld's description points to the collaborative nature of Martines's activities. By mentioning her ability to accompany from full scores, he invites the reader to imagine the music that she and her guests and fellow musicians perform. His use of the verb *bilden* to describe how Martines assists her singing students denotes her interest in music as a source of edification and the fostering of musicianship in other women.[61] Additionally, Schönfeld's use of the term *Unterhaltung* connotes not only amusement, but also conversation and sociability. It seems that the same sense of mutual support was at play in Martines's assessment of the music of Maria Rosa Coccia and in her apparent openness to playing the music of other composers and evaluating them in positive terms.[62]

Music and sociability merge in numerous other accounts of Martines's salon in the years following Metastasio's death. Hester Thrale Piozzi's account, quoted in chapter 1, describes Martines as one of Vienna's "ladies of fashion . . . eminent for their musical abilities," and reported that she and her sister "set [Metastasio's] poetry and sing it very finely, appearing to recollect his conversation and friendship, with infinite tenderness and

60. "Sie ließt vom Blatte, accompagnirt aus der Partitur, ist eine vortreffliche Sängerinn, streng gramatikalisch in Komposizion und Exekuzion, ihr Geschmack ist hauptsächlich nach der ältern italiänischen Manier. Aus Unterhaltung und aus Liebe für die Kunst hat sie fast immer eine eigene Singschule, worinn sie vortreffliche Sängerinnen bildet, unter welchen sich die so zeitig vom Tode hingeraffte Frau von Dürfeld, geb. Fräulein von Hacker sich auszeichnete. Sie hat Messen und sehr viele Arien komponirt, die zuweilen dem Jomelischen Styl nahe kommen, und ist in jedem Betrachte eine große Stücke der Tonkunst." Schönfeld, *Jahrbuch der Tonkunst von Wien und Prag*, 41–42. Translated in Godt, *Marianna Martines*, 199.

61. See Godt, *Marianna Martines*, 199–201.

62. Harer, "Alte Musik in Wien um 1800." Schönfeld's description of Martines herself as an "excellent singer" calls into question the claim, put forward by Godt, that Martines had lost her voice by this point; see Godt, *Marianna Martines*, 199–201. However, Marchese Cesare Lucchesini provided an account in a letter dated January 5, 1793, that describes Martines and her sister as "due vecchie sorelle," and judges Martines's voice "strident and shaky" (stridula e tremante). See John A. Rice, "Marianna's Weekly Conversazione: An Account by an Italian Visitor to Vienna in 1793," https://sites.google.com/site/johnaricecv/marianna-s-weekly-conversazione (accessed July 19, 2020).

delight."[63] Michael Kelly, the Irish tenor who sang in the Viennese opera buffa between 1783 and 1787 and premiered *Le nozze di Figaro*, among other works, was likewise a regular guest in the Martines salon. The memoir attributed to him referred to her as a "deep blue"—that is, a Bluestocking—and recalled her performances of keyboard duets with Mozart. As discussed in chapter 1, Kelly's memoir further noted that he had met Piozzi in Martines's home, and it reported that the two women enjoyed conversation with one another. Kelly's report that Mozart played keyboard duets with Martines is quite plausible, since he was connected to numerous women of the professional class, middle class, and aristocracy, and he cultivated their educations in music.[64]

In all these descriptions, it is a sense of musical sociability and collaboration that dominates. While the descriptions of the salons that Martines had held in the 1760s and 1770s are fewer in number, there is no reason to assume, with Godt, that these earlier events featured conversation or sociability any less. During those years, with Metastasio and Martines in the same home, greeting their guests together, it is easy to imagine that the active conversation that Burney experienced during his visit to Vienna in 1772 was the rule rather than the exception. Indeed, the collaborative relationship that Martines and Metastasio enjoyed—one manifested, as I have argued, in Martines's musical settings of Metastasio's poetry—is echoed in accounts of her continued musical sociability and support of other musicians in her later years.

Conclusion

That Martines was widely admired by professional musicians, amateurs, and members of Vienna's nobility attests not only to her skill as a composer and performer, but also to her successful negotiation of the social expectations of women in music in the eighteenth century. While other women endured derision as a result of their acquisition of skill in composition and their forays into the public sphere, Martines employed the liminal space

63. Hester Lynch [Thrale] Piozzi, *Observations and Reflections Made in the Course of a Journey, through France, Italy, and Germany* (London: A. Strahan and T. Cadell, 1789), 2:306.

64. Morrow writes that Mozart maintained a "dizzying schedule of appearances" in musical salons; see Morrow, *Concert Life in Haydn's Vienna*, 18. The literature on Mozart and musical women is too expansive to cite in full here, but a recent account is in Jane Glover, *Mozart's Women: His Family, His Friends, His Music* (Oxford: Macmillan, 2005).

of the musical salon to cultivate her image in a way that would facilitate social ascent. Within an environment that allowed for diligent study even among amateurs, Martines came to embody the 1808 report in the *Vaterländische Blätter* that, in Vienna, music enabled sociability among all classes of people: "Each day here, music brings about a wondrous event that one can only attribute to love: it makes all social positions equal—nobility and bourgeoisie, princes and their vassals, superiors and their underlings, sit at *one* stand together and, with the harmony of tones, forget about the disharmony of their positions."[65]

65. S.n., "Uebersicht des gegenwärtigen Zustandes der Tonkunst in Wien," 39. Translated in Painter, "Mozart at Work," 196.

CHAPTER FIVE

*

The Cultural Work of Collecting and Performing in the Salon of Sara Levy

In 1798, the Jewish writer Wolff Davidson published his treatise *Über die bürgerliche Verbesserung der Juden*, intended to justify the emancipation of Jews in Prussia and their full integration into the predominantly Christian society around them. Borrowing his title from a 1781 publication by Christian Wilhelm von Dohm, Davidson joined an ongoing discussion among both Jewish and Christian thinkers of the Enlightenment concerning the merits of Jewish emancipation and the participation of Jews in civic and cultural life. By way of justifying Jewish emancipation, Davidson cited a long list of Jews, from philosophers and educators to practitioners of the mechanical arts, who were already making significant contributions to society. Some were professional musicians, but more were in the emerging category of "Dilettanten."[1] Within that group, he wrote, "well known as prodigious keyboardists here in Berlin are Madame Lewy, Madame Wolff, and Madame Boser *née* Flies."[2]

These women have emerged in recent scholarship as important figures in the musical history of the late eighteenth century, especially because of their close connections to the Bach family. Zippora Wulff, *née* Itzig

1. On the rise of musical amateurism in late eighteenth-century Berlin, see Celia Applegate, *Bach in Berlin: Nation and Culture in Mendelssohn's Revival of the "St. Matthew Passion"* (Ithaca, NY: Cornell University Press, 2005), ch. 4, "Musical Amateurism and the Exercise of Taste." See also the discussion of dilettantism in chapter 4 of this volume.

2. "Hier in Berlin sind als vortreffliche Klavierspielerinn, Madame Lewy, Madame Wolff und Madame Boser, gebohrne Flies bekannt." Wolf Davidson, *Ueber die bürgerliche Verbesserung der Juden* (Berlin: Ernst Felisch, 1798), 109.

(later Cäcilie von Eskeles), and Karoline Luise Eleonore von Boser, *née* Flies, were well known in their day as talented keyboardists.[3] But it was Zippora's sister Sara Levy, *née* Itzig, who had the most lasting effect on musical performance and scholarship (fig. 5.1). A student of Wilhelm Friedemann Bach and a patron of both Friedemann and Carl Philipp Emanuel Bach, Sara Levy played, collected, and preserved a large quantity of their music, as well as music by Johann Sebastian Bach and many others of his generation—especially composers who lived and worked in Berlin.[4] Levy donated the majority of her holdings to the Sing-Akademie zu Berlin around 1815, when they were subsumed within the larger collection then being assembled by Carl Friedrich Zelter.[5] With the repatriation of the Sing-Akademie collection to Berlin at the end of the Cold War, the archival work of such scholars as Christoph Wolff and Peter Wollny has solidified Levy's position as a crucial link in the Bach tradition in the generation before the revival of the *St. Matthew Passion*, initiated by her great-nephew, Felix Mendelssohn-Bartholdy.[6]

3. Biographical information on all three women is in Thekla Keuck, *Hofjuden und Kulturbürger: Die Geschichte der Familie Itzig in Berlin* (Göttingen: Vandenhoeck & Ruprecht, 2011). For the broader context, see Natalie Naimark-Goldberg, *Jewish Women in Enlightenment Berlin* (Portland, OR: Littman Library of Jewish Civilization, 2013).

4. On Levy's biography, collection, and impact on her musical environment, see especially Peter Wollny, *"Ein förmlicher Sebastian und Philipp Emanuel Bach-Kultus": Sara Levy und ihr musikalisches Wirken, mit einer Dokumentensammlung zur musikalischen Familiengeschichte der Vorfahren von Felix Mendelssohn Bartholdy* (Wiesbaden: Breitkopf & Härtel, 2010); Wollny, "Sara Levy and the Making of Musical Taste in Berlin," *Musical Quarterly* 77, no. 4 (winter 1993): 651–88; Wollny, "'Ein förmlicher Sebastian und Philipp Emanuel Bach-Kultus': Sara Levy, geb. Itzig, und ihr musikalischer Salon," in *Musik und Ästhetik im Berlin Moses Mendelssohns*, ed. Anselm Gerhard (Tübingen: Max Niemeyer, 1999), 217–55; Wollny, "Anmerkungen zur Bach-Pflege im Umfeld Sara Levys," in *"Zu groß, zu unerreichbar": Bach-Rezeption im Zeitalter Mendelssohns und Schumanns*, ed. Anselm Hartinger, Christoph Wolff, und Peter Wollny (Wiesbaden, Leipzig, and Paris: Breitkopf & Härtel, 2007), 39–50; Christoph Wolff, "A Bach Cult in Late-Eighteenth-Century Berlin: Sara Levy's Musical Salon," *Bulletin of the American Academy of Arts and Sciences* 58, no. 3 (spring 2005): 26–31; and Christoph Wolff, "Sara Levy's Musical Salon and Her Bach Collection."

5. On Zelter's collecting habits, see Matthias Kornemann, "Zelter's Archive: Portrait of a Collector," in *The Archive of the Sing-Akademie zu Berlin: Catalogue / Das Archiv der Sing-Akademie zu Berlin: Katalog*, ed. Axel Fischer and Matthias Kornemann (Berlin and New York: De Gruyter, 2010), 19–25; Levy's donation of her collection to the Sing-Akademie is discussed on p. 21.

6. On the repatriation of the collection, see Christoph Wolff, "Recovered in Kiev: Bach et al. A Preliminary Report on the Music Collection of the Berlin Sing-Akademie," *Notes*,

Figure 5.1 One of the Itzig daughters, probably Sara Levy, *née* Itzig. Silverpoint engraving by Anton Graff (1786). Reproduced in Otto Waser, *Anton Graff von Winterthur: Bildnisse des Meisters* (s.l.: Winterthur Kunstverein, 1903). Courtesy of Christoph Wolff with thanks to Peter Wollny.

Levy and her sisters had been performing together in their parents' home from the time they were teenagers. As noted in chapter 1, in his travel diary, August Hennings recalls hearing the Itzig daughters play music as one of the highlights of his visit to Berlin, and his mention of their "finely developed intellect" suggests that he conversed with them as well. Around the time of her marriage in 1783, Levy began hosting a salon in her home,

---

2nd series, 58, no. 2 (December 2001): 259–71; and Ulrich Leisinger, "The Bach Collection," in *The Archive of the Sing-Akademie zu Berlin*, 41–42 and passim. The complete literature on Mendelssohn's performance of the *St. Matthew Passion* is too extensive to list here; see, for example, Applegate, *Bach in Berlin*; Gottfried Eberle, *200 Jahre Sing-Akademie zu Berlin: "Ein Kunstverein für die heilige Musik"* (Berlin: Nicolaische Verlagsbuchhandlung, 1991), 87–99; and R. Larry Todd, *Mendelssohn: A Life in Music* (New York and Oxford: Oxford University Press, 2003), 193–98 and passim. See also Yael Sela-Teichler, "Longing for the Sublime: Music and Jewish Self-Consciousness at Bach's *St. Matthew Passion* in Biedermeier Berlin," in *Sara Levy's World*, 147–80.

and these regular gatherings continued well into the nineteenth century.[7] In addition to performances in both private concerts outside her salon and at the more public institution of the Sing-Akademie zu Berlin, founded in 1792, Levy's salon formed a platform from which she exercised her musical taste and made a mark on the musical life of her city.[8] Her salon was one of a number hosted by Jewish women in Berlin in this period, though hers is distinctive within this first generation of *salonnières* in its focus on music. While non-Jewish guests were included, even privileged, in these gatherings, Liliane Weissberg has noted that Jewish women were not welcome in the homes of gentile women. If these salons formed part of the attempt to put into practice the principles of tolerance that were so widely vaunted as a feature of the Enlightenment, their social lives—what Weissberg calls a "social one-way street"—demonstrated how far the reality was from that ideal.[9]

The complex relationship of the Bach family and Bach scholarship with Judaism underlies the story of Sara Levy and her circle.[10] In 2005, Wolff suggested that Levy had until then been "underemphasized, under-researched, or neglected if not suppressed by earlier historical German scholarship for reasons of an apparent anti-Semitic bias."[11] Until recently, Levy's role was most often discussed from the perspective of her contribution to the Bach legacy, rather than as an autonomous figure in her own right.[12] As noted throughout this volume, this problematic manner of thinking may be discerned in the historiography of many musical salon women, who have long been considered for their role in aiding the careers

7. Wollny, *"Ein förmlicher Sebastian und Philipp Emanuel Bach-Kultus"* (2010), 29–36.

8. Among the many sources on the Berlin Jewish salons, see Marjanne E. Goozé, "What Was the Berlin Jewish Salon Around 1800?" in *Sara Levy's World*, 21–38, which contains a lucid analysis as well as the most important citations on the topic.

9. Liliane Weissberg, "Literary Culture and Jewish Space around 1800: The Berlin Salons Revisited," in *Modern Jewish Literatures: Intersections and Boundaries*, ed. Sheila E. Jelen, Michael P. Kramer, and L. Scott Lerner (Philadelphia: University of Pennsylvania Press, 2011), 32.

10. These issues are explored in Michael Marissen, *Bach & God* (New York and Oxford: Oxford University Press, 2016); and in Marissen, *Lutheranism, Anti-Judaism, and Bach's* St. John Passion: *With an Annotated Literal Translation of the Libretto* (New York and Oxford: Oxford University Press, 1998).

11. Wolff, "A Bach Cult in Late-Eighteenth-Century Berlin," 26.

12. Cypess and Sinkoff, eds., *Sara Levy's World*, brings together work by scholars from musicology, Jewish studies, history, literature, and philosophy in an attempt to treat Levy from the multidisciplinary perspectives that her biography warrants.

of male composers, rather than for their own interests, talents, and goals. In the case of Levy, however, this approach is especially troubling, as it carries the added baggage of an apparent anti-Jewish bias. In fact, this manner of thinking was initiated by Davidson, among others, who suggested that emancipation and tolerance were justified by—and, by implication, contingent upon—the "usefulness" of Jews to society. If Levy and her circle had not made "contributions" to Prussian cultural and intellectual life, would the emancipation of the Jews not have been justified?[13]

In addition to raising questions about the complex position of Jews and Judaism in Enlightenment Berlin, the case of Sara Levy brings into focus new questions of agency and authorship. Chapters 3 and 4 of this volume considered *salonnières* who were also composers, taking their compositions as indicators of their musical priorities and values. By contrast, Levy is not known to have composed; at least, she never signed her name to any compositions. Locating her agency, therefore, requires a different approach. This chapter will consider the two aspects of her musicianship most central to her salon: performing and collecting. While these activities were not unique to her, they take on new meaning in light of her adherence to Judaism—strong, even insistent, compared with many other men and women in her family and social circle, many of whom chose radical assimilation or conversion—and her advocacy of and engagement with the Jewish Enlightenment (*Haskalah*).[14] Indeed, recent archival work by Natalie Naimark-Goldberg has underscored the significance of Levy's patronage of *Haskalah* intellectual causes and Jewish communal institutions, which suggests a purposeful Jewish self-identification.[15] As a result of her awareness of *Haskalah* ideas on music—a point to which I will return below—Levy is likely to have known of the persistent and sometimes contentious debates over the history of Jews in music and over the potential of contemporary Jews to be musical.

13. On the problems of the "contribution discourse" in Jewish history, see Moshe Rosman, *How Jewish Is Jewish History?* (Oxford and Portland: OR: Littman Library of Jewish Civilization, 2007), 111–30.

14. On the tendency toward conversion among Levy's generation of enlightened German Jews, see Amos Elon, *The Pity of It All: A Portrait of the German-Jewish Epoch, 1743–1933* (New York: Picador, 2002), 81–86 and passim. Elon's observation that "before conversion most converts were nonpracticing Jews; after conversion they were nonpracticing Christians" (82) highlights the distinctiveness of Levy's situation.

15. Natalie Naimark-Goldberg, "Remaining Within the Fold: The Cultural and Social World of Sara Levy," in *Sara Levy's World*, 52–74.

Levy's collection of musical scores and the performances that she presented and hosted in her salon accomplished what scholars of performance studies have described as "cultural work."[16] By collecting music and performing it within her salon, Levy endowed it with new associations and new meanings. As other Jewish women of Levy's generation engaged with the process of *Bildung* essentially for the first time, Levy helped open Prussian musical culture to participation by Jews. The collection of notated scores and the music-making that they enabled within her salon can be understood as examples of the complementary phenomena of artistic creation and cultural memory—the written text and the embodied performance, or what performance theorist Diana Taylor has called the "archive" and the "repertoire."[17] Taylor locates the impetus behind textual archives in the desire to frame cultural memory, and the act of performance as a site of embodied meaning. Levy engaged with both of these. She accumulated a collection—a textual archive—that attests to her agency and asserts her place in the German cultural patrimony. And, through the act of performance, she reconstituted the contents of her collection as a component of Jewish culture. Both her collection and her performances served to loosen the bonds tying this music to a pre-Enlightenment past, giving it new life within the context of an enlightened society. In collecting, playing, and transmitting this music, Levy reframed it as a component of Jewish history, thus fulfilling the call by some leaders of the *Haskalah* for members of the Jewish community to engage with all the arts and sciences. By playing and collecting, Levy sought to forge a common musical history accessible to both Christians and Jews.

Sara Levy's Collection and Her Musical Salon Practices

The evidence from Sara Levy's musical salon is fragmentary. Unlike some women in her social circle, most notably her younger contemporary Rahel Varnhagen, Levy seems not to have kept a diary, and very little of her correspondence survives to document her thoughts and intentions.[18] Eyewit-

16. See, for example, Ruth Solie, "Whose Life? The Gendered Self in Schumann's *Frauenliebe* Songs," in *Music and Text: Critical Inquiries*, ed. Steven P. Scher (Cambridge: Cambridge University Press, 1992), 219–40; and Suzanne Cusick, "Gender and the Cultural Work of a Classical Music Performance," *repercussions* 3, no. 1 (Spring 1994): 77–110.

17. Diana Taylor, *The Archive and the Repertoire: Performing Cultural Memory in the Americas* (Durham, NC, and London: Duke University Press, 2003).

18. Varnhagen's writings have been published in modern editions in Rahel Levin Varn-

ness accounts of her musical practices from friends and visitors remain on a general level. Therefore, information must be pieced together largely from nonverbal sources—especially her collection of scores. Hundreds of musical manuscripts survive that bear either her handwritten name, or, more commonly, her distinctive *ex libris* stamp, which reads "SSLev^{i}" (Sara and Samuel Salomon Levy), as shown in fig. 5.2.[19] These manuscripts appear to be directly tied to her musical practice. Some of them, especially scores for solo keyboard, attest to her private music-making, while her chamber and orchestral music apparently reflects her salon practices. These chamber and orchestral pieces were copied out in part books, indicating that they were created for use in performance and not simply as scores for silent reading or mere posterity.

Levy's collection displays at least two stages of conscious selection and classification. The first stage occurred when she had pieces copied and preserved them in her collection. Levy did not collect all kinds of music; rather, she showed a clear inclination toward certain composers and genres. The second stage occurred when she selected which of her manuscripts to donate to the Sing-Akademie. The works that she donated appear to reflect the practices of her salon: they consist almost entirely of chamber or orchestral music, not music for solo keyboard, and thus project an image of her musicianship as rooted in sociability.

The first stage of selection is evident in Levy's preference for composers from Berlin, whether from her own generation or from an earlier time, and for music from the Bach family. As is well known, the Prussian court and its environs under Frederick the Great were strongholds of the Bach tradition in the generation after Johann Sebastian Bach's death, with figures such as C. P. E. Bach, Johann Adam Hiller, Johann Friedrich Agricola, and Johann Philipp Kirnberger carrying on the teachings of the elder Bach even as they adapted those teachings to the enlightened, galant tastes of their patron.[20] As the influence of the Prussian court declined after the Seven Years' War, salons began to fill some of the resulting gap in the cultural and social life

---

hagen, *Edition Rahel Levin Varnhagen*, ed. Barbara Hahn and Ursula Isselstein (Munich: Beck Verlag, 1997–); and Rahel Levin Varnhagen, *Rahel: Ein Buch des Andenkens für ihre Freunde*, ed. Barbara Hahn, 6 vols. (Göttingen: Wallstein Verlag, 2011).

19. Levy's collection and the collections of her family members are catalogued and discussed extensively in Wollny, *"Ein förmlicher Sebastian und Philipp Emanuel Bach-Kultus"* (2010).

20. Wolff surveys these tastes as evidence of Levy's musical context in Wolff, "Sara Levy's Musical Salon and Her Bach Collection," 40.

Figure 5.2 Cover page of Johann Schobert, "Sonatina a quatuor," op. 7 no. 1 in E-flat major in the manuscript owned by Sara Levy. D-Bsa SA 4858. Note Levy's distinctive *ex libris* stamp. The remainder of the manuscript is in part books for the individual instruments. Image courtesy of Staatsbibliothek zu Berlin—Preußischer Kulturbesitz, Musikabteilung mit Mendelssohn-Archiv, Depositum Archiv der Sing-Akademie zu Berlin, Germany.

of Berlin, including musical patronage and performance. Levy's affinity for the Bach tradition was certainly influenced by this environment, and especially by her studies with Wilhelm Friedemann Bach; she was apparently his only student during his period in Berlin, which spanned the last decade of his life. This relationship is recorded most poignantly in a note appended to a manuscript of J. S. Bach's B-major Fugue from book two of the *Well-Tempered Clavier* once owned by Levy. There, the copyist, Justus Amadeus Lecerf, labeled the piece as a "Fugue from the Well-Tempered Clavier from the estate of the beloved student of Friedemann Bach, Madame Sarah Levy, née Itzig, in Berlin."[21]

This excerpt from the *Well-Tempered Clavier* (a work that would later become such an important vehicle for Lea Mendelssohn and her children) was one of many manuscripts for solo keyboard that Levy owned. Her full collection must have included sonatas (her name appears on the subscription list for C. P. E. Bach's sonatas *für Kenner und Liebhaber*), suites, and fantasies, though very few of these were included in her gift to the Sing-Akademie.[22] This lost portion of Levy's collection may be inferred from works collected by her sister Zippora, who owned the solo keyboard works in the *Konvolut* GB-Lcm Ms. 2000, which includes Sebastian Bach's French suites and Partita in E minor, as well as fugues and fantasies by Friedemann and Philipp Emanuel Bach. Some, but not all, of these works survive in copies with Levy's *ex libris*, suggesting that others may no longer be extant or may never have been marked with her name. Yet the care that Levy took in assembling her collection is evident from the letter that Johanna Maria Bach, widow of Carl Philipp Emanuel Bach, sent to Levy in 1789, which implies that Levy wished to own a complete collection of Philipp Emanuel's music.[23]

The second stage of selection and organization of Levy's collection occurred when she donated the majority of her manuscripts to the Sing-Akademie starting in the mid-1810s. At this point, she held some scores back, whether because she wished to continue using them or because they

21. "Fuge aus dem wohltemperirten Clavier aus dem Nachlaß der Lieblingsschülerinn Friedemann Bachs, der Madame Sarah Levy geb. Itzig zu Berlin. Justus Amadeus Lecerf." Case MS 6A 72, Newberry Library, Chicago.

22. On the place of the *Well-Tempered Clavier* in the Mendelssohn family, see R. Larry Todd, *Mendelssohn Essays* (New York: Routledge, 2008), 118.

23. The letter is transcribed in Wollny, *"Ein förmlicher Sebastian und Philipp Emanuel Bach-Kultus"* (2010), 49–51; see also Wollny, "Sara Levy and the Making of Musical Taste in Berlin," 657.

did not reflect the aesthetic values that she sought to construct and convey in her donated collection. Eventually, the scores that remained outside the Sing-Akademie collection made their way into the hands of Abraham Mendelssohn, August Wilhelm Bach, Justus Amadeus Lecerf, and others.[24]

The collection for the Sing-Akademie—preserved there as a testament to her participation in Berlin's musical life—largely eschews solo keyboard genres, focusing instead on chamber music—sociable music to be made in company. As I noted in chapter 2, some of these scores attest to the specific nature of Levy's salon and her musicianship. Her strong interest in keyboard duets and concertos for two and three keyboards reflects this sociability: these concertos could serve as vehicles for the articulation of her relationship with her sisters in particular, even as they displayed the sisters' impressive technical proficiency as keyboardists.[25] Several solo, double, and triple concertos by the Bach family are known to have been included in Levy's collection and those of her sisters. That Levy is thought to have commissioned the double concerto for harpsichord, fortepiano, and orchestra by C. P. E. Bach (Wq. 47)—his last known composition—attests to this strong interest in music for two keyboards as a vehicle to enact musical sociability through compositions tied by nature to Levy's salon.[26] In addition, it confirms her continuing interest in the harpsichord alongside other keyboard instruments. As late as the 1790s, she corresponded with the Strasbourg workshop of the Silbermann atelier, inquiring about the purchase price of harpsichords, fortepianos, and clavichords.[27] According to Ludwig Rellstab, Levy favored the harpsichord long into the nineteenth century, when most keyboardists had abandoned it as a relic of the past.[28]

The collection of scores that Levy donated to the Sing-Akademie includes copies of no fewer than 77 quartets that would have been suitable for performances in her own salon, as well as the other concerts in which she participated.[29] That Levy's husband was apparently a flutist helps explain why so many of these quartets and other works include prominent

24. Wollny, *"Ein förmlicher Sebastian und Philipp Emanuel Bach-Kultus"* (2010), 37.

25. The meanings of keyboard duos in the collection of Sara Levy are discussed in Rebecca Cypess, "At the Crossroads of Musical Practice and Jewish Identity: Meanings of the Keyboard Duo in the Circle of Sara Levy," in *Sara Levy's World*, 181–204.

26. The manuscript is D-B N. Mus. SA 4.

27. A letter from Johann Friedrich Silbermann to Sara Levy laying out these prices is in Wollny, *"Ein förmlicher Sebastian und Philipp Emanuel Bach-Kultus"* (2010), 53–54.

28. Ludwig Rellstab, *Aus meinem Leben* (s.l.: J. Guttentag, 1861), 1:117.

29. See, for example, the description of "quartet evenings" in Rellstab, *Aus meinem*

flute parts, though quartets including flutes and strings were popular in Berlin.[30] Levy's collection preserved the unique copy of the six quartets by Johann Joachim Quantz (QV 4:8–13),[31] as well as quartets by Christoph Schaffrath, Johann Samuel Schroeter, Carl Heinrich and Johann Gottlieb Graun, and Georg Philipp Telemann. In addition, she is known to have owned the autograph manuscript of two of the late quartets of C. P. E. Bach (Wq. 94–95, fig. 5.3), scored for flute, viola, and obbligato keyboard (the right hand and left hand of the keyboard part each constitute an individual line to form the quartet texture).[32] In fact, it is likely that Levy commissioned these works, and Steven Zohn has presented a reading that views them as reflections of Levy's salon sociability (audio ex. 5.1 ♫).[33] The "Sonatina a quatuor" scored for keyboard, viola, and violin by Johann Schobert, whose title page is shown above in figure 5.2, would seem to provide a precursor for C. P. E. Bach's quartets with obbligato keyboard.[34] In Paris and Amsterdam, where Schobert's opus 7 was first published, this piece would have been understood as a keyboard sonata with accompaniment of two violins and cello. The transcription of the second violin line for viola shown in Levy's manuscript copy is typical of the apparent interest in her circle in the viola as a contrapuntal instrument.

Indeed, Levy's salon performances, which featured participants from her amateur circle as well as professional players, must have boasted more than one extremely skilled violist. Not only would those players have been able to manage the difficult viola parts in C. P. E. Bach's quartets, but they would also have played such works as the duets for two violas by W. F. Bach, Fk. 60–62, of which she owned both the autograph and a manuscript copy. This copy was produced on especially high-quality paper, as directed

---

Leben, 1:117. Rellstab's concerts are also described in Karla Höcker, *Hauskonzerte in Berlin* (Berlin: Rembrandt Verlag, 1970), 13–18.

30. On Levy's husband as a flutist, see Wollny, *"Ein förmlicher Sebastian und Philipp Emanuel Bach-Kultus"* (2010), 25–28. I have discussed manuscripts from Sara Levy's collection that preserve arrangements including flute in Rebecca Cypess, "Arrangement Practices in the Bach Tradition, Then and Now: Historical Precedent for Modern Practice," *Journal of Musicological Research* 39, nos. 2–3 (2020): 187–212.

31. The Quantz quartets are preserved in D-Bsa SA 2930–34. See Mary Oleskiewicz, "Quantz's *Quatuors* and Other Works Newly Discovered," *Early Music* 31, no. 4 (November 2003): 484–504.

32. The manuscript is D-Bsa SA 3328.

33. See Zohn, "The Sociability of Salon Culture."

34. Levy's manuscript copy of the Schobert quartet is preserved in D-Bsa SA 4858.

Figure 5.3 Carl Philipp Emanuel Bach, Quartet for flute, viola, and keyboard in D major, Wq. 95. Autograph manuscript, D-Bsa SA 3328. Image courtesy of Staatsbibliothek zu Berlin—Preußischer Kulturbesitz, Musikabteilung mit Mendelssohn-Archiv, Depositum Archiv der Sing-Akademie zu Berlin, Germany.

in a letter from Levy's husband to their copyist, a Herr Krieger.[35] Her collection also included numerous works by composers who are little known today but whose compositions formed the principal fare of Berlin's musical life; she owned, for example, more than 40 manuscripts of works by Johann Gottlieb Janitsch. String players, flutists, and keyboardists are all called for, variously, in the many solo and trio sonatas with continuo, obbligato duets, and concertos, the last of which would have been accompanied by a small orchestra. (Starting in 1806, the year in which her husband died and Napoleon's armies marched into Berlin, Levy began performing publicly at the Sing-Akademie, playing concertos by members of the Bach family.[36])

Levy's collection favored instrumental music heavily over vocal music, but, as I have shown elsewhere, vocal music was not absent from the collections and musical practices of Sara and her sisters. In at least one case—the *Wechselgesang der Mirjam und Debora* by Justin Heinrich Knecht—there is reason to think that the sisters took an interest in the piece because it was thought of as encapsulating "the true taste of the ancient Hebrew poetry," and the composition as constituting the ideal synthesis of ancient poetry and modern music.[37] And, as I suggested there, it seems possible that the handful of other vocal works in the collection of Levy and her sisters may likewise have held special meaning for the enlightened Jews of Berlin. Conspicuously absent are Johann Sebastian Bach's sacred cantatas, which are firmly entrenched in a traditional Lutheran perspective, and thus do not open themselves to the kinds of enlightened interpretation that would have been facilitated by performance through Levy's hands. While Levy did not eschew sacred Christian music entirely, such works are the exception within her collection.[38]

35. The viola duets are preserved in D-Bsa SA 3912, 3913, 3914, and 3921. Samuel Salomon Levy directed Herr Kriger to write the pieces out "as in the original, Primo and Secondo on a single sheet," using "good white paper; I will gladly pay somewhat more for it" ("so wie im Original, Primo und Secondo auf einem Bogen"; "gutes weißes Papier, ich zahle gerne etwas mehr dafür"). Quoted in Wollny, *"Ein förmlicher Sebastian und Philipp Emanuel Bach-Kultus"* (2010), 39.

36. Kornemann, "Zelter's Archive," 21.

37. See Rebecca Cypess, "Ancient Poetry, Modern Music, and the *Wechselgesang der Mirjam und Debora*: The Meanings of Song in the Itzig Circle," *Bach: Journal of the Riemenschneider Bach Institute* 47, no. 1 (2016): 21–65.

38. On Levy's approach to sacred music, and its implications for Felix Mendelssohn-Bartholdy's revival of the *St. Matthew Passion*, see Naimark-Goldberg, "Remaining Within the Fold."

Levy stamped hundreds of scores with her *ex libris*, but she did this sometimes long after a given score had first entered her collection. Such is the case, it seems, with the manuscript SA 1584, which bears an annotation in the hand of her sister Zippora Wulff in which Sara is called "Sara Itzig mariée pointe" (Sara Itzig, not married at all [i.e. with only a maiden name]),[39] but which was later stamped with the *ex libris* showing Sara's married name. How many scores survive that were once in her possession, but that were never marked with her name? Peter Wollny has suggested that this is true for the manuscript SA 274, the *Konvolut* containing Friedemann Bach's song "Herz, mein Herz, sey ruhig," Fk. 97. Wollny has proposed that Friedemann wrote the song, described in the manuscript as a *cantilena nuptiarum consolatoria*, in honor of Levy's marriage.[40]

The two stages of collection that I am positing here—the first in the initial selection of the music that she wished to own, play, and preserve, and the second in the shaping of a portion of that collection for donation to the Sing-Akademie—were, I propose, undertaken consciously and intentionally. To add her *ex libris* to a score was to take ownership of it, to declare it part of her collection. To donate a score with her name on it to the Sing-Akademie was to render it part of the larger collection there, and to connect herself with it for posterity. While Levy was not alone in her affinity for the kinds of music reflected in her collection, the size of her collection and her apparent desire to connect herself to this music in the long run is remarkable.

Overall, Levy's collection displays what Peter Wollny has characterized as a "conservative-enlightened musical taste."[41] This is especially apparent in her strong interest in music historicism, which led her to collect manuscripts that preserve music from previous generations. Of course, Levy was not alone in her interest in early music during this period; a similar preservationist tendency can be seen, for example, in the collection of the Princess Anna Amalia. Wolff has connected this music historicism to the Concerts of Antient Music in London, though musicians and music collec-

39. See Cypess, "Ancient Poetry, Modern Music, and the *Wechselgesang der Mirjam und Debora*."

40. Wollny, "Sara Levy and the Making of Musical Taste in Berlin," 659; and Wollny, *"Ein förmlicher Sebastian und Philipp Emanuel Bach-Kultus"* (2010), 74. David Schulenberg is more circumspect in connecting the song to Levy; see Schulenberg, *The Music of Wilhelm Friedemann Bach* (Rochester, NY: University of Rochester Press, 2010), 263.

41. See Wollny, "Sara Levy and the Making of Musical Taste in Berlin," 659.

tors in other cities, including Marianna Martines and Baron von Swieten in Vienna, displayed similar tendencies.

If Levy's collection reflects a conservative approach to music, I argue that her conservatism must be understood within the decidedly progressive context of her salon, which enabled her to connect herself to the musical life of the Prussian capital despite her Judaism. Her guests included a wide range of individuals, including Jews and non-Jews. Within this environment, Levy's engagement with music from the Bach family and local composers from the musical past and present carried important implications for the integration of Jews into Prussian society and their inclusion in Prussian culture. An understanding of these implications requires exploration of the debates over the potential of Jews to be musical at all. It is to that context that I now turn.

Polemics on Ancient Hebrew Music and the Music of the "neue Juden"

Numerous thinkers of the Enlightenment wrote about the history of music among the ancient Israelites. Basing their observations on the poetry of the Hebrew Bible, including passages such as the Song at the Sea (Exodus 15), the Song of Deborah (Judges 5), the Song of Solomon, and the book of Psalms as a whole, historians and literary theorists of the latter half of the eighteenth century described the sung poetry of the ancient Hebrews as a pinnacle of artistic creation. Johann Gottfried Herder's *Vom Geist der Ebräischen Poesie* (1782–1783) cast the poetic song of the ancient Israelites as an ideal mode of "natural" expression: "Since Hebrew musick was probably free from the restraints of artificial rules, it could on that account approximate more nearly to the movements of the heart."[42] For Herder, the spirit of the Hebrew Bible was one of idyllic simplicity, primitive yet more expressive than the poetry of his own day. Moreover, music and poetry were perfectly united in the biblical art, and neither dominated the other:

42. "Da die ebräische Musik wahrscheinlich noch ohne ermattende Kunst war, so konnte sie sich desto mehr dem Schwunge des Herzens nähern." Johann Gottfried Herder, *Vom Geist der Ebräischen Poesie: Eine Anleitung für Liebhaber derselben und der ältesten Geschichte des menschlichen Geistes* (Dessau: Buchhandlung der Gelehrten, 1783), 2:27–28. Translated in Herder, *The Spirit of Hebrew Poetry*, trans. J. Marsh (Burlington, VT: Edward Smith, 1833), 2:25–26.

"So soon as musick was invented, poetry acquired a new power, a more graceful movement, and greater harmony of sound."[43]

Although the study of Hebrew letters had long been part of humanist education, the eighteenth century saw a rising interest in the incorporation of Hebraist learning among Christian scholars, and Herder's text is an example of the elevation of the biblical art of poetry within the new field of aesthetics. For many writers of the period, analysis of the ancient Hebrew text had practical ramifications for contemporary artistic creation. Herder celebrated poets who captured the "spirit of Hebrew poetry" by imitating its classical forms and styles. Although, he explained, the German language was not naturally conducive to the pure expression and simple constructions of Hebrew, he praised Friedrich Gottlieb Klopstock, among others, as a latter-day King David, since Klopstock had captured some of the eloquence of the Psalms in his German odes and in his epic *Der Messias*.[44] Herder and other admirers of biblical poetry no doubt understood the ancient Hebrews as proto-Christians, and for that reason, admiration of the ancient art in no way undermined their own adherence to Christianity. Yet for Herder, the artistic value of the Hebrew Bible had implications for Jews in the eighteenth century as well; as he wrote, "Can a nation be called barbarous, that has even a few such national songs?"[45]

Johann Nikolaus Forkel, too, admired the loftiness of the sung poetry of the ancient Hebrews. Yet Forkel's account is a darker one, reflecting the biases that had dominated Lutheran Germany until the age of Enlightenment, and that continued as a prominent theme even after ideals of enlightened tolerance had begun to take shape. Forkel's *Allgemeine Geschichte der Musik* (1788) includes an impressively detailed history of ancient Hebrew music that draws on a wide range of previous scholarship, some written by Jews such as the seventeenth-century Mantuan writer Abraham Ben

43. "Sobald Musik erfunden war, bekam die Poesie neuen Schwung, Gang und Wohllaut." Herder, *Vom Geist der ebräischen Poesie*, 2:25. Translated in Herder, *The Spirit of Hebrew Poetry*, 2:23.

44. Herder, *Vom Geist der ebräischen Poesie*, 2:343. On Justin Heinrich Knecht's setting of Klopstock's *Wechselgesang der Mirjam und Debora*, held in the collection of the Itzig daughters, and its relationship to the aesthetics of the Hebrew Bible, see Cypess, "Ancient Poetry, Modern Music, and the *Wechselgesang der Mirjam und Debora*."

45. "Könnte man ein Volk barbarisch nennen, das nur einige solche Nationalgesänge hatte?" Herder, *Vom Geist der Ebräischen Poesie*, 2:334. Trans. in Herder, *The Spirit of Hebrew Poetry*, 2:2.

David Portaleone (1542–1612), and some by Christians, including Athanasius Kircher, Charles Burney, and many others. At least one of the texts by Jewish writers had not been translated, so Forkel may have read it in the original Hebrew.[46] His discussion treated the poetic structures of biblical song, with special emphasis on the book of Psalms. Indeed, discussion of the Psalms formed the greatest part of Forkel's history of ancient Hebrew music, for he viewed this work, understood to have been composed and assembled during the reign of King David, as the pinnacle of the art of Hebrew poetry. Furthermore, as in the earlier sources that he cited, evidence from the Psalms allowed Forkel to discuss the identity of the instruments used in the ancient world—especially during the reigns of David and of Solomon, who, tradition holds, built the first Temple in Jerusalem, where music was an important part of liturgy and ritual. He wove interpretations by Christian theologians together with sources by Jewish writers from the medieval era to the seventeenth century.

Forkel introduced and concluded his discussion of Hebrew poetry and music with observations on the music of Jews during his own day, and sprinkled references to the *neue Juden* (modern Jews) throughout the text. At the beginning of his chapter, he noted how different ancient music must have been from anything heard in his own lifetime. Citing Herder's work, Forkel explained that "the nature of music is, like the nature of speech, as easily changeable as a breeze. . . . it floats in on a whim and on a whim it flies away."[47] He contrasted the changeable nature of music with the more static nature of the other arts. For example, whereas speech may be preserved through writing, "only music must live, that is, it must sound or it is no music."[48]

Forkel's reasons for starting with these statements were on one level entirely methodological: he needed to establish that the music of the ancient

46. Forkel's discussion of ancient Hebrew music appears in Johann Nikolaus Forkel, *Allgemeine Geschichte der Musik* (Leipzig: im Schwickertschen Verlage, 1788), 1:99–184; the bibliography occupies 174–84. The author whose work had not yet been translated was Shabbethai ben Joseph "Bass" (1641–1718), a singer who had started his career at the Great Synagogue in Prague, later moving throughout Europe; he printed Hebrew books and wrote a supercommentary on the Pentateuch, known in Hebrew as the *Siftei Ḥachamim*.

47. "das Wesen der Tonkunst ist, wie das Wesen der Sprache, ein fein modificirter Hauch, der . . . auf den Lüften schwebt, und auch mit den Lüften vorüber fliegt." Forkel, *Allgemeine Geschichte*, 1:99.

48. "allein die Musik muß leben, das heißt: sie muß klingen, oder sie ist keine Musik." Forkel, *Allgemeine Geschichte*, 1:99.

Hebrews was lost, and that attempts to recover it were therefore speculative and uncertain. Yet, on another level, this portion of his history was not merely academic, but rather polemical: through it, he sought to discredit the music of the Jews in the eighteenth century, and in doing so, to delegitimize Judaism itself. This point is made clear at the end of the chapter, where he connected the loftiness of ancient Hebrew music and poetry to the high spiritual and ethical status of the ancient Jews. Conversely, he cited the *unmusicality* of contemporary Jews, using it as evidence of their immorality and their errant ways. Since the Jews had been dispersed among other nations, they had been unable to preserve their own musical–poetic tradition. Their resulting unmusicality was both a function and a reflection of their spiritual baseness. Mixing his words with those of Claude François Xavier Millot, whose *Élémens d'histoire generale* accused ancient Jews of the most heinous crimes, including human sacrifice, as well as purposeful ignorance of all the arts and sciences,[49] Forkel confirmed that the loss of the Hebrew musical tradition by Jews across the millennia was the fault of the Jews themselves:

> In the end, even the music of the prophets of every nation progresses only hand in hand with the other arts and sciences, as with the culture of customs. Above all, good and pure feelings of the heart are the most fertile soil for it [i.e., music]. But how were the sciences, arts (excluding poetry), traditions, and feelings of the Hebrews obtained? General opinion sees them as ignorant. All strangers, their languages, arts, sciences, and so forth, were for them [the Jews] objects of contempt or detestation. . . . Our holy books give us many examples of their inhuman barbarism; no less of their affinity for superstition and for unfaithfulness to God, who overwhelms them constantly with benefactions. In short, even with the direct guidance of Heaven the culture of this people remained in every respect so far behind that it has hardly earned the right to be counted among the number of cultivated nations.[50]

49. See Claude François Xavier Millot, *Élémens d'histoire generale* (Paris: Durand, 1778), 1:152–60.

50. "Endlich ist auch die Musik von jeher bey allen Nationen nur mit andern Künsten und Wissenschaften, so wie mit der Kultur der Sitten, Hand in Hand vorwärts gegangen. Vorzüglich sind gute und reine Empfindungen des Herzens der fruchtbarste Boden für sie. Aber wie waren die Wissenschaften, Künste, (Poesie abgerechnet) Sitten und Empfindungen der Hebräer beschaffen? Ein fast allgemeines Urtheil erklärt sie für unwissend. Alle Fremde, ihre Sprache, Künste, Wissenschaften, u. s. f. waren für sie Gegenstände der

In Forkel's view, consistent with widespread understandings across the Christian world, while the ancient Hebrews were of a high ethical standing, their place in modern times had been supplanted by Christians, who followed the true calling of God. The alleged ignorance of the Jews in music, and in every other art and science, was a result of the Jews' own contempt for other nations—a circumstance that they brought upon themselves. It was unlikely that their traditions could ever be rehabilitated, for they were "without sciences, without customs, without fine feelings of the heart, without good instruments, without a singable language, without an art of musical notation [*Schreibekunst*]."[51]

Forkel's history of Hebrew music was not the first in the Western tradition to assert that contemporary Jews were inherently unmusical. As Ruth HaCohen has shown, European music history is littered with examples of a "music libel against the Jews," which held that while Christianity produced music that was beautiful and spiritually edifying, Jews were capable of nothing but noise.[52] Indeed, while Forkel acknowledged that there were some "Virtuosen" in the tradition of synagogue music, these were "rare." In general, "in the synagogue itself, modern Jewish music is nothing but either a musical prayer, which is more or less growled or muttered in a few tones, or (when a chorus joins in) a frightful shouting."[53]

The educated Jews of Prussia were doubtless aware of these characterizations of synagogue music. They were also aware that they lacked a unified national or religious music that could be compared with the Christian church traditions. In German and in Hebrew, Jewish writers lamented the loss of their ancient music. Moses Mendelssohn's German translation of the

---

Verachtung oder der Verabscheuung. . . . Von ihrer unmenschlichen Grausamkeit werden uns in den heil. Büchern eine Menge Beyspiele erzählt; nicht weniger von ihrer Neigung zum Aberglauben und zur Untreue gegen Gott, der sie ununterbrochen mit Wohlthaten überhäufte. Kurz, selbst mit dem unmittelbaren Unterrichte des Himmels blieb die Kultur dieses Volks in jeder Rücksicht doch so weit zurück, daß es kaum unter die Zahl der kultivirten Nationen gerechnet zu werden verdiente." Forkel, *Allgemeine Geschichte*, 1:172. My thanks to Douglas Johnson for his assistance with this translation.

51. "ohne Wissenschaften, ohne Sitten, ohne feine Gefühle des Herzens, ohne gute Instrumente, ohne eine singbare Sprache, ohne eine musikalische Schreibekunst." Forkel, *Allgemeine Geschichte*, 1:172.

52. HaCohen, *The Music Libel Against the Jews*.

53. "In den Synagogen selbst ist die heutige jüdische Musik nichts, als entweder ein musikalisches Beten, welches in einerley Ton gleichsam gebrummt oder gemurmelt wird, oder (wenn der Chor einfälle) ein fürchterliches Geschrey." Forkel, *Allgemeine Geschichte*, 1:162.

Psalms, published in 1783, attempted to minimize the gap between the Jewish and Christian traditions of sung poetry. The work, intended for both Jewish and non-Jewish readers, presented the Psalms in a new guise—"as a great work of lyric religious poetry that could inspire both Jews and Christians rather than as a repository of Christian or Jewish messianic predictions."[54] Indeed, in the text of his dedication to the poet Karl Wilhelm Ramler, Mendelssohn placed the project of his Psalm translations within the context of his famous friendship with the Christian writer Gotthold Ephraim Lessing—a friendship that epitomized and exemplified the promise of enlightened tolerance.[55] Mendelssohn's translation departed from both Jewish and Lutheran traditions, but it did so by reaching into their common history. In its multiconfessional aims, it sought to reclaim the Psalms as an aesthetic space available to both religions, and one that could bridge the gap between them.[56]

The potential of the Psalms to unite Christians and Jews was tested by Johann Philipp Kirnberger, with whom Mendelssohn studied music and who attempted to put Mendelssohn's aesthetic theories into practice.[57] Kirnberger's settings of some of Mendelssohn's Psalm translations attested to the interest among a small group of Christian artists and aestheticians in

54. Michah Gottlieb, prefatory note to the Psalm translations, in Moses Mendelssohn, *Writings on Judaism, Christianity, and the Bible*, ed. Michah Gottlieb, trans. Curtis Bowman, Elias Sacks, and Allan Arkush (Waltham, MA: Brandeis University Press, 2011), 182.

55. Mendelssohn's German translations of the Psalms are in Mendelssohn, *Die Psalmen*, in *Gesammelte Schriften: Jubiläumsausgabe* (hereafter *JubA*), ed. Fritz Bamberger et al., 24 vols. (Stuttgart-Bad Canstatt: Frommann, 1971), 10.1. Further on the Psalm translations, see David Sorkin, *Moses Mendelssohn and the Religious Enlightenment* (London: Peter Halban, 2012), ch. 5, "Psalms." On Mendelssohn's friendship with Lessing, see Alexander Altmann, *Moses Mendelssohn: A Biographical Study* (Tuscaloosa: University of Alabama Press, 1973), 36–50, 66–71, 553–81, and passim. On the persistence of anti-Judaism even in the thought of Lessing, see Martha Helfer, *The Word Unheard: Legacies of Anti-Semitism in German Literature and Culture* (Evanston, IL: Northwestern University Press, 2011), ch. 1, "Lessing the Limits of Enlightenment."

56. On the role of Psalms in Mendelssohn's thought, see Yael Sela, "The Voice of the Psalmist: On the Performative Role of Psalms in Moses Mendelssohn's *Jerusalem*," in *Psalms In/On Jerusalem*, ed. Ilana Pardes and Ophir Münz-Manor (Berlin: De Gruyter, 2019), 109–34; and Yael Sela, "Songs of the Nation: The Book of Psalms in Late Eighteenth-Century Jewish Enlightenment," *Musical Quarterly* 101, no. 4 (winter 2018): 331–62.

57. See the account in Laurenz Lütteken, "Zwischen Ohr und Verstand: Moses Mendelssohn, Johann Philipp Kirnberger und die Begründung des 'reinen Satzes' in der Musik," in *Musik und Ästhetik im Berlin Moses Mendelssohns*, ed. Anselm Gerhard (Tübingen: Max Niemeyer Verlag, 1999), 135–63.

Mendelssohn's project. As Yael Sela writes, Mendelssohn's translations were "non-literal, emphasizing the significance of aesthetic and oral qualities of Hebrew Scripture to the meaning of its content."[58] As Sela further notes, Mendelssohn located the original aesthetic power of the Psalms in their musical origins. In his commentary on the English theologian Robert Lowth's *Lectures on the Sacred Poetry of the Hebrews*, Mendelssohn explained that the Psalms, created in the days of King David, had since been "robbed of their most noble adornment, since we have not the slightest clue about their instruments or their music."[59] Kirnberger's musical settings of Mendelssohn's Psalm translations thus presented ancient poetry in a modern guise—one designed to preserve its aesthetic essence. That these Psalm settings could be performed in a secular or cross-confessional context—including a domestic context or a salon—is suggested by the inclusion of Kirnberger's setting of Mendelssohn's translation of Psalm 137 in his *Oden mit Melodien*, published in 1773, even before Mendelssohn's Psalm translations had appeared in print.[60] This collection, which sought to perfect the art of text setting in music, was directed primarily at an audience of *Liebhabern*. In Kirnberger's collection, Mendelssohn's Psalm translation stands alongside strophic poetry in German and Greek as an example of a "pure" ancient art that could be renewed through modern musical practice.

In his Hebrew writings, too, Mendelssohn was explicit about the loss of a Jewish musical heritage. In his commentary on the Pentateuch, published as *Sefer netivot ha-shalom* ("Book of the Paths of Peace") but commonly known as the *Bi'ur* ("Explanation") (1780–1782),[61] Mendelssohn admitted

58. Sela, "The Voice of the Psalmist," 115. Two recorded examples of Kirnberger's settings of Mendelssohn's Psalm translations are "An den Flüssen Babylons," in Vocal Concert Dresden, directed by Peter Kopp, *Bachs Schüler: Motetten* (Carus 83.263 © 2008); and "Erbarm dich, unser Gott," in Rheinische Kantorei, directed by Hermann Max, *Johann Hermann Schein: Fontana d'Israel, "Israelis Brünnlein 1623"* (Capriccio 10 290/91 © 1990).

59. "sie sind ihres vornehmsten Schmuckes beraubt, weil wir weder von ihren Instrumenten noch von ihrer Musik die geringste Kenntniß haben." Moses Mendelssohn, "Robert Lowth: *De sacra poesi hebrauorum*. Oxford 1753: Rezension," *Bibliothek der schönen Wissenschaften und der freyen Künste* 1, no. 2 (1757): 277. Translated in Sela, "The Voice of the Psalmist," 115–16.

60. Johann Philipp Kirnberger, *Oden mit Melodien* (Danzig: Jobst Herrmann Flörcke, 1773).

61. On the significance of Mendelssohn's Pentateuch translation as the first German-language translation of the Hebrew Bible, see Abigail E. Gillman, "Between Religion and Culture: Mendelssohn, Buber, Rosenzweig and the Enterprise of Biblical Translation," in *Biblical Translation in Context*, ed. Frederick W. Knobloch (Bethesda: University Press of

that "we have lost this ancient musical science, and no remnant of the musical art used by our ancestors remains."[62] His introduction to Exodus 15, the Song at the Sea, includes a lengthy explanation of the poetics of the Hebrew Bible, but it, too, acknowledges that, with the passage of time and the geographical dispersion of the Jewish people, the oral traditions of the text—including its music—were lost. Still, he claimed, "there nevertheless remains in our sacred poetry much sweetness that is sensed by every wise reader, even if he does not grasp its cause. This sweetness is not merely auditory sweetness, which is intimately connected to the language in which a poem is composed. . . . Rather, it is the sweetness of the content, which is connected to the meaning and intention of the statement."[63] In fact, the aesthetic power of biblical poetry even in the absence of music provided Mendelssohn with a justification for translation of the text out of its original Hebrew. Just as the text alone, without its musical recitation, retained that original "sweetness of content," a translation into German would do the same. Although the poetry's "flavor is weakened and its fragrance made bitter by the translation, there nevertheless remains the sweetness of the content that we have mentioned."[64]

Mendelssohn's earlier writings on aesthetics indicate that, like other (non-Jewish) writers of the Enlightenment, he understood music, together with the other fine arts, as capable of shaping the ethical understanding

Maryland, 2002), 93–114; and Sorkin, *Moses Mendelssohn and the Religious Enlightenment*, ch. 6, "The Pentateuch."

62. "אבדנו חכמת המוזיקא הקדומה, ולא נשאר לנו שריד מכל מלאכת הנגון, אשר השתמשו בה קדמונינו." Mendelssohn, *Sefer netivot ha-shalom* [*Bi'ur*], in *JubA* 16:126. Trans. in Mendelssohn, *Writings on Judaism, Christianity, and the Bible*, 214. This narrative of communal loss of a musical culture had been articulated by Jewish writers such as Don Isaac Abravanel, *Perush Abravanel 'al ha-Torah* [Abravanel's commentary on the Torah] (Jerusalem: Ḥoreb, 5757 [=1996–1997]), 2:212. Abravanel's discussion of poetry is likewise placed in his commentary on the Hebrew Bible just before Exodus 15. For further references, see Rebecca Cypess and Lynette Bowring, "Orality and Literacy in the Worlds of Salamone Rossi," in *Music and Jewish Culture in Early Modern Italy: New Perspectives*, ed. Lynette Bowring, Rebecca Cypess, and Liza Malamut (Bloomington: Indiana University Press, 2022), 197–232.

63. "מכל מקום נשאר עריבות רב בשירי הקודש, נרגש לכל קורא משכיל אף אם לא ידע סבתו, והעריבות ההוא אינו עריבת אוזן בלבד, הדבק ונצמד בלשון אשר בו הוסד . . . כי אם עריבת ענין, דבק במובן וכוונת המאמר." Mendelssohn, *Sefer netivot ha-shalom* [*Bi'ur*], in *JubA* 16:126. Trans. in Moses Mendelssohn, *Writings on Judaism, Christianity, and the Bible*, 214–15.

64. "אף אם יפג טעמם הרב וימר ריחם ע"י ההעתקה, מכל מקום ישאר להם העריבות העינייני שזכרנו." Mendelssohn, *Sefer netivot ha-shalom* [*Bi'ur*], in *JubA* 16:127. Trans. in Mendelssohn, *Writings on Judaism, Christianity, and the Bible*, 215.

and behavior of the listener: "Through different senses, poetry, rhetoric, beauties in shapes and sounds pervade our soul and dominate all its inclinations."[65] Yet he cautioned that Jews should not think the music they heard around them was anything like the music of the ancient Hebrew poets and instrumentalists:

> On account of our great suffering and dislocation, all of this wondrous science . . . has been lost from us, including the art and form of these instruments, the system of voices, the modes of playing, and the pleasantness of the music. Nothing remains for us except the names of the instruments and songs, which in most cases are mentioned in the book of Psalms by the sweet singer of Israel [King David]. Yet we know that this science was widely disseminated within the nation, and that the great men, sages, and prophets of the nation were experts in poetry, excellent performers of music, and exceedingly learned in this science. . . . Do not liken the musical art [*muzika*] that we possess today to the glorious science that these perfect individuals used, since it appears that there is absolutely no resemblance between the two.[66]

It is significant that Mendelssohn attributed the loss of the science of music among the Jews to their "suffering and dislocation." This narrative pervaded the discourse of *Haskalah* writers and their Christian allies in the causes of Enlightenment and emancipation, and it stood in sharp contrast to the narrative of moral degeneracy adopted by Forkel and others. For Men-

65. "Die Dichtkunst, die Beredsamkeit, die Schönheiten in Figuren und in Tönen dringen durch verschiedene Sinne zu unserer Seele, und beherrschen alle ihre Neigungen." Moses Mendelssohn, "Ueber die Hauptgrundsätze der schönen Künste und Wissenschaften," in *JubA* 1:428. Trans. in Mendelssohn, "On the Main Principles of the Fine Arts and Sciences," in *Philosophical Writings*, trans. and ed. Daniel O. Dahlstrom (Cambridge: Cambridge University Press, 1997), 169–70.

66. "והנגונים נשכחו ממנו באורך הגלות, ומרוב העוני והטלטול אבדה ממנו כל החכמה הנפלאה ההיא, מלאכת הכלי' ותבניתם, מערכת הקולות ואופני הנגון ונעימות הזמירה אשר השתבחו בה גדולי עמנו , ולא נשאר לנו כ"א שמות הכלים והשירי' לבד, הנזכרים על הרוב בספר תהלות נעים זמירות ישראל. ואולם ידענו שהיתה החכמה ההיא מפורסמת באומה, וגדולי העם וחכמיו ונביאיו היו יודעי שיר מטיבי נגן ובקיאי' מאוד בחכמה ההיא. . . . ואל תדמה בנפשך מלאכת המוזיק' המצוי' בידינו היום אל החכמה המפוארה אשר השתמשו בה השלמי' ההם, כי הנראה שאין דמיון ביניהם כלל."
Mendelssohn, *Sefer netivot ha-shalom* [*Bi'ur*], in *JubA* 16:126. Trans. in Mendelssohn, *Writings on Judaism, Christianity, and the Bible*, 213.

delssohn, the musical disarray and the loss of musical history of the Jewish community was a result of the oppressive regimes that had kept them shrouded in darkness. Logically, then, a regeneration of music among the Jews required both a lifting of oppression by means of emancipation and an intellectual awakening among the Jews themselves.

The place of music in the budding Jewish Enlightenment was at first uncertain, as Yael Sela has noted.[67] The program of enlightenment that Mendelssohn's collaborator, Naphtali Herz (Hartwig) Wessely, presented in his *Divrei Shalom Ve-'Emet* (Words of Peace and Truth, 1782) did not mention music. It was in the letter of endorsement provided for Wessely's work by a group of Venetian rabbis that music was first advocated as a component of the Jewish Enlightenment. These rabbis strongly favored the involvement of Jews in all fields of inquiry, including *muzika* (music), a category that encompassed both the sung poetry (*shira*) of the Hebrew Bible and the art of instrumental performance. Both, they argued, could be fruitfully revived, along with all other fields of inquiry, among an enlightened, emancipated Jewish population in the diaspora. They cited a long list of stories and characters from the Hebrew Bible that attest to the importance of music for Jewish worship and tradition, on the basis of which they asked, "why should a person who wishes to learn [music] be chastised, after he has filled his stomach with meat and wine, which are the written Torah and the oral Torah? And if he has inclination to learn it, why should he not occupy himself with it? For also today there is a need for this science."[68] Yet Wessely's silence on the matter betrays his own ambivalence or indifference about use of "the arts for the sake of aesthetic pleasure," as advocated by Mendelssohn.[69] Although Wessely's treatise emphasized the need to revive the science of music in the context of Jewish worship, his nephew Bernhard Wessely epitomized, at least temporarily, professional Jewish engagement with music outside the synagogue. Before Bernhard's conversion to Christianity, his cantata commemorating

67. Sela, "Songs of the Nation," 333–34.

68. "למה יגונה מי שהוא חפץ ללמוד אותה, אחר שימלא כרסו בשר ויין, זו תורה שבכתב, ותורה שבעל פה, ויהיה לו הכנה ללמדה, למה לא יתעסק בה? וכי גם בזמן הזה איכא מצטרכת החכמה הזאת?" Naphtali Herz Wessely, ed., *Divrei shalom ve-emet* (Berlin: Ḥevrat Ḥinuch Ne'arim, 1782), 3:29.

69. Yael Sela-Teichler, "Music, Acculturation, and Haskalah Between Berlin and Königsberg in the 1780s," *Jewish Quarterly Review* 103, no. 3 (2013): 376.

the death of Moses Mendelssohn in 1786 was celebrated by enlightened Jews and Christians alike.[70]

If Naphtali Herz Wessely equivocated about the need to incorporate music into contemporary Jewish learning, Mendelssohn's lament for the lost art of *muzika* underlies a remarkable Hebrew-language publication that appeared in five volumes between 1785 and 1791, and that engaged directly with Forkel's history of ancient Hebrew music in the *Allgemeine Geschichte der Musik*. Intended for a Jewish readership, this collection, entitled *Sefer zemirot Yisra'el* (Book of the Songs of Israel), included the text of the original Hebrew Psalms alongside Mendelssohn's German translation. However, like Mendelssohn's translation of the Pentateuch, the *Zemirot Yisra'el* printed the German text in Hebrew characters, thus endowing the work with a sense of traditionalism despite its radical departure from Jewish tradition, which had resisted translation to the vernacular until Mendelssohn's lifetime.[71]

The introduction to the *Sefer zemirot Yisra'el*, which appeared in the volume of 1791, was written by one of Mendelssohn's disciples and followers in the *Haskalah* movement, Joel Bril Löwe. Bril's contribution dealt first with biblical poetics (*melitza*), emphasizing the manifestation of poetic principles in the book of Psalms.[72] He described linguistic devices and constructions that had already been observed by Christian Hebraists such as Herder, as well as in the German-language writings of Mendelssohn.[73]

70. Sela-Teichler, "Music, Acculturation, and Haskalah," 352–84; and David Conway, *Jewry in Music: Entry to the Profession from the Enlightenment to Richard Wagner* (Cambridge: Cambridge University Press, 2012), 148–49.

71. On a similar choice in the print layout of the *Bi'ur*, see Gillman, "Between Religion and Culture," 100–104.

72. Mendelssohn is listed on the title page as an author of the *Sefer zemirot Yisra'el*, along with Bril. See *Sefer zemirot Yisra'el: hu sefer Tehilim 'im targum Ashkenazi me-ha-rav Rabenu Moshe Ben Menaḥem* [Book of the Songs of Israel: That is, Book of Psalms with a German Translation by the rabbi, our teacher Moses son of Menaḥem] (Berlin: Shoḥarei ha-tov veha-tushiyah, 1791), ed. with introduction by Joel Bril Löwe. An extended discussion of this volume is in Sela, "Songs of the Nation."

73. Mendelssohn's review of the *Praelectiones academicae de sacra poesi Hebraeorum* (1753) by Robert Lowth synthesized many of the issues in biblical poetics, and it allowed Mendelssohn to articulate his deviation from Lowth and other Christian writers based on Mendelssohn's own Jewish identity and adherence to Jewish tradition. See Moses Mendelssohn, review of *Robert Lowths akademische Vorlesungen von der heiligen Dichtkunst der Hebräer; nebst einer kurtzen Widerlegung des harianischen Systems von der Prosodie der Hebräer*, in *Bibliothek der schönen Wissenschaften und der freyen Künste* 1, no. 1 (1757): 122–55, and no. 2

And, like Herder, Mendelssohn, Robert Lowth, and numerous other writers of the period, Bril identified the pinnacle of the biblical art in its union of poetry and music. In Bril's words, "When these two sciences are joined together—poetics and music—each one strengthens the other . . . and from this is born the most pleasant category of poetics, that is *shir*, or what is known in the vernacular as lyric poetry [*lirische poesie*]."[74]

In the second section, however, Bril presented a history of ancient Hebrew music proper, considered as a separate subject from poetic text. Given the importance of Forkel's *Allgemeine Geschichte* for the music-historical narrative of the *Aufklärung*, it comes as no surprise that Forkel's is one of two German sources that Bril cited at the outset of his essay. The other was August Friedrich Pfeiffer's *Ueber die Musik der alten Hebraër* (1779), which served as the basis for Bril's illustrations of the instruments used by the ancient Israelites;[75] indeed, a discussion of the identity of the biblical instruments dominates this portion of the *Sefer ẓemirot Yisra'el*. Bril began his history of music with Jubal (Genesis 4) and proceeded through the destruction of the Temple.[76] Like Herder and other Christian writers, he identified the art of King David, to whom most of the Psalms are ascribed, as the most accomplished musician in the Jewish tradition. Like Mendelssohn, Bril acknowledged that the greatest music of the Jews had been lost to time. Yet he argued that it would be worthwhile to attempt to reconstruct the history of the art as much as possible: "Still, it is proper to investigate even these

---

(1757): 269–97. See also Cypess, "Ancient Poetry, Modern Music, and the *Wechselgesang der Mirjam und Debora*."

74. "כאשר יצטרפו שתי אלה החכמות יחד, המליצה והנגון, יחזקו זו את זו. . . . ומזה יולד החלק היותר נעים שבמליצה, זהו השיר, המכונה בל"ז (לירישי פאעזיא)."

Bril, introduction to *Sefer ẓemirot Yisra'el*, 8b–9a. On the history and significance of the *Sefer ẓemirot Yisra'el*, see Sela, "Songs of the Nation"; and Natalie Naimark-Goldberg, "Entrepreneurs in the Library of the Haskalah: Editors and the Production of Maskilic Books" (Hebrew), in *The Library of the Haskalah: The Creation of a Modern Republic of Letters in Jewish Society in the German-Speaking Sphere*, ed. Shmuel Feiner, Zohar Shavit, Natalie Naimark-Goldberg, and Tal Kogman (Tel Aviv: Am Oved Publishers, Ltd., 2014), 112–16.

75. While Naimark-Goldberg is correct that the presentation of these illustrations is similar to that of Daniel Chodowiecki in Bernard Basedow's *Elementarwerk* (Dessau: Crusius, 1774), Bril's images closely resemble Pfeiffer's. See Naimark-Goldberg, "Entrepreneurs in the Library of the Haskalah," 112–16.

76. Tracing the origins of music to the biblical figure of Jubal was common in works of this era; compare, for example, Leopold Mozart, *Versuch einer gründlichen Violinschule* (Augsburg: Johann Jacob Lotter, 1756), 11.

few words that are before us, and to seek as far as we can in these matters, for even from this little bit will emerge a great reward in the understanding of some Scripture."[77]

Sara Levy and the Cultural Work of Collecting and Performing

If the topic of scholarship on ancient Hebrew music seems far from my starting point—the collection of music assembled by Sara Levy and her salon performances—the *Sefer zemirot Yisra'el* brings my discussion full circle. For among the long list of names printed in the subscription list of Bril's Hebrew edition of Mendelssohn's Psalm translations is that of Sara Levy. As Natalie Naimark-Goldberg has shown, the presence of Levy's name on this list should be understood within the context of her extensive philanthropy in the Jewish community of Berlin, and especially her active support for and intellectual engagement with the *Haskalah* movement, which exceeded that of other women in her circle. Although it is unclear whether Levy read Hebrew, she must have been aware of the contents of the *Sefer zemirot Yisra'el*, along with the other Hebrew-language books that she supported. Whether through the text itself or through the discussions with *maskilim* (adherents of the *Haskalah* movement) and other Jewish intellectuals whom she hosted in her home, she was surely aware of the aims and purposes of the quest for Jewish Enlightenment, as well as this music-historical project in particular.[78]

Among the goals of the *Haskalah* was the recovery and conceptualization of Jewish history. Indeed, Shmuel Feiner has located in the maskilic texts a concerted effort to legitimize academic history and introduce a historical consciousness into Jewish discourse, and Elias Sacks has argued that Mendelssohn's framing of contemporary Jewish practice relies upon this historical consciousness.[79] Whereas Jewish writers in the preceding thou-

77. "מכל מקום ראוי להתבונן גם במעט הדברים האלה אשר לפנינו, ולחקור כפי אשר תשיג ידנו בענינים האלה, כי גם מזה המעט יצא לנו תועלת רבה בהבנת כמה כתובים."
Bril, introduction to *Sefer zemirot Yisra'el*, 14b.

78. See Naimark-Goldberg, "Remaining Within the Fold." On the reading habits of women in Levy's circle, see Naimark-Goldberg, *Jewish Women in Enlightenment Berlin*, 64–101. One example of a *maskil* who socialized with Sara Levy was Solomon Maimon; see Sabattia Joseph Wolff, *Maimoniana: oder Rhapsodien zur Charakteristik Salomon Maimon's aus seinem Privatleben gesammelt* (Berlin: G. Hayn, 1813), 108–13 and passim.

79. See Shmuel Feiner, *Haskalah and History: The Emergence of a Modern Jewish Historical Consciousness*, trans. Chaya Naor and Sondra Silverston (Oxford and Portland, OR: Littman Library of Jewish Civilization, 2002), 1–70; and Elias Sacks, *Moses Mendelssohn's*

sand years or more had viewed the field of history predominantly as an instrument of theology, designed to connect Jews to their ancient forebears and traditions, the *maskilim* sought to understand Jewish history, alongside the general history of humanity, for its own sake. The history of music presented in Bril's introduction to the *Sefer zemirot Yisra'el* should be understood in this context: written in Hebrew, engaging both Jewish and Christian sources, but carefully distinguishing itself from the polemics and *a posteriori* justifications of the Christian discourse on music, Bril's introduction to the Psalms represents an important step in Jewish efforts to reclaim their own musical history.

The maskilic historical consciousness did not manifest itself only in written treatises and histories like Bril's. Mendelssohn's German Psalm translations of 1783 display a similarly strong historical consciousness, and they update the ancient poetry of the Psalms for the modern day. In this work, as noted above, Mendelssohn reached into the history of both Christianity and Judaism for his source material, reframing it for the aesthetic, ethical, and spiritual needs of his own generation. In loosening the Psalms from a distinct religious context—whether Christian or Jewish—Mendelssohn presented a sacred text valued by both groups in a new and neutral guise. He described his emotional reactions to the Psalm translations as aesthetic works in a letter to his friend Sophie Becker in 1785. The Psalms had, he wrote, "sweetened many a bitter hour for me, and I pray and sing as often as I feel the need in me to pray and sing." Moreover, the Psalms were not merely for prayer to God; instead, they were the spontaneous eruptions of a soul that needed to sing:

> The most common person, it seems to me, does not sing so that God hears him and finds pleasure in his melodies. We sing for our own sake, and this does as much good for the wise man as it does for the fool. Have you ever read the Psalms with this purpose? It seems to me that many Psalms are of such a type that they must be sung with true edification by the most enlightened people [*sie von den aufgeklärtesten Menschen mit wahrer Erbauung gesungen werden müssen*]. I would once again recommend to you my translation of the Psalms, if this would not betray too much of the frailty of an author.[80]

Living Script: Philosophy, Practice, History, Judaism (Bloomington: Indiana University Press, 2017).

80. "Der gemeinste Mensch, dünkt mich, singt nicht, daß Gott ihn höre und an seinen Melodien Gefallen finde. Wir singen unserthalben; und das thut der Weise so gut als der

It is significant that Mendelssohn did not merely advocate reading his Psalm translations silently. Instead, he explained that they need to be *sung aloud*.[81] This idea is very much in keeping with Mendelssohn's claim that the Bible should be sung using the traditional Jewish cantillation system; as Elias Sacks has noted, in Mendelssohn's view, this act of singing aloud helps impress the meanings of the words on both the singer and the listener.[82] Moreover, the experience of the Psalms as a performed work of art was not limited to either Jews or Christians; instead, the Psalms were available to all "the most enlightened people." As noted above, Mendelssohn made this point clear when he dedicated his translation to Ramler and discussed his friendship with Lessing in the text of the dedication. Reaching into their common history, Mendelssohn offered his friends and readers a work of poetry that would both fulfill a spiritual need and create a bridge between them. It was through this experience of a historical artwork, read in a modern, cross-confessional translation and shared through sounding performance, that such a bridge could be forged.

If sounding performances of Mendelssohn's Psalm translations had the power to reclaim biblical poetry as a neutral aesthetic space available to both Christians and Jews, then Sara Levy's acts of "musicking"—especially her creation of a collection and her salon performances—may be understood as having a similar force. Both Mendelssohn and Levy engaged with what Diana Taylor has called the "archive" and the "repertoire"—that is, written culture and performance—both of which, as Taylor argues, carry the potential to create meaning.

Taylor's theory of the archive and the repertoire is rooted in the tensions at play in Latin America, where the written culture of colonial settlers served to supplant the practices of indigenous peoples, which transmitted knowledge through oral culture and embodied performance. In some respects, this case seems incongruous with Levy's; after all, Levy was a literate musician as well as a performer, and she had the financial means to curate a collection of scores, along with the instruments and personnel needed to use them in

---

Thor. Haben Sie je die Psalmen in dieser Absicht gelesen? Mich dünkt, viele Psalmen sind von der Art, daß sie von den aufgeklärtesten Menschen mit wahrer Erbauung gesungen werden müssen. Ich würde Ihnen abermals meine Uebersetzung der Psalmen vorschlagen, wenn es nicht zu viel Autorschwachheit verriethe." Moses Mendelssohn to Sophie Becker, December 27, 1785, in *JubA*, 13:334. Cited and translated in Elias Sacks, "Poetry, Music, and the Limits of Harmony: Mendelssohn's Aesthetic Critique of Christianity," in *Sara Levy's World*, 122.

81. See Sela, "The Voice of the Psalmist."

82. Sacks, "Poetry, Music, and the Limits of Harmony."

performance within the elite institution of the salon. And yet, recall Forkel's argumentation about the unmusicality of Jews: one of his proofs for the inferiority of Jews in music was their lack of a "musikalische Schreibekunst."[83] Levy's collection, then, may be seen as undermining this claim and demonstrating that Jews could indeed participate in a literate musical culture. Through her collection, Levy inserted herself into the tradition of the archive, drawing on her wealth, her education, and her family's connections, though the latter were attenuated by their Jewish faith. In forming her collection, Levy was not just the passive recipient of an objective musical culture, but a mediator; in Taylor's words, "What makes an object archival is the process whereby it is selected, classified, and presented for analysis."[84]

In Levy's case, this process of selection, classification, and presentation involved stamping most of her collection with her distinctive *ex libris*. Although she was not a composer *per se*, the assembly of a collection may be understood as a creative act in its own right—perhaps even an act of "authorship." By collecting these manuscripts and marking them with her *ex libris*, Levy asserted her place in the tradition of German music—indeed, as a "grand-student" of Johann Sebastian Bach and, through patronage of his sons, an innovator in his tradition. By reviving the sounds of music from the Bach family and the Prussian tradition through her own performances, Levy had the capacity to remake them as part of her own musical inheritance, and to make them accessible to her listeners.

This point leads to consideration of the implications of Taylor's theory of performance, which is especially fruitful in light of the enlightened, cosmopolitan environment of Levy's salon, in which Jews and non-Jews mixed and socialized over music. Taylor's understanding of what she calls the "repertoire"—the embodied acts of performance that transmit knowledge and help create identity—foregrounds performance as a site of meaning. In Taylor's words:

> The repertoire . . . enacts embodied memory: performances, gestures, orality, movement, dance, singing—in short, all those acts usually thought of as ephemeral, nonreproducible knowledge. Repertoire . . . allows for individual agency. . . . The repertoire requires presence: people participate in the production and reproduction of knowledge by "being there."[85]

83. Forkel, *Allgemeine Geschichte*, 1:178; see note 51 above.
84. Taylor, *The Archive and the Repertoire*, 19.
85. Taylor, *The Archive and the Repertoire*, 20.

While recognizing, again, that the social situation of Levy's salon was quite different from that of Taylor's subjects, the lessons that she proposes—especially about the capacity of performance to create and transmit meaning—can be productively applied to Levy's situation. Within the environment of her salon, Levy's performances had the capacity to reinterpret the music she played. Rather than seeing her merely as a receptacle—as a vehicle for the transmission of notated musical scores—we should understand her as an agent capable of spreading new understandings of older music. Indeed, while the music that she played and collected was not composed by Jews, her acts of playing and collecting these works rendered them part of Jewish life and Jewish history.

How can we envision such a transformation taking place? As noted above, past writers have observed two apparently contradictory cultural tendencies in Levy's world. On one hand is Wollny's description of Levy's musical tastes as displaying a "conservative-enlightened" approach.[86] Indeed, if one considers the music on its own terms, divorced from Levy's performances and their social context, this assessment seems accurate, and it is exemplified most obviously by the strong interest in music from the past that her collection displays. By contrast, however, the social implications of the salons that she and other Jewish women held in their homes were decidedly progressive. Levy's salon involved a heterogeneous group, including Jews and Christians, men and women, philosophers and socialites, artists, scientists, diplomats, and intellectuals. Jews and non-Jews gathered to share cultural experiences, to discuss literature and the sciences, to read poetry, to hear music. That Jewish women were figureheads and hostesses at these gatherings attests to the significance of the salons in loosening earlier social hierarchies. Ruth Dawson has emphasized women's "cultural roles," rather than merely their scholarly production (or perceived paucity thereof), as vehicles for their participation in the Enlightenment, and the salon gatherings hosted by Levy and her peers exemplify these alternative modes of engagement with the social and intellectual trends of the era.[87] While it would be unwise to over-idealize the social harmony that the Berlin Jewish salons seem to imply, there can be no doubt as to the general progressiveness of their agendas.

When considered within this social context or the equally heterogeneous performances that Levy gave at the Sing-Akademie, the apparently

86. See Wollny, "Sara Levy and the Making of Musical Taste in Berlin," 659.

87. Dawson, "'Lights Out! Lights Out!,'" 236–38.

conservative music that she favored takes on a new aspect. In performing music, Levy may indeed have retained most of the notes on the page, perhaps reviving the works as they were heard in the lifetime of Quantz or Sebastian Bach, or in the heyday of musical life at the court of Frederick the Great. (As noted in chapter 2, aspects of performance practice, especially with respect to instrumentation, seem to have changed in Levy's hands.) Yet the very act of performance within a new social context endowed this older music with different meaning, accomplishing what Ruth Solie and Suzanne Cusick, among others, have referred to as "cultural work"—work that may include the affirmation of or resistance to received understandings and associations.[88]

Writers focused on the act of performance have sought to challenge the hermeneutic tradition centered around the musical text or the "composer's voice."[89] Addressing the tension between the composer's intent and the performer's own persona, Cusick argues for an understanding that accounts for both, "redefin[ing] interpretation as a complex negotiation between performer and script, in which both have agency."[90] For Taylor, too, "the archive and the repertoire have always been important sources of information, both exceeding the limitations of the other."[91] Attention to the moment of performance—and to shifting circumstances of performance over decades and centuries—highlights the changeable nature of musical meaning, even for works that have long been thought to form part of a stable "canon." Indeed, in this respect, it is significant that Sara Levy's lifetime was a formative age for the musical canon; the performances and performance practices in which she participated were among the factors that led to canon formation. Repeated performance within a group of connoisseurs of mixed religions may have contributed to the inscription of this music within the cultural consciousness of the enlightened Berlin community. The radical re-readings that Cusick advocates might be out of place in Levy's historical situation, but a nuanced understanding that accounts for *both* the

88. Solie, "Whose Life?"; and Cusick, "Gender and the Cultural Work of a Classical Music Performance."

89. See, for example, Carolyn Abbate, "Music—Drastic or Gnostic?," *Critical Inquiry* 30, no. 3 (spring 2004): 505–36; and the colloquy "Studying the Lied: Hermeneutic Traditions and the Challenge of Performance," convened by Jennifer Ronyak, *Journal of the American Musicological Society* 67, no. 2 (2014): 543–81. The challenge is particularly to Edward T. Cone, *The Composer's Voice* (Berkeley: University of California Press, 1974).

90. Cusick, "Gender and the Cultural Work of a Classical Music Performance," 99.

91. Taylor, *The Archive and the Repertoire*, 21.

conservative contents of her music collection and performing habits *and* the progressive nature of her social practices would be very much in keeping with her historical moment. Through her cultivation of a collection of scores and the resounding of that music in performance within her salon, Levy marked these works as objects of her admiration, and she also left her own mark on them—rendering them vehicles of expression and sociability available to Jews as well as to Christians. As Mendelssohn did when he translated the Psalms into German and advocated their sounding performance as the best method to absorb their meaning, Sara Levy reframed and reinterpreted the music she played, translating it for a modern, enlightened, sociable situation. She loosened the bonds that linked the German musical tradition to Christianity, forging a common musical heritage that would be accessible to both Christians and Jews.

Conclusion

We should not assume that Levy and other modernizing Jews would have walked away from Christians who viewed them skeptically or disparagingly. Indeed, Levy's name appeared not only on the subscription list of Brill's *Sefer ẓemirot Yisra'el*, but also on the subscription list for Forkel's published variations on "God Save the King."[92] Whether she was also aware of Forkel's disparaging views of Jews or of Carl Friedrich Zelter's anti-Jewish sentiments is unclear,[93] but it seems that anti-Judaism was simply a fact of life. This point is made evident by Davidson's book, quoted at the outset of this chapter. His special pleading for recognition of Jewish contributions to Prussian society must have been a response to the many people around him who refused to grant such recognition—who refused the enlightened call for tolerance across religions. I suggest that Sara Levy navigated this complex social and religious terrain by modestly but seriously staking out her claim in German musical history.

92. Johann Nikolaus Forkel, *Vier und ẓwanẓig Veränderungen fürs Clavichord oder Fortepiano auf das englische Volkslied: God Save the King* (Göttingen: beym Autor, und in der Vandenhoek-Ruprechtischen Buchhandlung, 1791).

93. See Leon Botstein, "The Aesthetics of Assimilation and Affirmation: Reconstructing the Career of Felix Mendelssohn," in *Mendelssohn and His World*, ed. R. Larry Todd (Princeton, NJ: Princeton University Press, 2012), 21; also Jeffrey S. Sposato, *The Price of Assimilation: Felix Mendelssohn and the Nineteenth-Century Anti-Semitic Tradition* (Oxford: Oxford University Press, 2006), 52–53 and passim.

CHAPTER SIX

*

Musical Improvisation and Poetic Painting in the Salon of Angelica Kauffman

In 1794, the painter Angelica Kauffman made a self-portrait in which she depicted herself struggling over the choice between the careers of painting and music. The *Self-Portrait of the Artist Hesitating between the Arts of Music and Painting* (fig. 6.1) has been viewed as a reinterpretation of the "Choice of Hercules" *topos*, in which the hero wavers between two competing inclinations.[1] In the classical iteration of this myth, Hercules must overcome his temptation to enjoy a life of ease and pleasure, pursuing instead a path of hardship, virtue, and honor. Kauffman's self-portrait builds on this theme, depicting painting as the more difficult and virtuous of the two arts. The allegorical figure who represents Painting points upward, to a temple situated at the top of a nearby mountain, suggesting that, though the path to success as a painter may be arduous, its traversal will yield well-earned glory. The figure representing Music, by contrast, remains seated at the bottom of the mountain, a score open on her lap. Showing no inclination toward exertion, Music looks up at Kauffman, pleading with her to remain. Although Kauffman looks at Music with apparent regret, her choice takes her in the direction of Painting.

And yet, the choices of Hercules and Kauffman diverge in one respect. Whereas the classical myth of Hercules shows the hero choosing absolutely between the paths of virtue and vice, abandoning worldly pleasures entirely,

1. Wendy Wassyng Roworth, "Kauffman and the Art of Painting in England," in *Angelica Kauffman: A Continental Artist in Georgian England*, ed. Wendy Wassyng Roworth and David Alexander (London: Reaktion Books, 1992), 16–17; Rosenthal, *Angelica Kauffman*, 272–74.

Figure 6.1 Angelica Kauffman, *Self-Portrait of the Artist Hesitating between the Arts of Music and Painting.* Signed on the artist's sash: Angelica Kauffn. Sc. & P. Pinxit, Rome, 1794. Nostell Priory, Yorkshire, United Kingdom. © National Trust Images/John Hammond. Image no. 81290.

Kauffman never abandoned music. Kauffman was trained in singing from an early age, and as her friend and biographer Giovanni Gherardo De Rossi would explain following her death, "her voice was extremely sweet, her expression touched the heart, her bravura astonished."[2] While she eschewed "the applause, the pleasures, the riches" that a career as a professional musician promised,[3] eyewitness accounts confirm that music-making formed an important part of her artistic practice and social life.[4] Starting with a

2. "la sua voce era dolcissima, la sua espressione toccava il cuore, la sua bravura sorprendeva." Giovanni Gherardo De Rossi, *Vita di Angelica Kauffmann, pittrice* (Florence: A Spese di Molini, Landi, e Comp., 1810), 16.

3. "il plauso, i piaceri, le ricchezze." De Rossi, *Vita*, 16.

4. Evidence of Kauffman's continued engagement with music throughout her life might call into question the interpretation of the *Self-Portrait of the Artist Hesitating between the Arts of Music and Painting* as enacting a definitive and final choice. Wendy Wassyng Roworth, for example, writes that this self-portrait of Kauffman enacting the "choice of Hercules" trope represents a clear rejection of Music in favor of Painting, the latter of which assumes "the stern, heroic posture of Virtue. . . . Kauffman's purposeful rejection of such an image . . . places her within the tradition of great male artists such as Poussin, who represented

self-portrait as a singer made at the young age of thirteen, she returned to the theme of music again and again throughout her career, exploring its relationship to her own artistic life and the lives of those in her circle.

Born in Switzerland, Kauffman lived and trained in Italy under the guidance of her father, also a professional painter, in the early 1760s. In the mid-1760s she moved to London, where she quickly became connected with some of the most important artists of her generation, experienced substantial success, and helped found the Royal Academy. "Rome," however, was "always in her thoughts,"[5] and she returned there in 1782 to live among that city's artistic treasures and flourishing artistic culture.[6] During these later years in Rome, Kauffman joined numerous other women in the common practice of hosting *conversazioni*. These salons, which arose as the dominance of the Catholic church on Roman social and cultural life weakened, attracted a wide range of intellectuals, poets, scientists, and artists living in Rome, along with the many visitors who traveled to that ancient city on the grand tour.[7] While Kauffman's Roman salon has been considered in the past in light of her artistic practice, in this chapter I propose to consider it within the framework of *musical* salons. Even if music was not the primary focus of her *conversazioni*, it was an important component of

---

Hercules's Choice for its theme of masculine moral judgment." See Roworth, "Kauffman and the Art of Painting," 16–17. By contrast, Angela Rosenthal acknowledges that in this painting, Kauffman "render[s] equivalent painting and music," thereby "clos[ing] the gap between the disciplines"; see Rosenthal, *Angelica Kauffman*, 272. Admittedly, Kauffman herself described this painting as one in which she "is holding Music's hand as a final adieu" before "giv[ing] herself up entirely to Painting." However, this tender "adieu" perhaps indicates greater complexity in the situation. This description is from the inventory that Kauffman or her husband made of her Roman paintings and translated in Victoria Manners and George C. Williamson, *Angelica Kauffman, R. A., Her Life and Her Works* (New York: Brentano's, s.d.), 160; see also Wendy Wassyng Roworth, "Angelica Kauffman's 'Memorandum of Paintings,'" *The Burlington Magazine* 126, no. 979 (October 1984): 627–30.

5. De Rossi, *Vita*, 26. See also Anthony M. Clark, "'Roma mi è sempre in pensiero,'" in *Studies in Roman Eighteenth-Century Painting*, ed. Edgar Peters Bowron (Washington, DC: Decatur House Press, 1981), 125–38.

6. On Kauffman's motivations for returning to Rome, see Wendy Wassyng Roworth, "'The Residence of the Arts': Angelica Kauffman's Place in Rome," in *Italy's Eighteenth Century: Gender and Culture in the Age of the Grand Tour*, ed. Paula Findlen, Wendy Wassyng Roworth, and Catherine M. Sama (Stanford, CA: Stanford University Press, 2009), 156–57.

7. Maria Pia Donato, "The Temple of Female Glory: Female Self-Affirmation in the Roman Salon of the Grand Tour," in *Italy's Eighteenth Century*, 59–78.

Figure 6.2 Angelica Kauffman, *Fortunata Sulgher Fantastici* (1792). Oil on canvas. Inventory no. 4339, Palazzo Pitti, Galleria Palatina, Florence, Italy. By permission of the Ministero per i beni e le attività culturali e per il turismo, Gallerie degli Uffizzi, Florence, Italy.

them. Thinking through her musical environment and interests sheds new light on Kauffman's total artistic practice and persona.

Kauffman's Roman salon was well known not only for its discussions of art but also for the musical performances that it featured. The painter herself performed for her guests, and she also hosted performances by other musicians and poets. Among these were the famed singer–improvisers Fortuna Sulgher Fantastici and Teresa Bandettini Landucci, whom she painted in the 1790s (figs. 6.2 and 6.3). Both these portraits depict their subjects in the moment of performance, as denoted by their postures and gestures. The

Figure 6.3 *Portrait of the Impromptu Virtuoso Teresa Bandettini Landucci as Muse* (1794). Kunstpalast Düsseldorf, Werner G. Linus Müller Bequest, inv. no. mkp M 2008–2. © Düsseldorf, Germany, Kunstpalast. Photo: Horst Kolberg—ARTOTHEK.

garland in Bandettini's hair and the emblem showing Terpsichore on Fantastici's belt connect these women with the long heritage of aulic poets and bards in Italy, and indeed, the practices of such *improvvisatrici* were understood to be linked with ancient tradition.[8] Kauffman's home, bedecked with exquisite paintings designed to display her own tastes and talents, served as an ideal backdrop for the improvised performances of Bandettini and Fantastici. The convergence of painting, poetry, and music in Kauffman's salon echoed the view of the Arcadian Academy, of which all three women were members, that these arts were necessary complements to one another. That the *improvvisatrici*'s performances relied upon music resonated both with the hostess's own inclinations and, as I will explain, with the sociability of her salon. By way of explicating these resonances, I offer new evidence and reconstructions of the art of eighteenth-century *improvvisatrici* based on a little-known manuscript written in the decade in which these two women appeared in Kauffman's salon.

Kauffman fashioned her salon as a place where the fleeting sounds of women's music-making gained a permanent presence through painted art. The musical performances of women in her salon constituted a sonic parallel to the visual dimension, bridging the senses of sight and sound and linking modernity with the ethos of antiquity. Musical performance, and especially the fleeting art of sung poetic improvisation, destabilized the permanence of painting, rendering the total artistic experience of Kauffman's salon more temporal—more delicate and fleeting—than the visual dimension alone would suggest. In turn, Kauffman's self-portrait showing the tension between painting and music, as well as her portraits of the famed improvisers Bandettini and Fantastici, provide a sense of permanency to the art of music. And, in casting some of these female singers in a classical guise, Kauffman evoked the longevity and gravitas of the ancient arts, endowing her subjects with a sense of timelessness and ancient inspiration that helped frame their intellectual acumen and skill. Thus, within her Roman salon,

8. The literature on *improvvisatrici* is large and growing. Among others, see Alessandra Di Ricco, *L'inutile e maraviglioso mestiere: poeti improvvisatori di fine Settecento* (Milan: Franco Angeli, 1990); Alessandra Di Ricco, "Poeti improvvisatori aulici in età moderna," in *Cantar ottave: Per una storia culturale dell'intonazione cantata in ottava rima*, ed. Maurizio Agamennone (Lucca: Libreria Musicale Italiana, 2017), 113–34; Benedetto Croce, "L'Arcadia e la poesia del settecento," *Quaderni della critica* 6 (1946): 1–10; and Paola Giuli, "Women Poets and Improvisers: Cultural Assumptions and Literary Values in Arcadia," *Studies in Eighteenth-Century Culture* 32, no. 1 (2003): 69–92. Other citations appear below.

Kauffman used music to animate her paintings and crystallized for posterity the inherently unstable art of sung poetic improvisation. Women's voices resonated, echoed, and achieved a state of permanence.

Angelica Kauffman's Salon as a Site of Musical Sensibility

Angelica Kauffman received much of her early training in Italy under the eye of her father, also a professional painter. Following her mother's death in 1754, father and daughter moved to Milan, and their travels took them throughout Italy, where Angelica was celebrated for her talent as an artist and musician. She spoke multiple languages, which helped equip her for a cosmopolitan life; her studio would become a way station for elite men and women of numerous nationalities. The early 1760s saw her reputation rise across Italy; during this period she was accepted as a member of the Accademia di belle arti in Florence, and she received important commissions from leading aristocrats and intellectuals. One of these, the classicist Johann Joachim Winckelmann, described her in a letter in 1764, making special note of her prestige, her talents as an artist, her skills as a linguist, and her excellence in music:

> She is very strong at portraits in oil, and the least expensive costs 30 zechins. This young lady of whom I speak . . . was brought to Italy by her father, who is also a painter. Therefore she speaks German so well that she sounds like she was born in Saxony. She also speaks polished French and English, so that she paints all the English people who come here. She can be called pretty, and she sings on a level that competes with our best virtuosos. Her name is Angelica Kauffman.[9]

The sociable artistry implicit in Winckelmann's description would serve Kauffman well throughout her life and career. Her studio was a meeting

9. "Sie ist sehr stark in Porträts in Ol, und das meinige kostet 30 Zecchini . . . Das Mädchen, von welcher ich rede, ist . . . von ihrem Vater, der auch ein Maler ist, nach Italien geführet worden, daher sie wälsch so gut als deutsch spricht; sie spricht aber dieses, als wen[n] sie in Sachsen geboren wäre. Auch spricht sie fertig französisch und englisch, daher sie alle Engeländer, welche hierher kommen, malet. Sie kan[n] schön heissen, und singet um die Wette mit unsern besten Virtuosen. Ihr Name ist Angelica Kauffmannin." Johann Joachim Winckelmann, letter of August 18, 1764, in Johann Winckelmann, *Johann Winckelmanns sämtliche Werke. Einzige vollständige Ausgabe*, ed. Joseph Eiselein (Donauöschingen: im Verlag deutscher Classiker, 1825), 96–97.

Figure 6.4 Engraving based on Richard Samuel, *The Nine Living Muses of Great Britain*. Printed in *The Ladies New and Polite Pocket Memorandum-Book, for the Year of Our Lord 1778: Being the Eighteenth of King George III and the Twenty Seventh of the New Stile of Great Britain: Embellished With a Beautiful Copper Plate Representing the Nine Living Muses of Great Britain in the Temple of Apollo* (London: J. Johnson, 1777), foldout plate. Courtesy of the Folger Shakespeare Library. LUNA: Folger Digital Image Collection, call number 193-495q.

place for men and women from across the European continent; her success in obtaining commissions was intertwined with her ability to interact sociably with her guests in multiple languages. This cosmopolitan sociability, which allowed her to transcend a narrowly defined national identity, played a role in her professional and social success when she moved to England in 1765. There, she became an intimate friend of Sir Joshua Reynolds, and they painted each other's portraits. Her connection with Reynolds led to her inclusion among the founding members of the Royal Academy in 1769.

While this context does not allow me to dwell on Kauffman's extensive artistic practice in London, it is worth pausing over her presence in the celebrated painting by Richard Samuel titled *The Nine Living Muses of Great Britain* (1779), which assumed iconic status in its engraved form (fig. 6.4). This image solidified Kauffman's position in the British pantheon of female artists. Seated at her easel, Kauffman is joined by other notable female artists, performers, and writers of the age, with the singer Elizabeth Linley assuming center stage.

This image has yielded divergent interpretations among contemporary scholars. For some, Samuel's depiction of contemporary women as muses denies them agency: as Matthew Head and others have argued, they appear as featureless, flattened characters, placed on pedestals that restrict their creativity and allow the (male) beholder to congratulate himself on his admiration of them. Samuel's painting represents one well-known manifestation of the woman-artist-as-muse trope; as Head and others have suggested, this trope was widely used by male critics across Europe as a means of reinforcing their own dominant position. By contrast, Elizabeth Eger understands the muse trope as one that allowed eighteenth-century viewers to relate contemporary women artists to classical heroines, and in doing so, it made such female artists more easily understood and accepted. Kauffman herself—together with other women in her orbit—used the muse trope to frame her own work. Kauffman cast herself and other female artists in classical guise, using the fashionable interest in the ancient art and architecture inspired by scholars such as Winckelmann to link her own work to the creativity of the ancient and storied muses.

Nowhere was this link more pronounced than in Rome, where, together with her husband, Antonio Zucchi, Kauffman moved in 1782. There, her home became a meeting place for visitors from across the continent, and the sociability of the painter's studio blended with the sociability of her *conversazioni*. The hosting of such gatherings was common among both professional-class and aristocratic women of Rome. Hester Thrale Piozzi visited Kauffman's salon during her tour of Europe and explained that though Kauffman was "neither English nor Italian . . . [she] has contrived to charm both nations, and shew her superior talents both here and there. Besides her paintings, of which the world has been the judge, her conversation attracts all people of taste to her house, which none can bear to leave without difficulty and regret."[10]

Kauffman's *Self-Portrait of the Artist Hesitating between the Arts of Music and Painting* (fig. 6.1, above), produced during this Roman period, is one in a long series of paintings that draw on music as a symbol or music as a practice. Two additional self-portraits are especially instructive in this re-

10. Piozzi, *Observations and Reflections Made in the Course of a Journey through France, Italy, and Germany*, 2:410.

Figure 6.5 Angelica Kauffman, *Self-Portrait* (ca. 1764). © National Trust Images/John Hammond. Saltram, Devon, United Kingdom. Image reference 49685.

spect. First is her self-portrait with a guitar (fig. 6.5, ca. 1764), which shows Kauffman in contemporary garb and in the midst of a musical performance. Although her mouth is closed, it is likely that she used this instrument to accompany herself in song. Neglecting the open music book on the table next to her, her eyes instead hold the gaze of the viewer. The book, covered in shadow, does not circumscribe her performance, as she gains inspiration for her music without reference to the text.

Figure 6.6 *The Artist in the Character of Design Listening to the Inspiration of Poetry* (1782). Inscribed (top): "For George Bowles Esq." English Heritage, Kenwood (The Ernest Edward Cook Bequest Presented by the National Art-Collections Fund). Kenwood House accession number 88029077. Photo credit: Historic English Archive.

If that portrait shows Kauffman as a practitioner of contemporary music, *The Artist in the Character of Design Listening to the Inspiration of Poetry* (fig. 6.6) takes a very different approach. Here, Kauffman presents herself as a medium for the ancient arts—a modern-day muse who could channel the sights and sounds of antiquity for an audience ready to receive inspiration. This work shows Kauffman's use of the muse trope as a deliberate means of legitimizing, framing, and advancing her own practice.

Throughout her career, Kauffman blended the arts in what art historian

Angela Rosenthal has called a "sensible studio."[11] As Rosenthal argues, the artwork that Kauffman hung in her studio created an atmosphere that helped mediate between the artist and her visitors or sitters. The effect—supported by Kauffman's sumptuous furniture and the impressive array of artworks displayed throughout the house—was enhanced by poetic readings and musical performances by both Kauffman and her guests.[12] Rosenthal cites a number of accounts that highlight the multimedia nature of Kauffman's artistic environment. Helfrich Peter Sturz, for example, described Kauffman's performance of Pergolesi's *Stabat mater* on the glass armonica—an instrument associated with feminine sensibility and an "other-worldly" female voice.[13] Catherine Wilmot wrote that Kauffman's "sweetness of voice soothes one like the effect of plaintive musick."[14] Kauffman's last will and testament indicates that she also owned an English piano (probably a square piano of the sort owned by Madame Brillon, as discussed in chapter 3), which she must have used in performances for her guests.[15]

Poetic readings in Kauffman's Roman studio might have included excerpts from the *Odyssey*, perhaps in the translation by Pope, which she owned. In fact, Rosenthal argues, Kauffman's engagement with the *Odyssey* prompted her to fashion herself as a latter-day Penelope, weaving narratives of the past.[16] Other poetic works that must have been performed included those of Goethe, who became an intimate friend of Kauffman during his Italian journey, which started in 1786. A reading of Goethe's *Wanderer* evidently sent Kauffman into a state of poetic ecstasy, "as if through a violent electrical shock."[17] It was through *sound*—through listening to a

11. Rosenthal, *Angelica Kauffman*, 90–99.

12. Roworth, "'The Residence of the Arts,'" 151–71.

13. On these associations of the glass armonica, see Hadlock, "Sonorous Bodies"; and Richards, "Ghost Music."

14. Peter Helfrich Sturz, *Schriften* (Leipzig: Weidmanns Erben und Reich, 1786), 162–63; and Catherine Wilmot, *An Irish Peer on the Continent (1801–1803). Being a Narrative of the Tour of Stephen, 2nd Earl Mount Cashell, Through France, Italy, etc., as Related by Catherine Wilmot*, ed. Thomas U. Sadleir (London: Williams and Norgate, 1920), 178. Both quoted in Rosenthal, *Angelica Kauffman*, 91–92.

15. Carl von Lutzow, "Das Testament der Angelica Kauffmann," *Zeitschrift für bildende Kunst* 24 (1889): 297.

16. Rosenthal, *Angelica Kauffman*, ch. 1, "Penelope and the Weaving of Narrative."

17. "wie durch einen gewaltigen elektrischen Schlag." Friedrich von Matthison, *Schriften* (Zurich: Orell and Füssli, 1835), 4:280. Translated in Rosenthal, *Angelica Kauffman*, 92.

live performance—that she became transported. Her own reaction, with all of its gendered and erotic implications, was itself a kind of performance, in which the sound of Goethe's poetry came to possess her in an ecstatic display of sentiment.

Storytelling was more than an ancillary feature of Kauffman's art. Indeed, perhaps the most remarkable aspect of her artistic practice was her primary focus on history painting. While Kauffman's work as a portrait artist formed a significant part of her *oeuvre* and her successful career, she viewed history painting as her primary calling.[18] Her success in this genre was highly unusual for women artists, but Kauffman reportedly succeeded through a combination of hard work, natural talent, and inspiration. In De Rossi's words, "She was felicitous in the choice of subjects, having read the best historians and poets of many nations and being endowed with a penetrating genius, with a lively imagination, a most feeling heart, a felicitous memory, she had impressed in her those traits by which she had been struck vividly; and those were the ones that she would choose from, which somehow became part of herself, [from which] she produced new and very elegant ideas."[19]

As Roworth has explained, the profession of history painting was one largely closed off to female artists. Portraiture and still-life painting required only the ability to imitate forms and objects found in nature or those of the sitter posing for the artist. By contrast, "in academic theory since the Renaissance, history painting was classified as the noblest and most difficult genre—the equivalent of the epic form in poetry—and a highly unusual choice for a woman artist." While portraiture and still life "did not require knowledge of history or literature, extensive study of human anatomy, or the ability to portray complex multifigured actions in large-scale compositions," history painting presented challenges to women artists because they were, "for the most part, denied access to academic training and the freedom to travel."[20] Indeed, Kauffman was at a basic disadvantage

18. De Rossi, *Vita*, 21.

19. "Era felice nella scelta degli argomenti, perchè avendo letto i migliori storici e poeti di molte nazioni, dotata di un penetrante ingengo, di una vivace fantasia, di un cuore sensibilissimo, di una felice memoria, avea vivamente impressi quei tratti, da'quali era stata maggiormente colpita, e quelli sceglieva, e su quelli, ch'erasi in certo modo fatti suoi, produceva nuove e leggiadrissime idee." De Rossi, *Vita*, 21–22.

20. Roworth, "'The Residence of the Arts,'" 154; see also Roworth, "Kauffman and the Art of Painting," 21–24.

in comparison to male artists because she was excluded from studying male figures in the nude.[21]

In keeping with the ethos of history painting as an art designed to cultivate moral virtue, as theorized by the 3rd Earl of Shaftesbury, Kauffman told stories that would be uplifting and edifying. The weaving of such tales also bespeaks an interest in creating motion and narrative in her art. This is true, I would argue, even of some of her portraits, which seem to embrace a narrative sensibility. In her *Self-Portrait as the Art of Design Listening to the Inspiration of Poetry* (fig. 6.6) and the *Self-Portrait of the Artist Hesitating between the Arts of Music and Painting* (fig. 6.1), she cast herself as a living embodiment of the *paragone* between music and painting. These portraits show events occurring in real time: What, the viewer might ask, could poetry be whispering in Kauffman's ear? With what words, what arguments, are Music and Painting attempting to convince Kauffman of the virtues of their respective paths? The sounds of words and music seem to live in these paintings, just beyond the viewer's hearing.

The Musical Art of the *Improvvisatrice*

If the visual dimension of Kauffman's salon enticed visitors with the promises of sound, its aural dimension provided a necessary complement. As we have seen, Kauffman and her guests played, sang, and read aloud to each other. These equivalencies and resonances between the arts were central components of the theories espoused by the Arcadian Academy during the period known as the *Seconda Arcadia* (1770s–1780s), in which "Enlightenment principles dominated and scientific and philosophical inquiry flourished."[22] Granting membership to numerous highly talented women, "the Arcadian Academy created a cultural space where the literary and artistic spheres comingled." Furthermore, "these same concerns were central to the project of history painting at which Kauffmann excelled."[23]

Improvised musical–poetic performances by Fantastici and Bandettini

21. Wendy Wassyng Roworth, "Anatomy Is Destiny: Regarding the Body in the Art of Angelica Kauffman," in *Femininity and Masculinity in Eighteenth-Century Art and Culture*, ed. Gill Perry and Michael Rossington (New York: Manchester University Press, 1994), 42–43.

22. Melissa Dabakis, "Angelika Kauffmann, Goethe, and the Arcadian Academy in Rome," in *The Enlightened Eye: Goethe and Visual Culture*, ed. Evelyn K. Moore and Patricia Anne Simpson (Amsterdam and New York: Rodopi, 2007), 32.

23. Dabakis, "Angelika Kauffmann, Goethe, and the Arcadian Academy in Rome," 34.

were also part of the proceedings in Angelica Kauffman's Roman salon, and these two *improvvisatrici* maintained friendships with Kauffman for years. Frederike Brun recalls a performance by Bandettini in 1796, two years after Kauffman had painted Bandettini's portrait, in which she "sang about subjects, which were given to her on the spot. . . . Already her portrait by Angelica attracted me. She has a wonderful [*herrliches*], fiery eye, and a flaming, though never wild, gaze; her positions are nice, and she opens her mouth like an inspired one."[24] Friedrich von Matthisson viewed Kauffman's portrait of Bandettini and reacted to what he perceived as its inherent musicality, claiming that it was "transferred to the canvas with entrancing harmony."[25]

Giovanni Gherardo De Rossi described Kauffman's home and her *conversazione*, making note of the music that Kauffman cultivated there and mentioning, in particular, the performances by Bandettini and Fantastici:

> People of letters, or who were distinguished by some talent, received the warmest reception from her, and since her love for music was not extinguished from her heart, she delighted in hearing its most excellent practitioners. When, at different times, the two renowned extemporaneous poets, Fortunata Fantastici and Teresa Bandettini, came to Rome, they wished to know Angelica, and became dear to her; thus she desired to paint their portraits, and she gave them her work as gifts. I remember hearing each of these valorous women improvising in Kauffman's home, and perhaps neither of them ever sang better than in these moments. In fact, their inspiration must have ignited and burned in a place that could almost be called the temple of female glory.[26]

24. "Darauf sang die berühmte Improvisatrice Bandettini nach Sujets, die ihr auf der Stelle gegeben wurden. . . . Schon ihr Portrait von Angelika hatte mich angezogen. Sie hat ein herrliches feuervolles Auge, und einen flammenden, doch nie wilden Blick; ihre Stellungen sind schön, und sie öffnet den Mund wie eine Begeisterte." Friederike Brun, *Tagebuch über Rom 1795–1796* (Zurich: Orrell, Füssli, and Company, 1800), 1:234. Translated in Rosenthal, *Angelica Kauffman*, 183.

25. "Mit bezaubernder Harmonie auf Leinwand übertragen." Matthison, *Schriften*, 5:39. Translated in Rosenthal, *Angelica Kauffman*, 183.

26. "Le persone di lettere, o distinte per un qualche talento, riceveano da lei le più affettuose accoglienze, e non essendo spenta nel suo cuore la passione per la musica, deliziavasi nell'ascoltare chi con eccellenza la professava. Quando in diverso tempo le due rinomate poetesse estemporanee, Fortunata Fantastici, e Teresa Bandettini vennero in Roma, desiderarono di conoscere Angelica, e furono ad essa carissime; onde volle ritrarre ambedue, e

De Rossi's mention of the "temple of female glory," like the trope of the female artist as muse, is a phrase that can be interpreted in different ways; this is a point to which I will return below. First, though, it is worth considering why the performances of Fantastici and Bandettini fit so comfortably within the environment of Kauffman's salon. What was it about this environment that inspired such superlative performances?

To answer this question, it will be helpful to consider the musical dimension of the *improvvisatrici*'s performances in greater detail. While the art of musical–poetic improvisation was a closely guarded secret, aspects of it were captured by eyewitnesses. The most extensive accounts from the second half of the eighteenth century describe the performances of Maria Maddalena Morelli (1727–1800), known by her Arcadian name, "Corilla Olimpica," who was slightly older than Fantastici and Bandettini; as Hester Thrale Piozzi confirmed in 1789, Corilla was still hosting salons at the time that Fantastici and Bandettini were active in performance: "We are called away to hear the fair Fantastici, a young woman who makes improviso verses, and sings them, as they tell me, with infinite learning and taste. She is successor to the celebrated Corilla, who no longer exhibits the power she once held without a rival: yet to *her* conversations every one still strives for admittance, though she is now ill, and old, and hoarse with repeated colds."[27] Corilla's training and performance practices are better documented than those of Fantastici and Bandettini, and this documentation is worth exploring for what it tells us about the intersection of music, poetry, and sociability in the world of the *improvvisatrici*. These lessons, in turn, elucidate an understanding of the improvised performances in Kauffman's salon as resonating with the multimedia, multisensory nature of her artworks.

Corilla's supremacy as a poetic improviser was recognized in 1775 with her coronation on the steps of the Roman Capitol. Two volumes commemorating the occasion offer ample evidence both of Corilla's intellectual achievements and of the importance of musical performance to her poetic

ad ambedue fece poi dono del suo lavoro. Mi ricordo di aver udito sì l'una che l'altra valorosa donna improvisare in casa della Kauffmann, e l'una e l'altra forse mai non cantarono meglio, che in quei momenti: ed in fatti l'estro dovea riscaldarsi, ed accendersi in un luogo, che quasi poteasi dire il tempio della gloria muliebre." De Rossi, *Vita*, 76.

27. Piozzi, *Observations and Reflections Made in the Course of a Journey through France, Italy, and Germany*, 318.

art.[28] One of these, the *Atti della solenne coronazione fatta in campidoglio della insigne poetessa D.na Maria Maddalena Morelli*, consists largely of poetic tributes by members of the Arcadian Academy, but its introductory material outlines the extensive testing that she underwent in order to be admitted to the academy, as well as the manner in which she demonstrated her expertise. The *Atti* begin by offering proof of Corilla's encyclopedic command of every field of human knowledge. Outlining Corilla's virtues as an improviser, this volume explained that her fame rested on her ability

> to improvise upon any subject, whether philosophical, poetic, or historic, that was offered to her, with refined elegance of phrase, with marvelous variety of meters, with flights of fantasy truly rare and sublime, with the most lively and colorful images and expressions, with astonishing speed, such that the instrument could barely keep up in accompanying the many sweet modulations of her singing voice, and, in sum, with all the graces that can hardly be expressed and imagined, except by those who have had the chance to hear it often.[29]

Further detail on the centrality of music to Corilla's performance practices appears in the *Atti*'s description of her examination by members of the *Arcadi*, in which she improvised poetry on the subject of "all the various scientific subjects proposed to her."[30] In addition, this source indicates that Corilla's teacher, "il signor Pietro Nardini, incomparabile Sonatore di Vio-

28. The two volumes are *Adunanza tenuta dagli Arcadi per la coronazione della celebre Pastorella Corilla Olimpica* (Rome: Dalle Stampe del Salmoni, 1775) and Giambattista Bodoni, Domenico Cagnoni, and Evangelista Ferrari, *Atti della solenne coronazione fatta in campidoglio della insigne poetessa D.na Maria Maddalena Morelli Fernandez Pistoiese tra gli Arcadi Corilla Olimpica* (Parma: Impresso nella Stamperia reale di Parma, 1779). While the date of Corilla's coronation is sometimes given as 1776, the production of the *Adunanza* in 1775 clarifies the year of the event.

29. "improvvisare sopra qualunque soggetto o filosofico, o poetico, o storico, che veniale proposto, con iscelta eleganza di frasi, con varietà meravigliosa di metri, con voli di fantasia veramente rari e sublime, con le più vive e colorite immagini ed espressioni, con celerità sorprendente, e tale, che l'istromento potea appena tener dietro, e accompagnare le varie soavissime modulazioni della sua voce canora, e in fine con tutte le grazie, che mal si possono esprimere ed immaginare, se non da chi ha avuto in sorte di sovente ascoltarla." Bodoni et al., *Atti della solenne coronazione*, 6–7.

30. "tutte le varie scientifiche materie a lei proposte." Bodoni et al., *Atti della solenne coronazione*, 21.

lino," was present at her coronation and played with her: "He left Florence in order to accompany the improvised poetry of the very valorous poet on the day of her coronation at the Capitol."[31]

Nardini's name appears, too, in the account of Charles Burney, who visited Corilla years before her momentous coronation, by which point her reputation had already been established in Rome and abroad: "At another great *accademia*, at the house of Signor Domenico Baldigiani, I this evening met with the famous *Improvvisatrice*, Signora Maddalena Morelli, commonly called *La Corilla*, who is likewise a scholar of Signor Nardini, on the violin; and afterwards I was frequently at her house." In a footnote, Burney adds, "She has, almost every evening, a *conversazione*, or assembly, which is much frequented by the foreigners, and men of letters, at Florence." He continues in the text, "Besides her wonderful talent of speaking verses *extempore* upon any given subject, and being able to play a *ripieno* part, on the violin, in concert, she sings with a great deal of expression, and has a considerable share of execution." In his unpublished diary, Burney went even further in describing her performance practices and their relationship to her posture as *improvvisatrice*: there, too, he notes that she is "a scholar of Nardini, on the Violin," but adds that "she plays [the violin] on her lap, and looks like a 10th Muse, which she has often been called."[32]

This unusual manner of playing the violin is confirmed by a note in Anna Brownell Jameson's *Diary of an Ennuyée*, published originally in 1826. Describing an evening of listening to a male improviser, the narrator recalls aspects of the history of this art, including certain practices of eighteenth-century *improvvisatrici* such as Corilla and Fantastici: "It is seldom that an *improvvisatore* attempts to recite without the assistance of music. When Dr. Moore heard Corilla at Florence, she sung to the accompaniment of two violins. La Fantastici preferred the guitar; and I should have preferred either to our jingling harpsichord." An editorial footnote explains, "Corilla (whose real name was Maddalena Morelli) often accompanied herself on the violin; not holding it against her shoulder, but resting it in her lap. She

31. "Egli partì da Firenze per accompagnare il Canto improvviso della valorosissima Poetessa nel giorno della Coronazione Capitolina." Bodoni et al., *Atti della solenne coronazione*, 288.

32. Charles Burney, *Dr. Burney's Musical Tours in Europe*, ed. Percy Alfred Scholes (Oxford: Oxford University Press, 1959), 1:188.

was reckoned a fine performer on this instrument; and for her distinguished talents was crowned in the Capitol in 1779 [*sic*]."[33]

The *Atti* commemorating Corilla's coronation describe her performances. In this account, she begins her improvisation slowly, as if searching for inspiration; in one case she first "invoked the great name of GOD, which produced a tender emotion in the audience."[34] Gradually overcoming her modesty, she is soon transported by rhapsodic enthusiasm:

> To understand the enthusiasm of CORILLA it is enough to have heard her sing a few times, and [it is enough] to discern, through the effects that we experience within us, the nature and force of this fire that illuminates the senses, enchants the soul, exhilarates it, charms it, and floods it with an intimate, very sweet pleasure. . . . Who has not seen her stand quiet and listless, begin slowly and uncertainly, from there, in an instant, igniting, rekindling, lifting herself on wings, hastening her gestures and her voice, shaking with motion, and, with a crowd of conceits and rhymes, from the flow and waves of her picturesque images, say things that are new, surprising, admirable, adapting the most pleasing harmony to the poetic meters, speaking a language completely heavenly and superhuman, and, as if in an immense, swollen torrent of waters, launches her poetry forth so rapidly that the sound of the instrument can barely keep up![35]

33. Anna Brownell Jameson, *The Diary of an Ennuyée: A New Edition* (Paris: Baudry's European Library, 1836 [original publication 1826]), 133. Cited in Cristina Ghirardini, "*L'improvvisatore* in Genre Scenes by Foreign and Italian Artists in the 19th Century," *L'Idomeneo* 21 (2016): 47.

34. "invocò il gran nome di DIO; il che produsse una tenera commozione nell'udienza." Bodoni et al., *Atti della solenne coronazione*, 21.

35. "A ben conoscere l'entusiasmo di CORILLA basta averla udita alcuna volta cantare, e dagli effetti sperimentati in noi stessi argomentare qual sia la natura e l'impeto di quel fuoco, che accende i sensi, incanta l'anima, e l'inebria, e l'innamora, e l'inonda di un'intima soavissima voluttà. . . . Chi non la vide star cheta prima e svogliata, incominciar languida e incerta, indi in un punto accendersi, ravvivarsi, levarsi sull'ale, affrettare il gesto e la voce, vibrare i moti, e tra l'affollamento de' concetti e delle rime, tra l'affluenza e l'ondeggiamento delle immagini pittoresche, dir cose nuove, sorprendenti, mirabili, adattare ai metri l'armonia più felice, parlare un linguaggio tutto celeste e sovrumano, e a guisa di torrente, che serve immenso e turgido d'acque, lanciare i carmi con tanta rapidità, che il suono dello strumento potea [raggiungerla] appena!" Bodoni et al., *Atti della solenne coronazione*, 48–49. See also the accounts in Di Ricco, "Poeti improvvisatori."

In this description, Corilla begins timidly and progresses to greater fluency as she is overcome by the fire of inspiration. The effect of her improvisation on her audience, moreover, is dependent on both sight and sound. Her "enthusiasm" can be sensed after "hearing her sing just once," and one must "see her start quietly." Once she has been transported to the heights of enthusiasm, and her song flows rapidly and fluidly, the instrumental accompaniment can only just follow her. As Paola Giuli points out, these descriptions of the improviser's "enthusiasm" as she is transported to a higher plane of inspiration and expression are modeled after Saverio Bettinelli's treatise *Entusiasmo* (1769).[36] As Giuli notes, the improviser's performance was an "almost sacred moment in which one could witness the genius' creative energy and inspiration take poetic shape and come forth right in front of one's eyes."[37] The description of Corilla's enthusiasm reverberates in the words of the heroine of Germaine de Staël's 1806 novel *Corinne*, based in part on the historical figure of Corilla, who explains that, during improvisation, "I think I experience a supernatural enthusiasm and I have the definite feeling that the voice within me is of greater worth than myself."[38]

What these musical accompaniments and improvisations sounded like was a subject shrouded in mystery and an object of much speculation in the eighteenth century. In his private diary Burney expressed annoyance at his frustrated attempts to learn more about the improviser's musical art when he described an evening at the home of Corilla:

> There was Nardini, the little [Thomas] Linley, Signor Frei and 2 or 3 more of her particular friends and we begun to be very comfortable and *she* in a very good disposition to satisfy my great curiosity concerning the manner of pronouncing and accompanying poems *al l'improvistà*, when, behold! a heap of disagreeable people came in and spoilt all—

36. Saverio Bettinelli, *Dell'entusiasmo delle belle arti* (Milan: Galeazzi, 1769).

37. Giuli, "Women Poets and Improvisers," 75; see also Di Ricco, *L'inutile e maraviglioso mistiere*, 40.

38. Germaine de Staël, *Corinne, or Italy*, trans. Sylvia Raphael, with intro. by John Isbell (Oxford and New York: Oxford University Press, 1998), 46. While the attribute of modesty was also attributed to male improvisers, such descriptions assume a decidedly gendered aspect in relation to female *improvvisatrici*. For a description of the *improvvisatore* Bernardino Perfetti as modest, see Domenico Cianfogni, introduction to Bernardino Perfetti, *Saggi di poesie parte dette all'improvviso, e parte scritte* (Florence: Nella Stamperia Bonducciana, 1774).

there was nothing but politicks going forward, and every other subject but music and poetry.[39]

While Burney's frustration might seem understandable, one wonders whether it might not have been possible for him to inquire about Corilla's improvisational practices when he attended private soirées with her and Nardini. Again writing in his private diary, Burney noted that "on quiet nights [Corilla] had often only Nardini and me—and we played trios. Nardini 1st Violin, the Corilla 2nd and I accompanied them on the Tenor."[40] While some of these trios might well have been compositions by Nardini, his teacher, Tartini, or other Italian composers, it also seems plausible that, on these occasions, Corilla would have sung as well; as I will discuss below, the use of two violins and bass to accompany improvised song was quite common.

Nevertheless, the aura of mystery surrounding the art of the *improvvisatrice* was essential to its effect. Yet some writers did attempt to notate examples of their musical and poetic practices. Among these is a series of four plates appended to the second volume of Carl Ludwig Fernow's *Römische Studien* of 1806, which includes a lengthy article on Italian improvisers, including Corilla, Fantastici, and Bandettini.[41] The first of Fernow's four examples is titled "Passagallo Romano" (fig. 6.7); the word "passagallo" seems to be used here simply to indicate a repeating harmonic progression. As Melina Esse notes, the text is an invocation of a muse; in fact, these are the first four lines of the second stanza of Torquato Tasso's *Gerusalemme liberata*, one of the most famous Italian epics entirely in *ottava rima* form.[42] The speaker's plea for assistance from a supernatural being is echoed in Corilla's invocation of God, suggesting that this was a common practice among *improvvisatori*: "O Muse, [you] who do not string a garland of / the fading laurel fronds of Helicon, / but far in heaven among the blessed choirs / wreathe deathless stars into a golden crown"; the second half of the stanza, unnotated in Fernow's transcription, asks the Muse to "breathe into my heart the fire of heavenly love, / illuminate my song, and if I have

39. Burney, *Music, Men, and Manners in France and Italy*, 118.

40. Burney, *Dr. Burney's Musical Tours*, 188.

41. The article is Carl Ludwig Fernow, "Über die Improvisatoren," *Römische Studien* 2 (1806): 303–416.

42. Melina Esse, "Encountering the *Improvvisatrice* in Italian Opera," *Journal of the American Musicological Society* 66, no. 3 (Fall 2013): 752.

Figure 6.7 Musical formula titled "Passagallo Romano," from Carl Ludwig Fernow, *Römische Studien* 2 (1806), unpaginated appendix. Courtesy of Bayerische Staatsbibliothek, Munich, Germany.

sewn / embroideries of the truth in any place, / I ask forgiveness for their lesser grace."[43]

Since the text of this example is taken from a preexisting source, its purpose is not to demonstrate the verbal practices of any improviser from Fernow's lifetime, although poems such as the "Invito al canto" (invitation to song) by Fortunata Fantastici, which assumes a similar tone to the excerpt from Tasso, seem well suited to such a musical setting.[44] Indeed, as Esse notes, the invocation that Fernow records "bears a striking resem-

43. Translated in Torquato Tasso, *Jerusalem Delivered / Gerusalemme liberata*, ed. and trans. Anthony M. Esolen (Baltimore and London: Johns Hopkins University Press, 2000), 17.

44. Fortunata Sulgher Fantastici, *Poesie* (Florence: Nella Stamperia Granducale, 1796), 77.

blance to recitative, with held chords supporting a speech-like and more rhythmically free recitation style."[45] Burney confirms that Corilla, for one, was fully capable of singing in modern operatic styles, and in fact that her expertise in improvisation may have aided in her execution of opera: "I heard the Corilla in a *scena* of an opera by *Latilla* with recitativo and air both accompanied by Nardini and [Thomas] Linley in which the music was charming—full of expression and new passages."[46] One noteworthy feature of Fernow's first example is its wide range; the melody quickly traverses high and low registers of the voice in succession. In addition, the notation of sixteenth notes and appoggiaturas suggests that the improviser's voice was agile and precise. The use of Tasso's poetry, combined with a recitative style that evokes contemporary opera, associates this example with aulic improvisation.

Simpler, more straightforward melodies appear in Fernow's three other examples, as Esse points out. These are "melodious galant-style pieces, often in rounded binary form"; they are "nearly folklike in their tuneful simplicity and, when repeated for multiple stanzas of poetry, their links to the strophic ballad must have been audible."[47] The example that Fernow associates with Corilla (fig. 6.8) is a tuneful composition with regular phrase structures and a more active bass line. The harmonies are still quite simple, but the form is slightly more complicated, as it provides a template to accommodate eight-line stanzas (rather than the music to accommodate only four lines shown in fig. 6.7, which must be repeated in order to accommodate a single stanza of *ottave*) with a tonicized half cadence and a double bar at the midpoint.

The text of this example is the third stanza from a canzonetta, "Grazie agl'inganni tuoi," by one of the most revered Arcadians of the eighteenth century, Pietro Metastasio. As discussed in chapter 4, Burney had heard Metastasio's own musical setting of this poem and discussed it with him when Burney visited Vienna in 1772. Metastasio confirmed at that time that the composition (or "something like it") was indeed his. When Burney published Metastasio's setting in his biography of 1796, he observed that many other composers had set the same text, but Metastasio's was "superior to most of them in elegant simplicity."[48] Viewed in comparison to Metasta-

45. Esse, "Encountering the *Improvvisatrice*," 752.

46. Burney, *Music, Men, and Manners in France and Italy*, 128.

47. Esse, "Encountering the *Improvvisatrice*," 754.

48. Burney, *Memoirs of the Life and Writings of the Abate Metastasio*, 1:127.

Figure 6.8 Musical formula titled "Corilla," from Carl Ludwig Fernow, *Römische Studien* 2 (1806), unpaginated appendix. Courtesy of Bayerische Staatsbibliothek, Munich, Germany.

sio's setting (fig. 4.3), Fernow's transcription of Corilla's song is considerably simpler, enabling clear declamation of the text and elaboration of the melody over the course of the stanzas. In linking Corilla to Metastasio's text, Fernow affirms her place in the Arcadian tradition.

In fact, the poetic meter of Metastasio's text is exceedingly common, confirming that this melody could easily have accommodated other stanzas—whether improvised or precomposed—in a similar meter and style. An excerpt from a published poem by Fortunata Sulgher Fantastici will serve as an example (ex. 6.1 and audio ex. 6.1 ♫). Like Metastasio's canzonet, Fantastici's poem consists of eight-line stanzas of *settenari* (seven-syllable lines), in which the fourth and eighth lines are *tronchi* (that is, they omit the final syllable of the seven by ending on an accented syllable). The fourth and eighth lines also rhyme, making the full eight lines a single unit. Each

Example 6.1 Text by Fortunata Sulgher Fantastici, "Anacreontica," from *Poesie* (Florence: Nella Stamperia Granducale, 1796), 68, set to the musical formula labeled "Corilla," from Carl Ludwig Fernow, *Römische Studien* 2 (1806), unpaginated appendix.

subsequent set of eight lines uses a different rhyme scheme from the preceding one. Thus the poetic rhymes map neatly onto the bipartite musical form of Fernow's example; line four ends at the first double-bar, and line eight corresponds to the end of the setting.

Solo, distinto, e nobile
    Domina ancor le fere,
    E tutto a suo piacere
    Frenando regger sà;
Ma dalle Donne vinto

Figure 6.9 Musical formula titled "Bandettini," from Carl Ludwig Fernow, *Römische Studien* 2 (1806), unpaginated appendix. Courtesy of Bayerische Staatsbibliothek, Munich, Germany.

> Per man del Dio d'amore,
> De' bruti al domatore
> Dà Leggi la beltà.[49]

(Alone, distinctive, and noble / he still dominates the beasts / and he knows how, at his will, / to handle everything by restraining it. // But, conquered by women / through the hand of the God of Love, / Beauty imposes the laws / of brutes to the tamer.)

Another of Fernow's examples is labeled "Bandettini" (fig. 6.9). Again, the text is taken from a canzonetta by Metastasio, "Or che niega i doni suoi," indicating that it is the music, not the words, that reflects Bandet-

49. Fantastici, *Poesie* (1796), 68.

tini's particular approach to improvisation. The harmonic language is very simple; the third line (mm. 11–12) contains a momentary tonicization of the dominant chord, but otherwise the formula remains firmly in A major, oscillating between tonic, subdominant, and dominant harmonies throughout. Of particular note in this example is the florid ornamentation (perhaps especially suited to the text, which is about springtime, the "season of flowers"), featuring triplet figuration, dotted figures, and appoggiature that give the melody a sense of lightness. A fermata on a dominant seventh chord in m. 16 calls attention to the fact that the notated "improvisation" is incomplete: Bandettini would likely have inserted a different cadenza at this point in each stanza of her recitation, just as she would likely have used different ornamental *passaggi* throughout.

It is worth noting that in Fernow's first example (fig. 6.7), the chordal accompaniment is fully written out, suggesting that it would have been executed on a guitar, mandolin, lute, or harp. Indeed, some improvisers preferred plucked instruments as their modern stand-in for the classical lyre, rather than bowed instruments. As noted above, Jameson reported that "La Fantastici preferred the guitar." The male improviser Bernardino Perfetti is also reported to have accompanied his singing with "the gracious sound of the musical instrument which we commonly call *chitarra*," which complemented "a sonorous, gracious voice."[50] The use of a guitar or mandolin, although common among the upper classes of the eighteenth century, may still have had resonances with the improvised folk-song traditions that persisted on the streets of Italy.[51] In any case, the plucked strings would have evoked the classical lyre so commonly associated with the ancient bards on whom the *improvvisatrici* modeled themselves.

By contrast, the other examples in Fernow's book contain only notated

50. "grato suono del musicale istrumento, che da noi chiamasi volgarmente chitarra"; "una voce sonora, e graziosa." Cianfogni, introduction to Perfetti, *Saggi di poesie*, vi. The use of a lute is attested in the *Atti* commemorating Corilla's coronation; she is first described as singing with the accompaniment of violins, and then pausing her performance "to give time for the lutenist to prepare his instrument" (per dar luogo al lauto rinfresco ivi preparato). Bodoni et al., *Atti della solenne coronazione*, 22. Bandettini is reported to have been accompanied by a pianoforte at a performance for the Accademia degli Oscuri in 1794; see Susanne Winter, "Performatività e improvvisazione: L'artista Teresa Bandettini Landucci," *Italica Wratislaviensia* 10, no. 2 (2019): 166n5.

51. I thank Robert Holzer for pointing out that in Wolfgang Amadeus Mozart's *Don Giovanni*, the title character's aria "Deh vieni alla finestra," accompanied by mandolin and pizzicato strings, approximates the song of an *improvvisatore*.

bass-line accompaniments, and so it is left to the reader to imagine what other instrumental accompaniments might have been included. In the case of Corilla, the violin was apparently an essential component in the projection of a classical persona; this can be seen from her connection to Nardini, her performances with him at her coronation and with Burney, and especially in her practice of holding the violin on her lap, looking "like a 10th Muse."

A manuscript source discussed by the Italian literary historian Benedetto Croce and, more recently, by Cristina Ghirardini elucidates what roles violins might have played in accompanying the performances of *improvvisatrici*. The manuscript, photos of which are now held in an archive in Milan, is titled *Musiche per poesie estemporanee ad uso di Nicola Nicolini*.[52] Nicolini, a jurist and legal scholar, was also a trained amateur musician. According to a nineteenth-century biographical sketch, Nicolini devoted himself, between 1789 and 1802, to studying the practice of improvised sung poetry.[53] This account suggests that the contents of the manuscripts date precisely to the heyday of Bandettini and Fantastici.

Nicolini's manuscript contains accompaniments for improvised poetry, arranged for two violins and *basso* in a style thoroughly consistent with the trio texture of the eighteenth-century galant style. Its contents are organized according to poetic meter, with sections for accompaniments designed for *endecasillabi*, *decasillabi*, *ottonari*, *settenari*, *senari*, and *quinari*. Some, like Fernow's example of Corilla's poetry, accommodate an eight-line poetic phrase structure, so that a single four-line stanza occupies one complete iteration of the music. In other cases, the setting offers only four lines of music, which must be repeated to accommodate an eight-line stanza. The difference can be seen in examples 6.2 and 6.3 and heard in audio examples 6.2 and 6.3: here I have used two of Nicolini's instrumental accompaniments to set a single stanza of *ottave rime* by Teresa Bandettini. ♫

I am speculating here that the *improvvisatrice* would largely have doubled the violin 1 part, elaborating on it with increasing complexity as she proceeded through her poem. Certainly, it is possible that the singer and the

52. Milan, Archive of the Istituto Nazionale per la Storia del Movimento di Liberazione in Italia, Fondo Malvezzi, b. 12, fasc. 43/17. My deep thanks to Cristina Ghirardini for sharing photos of this manuscript with me. It is also mentioned in Benedetto Croce, "Gl'improvvisatori," *Quaderni della critica* 6 (November 1946): 46.

53. Giuseppe Madia, introduction to Nicola Nicolini, *Quistioni di dritto, novella edizione* (Naples: Nicola Jovene and C. Pedone Lauriel, 1870), ii.

Example 6.2 Text by Teresa Bandettini, "La morte d'Ercole," from *Rime estemporanee di Amarilli Etrusca conservate in varie città* (Lucca: Presso Francesco Bertini, 1807), 56. The musical formula, codified in the manuscript Nicola Nicolini, *Musiche per poesie estemporanee ad uso di Nicola Nicolini* (Parri, Fondo Malvezzi, b. 12, fasc. 43/17), 2–3, must be repeated to accommodate the full eight-line stanza.

Example 6.3A Text by Teresa Bandettini, "La morte d'Ercole," from *Rime estemporanee di Amarilli Etrusca conservate in varie città* (Lucca: Presso Francesco Bertini, 1807), 56. The musical formula, codified in the manuscript Nicola Nicolini, *Musiche per poesie estemporanee ad uso di Nicola Nicolini* (Parri, Fondo Malvezzi, b. 12, fasc. 43/17), 4–5, can accommodate the full eight-line stanza.

Example 6.3B

violinists might have coordinated, in broad strokes, some of the variants in advance, but I think it is just as likely, if not more so, that they would have allowed deviations in their melodic decorations to occur spontaneously. Even if these deviations happened in moments when they would otherwise have played and sung in unison, these momentary "clashes" would probably have been understood as unproblematic and even pleasing. Such apparent errors, in fact, might heighten the impression of authenticity in the improvisation, demonstrating that it was truly unprepared and inspired by the moment of enthusiasm.

The suggestion that the singer would have doubled the violin 1 part is supported by formulas in the Nicolini manuscript in which the violin 1 part is melodic in nature, while the violin 2 part is predominantly accompanimental. This is true, for instance, in example 6.4 (heard in audio ex. 6.4 ♫). Here, I offer a version of the voice part in which I show how I think the melody could have been varied; a variant like this could be used, for example, after the first stanza. The ornamentation is based on the ornaments in Fernow's examples as well as general eighteenth-century practices of embellishment. The text I use here describes an imagined encounter between Petrarch and his beloved, Laura.

Example 6.4A Text from "Incontro di Petrarca e M. Laura," in Amarilli Etrusca [Teresa Bandettini], *Saggio di versi estemporanei* (Pisa: Antonio Peverata, 1799), 7. The musical formula for violin 1, violin 2, and *basso* is codified in the manuscript Nicola Nicolini, *Musiche per poesie estemporanee ad uso di Nicola Nicolini* (Parri, Fondo Malvezzi, b. 12, fasc. 43/17), 66–67. The elaborated voice part, shown in small notes, is my suggestion.

Example 6.4B

In example 6.5 and audio example 6.5 ♫, I show how one of Fernow's examples (fig. 6.10) mirrors and can be merged with string accomaniments recorded in Nicolini's manuscript. Fernow gives this plate the rubric "terzine," indicating that it should be used to accompany poetry in *terza rima*; the string parts are likewise found in Nicolini's section devoted to *terza rima* accompaniments. The boxes in example 6.5 show the two places where the harmonies in the sources diverge slightly. Otherwise, the clear similarities of Fernow's print and Nicolini's manuscript confirm that this formula was well known.

The juxtaposition of sources in example 6.5 further elucidates the extent to which the *improvvisatrice* might have doubled a violin part in performance. At some points (for example, the first few notes), Fernow's vocal melody and Nicolini's violin 1 part double each other exactly. In the second beat of m. 3, however, the violin 1 has ornamental sixteenth notes, which decorate the singer's melody as shown in Fernow's plate. Similarly,

Example 6.5 Juxtaposition of the voice and bass parts from the "Terzine" formula codified in Carl Ludwig Fernow, *Römische Studien* (fig. 6.10), and the string parts in the manuscript Nicola Nicolini, *Musiche per poesie estemporanee ad uso di Nicola Nicolini* (Parri, Fondo Malvezzi, b. 12, fasc. 43/17) [unpaginated]. The boxes show two slight deviations in harmony between the two sources.

Figure 6.10 Musical formula titled "Terzine," from Carl Ludwig Fernow, *Römische Studien* 2 (1806), unpaginated appendix. Courtesy of Bayerische Staatsbibliothek, Munich, Germany.

the decorations in m. 10 of the violin part are more elaborate than the dotted figures in Fernow's melody. One can easily imagine that, during their private evenings of music-making together, Nardini, Corilla, and Burney augmented their playing of notated trios with poetic–musical recitations akin to those shown in example 6.5. Burney's report that Corilla could "play a *ripieno* part, on the violin, in concert" suggests that she was quite capable of playing and singing at the same time, with Nardini and Burney adding their accompaniments to support her inspired performances.

Angelica Kauffman's Musical–Poetic Art

Maria Pia Donato has proposed that Fortunata Sulgher Fantastici and Teresa Bandettini found in Kauffman's salon the "reciprocal benefits" of female friendship and support. "For these literary women," Donato writes, "the salon held by [Kauffman] offered social and cultural legitimization of their activities and a guarantee of their honor since the salon was, by its nature, sexually mixed and therefore (despite the ferocious criticisms of the conservatives) morally protected." In Donato's estimation, Kauffman's salon "acted as a bridge between different worlds—linked by neoclassical culture, even if divided by gender, by class, by wealth, by nationality."[54] Kauffman had a long history of relationships with other female artists, which she had cultivated during her travels and her long stay in London. However, beyond the general camaraderie that may have developed among women who were practicing artists, I suggest that there were special resonances between Kauffman's artistic practice and the performance practices of these two *improvvisatrici* that rendered them ideally suited to appear in Kauffman's salon. Some of these resonances are recorded in their correspondence or in eyewitness accounts.

A surface-level similarity lies in the way that Kauffman, Bandettini, and Fantastici cast themselves as living muses. As noted above in relation to Richard Samuel's famous work *The Nine Living Muses of Great Britain*, modern scholars have debated the significance of the muse trope as applied to women in the arts. However, in the cases of Kauffman and the *improvvisatrici*, it was the women themselves who used this trope. Presenting themselves as muses, women artists could become unfettered from social norms that would have made their observers question their education, their command of public attention, and any expressions of their creativity.

When Giovanni Gherardo De Rossi wrote of Fantastici and Bandettini performing in Kauffman's salon, he claimed, first, that "neither of them ever sang better than in these moments"; second, that they appeared "in the heat of their inspiration"; and third, that "they ascended to the place that can be called the temple of female glory." The "temple of female glory" is, I think, an allusion to the classical associations of their art, as well as a recognition that women as a whole were generally restricted from achievement that relied so heavily on intellectual learning and long years of study. Thus the "heat of inspiration" formed a rhetorical key to their success: it helped excuse and explain their attainment of such heights and endowed their improvisations with an oracular sense, as they purposefully projected an image of themselves as vehicles for the ancient Muses. These three clauses from De Rossi's biography might seem formulaic, but in fact they allude to

54. Donato, "The Temple of Female Glory," 75.

central components of the artistry of these women. If they "never sang better than in these moments," then it was surely the result of the environment that Kauffman's salon afforded—one that joined sensibility with intellectual stimulation and achievement.

This dimension of intellectual achievement is worth considering at greater length. The celebrity of female *improvvisatrici* during the second half of the eighteenth century was a remarkable phenomenon in light of the fact that these women were often required to find their own way through the arduous process of learning that their art required. Since audience members could propose virtually any subject as a subject of sung poetry, the improviser was required to have a virtuosic command of all the arts, sciences, and humanities. This point is made clear from the description of Corilla's achievements in the *Atti* commemorating her coronation: before having this honor conferred, she was examined by a panel of a dozen Arcadians, whose questions covered "religious history, revelation, moral philosophy, physics, metaphysics, heroic poetry, law, eloquence, mythology, harmony, fine arts, pastoral poetry."[55]

Indeed, in their volume commemorating the proceedings that led to Corilla's coronation, members of the Arcadian Academy made special note of Corilla's intellectual achievements as an instance of a woman surmounting social norms: "Ancient and modern societies have always admired those women who, overcoming the unjust obstacles invidiously imposed on their sex, were able to distinguish themselves in their pursuit of literary glory."[56] Noting that the modern age offered numerous examples of brilliant—albeit still exceptional—women, the preface to the published proceedings by Abate Ceruti framed the honors paid to Corilla as an opportunity to let "poetry flourish again" and to give comfort to "the afflicted Muses."[57] As Paola Giuli notes, these statements reveal the distinctly gendered nature of Corilla's performances (and, by extension, those of other *improvvisatrici*): for such women, in contrast to male *improvvisatori*, the ascent to intellectual and expressive achievement that had rightly been the domain of the

55. "Storia sacra, religione rivelata, filosofía morale, fisica, metafisica, poesía eroica, legislazione, eloquenza, mitología, armonía, belle arti, poesía pastorale." Bodoni et al., *Atti della solenne coronazione*, 18.

56. "Sempre l'antica e la moderna etade ammirò quelle donne che superando gli ostacoli ingiusti al loro sesso invidiosamente prescritti, si distinsero nelle lettere, e nel bel sentiero della gloria." *Adunanza tenuta dagli Arcadi per la coronazione della celebre Pastorella Corilla Olimpica*, 30. Translated in Giuli, "Women Poets and Improvisers," 77.

57. "sorga la poesia"; "le afflitte muse."

ancient Muses was now marked by the injustices of eighteenth-century society. And, as Giuli notes, this fact was the basis of the opposition that Corilla faced: slandered for her audacity and licentiousness for her public performances, as well as her low birth and allegedly base manners, Corilla became a figure who divided Italian critics.[58]

While the descriptions of *improvvisatrici* often figure women's intellectual acumen as a product of divine inspiration and fulfillment of the promise of the Muses, these rhetorical stances served as cover for the fraught phenomenon of women's learning. As Marta Cavazza argues, in eighteenth-century Italy, "women's access to instruction was a new Pandora's box, the opening of which could cause a series of explosive consequences for power relations between the sexes in the family and in society." Male critics of women's education attacked learned women for, among other offenses, "aspiring to cultivate the sciences while neglecting their duties as wives and mothers."[59] Cavazza argues that, during this era, women's learning became "spectacularized." Educated women inspired both praise and disdain, and these debates assumed a decidedly public form.

Accounts of the educations of Bandettini and Fantastici emphasize the two women's origins in the working classes. Fernow, for example, notes that they were both the daughters of merchants, and they both studied assiduously in order to attain the intellectual heights required of them.[60] He dwells at length on Banettini's training in dance and theater—elements that became incorporated into her performance style as an *improvvisatrice*. Her expertise in dance is no doubt why Kauffman depicted her in motion. Indeed, this portrait, in Fernow's view, was a product of the sympathy between the painter and her subject: "In such a moment [of inspiration], Angelica Kauffman painted [Bandettini's] picture, improvising, with an expression of enthusiasm, that perhaps only Angelica

58. Susanne Winter notes that musical–poetic improvisation was one field where women's achievement was allowed and rewarded; she attributes the critical inattention to figures such as Bandettini to nineteenth-century critics' valorization of the written word over oral poetry. This stance does not fully account for the heated debates over the value of women's improvisations during the second half of the eighteenth century. See Winter, "Performatività e improvvisazione," 161–74.

59. Marta Cavazza, "Between Modesty and Spectacle: Women and Science in Eighteenth-Century Italy," in *Italy's Eighteenth Century: Gender and Culture in the Age of the Grand Tour*, 279.

60. Fernow, "Über die Improvisatoren," 2:379 and 2:384.

was in a position to sense so deeply, and to communicate so truly and vividly."[61]

In Fernow's view, then, the live experience of Kauffman's salon is frozen in time in her portrait of Bandettini. Indeed, the negotiation of time as a whole was a central issue in Kauffman's salon, and it helps explain why the mutually elaborative arts of music, poetry, and painting dwelled so comfortably together there. If Bandettini and Fantastici drew upon the ancient traditions of learning and poetic recitation that had formed part of the art of the *improvvisatore* for centuries, then Kauffman, too, sought to revive the ancient arts in her Roman studio. All three cast themselves as contemporary artists in the garb of ancient Muses—a gesture that was simultaneously a practical strategy, in that it provided them with a suitable frame for their creativity and public display, and a source of artistic inspiration.

The issue of time was a persistent topic of discussion for Kauffman and Fantastici, who became close friends and correspondents. On May 25, 1792, Kauffman wrote to Fantastici, "The same day that I left you, I began to calculate the time until I would be gratified by receiving your news. The punctuality with which you graciously favored me proves that you preserved the memory of your absent friend."[62] And, reflecting on Fantastici's written poems, she explained that "when reading [your works] I think I am hearing the harmonious voice of my most beloved friend, I cherished the beauty of their verses and thought—and speaking of you consoles me."[63] If Kauffman sought to remember Fantastici's voice, Kauffman also hoped that her own portrait of the *improvvisatrice* would preserve the memory

61. "In einem solchen Moment hat Angelika Kaufman ihr Bild als Kniestük gemalt; improvisirend, mit einem Ausdruk von Begeisterung, die vielleicht nur Angelika so innig zu empfinden und so wahr und lebendig auszudrücken im Stande war." Fernow, "Über die Improvisatoren," 2:388–89.

62. "Il medemo [*sic*] giorno della di lei partenza cominciai a calcolare il tempo nel quale potevo lusingarmi recevere le sue nuove, la puntualità con la quale ella si è compiaciuta favorirmi prova che ella à conservato memoria del absente amica." Kauffman to Fantastici, Rome, May 25, 1792. Transcribed in Angelica Kauffman, *"Mir träumte vor ein paar Nächten, ich hätte Briefe von Ihnen empfangen": Gesammelte Briefe in den Originalsprachen*, ed. with commentary and notes by Waltraud Maierhofer (Lengwil am Bodensee: Libelle Verlag, 2001), 170.

63. "leggendo li medesimi mi sembra udir l'armoniosa voce della amatissima amica, ammiro in essi il bel verso—ed il pensiero. e mi consola il parlar di lei." Kauffman, *"Mir träumte,"* 170.

of her friend eternally: "although your image is vividly impressed in my mind, I will keep a copy of the portrait that I have painted of you, which is destined for you."[64] On October 12 of the same year, she begged Fantastici to "preserve me in your memory," and she wrote further of the delivery of the portrait—a document that would preserve remembrance between the two and recall a time when they were together.[65] On the 27th she asked that Fantastici "preserve her" in her heart, "just as I will always preserve you in mine."[66] In framing her portrait and her letters as a means of keeping her distant friend present, Kauffman echoed a tradition dating back to the Renaissance that viewed portraiture as an artform designed "to substitute itself for life."[67]

Resonances of classical and Renaissance art theory can be discerned, too, in the poem that appears in Kauffman's portrait of Fantastici. Echoing Horace's dictum "ut pictura poesis" (as painting, so poetry), and Plutarch's statement that poetry was "eloquent painting" while painting was "mute poetry," this poem elaborates on the *paragone* of the arts that was so central to the *Seconda Arcadia*:[68]

> Ne bei carmi Temira pari é alle Ascree Sorelle
> Tutta vorébbe Angelica L'Arte del grand Apelle

64. "benche nella mia mente sia rimasta vivamente impressa l'imagine sua, terrò copia del ritratto che ò dipinto di lei, e destinato per le." Kauffman, *"Mir träumte,"* 170.

65. "conservarmi nella vostra rimenbranza." Kauffman, *"Mir träumte,"* 176.

66. ". . . nel vostro cuore. nel quale vorrei essere conservata—come sempre vi conserverò cara nel mio." Kauffman, *"Mir träumte,"* 177.

67. This phrase is from David Rosand, "The Portrait, the Courtier, and Death," in *Castiglione: The Ideal and the Real in the Renaissance*, ed. Robert W. Hanning and David Rosand (New Haven, CT: Yale University Press, 1983), 92. See also the words of the Renaissance theorist Leon Battista Alberti, which still rang true in the eighteenth century: "through painting, the faces of the dead go on living for a very long time" ("Itaque voltus defunctorum per picturam quodammodo vitam praelongam degunt"). Leon Battista Alberti, *De pictura* 2.25, trans. in Leon Battista Alberti, *On Painting and On Sculpture: The Latin Texts of "De pictura" and "De statua,"* ed. and trans. with notes by Cecil Grayson (London: Phaidon Press, 1972), 60–61.

68. See Rensselaer W. Lee, "*Ut pictura poesis*: The Humanistic Theory of Painting," *Art Bulletin* 22, no. 4 (December 1940): 197. The source of Plutarch's statement is his *De Gloria Atheniensum*, cited in Lee, "*Ut pictura poesis*," 197. Plutarch's idea was transmitted through Renaissance writers such as Giovanni Paolo Lomazzo, *Trattato dell'arte della pittura, scoltura, et architettura . . . diviso in sette libri* (Milan: Paolo Gottardo Pontio for Pietro Tini, 1585), 486.

Quella dispiega il canto, e col pennel maestro
Questa ne pinge il volto nei momenti dell'estro
Di due si rare donne stringe amistade i cori
E si fan mutuo dono di versi, e di colori
Mira la viva tela, ascolta i carmi suoi
E' chi fe maggior dono decidi pur se puoi.

(In beautiful songs, Temira equals the sisters of Ascra, / Angelica aspires to all the art of the great Apelles. One recites the verse, and with masterful brush / The other paints the face in moments of fantasy. / It tugs, with friendship, the hearts of two most rare women / As they exchange gifts of verses and of colors. / Marvel at the living canvas, listen to her songs / And decide for yourself if you can which is the greater gift.)[69]

In return, Fantastici wrote a lengthy poem in honor of Kauffman, later published. In it, she, too, made overt reference to the *paragone* of their two arts, and she acknowledged the importance of Kauffman's portrait in granting her life after death.

Di Te, Donna sublime,
Volea narrar sulla mia cetra umìle
La bontà, la virtute, il senno, i dolci
Tuoi candidi costumi, e l'alto ingegno,
Indi pinger la fronte, il crine, il volto,
Ove l'incanto è accolto
Delle grazie più belle in quel sorriso,
E già chiedeva al biondo Nume il canto;
Volea spiegarti quanto
Grata all'opra son'io, con cui mi doni
Nuova vita, e sicura
La nell'età futura,
Ond' è ch'io prendo a vile
Il fero stral di morte. . . .[70]

69. Transcribed and translated in Rosenthal, *Angelica Kauffman*, 176.

70. Fortunata Fantastici, *Poesie* (Livorno: Nella Stamperia di Tommaso Masi e Comp., 1794), 87.

(Of you, sublime lady, / I wish to tell, with my humble lyre, / The goodness, the virtue, the judgment, your sweet, / pure manners, and lofty wisdom. / Then paint the brow, the hair, / the face, whose smile welcomes / the charm of the most beautiful Graces, / and I was already invoking the song of the blond Numen / to explain to you how / grateful am I for the work, with which you have given me / new and secure life / in future times. / Thus, I deem as worthless / the cruel arrow of death. . . .)

While this poem is composed of *versi sciolti* (i.e., it contains a mix of seven- and eleven-syllable lines)—a common configuration in Bandettini's and Fantastici's published poems—it can be easily made to conform to a recitational formula such as the "Passagallo Romano" recorded by Fernow, and I attempt such an adaptation in example 6.6 and audio example 6.6. ♫ In fact, it is not inconceivable that this poem originated as an improvisation in Kauffman's salon: perhaps one of her guests challenged Fantastici to improvise a poem in honor of their esteemed hostess. Whether or not this scenario actually took place, in publishing this poem, Fantastici codified and preserved her admiration for Kauffman in the permanent medium of print. In this respect, her published poem serves a purpose analogous to Kauffman's portrait of her friend.

The tensions between publication and improvisation were not lost on the *improvvisatrici* themselves; as Alessandra Di Ricco has written, "improvisation is . . . structurally opposed to the literary discipline."[71] When Bandettini's poems were published, a preface by Francesco Franceschi cautioned that they could not hope to reproduce her improvised art:

> It would be totally useless to try to capture the incredible beauties with which this unique lady has adorned her improvisations. . . . I need only remind the reader that these verses were created in the moment by an imagination heated by the fire of Apollo and which [the imagination] did not polish with a file, nor did it have the time to do so. . . . Whoever wishes to take offense at the few and slight stains that they happen to find here, besides setting the impossible as the boundary of perfection by expecting the ideal best instead of the good, of which the former is often the enemy, should end by believing that this art of poetry was prepared by art, rather than being a daughter of nature. Thus we admire the

71. Di Ricco, *L'inutile e maraviglioso mestiere*, 40.

Passagallo Romano

Example 6.6 Music from the "Passagallo Romano," from Carl Ludwig Fernow, *Römische Studien* 2 (1806), unpaginated appendix, accommodated to the *versi sciolti* in Fortunata Fantastici's poem dedicated to Angelica Kauffman, printed in Fortunata Fantastici, *Poesie* (Livorno: Nella Stamperia di Tommaso Masi e Comp., 1794), 87.

products of [nature], finding no fault in the little irregularities, which are, in substance, nothing more than the sure mark of the legitimate origin of their marvelous mother.[72]

72. "Sarebbe del tutto inutile, ch'io mi accingessi a rilevare le quasi incredibili bellezze, di cui questa donna unica ha saputo adornare i suoi improvvisi. . . . Io non debbo ricordare a chi legge se non che questi son versi creati sul momento da una immaginazione calda di tutto il fuoco d'Apollo, la quale non ha, nè può avere il tempo di ripulir colla lima ogni benchè minimo angolo del suo difficil lavoro. Chi volesse pertanto mostrarsi of-

Hester Thrale Piozzi was less willing to read the faults in such poetry generously: in her published travel diary she praised practitioners of this art but explained that "the whole secret of improvisation . . . seems to consist in this; that extempore verses are never written down, and one may easily conceive that much may go off well with a good voice in singing, which no one would read if they were once registered by the pen."[73] Thus while Franceschi casts the imperfections of Bandettini's recorded poetry as evidence of the genius of their creator and a marker of their authenticity as improvisations, Piozzi views these blemishes in a different light. Without claiming that they render the improvisations unacceptable, she claims that it is their performance—and, indeed, their music, done "with a good voice in singing"—that excuses errors that could never be accepted in written poetry.

Inherent in the judgments of Franceschi and Piozzi is a recognition that the art of the *improvvisatrice* was an inherently social one. This is true not only in the sense that she would accept topics of improvisation from her audience, and that she was inspired by their responses, though these factors are certainly true. More, the art of the *improvvisatrice* was social in that it was fleeting, vanishing in a moment. Without listeners, the art would be entirely lost to time. Thus Madame de Staël's Corinne: "it is to my friends that I owe the greatest part of my talent in this field. Sometimes the passionate interest aroused in me by a conversation on the great, noble questions about man's moral being, his destiny, his objective, his duties, his affections, raises me above my powers, enables me to discover in nature, in my own heart, bold truths, expressions full of life, which solitary reflection would not have produced."[74] And thus another dimension of Angelica Kauffman's

---

feso delle poche, e lievissime macchie, che per avventura vi ritrovasse, oltre il prescrivere l'impossibilità per confine alla perfezione esigendo il meglio ideale in luogo del bene, a cui sovente il primo è nemico, dovrebbe finire col credere preparata dall'arte quella poesia, che soltanto fu figlia della natura. Ammiriamo dunque i bei getti di questa, lasciandovi senza pena le piccole irregolarità, che non sono in sostanza, che le marche sicure dell'origin legittima dalla maravigliosa lor madre." Francesco Franceschi, "A chi leggerà," introduction to Amarilli Etrusca [Teresa Bandettini], *Rime estemporanee* (Lucca: Francesco Bertini, 1807), iii–iv. Further discussion of Bandettini "between improvisation and literature" is in Di Ricco, *L'inutile e maraviglioso mestiere*, 163–88.

73. Piozzi, *Observations and Reflections Made in the Course of a Journey Through France, Italy, and Germany*, 1:239–40.

74. De Staël, *Corinne*, 46.

salon that rendered it so ideal for the performances of Fantastici and Bandettini: as an oral art, the improvisation represented a shared, sentimental experience that belonged uniquely to those in attendance. Absence from the salon gathering at the time of an improvisation constituted a missed opportunity, and one that could never be recovered.

Piozzi's description of improvised poetry includes an astute observation: she wrote that it is "sung extemporaneously to some well-known tune, generally one which admits of and requires very long lines; that so alternate rhymes may not be improper, as they give more time to think forward, and gain a moment for composition."[75] This point is underscored by the musical examples that I have presented in this chapter, in which the formulas extend the recitation of poetry through a longer time than would be needed for speaking. With reference to Fernow's musical examples and written formulas for improvisation from the nineteenth century, Melina Esse has observed, similarly, that while some nineteenth-century writers "suggest that musical accompaniments played an important role, whether by setting the audience's mood or preparing the improviser to receive inspiration," it is likely that "music acted in a much more practical way: it gave the poet time. Time to think of the appropriate rhyme, to find the right word. Time, in other words, to tap into memory."[76] I suggest that both interpretations may be true—that the concern that Kauffman and Fantastici shared with the passage of time may be a persistent feature of the art of musical–poetic improvisation. This was an ancient art, both in reality and in the eighteenth-century imagination, and it was the job of the *improvvisatrice* to make the ancient art resound, in all of its transience, with all of its fragility and imperfection, in the modern day.

This, I think, is why it was so important that the proceedings of Kauffman's artistic salon featured music. Although she declined to pursue a career as a musician, the musical sensibility is palpable in her artwork. Indeed, the voice of the *improvvisatrice*, accompanied by her lyre, is almost audible in De Rossi's description of Kauffman as a "poetic" painter—one capable of freezing her subjects at the moment of inspiration and bringing them back to life with each new viewing: "taking up her brush, she was like a poet approaching her lyre and who, possessed by inspiration, became like

75. Piozzi, *Observations and Reflections Made in the Course of a Journey Through France, Italy, and Germany*, 1:238.

76. Esse, "Encountering the *Improvvisatrice*," 756.

another person, for whom anything is possible, and whose flights of the imagination know no bounds."[77]

Conclusion

I close by returning to Kauffman's two self-portraits discussed above: the self-portrait from 1764 with a guitar (fig. 6.5) and *The Artist in the Character of Design Listening to the Inspiration of Poetry* (fig. 6.6) made upon her return to Rome. In both, music has a nearly audible presence. In the early portrait, I suggest, it is no accident that the artist is looking away from her music book. She gazes at the viewer with her mouth closed. Whether she will sing or not, her fingers manipulate the instrument without reference to any text. In the later portrait, she is listening to the embodiment of Poetry—a figure adorned with a laurel wreath, perhaps in homage to Corilla, the *improvvisatrice* who was crowned in recognition of her intellectual and artistic achievements.[78] The lyre by her side stands for music: indeed, Poetry's art is clearly a musical one, and that same musical sensibility is whispered, softly and just for an instant, into the ear of the painter.

77. "prendeva il pennello, era simile ad un poeta, che si accosta alla cetra, e che invaso dall'estro diviene altr'uomo da quel di prima, e tutto è capace di tentare, e non conosce confine ai suoi voli." De Rossi, *Vita*, 112.

78. This idea appears in Dabakis, "Angelika Kauffmann, Goethe, and the Arcadian Academy in Rome," 34.

CHAPTER SEVEN

Reading Musically in the Salon of Elizabeth Graeme

In 1787, Elizabeth Graeme Fergusson, a member of the mid-Atlantic literary circle who was among the first published women poets in North America, completed a gift for her friend and fellow writer Annis Boudinot Stockton. The gift was a commonplace book—a manuscript compilation of poetry, essays, and correspondence that served as a repository of memory, a prompt to reflection, and a memento of friendship.[1] The contents of this commonplace book, now housed in the library at Dickinson College, attest to this purpose and, more broadly, to Fergusson's and Stockton's shared interests and worldview. The manuscript includes some of Graeme's original work. Her devotion to the natural world as seen through the lens of Protestant spirituality can be discerned in her odes to the seasons, to evening, and to immortality. Her poem commemorating the recent discovery of a star

1. The commonplace book, MC 2006.3 at the Archives and Special Collections, Dickinson College, can be viewed at http://archives.dickinson.edu/collection-descriptions/elizabeth-graeme-fergusson-commonplace-book (accessed July 24, 2020). Elizabeth Graeme Fergusson's life is chronicled in Ousterhout, *The Most Learned Woman in America*; see also Martha C. Slotten, "Elizabeth Graeme Ferguson: A Poet in 'The Athens of North America,'" *Pennsylvania Magazine of History and Biography* 108, no. 3 (July 1984): 259–88. On the purposes and construction of commonplace books in eighteenth-century America, see Susan M. Stabile, *Memory's Daughters: The Material Culture of Remembrance in Eighteenth-Century America* (Ithaca, NY, and London: Cornell University Press, 2004). Throughout this chapter, since I am dealing primarily with events that took place prior to her marriage, I refer to the subject as "Elizabeth Graeme." Her married name is rendered variously as "Ferguson" and "Fergusson."

represents her engagement with scientific learning and discovery in an age when enlightenment and reason seemed to offer a path forward in a nation struggling to define itself. Elegies for departed friends attest to the social and intellectual community in which she lived, and which she and Stockton sought to recall in their later years.

This commonplace book, like others in the genre, also includes writings by other authors whose work was meaningful to the copyist and the reader. Among these was a poetic elegy for the Scottish musician James Bremner. The elegy was originally penned by Graeme's friend, Francis Hopkinson, a leading intellectual in eighteenth-century Philadelphia, a statesman and theologian, and a signer of the Declaration of Independence. Hopkinson was also an amateur musician who advocated strongly for the role of music in shaping the character of the new country and developing the arts there. The year after Graeme completed her commonplace book for Stockton, Hopkinson published a set of songs dedicated to George Washington, in which Hopkinson claimed to be "the first Native of the United States who has produced a Musical Composition."[2] Yet this innovation was rooted in the rich musical culture that he and others had fostered for decades in Philadelphia. This musical culture was, in turn, supported by the practices of friendship and sociability in which Hopkinson, Graeme, Stockton, and Bremner had all participated. Bremner died in 1780, and Hopkinson's moving elegy for his teacher and friend harnesses the power of music—both as a symbol and as a sounding art—as a lasting tribute. The poem, "Sing to His Shade a Solemn Strain," describes Bremner as "the Swan of Schuylkill," referring to the Schuylkill River, which runs by Philadelphia. And it praises Bremner's command of "the magic pow'r of sound," which had contributed much to musical life in America.

By including a copy of Hopkinson's elegy for Bremner in her commonplace book for Annis Stockton, Graeme opens a window onto a certain type of eighteenth-century sociability: a sociability of memory, preserved in the written word. Indeed, in some cases Graeme seems to have used the medium of writing to perpetuate memories of her past friendships or to imagine friendships between herself and the poets whom she emulated. This poetics of memory is representative of women's practices in early America, as Susan Stabile has observed: "Based on a rhetorical tradition that considered

2. Hopkinson, *Seven [Eight] Songs*, unpaginated dedication. On the impact of these songs, see Catherine Jones, *Literature and Music in the Atlantic World 1767–1867* (Edinburgh: Edinburgh University Press, 2014), 56–57.

topoi, or places in the mind, as domestic spaces where one gathered, arranged, and displayed ideas, the commonplace book recuperates the house, and the female mind, as locales of knowledge and memory."[3] Graeme's commonplace book served to fix in writing the memories that both Graeme and Stockton held in their minds, and it included both women in the act of memorializing Bremner.

Beyond inscribing their friendship in her commonplace book for posterity, Graeme's inclusion of "Sing to His Shade a Solemn Strain" invited Annis Stockton to recall the lived sociability that she had shared with Hopkinson, Bremner, and other members of elite intellectual circles in the mid-Atlantic years earlier. Between 1765 and 1772, before her marriage to Henry Hugh Fergusson, the young Elizabeth Graeme had been hostess to regular social gatherings that included the leading intellectuals, philosophers, socialites, and statesmen of pre-Revolutionary Philadelphia. On Saturday evenings, this circle of friends had gathered in the house that Graeme shared with her father (her mother having recently died) on Chestnut Street in Philadelphia, to discuss new ideas in politics, literature, and the arts, in what would later be called the first literary salon in America. Decades later, as Stabile explains, Graeme would use the commonplace book as a "handwritten analogue to the salon," evoking salon sociability through the written text.[4] Chiara Cillerai has expanded on this metaphor, arguing that "the commonplace book is also a site where individuals develop memories to be shared, divided, and continually transformed."[5]

The place of music in Graeme's salon has scarcely been considered before. In some ways this is hardly surprising; until recently, Graeme was a figure all but lost to history, dismissed, like other women poets in eighteenth-century America and Britain, as amateurish and overly sentimental, and superseded by the nineteenth-century English Romantic writers such as William Wordsworth and Sir Walter Scott. Because it is primarily literary historians who have rescued Graeme from this obscurity, these historians have not yet attempted to understand how her poetic life intersected with music. An invitation for such consideration lies in Graeme's note that Hopkinson's elegy for Bremner should be sung to the popular

3. Stabile, *Memory's Daughters*, 9–10.

4. Susan Stabile, "Introduction: Elizabeth Fergusson and British–American Literary History," in Ousterhout, *The Most Learned Woman in America*, 5.

5. Chiara Cillerai, "Scribal Publication of Elizabeth Graeme Fergusson's Commonplace Books," *Studies in Eighteenth-Century Culture* 48, no. 1 (2019): 86n7.

Figure 7.1 Francis Hopkinson, "Sing to His Shade a Solemn Strain," from Hopkinson's manuscript titled *Duets / Songs*, Marian S. Carson Collection, Library of Congress ML96.H83 no. 2, Washington, DC, USA.

Scottish tune "The Lass of Peatty's Mill." Indeed, a separate manuscript in Hopkinson's hand, which survives in the Library of Congress, contains Hopkinson's musical setting of the same poem, with original music for the first part and "The Lass of Peatty's Mill" serving as the basis of the second part. The elegy appears in Hopkinson's musical manuscript as part of a larger collection of songs and instrumental pieces. Occupying a single modest page (fig. 7.1), the elegy would be easy to overlook, yet I suggest that it offers a window onto the art and practice of musical sociability in eighteenth-century America.

In this chapter I will argue that, while Graeme's salon focused primarily on literature, it warrants consideration as a musical salon as well. As I will show, music operated there on two separate and mutually reinforcing levels: like the neoclassical poets whom she encountered during her travels to Britain in 1764–1765, Graeme understood music as a potent symbol for the powers of poetry, and her work evokes a mythical past in which the timelessness of ancient music, both sacred and secular, merges with modern musical–poetic experience. I present new evidence from her poetic manuscripts—in particular, her manuscript copy book of her own paraphrases of the biblical Psalms—that demonstrates her keen, decades-long engagement with ideas of music as a means to achieve spiritual growth.

Yet it was not just on a symbolic level that Graeme embraced music. She was musically educated, owned a harpsichord, and is likely to have used it or encouraged others to use it during her salon gatherings. Her friendship with Hopkinson, Bremner, and others active in the growing public musical scene in Philadelphia and beyond meant that she had ready collaborators to foster music-making as a form of communal bonding and artistic creativity within her salon. Graeme's apparently simple gesture of copying this elegy in her commonplace book for Annis Stockton was, in fact, a complex act, rich in meaning. While the commonplace book was a private document, created by one friend for another, it links both writer and reader to a network of distant friends and bygone times. And, in evoking music—evoking, that is, a specific and significant melody derived from a familiar Scottish tune—it calls to mind the sounds of communal music-making that had once fostered friendship and sentiment in Graeme's salon circle. Ultimately, I argue, Graeme's poetry—even the poetry that she wrote after her salon ceased to meet—was informed by the musical poetics, sensibility, and sociability that she had cultivated there.

Elizabeth Graeme and Salon Sociability in Eighteenth-Century Philadelphia

Elizabeth Graeme (fig. 7.2) was born in 1737 to Dr. Thomas and Ann Graeme, devout Anglicans whose country estate, Graeme Park, still stands in Horsham, Pennsylvania, some 20 miles from Philadelphia. Her family was part of the elite, wealthy class in the mid-Atlantic region of the American colonies that maintained close ties to family and friends in Britain, and they socialized with some of the leading intellectuals in America. Ann Graeme, daughter of the Pennsylvania governor Sir William Keith, taught Elizabeth to read and write, to appreciate literature, and to exercise Christian devotion. In 1757, Elizabeth was engaged to William Franklin, son of Benjamin Franklin, over her parents' objections; however, the engagement was protracted, marriage was delayed, and William traveled to England with his father, where William married another woman. An obituary of Elizabeth by her friend Dr. Benjamin Rush, published in *The Port Folio* in

Figure 7.2 Anonymous portrait of Elizabeth Graeme, Graeme Park, Horsham, Pennsylvania, USA. Photo courtesy of Graeme Park, Pennsylvania Historical and Museum Commission.

1809, suggests that this disappointment in love prompted Graeme to begin writing poetry, starting with her English poetic translation of *Télémaque* from the French original; however, Rush's claim is clearly unfounded, as Elizabeth had begun writing poetry by the early 1750s.[6]

A formative experience in Graeme's creative development occurred in

6. Ousterhout, *The Most Learned Woman in America*, 44. Rush's biographical essay is in Benjamin Rush, "An Account of the Life and Character of Mrs. Elizabeth Ferguson," *The Port Folio* 1 (1809): 520–27.

1764–1765, when she took an extended journey to England and Scotland, encountering the rich social, artistic, and intellectual cultures there. She spent time not only in London but also in Lichfield, a town in the English countryside known for its cultivation of literature and its network of literary salons.[7] Graeme's travel diary from this period is lost, with excerpts surviving only in the commonplace book made by one of her friends, Milcah Martha Moore.[8] As a result, firm evidence about what she did and whom she met there is scant. However, remarkably, she met such venerable literary figures as Laurence Sterne, and she obtained an audience with King George III. She traveled extensively in both England and Scotland, her father's native country, where she still had family connections. During her visit there, her cousins on her father's side gave her a copy of the *Fragments of Ancient Poetry Collected in the Highlands of Scotland* attributed to Ossian, the legendary bard of ancient Scotland whose poetry was thought to represent the lyric tradition in its purest form. James MacPherson, who assembled the Ossianic *Fragments* primarily from oral sources, had lived in the home of Graeme's family in Scotland in the 1750s, serving as tutor to Graeme's young cousins.[9]

References to English writers in Graeme's poetry and copy books suggest that, during her travels in England, she met some members of the so-called Lichfield group, a network of men and women characterized by their neoclassical literary sensibilities and their salon sociability; members of this group included famous women such as Anna Seward and Hester

7. Stabile, "Salons and Power in the Era of Revolution," 136. On the Lichfield (also spelled "Litchfield") salons, see Amy Prendergast, *Literary Salons Across Britain and Ireland in the Long Eighteenth Century*, ch. 5, "Collaborative Hospitality and Cultural Transfers: Provincial Salons Across England and Ireland."

8. See Milcah Martha Moore, *Milcah Martha Moore's Book: A Commonplace Book from Revolutionary America*, ed. Catherine La Courreye Blecki and Karin A. Wulf (University Park: Pennsylvania State University Press, 1997); the excerpts from Graeme's travel diary are on 200–217.

9. Ousterhout, *The Most Learned Woman in America*, 99. A summary of the controversy over the authenticity of the Ossianic poetry assembled by MacPherson is in Sarah Clemmens Waltz, "Introduction," in *German Settings of Ossianic Texts, 1770–1815*, ed. Sarah Clemmens Waltz (Middleton, WI: A-R Editions, 2016), xii–xiii. On the relationship between the interest in Ossian and the rise of industrialization, see Eric Gidal, *Ossianic Uncomformities: Bardic Poetry in the Industrial Age* (Charlottesville: University of Virginia Press, 2015). Musical settings of Ossian from 1780 onward are considered in James Porter, *Beyond Fingal's Cave: Ossian in the Musical Imagination* (Rochester, NY: University of Rochester Press, 2019).

Figure 7.3 View of Graeme Park, Horsham, Pennsylvania, USA. Photo courtesy of Graeme Park, Pennsylvania Historical and Museum Commission.

Thrale (later Piozzi), as well as Dr. Samuel Johnson.[10] These writers had a palpable influence on Graeme's literary output, and, although it is difficult to show for certain that she visited their salons, it seems highly likely. Graeme's poem "Ode to the Lichfield Willow," written in 1789, figures the Lichfield literary circle as the venerable tree of the arts whose branches extended to America. The poem assembles the major figures of the Lichfield school in a figurative salon, praising each of their works in turn. Its seeds had been planted during her voyage to Britain more than two decades earlier, when she had reflected that "I love Engld. because it has given Birth to so many great & good Men, whose Writings have helped to form our Education in America."[11] When she returned to Philadelphia in 1765, she began referring to that city, in neoclassical terms, as "the Athens of North America," and she dedicated herself to fostering a flourishing of the arts and belles lettres there.

One way in which Graeme sought to ignite the culture of literature and

10. See Anne Hollingsworth Wharton, *Salons Colonial and Republican* (Philadelphia and London: J. B. Lippincott Company, 1900), 18; and Ousterhout, *The Most Learned Woman in America*, 2 and 299–300.

11. Moore, *Milcah Martha Moore's Book*, 216.

the arts in Philadelphia was through her own literary salon. Elizabeth's mother had long served as a hostess—especially in the family's country retreat of Graeme Park (fig. 7.3). According to Rush, Graeme Park "afforded [Elizabeth] the most delightful opportunities for study, meditation, rural walks, and pleasures, and, above all, for cultivating a talent for poetry." At this estate, Ann Graeme had welcomed friends and her husband's colleagues in their family's home, and she also made a place for her daughter's friends, as they were joined by "two or three young ladies from Philadelphia [who] generally partook with Miss Graeme of the enjoyments which her situation in the country furnished."[12] Following her mother's death, which took place while Elizabeth was traveling in Britain, Elizabeth assumed the role of hostess.[13] Like her mother, who had been responsible for cultivating Elizabeth's "uncommon talents and virtues," Elizabeth Graeme understood her social and intellectual lives as intertwined. Perhaps inspired by the salons of Lichfield, she regularized the social gatherings in the house that she shared with her father in Philadelphia, reserving every Saturday night during the winter for assemblies of friends. Rush described these Saturday evening salons in terms of both friendship and intellectual cultivation, recalling how Graeme's talents and imagination set the tone for the events:

> In her father's family she now occupied the place of her mother. She kept his house, and presided at his table and fire-side in entertaining all his company. Such was the character of Dr. Graeme's family for hospitality and refinement of manners, that all strangers of note who visited Philadelphia were introduced to it. Saturday evenings were appropriated for many years during Miss Graeme's winter residence in the city, for entertainment not only of strangers, but of such of her friends of both sexes as were considered the most suitable company for them. These evenings were, properly speaking, of the attic kind. The genius of Miss Graeme evolved the heat and light that animated them. One while she instructed by the stores of knowledge contained in the historians, philosophers, and poets of ancient and modern nations, which she called forth at her pleasure; and again she charmed by a profusion of original ideas, collected by her vivid and widely expanded imagination, and combined

12. Rush, "An Account of the Life and Character of Mrs. Elizabeth Ferguson," 521.
13. Ousterhout, *The Most Learned Woman in America*, 122–23.

> with exquisite taste and judgment into an endless variety of elegant and delightful forms. Upon these occasions her body seemed to evanish, and she appeared to be all mind.[14]

Rush reported elsewhere in this essay that Graeme's mother possessed a "masculine mind," by which he presumably meant intellectual talents that exceeded what was expected of women.[15] Elizabeth, too, in Rush's estimation, transcended the limitations of her female body—"her body seemed to evanish"—to reach a seemingly higher plane of intellectual achievement and inspiration.

Graeme's salon apparently stopped meeting around the time of her marriage in 1772 to Henry Hugh Fergusson. The marriage took place without the knowledge or permission of her father. When her father died a month later, he left his property to Elizabeth, but, since she was now a *feme covert*, the property legally belonged to her husband. Henry remained loyal to Britain during the Revolution and, in 1778, returned to England. Elizabeth remained in America, and her property was confiscated by the new government of the United States because it belonged to her husband, a traitor.[16] She was forced to leave Graeme Park and spent two years living with various friends while pursuing her claim to her home and property. She succeeded in asserting her right to the estate and was allowed to return in 1781, but a decade later she lacked the resources to continue its upkeep. The estate was sold, and she spent the last decade of her life living with a friend, a Mrs. Todd, in Horsham.

Graeme was a prolific writer, composing poetry throughout her adult life. In her work, she frequently referred to herself as "Laura," and her female friends adopted similar pseudonyms. While she published some of her work in periodicals, her primary method of sharing her poetry was through scribal publication—copying by hand. Her objectives were apparently

14. Rush, "An Account of the Life and Character of Mrs. Elizabeth Ferguson," 523.

15. An overview of women's education is in Linda K. Kerber, *Women of the Republic: Intellect and Ideology in Revolutionary America* (Chapel Hill: University of North Carolina Press, 2014), especially ch. 7, "'Why Should Girls Be Learned or Wise?' Education and Intellect in the Early Republic."

16. On the laws of coverture and the women who were disgraced as a result of their husbands' loyalty to the British crown, see Kacy Dowd Tillman, "Women Left Behind: Female Loyalism, Coverture, and Grace Growden Galloway's Empire of Self," in *Women's Narratives of the Early Americas and the Formation of Empire*, ed. Mary McAleer Balkun and Susan C. Imbarrato (New York: Palgrave Macmillan, 2016), 141–55.

twofold: first, to foster an environment for artistic creation in America, and second, to connect herself with friends through shared sentiment. Her commonplace books should be understood in this context. The genre of the commonplace book offered Graeme and her friends a means to commune, reflect on, and memorialize their experiences, linking themselves to each other through the medium of poetry.

Music in Elizabeth Graeme's World

Elizabeth Graeme's exposure to music began early on. Before her journey to Britain, in 1764, she reported to her friend Mary Campbell that she had been taking lessons with one of the music masters who had recently established himself in Philadelphia, though they got off to a rocky start. Apologizing for not writing to Campbell more often, she explains, "some of my engagements are of a nature to require a large share of my time":

> I have a French master attend in an hour each day; and leaves me employment for a couple more, and the new musick master who came over with Mr. Penn has also the disposal of part of my day; I often think we take of [*sic*] vast deal of pains to inform ourselves of what the wise king told us some thousand years ago; that in much knowledge there is much sorrow. And the conclusion of all is vanity: these are my notions when I have not perform'd my tasks and lessons as I might have done which is frequently the case.[17]

By the 1760s Philadelphia had begun to attract a population of enterprising professional musicians, who taught, sold sheet music and instruments, and performed publicly. Foremost among these was James Bremner, who immigrated to Philadelphia from Scotland by 1763. On December 1 of that year, the *Pennsylvania Gazette* ran an advertisement for Bremner's music school, "where young Ladies may be Taught the Harpsicord, or Guittar, on Mondays, Wednesdays and Fridays, from 10 o'Clock in the Morning till 12, at Twenty Shillings per Month, and Forty Shillings Entrance Money: Likewise young Gentlemen may be Taught the Violin, German Flute, Harpsicord, or Guittar, from 6 o'Clock in the Evening till 8, on Mondays,

17. Elizabeth Graeme to [Mary] Campbell, January 10, 1764. Pennsylvania Historical and Museum Commission, Pennsylvania State Archives, Manuscript Group 8, Pennsylvania Collection (Miscellaneous).

Wednesdays and Fridays, for the same price and Entrance Money."[18] Bremner also initiated and played in the first public concert series in Philadelphia, and it appears that the Graeme family attended them.[19]

Bremner's arrival in Philadelphia was part of a wave of Scottish immigration to Philadelphia between the 1750s and 1780s that had a palpable and lasting effect on the city and its intellectual and cultural life. Following the failed Jacobite Rebellion in 1745, during which Scottish nationalists had sought to restore the Stuart Prince Charles ("Bonny Prince Charlie") to the English throne, numerous Scottish families immigrated to the colonies, and there remained an active exchange of ideas and cultural traditions across the Atlantic.

Bremner's place in this trans-Atlantic network was crucial for Philadelphia's musical environment: he retained connections to institutions such as the Edinburgh Music Society, of which he had formerly been a member and paid employee, as well as a link to his brother, the London-based music printer and seller Robert Bremner.[20] Through his connections and travels across the Atlantic, Bremner helped enable Philadelphia's musical community to remain abreast of the latest developments across the ocean.[21] The lasting influence of these connections is made clear from the fact that Hopkinson and Robert Bremner continued to communicate after James Bremner's death in 1780. In 1783 Hopkinson wrote a letter intended for Robert Bremner, asking him to select a harpsichord for Thomas Jefferson's daughter—"an Instrument of the very best kind—a double Harpsichord with Merlin's forte-piano Stop and such other modern Improvements as

18. *The Pennsylvania Gazette*, December 1, 1763.

19. Osterhout, *The Most Learned Woman in America*, 124–25. On this concert series, see Krauss, "James Bremner, Alexander Reinagle and the Influence of the Edinburgh Musical Society on Philadelphia," 264–65; and Jones, *Literature and Music in the Atlantic World*, 43.

20. While many sources equivocate as to whether James and Robert Bremner were related, Anne McClenny Krauss has discovered convincing evidence from the payment records of the Edinburgh Musical Society to establish that the two were brothers, and their father, also named Robert, was likewise a member of the society. See Krauss, "James Bremner, Alexander Reinagle and the Influence of the Edinburgh Musical Society on Philadelphia," 261 and 273n8.

21. Bremner apparently resided in London between 1770 and 1775, during which years Hopkinson replaced him as organist at Christ Church in Philadelphia; see Krauss, "James Bremner, Alexander Reinagle and the Influence of the Edinburgh Musical Society on Philadelphia," 265; and Oscar G. Sonneck, *Francis Hopkinson, the First American Poet-Composer, 1737–1791 and James Lyon, Patrior, Preacher, Psalmodist, 1735–1794* (New York: Da Capo Press, 1967), 28.

you may think advantageous."[22] In 1785 Robert wrote to Hopkinson to chastise him for being unwilling to accept copies of his *Harpsichord or Spinnet Miscellany* on consignment: "Disappointments seldom ruffle my temper but I cannot help acknowledging being much hurt when I found you had returned the cases of music."[23] Clearly, Robert had come to expect better results from his communication with Hopkinson.

While Rush's description of Elizabeth Graeme's salon does not mention musical activities, other evidence suggests that music-making, whether by Graeme herself or by her friends, was an important component of her salon gatherings. Despite her confession, in the letter to Mary Campbell quoted above, that she did not practice music sufficiently, she was devoted to the art enough that she asked Francis Hopkinson to select a harpsichord for her when he traveled to London in 1766. A letter dated February 1767 indicates that Hopkinson had accomplished this task: "Long look'd for will I hope come at last. I have shipp'd your harpsichord on board of Capt. Sparks, and I heartily wish it may arrive safe and prove to your satisfaction."[24] It is likely that this instrument served her in her salon gatherings. That this instrument occupied an important place in her home is implied by the fact that it was included in the inventory of possessions that she drew up when attempting to recover her property from the American government in 1778.[25]

Further evidence for the cultivation of music in Graeme's salon comes from her poetry. She participated in the custom of writing new poetic texts for well-known Scottish tunes. Among these is her 1769 poem "Content in a Cottage, A Song to the Tune of The Lass of Peattys Mill," the same tune that Hopkinson would later use as the basis of the second part of his musical elegy for James Bremner.[26] The practice of writing new poetry to be sung to well-known tunes was designed to enable sociable music-making. By creating a new text that could be sung to such a melody, Graeme and

22. Francis Hopkinson to Robert Bremner, November 28, 1783, https://founders.archives.gov/documents/Jefferson/01-06-02-0285 (accessed July 22, 2020).

23. Robert Bremner to Francis Hopkinson, February 5, 1785. Quoted in J. S. Darling, "Preface," in Robert Bremner, *Harpsichord or Spinnet Miscellany: A Facsimile Reproduction of the Original Edition of About 1765, from a Copy Belonging to Colonial Williamsburg* (Williamsburg, VA: Colonial Williamsburg Foundation, 1972), v.

24. Francis Hopkinson to Elizabeth Graeme, February 21, 1767. Hopkinson Papers, Historical Society of Pennsylvania.

25. Ousterhout, *The Most Learned Woman in America*, 124.

26. "Content in a Cottage" is in the Library Company of Philadelphia, MS *Poemata Juvenalia*, vol. 2, no. 85, 13494.Q.

others who participated in this custom created a means for an easily shared communal experience. Such poetry could be sung by an individual or distributed among the participants in Graeme's salon gatherings, with Graeme herself or another of her musical friends at the harpsichord, to facilitate a spontaneous performance. Graeme's text, indeed, is tailored to reflect the rustic experience of the Pennsylvania countryside. Whether sung at Graeme Park or in the Philadelphia home that she shared with her father, the poem evokes an idealized—and musical—image of the American pastoral. It re-situates the song from the outdoor landscape of Scotland to the domestic comforts of the colonial hearth and home, as shown in the first of her eight stanzas:

The scenes of rural bliss,
An humble poet sings,
The *Shepherds* happy wish,
That mild *Contentment* brings.
Our vernal woods and groves,
A source of pleasure yield,
While soft delightful loves
Enliven every field.

The custom of using Scottish airs as the basis of new poetry is attested on both sides of the Atlantic, as Graeme surely knew, and it was especially popular in Philadelphia, where the influence of Scottish immigrants was so strong. The Lichfield poet Anna Seward, whom Graeme may have met during her journey to Britain, explained in a letter of 1764 that this practice was her "little musical recipe for love-sick melancholy." Sending to an unidentified friend a letter together with a poem, Seward explained, "The first verse is an old ditty to a gay and pleasing tune. The remaining stanzas are mine, following the lead of the original in its pretty, though quaint idea."[27] Although Seward wrote that she found both "pleasure" and "use" in singing the song to herself, she sent it to her friend with the expectation that they would be bound by the common experience that the musical poetry would enable. In a more humorous description of the same practice, Ben-

27. Anna Seward, *The Poetical Works of Anna Seward: With Extracts from Her Literary Correspondence . . . in three volumes*, ed. Walter Scott (Edinburgh: James Ballantyne and Co., 1810), 1:cx–cxi.

jamin Franklin wrote from London to chastise his brother, Peter, who had just sent him a newly written ballad text. As Benjamin wrote,

> I like your ballad, and think it well adapted for your purpose of discountenancing expensive foppery, and encouraging industry and frugality. If you can get it generally sung in your country, it may probably have a good deal of the effect you hope and expect from it. But as you aimed at making it general, I wonder you chose so uncommon a measure in poetry, that none of the tunes in common use will suit it. Had you fitted it to an old one, well known, it must have spread much faster than I doubt it will do from the best new tune we can get compos'd for it.[28]

Thus Franklin, too, demonstrates that the purpose of writing new words to familiar songs was to enable as many people as possible to partake of the experience of the music, in this case also absorbing the message of the text. Similarly, Franklin participated in this practice in the salon of Madame Brillon, as recorded in a manuscript from 1778; titled "Songs made for and sung at the Entertainment given us by M. Brillon," the manuscript includes a French-language poem titled "Le cheval et son maître," to be sung to the air "Il étoit une fille."[29] In all these cases, music fostered community, and the communal experience of music would serve to inspire new artistic creation. For Graeme, deeply invested in fostering the arts in Philadelphia, this practice would further her goals.

The music that was played and sung in Graeme's salon is not documented precisely; if she owned any musical scores, they were probably lost when her property was confiscated by the American government. However, given her close relationship with Hopkinson and his frequent presence in her salon, his collection of printed and handwritten music offers an idea of what music might have been heard in her salon.[30] Not surprisingly, the music of Handel figured prominently in his collection, as it did in the public concert scene in Philadelphia and throughout the British colonies.

28. Benjamin Franklin to Peter Franklin, before 1765. The letter was included in Benjamin Franklin, *Experiments and Observations on Electricity*, 473.

29. Benjamin Franklin, "Song for a Brillon Party," [ca. April 10, 1778?], https://franklinpapers.org (accessed June 4, 2021).

30. A portion of Francis Hopkinson's collection of music is held in the Kislak Center for Special Collections—Rare Book Collection of the University of Pennsylvania, Folio M1.A11 .H6. The library catalogue record is at https://franklin.library.upenn.edu/catalog/FRANKLIN_9922677353503681 (accessed July 22, 2020).

Figure 7.4 George Frideric Handel, "Let Me Wander Not Unseen," from *Handel's Songs Selected from His Oratorios for the Harpsichord, Voice, Hoboy or German Flute* (London: John Walsh, ca. 1765?).

Hopkinson owned five volumes (totaling 807 pages) of the series *Handel's Songs Selected from His Oratorios for the Harpsichord, Voice, Hoboy or German Flute*, published by the London printer John Walsh. While this collection included orchestral part books to enable performance in the original instrumentations, the vocal parts are contained in a keyboard-format layout that also functions as a chamber arrangement. The keyboardist is given bass figures to realize the harmony as well as melodic cues from the instrumental parts that also allow the keyboardist to cover those melodies when the singer rests; this can be seen in figure 7.4, Handel's setting of an adapted version of Milton's "Let Me Wander Not Unseen." This publication is ideally suited, then, for use in both public concerts and private salon gatherings where a full orchestra would have been impractical.

Other publications that Hopkinson collected attest to the predominantly British orientation of musical tastes in colonial Philadelphia, which included an embrace of both British and Italian composers. Hopkinson's volumes for string ensemble include works by Corelli, Geminiani, and Vivaldi. The solo keyboard music that he collected includes organ works for the Episcopal and Catholic churches. He also copied out three volumes of solo keyboard music including works by Handel and Scarlatti, as well as keyboard arrangements of music by Vivaldi, Geminiani, Galuppi, Corelli, and Stamitz.

Bremner clearly helped shape Hopkinson's musical tastes and practice, and Hopkinson's keyboard manuscripts include a stylistic fusion that reflects the tastes of their mutual social circle.[31] Music by the Italian composers featured in the Edinburgh Music Society and in the public concerts held in Philadelphia appear in keyboard reductions, often with inner voices thinned out to provide an easier texture for both playing and listening. The Hopkinson keyboard manuscripts also include music composed by James Bremner and one work by the Earl of Kelly, which Bremner would have provided. Solo keyboard works including lessons by Scarlatti are interspersed with English keyboard solos and popular songs.

Bremner's participation in Graeme's salon must also have influenced the repertoire heard there. Like other professional musicians who frequented musical salons, Bremner stood to gain an audience as well as a network of potential patrons or students. Part of his prestige lay in his experiences with interesting music. Bremner participated in the Edinburgh Music Society when it was giving public concerts that included repertoire by Handel, Corelli, Geminiani, and Vivaldi; he also played for Henry Home, Lord Kames, as well as the Sixth Earl of Kelly, one of the leading Scottish composers of the day. Krauss has demonstrated that through the earl, who traveled widely, Bremner also gained access to the repertoire and playing styles of the Mannheim school, meaning that he developed a truly international taste; this may explain the presence of music by Stamitz in the collection of Bremner's friend Hopkinson.

In addition to the sonatas and arrangements of orchestral music, oratorios, and choral music reflected in Hopkinson's collection and Bremner's practice, Graeme's salon must have featured performances of the Scottish airs for which she and many other poets wrote new texts. Publications of music containing Scottish airs—dozens or perhaps hundreds of them—proliferated and spread from the British Isles across the Atlantic. As with the work of Ossian, these songs assumed a nearly mythical status, as they

31. A thorough study of the practices of music manuscript production in early America is in Glenda Goodman, *Cultivated by Hand: Amateur Musicians in the Early American Republic* (New York and Oxford: Oxford University Press, 2020).

seemed to offer access to a simple, ancient, and authentic tradition of music that transcended a single time and place. In addition, as Bonnie Gordon has pointed out, the Scottish airs allowed elite Americans to conceptualize a "folk" tradition that was racialized as white. Wealthy elites like Graeme "[marked] themselves as metropolitan and cultivated, in opposition to the subordinated, enslaved, black, and mixed-race populations."[32] Indeed, like many members of the elite class in the mid-Atlantic region, the Graeme family held slaves in captivity.[33]

The link between the simplicity of the Scottish airs and the seemingly "natural" aesthetic that they encompassed is explained most clearly by Benjamin Franklin in a letter written from London to Lord Kames on June 2, 1765, and included in Franklin's published correspondence a few years later. For Franklin, much modern music was overly ornamented and artificial. Scottish melodies, by contrast, consisted of nothing but melodies composed in the pure intervallic ratios of the harmonic series. As he wrote to Kames,

> Many Pieces of [modern music] are mere Compositions of Tricks. I have sometimes at a Concert attended by a common Audience plac'd myself so as to see all their Faces, and observ'd no Signs of Pleasure in them during the Performance of much that was admir'd by the Performers themselves; while a plain old Scottish Tune, which they disdain'd and could scarcely be prevail'd on to play, gave manifest and general Delight. Give me leave on this Occasion to extend a little the Sense of your Position, That "Melody and Harmony are separately agreable, and in Union delightful;" and to give it as my Opinion, that the Reason why the Scotch Tunes have liv'd so long, and will probably live forever (if they escape being stifled in modern affected Ornament) is merely this, that they are really Compositions of Melody and Harmony united, or rather that their Melody is Harmony. I mean the simple Tunes sung by a single Voice. As this will appear paradoxical I must explain my Meaning. In common Acceptation indeed, only an agreable *Succession* of Sounds is called *Melody*, and only the *Co-existence* of agreeing Sounds, *Harmony*. But since the Memory is capable of retaining for some Moments

32. Bonnie Gordon, "What Mr. Jefferson Didn't Hear," in *Rethinking Difference in Music Scholarship*, ed. Olivia Bloechl, Melanie Lowe, and Jeffrey Kallberg (Cambridge: Cambridge University Press, 2014), 109.

33. See Ousterhout, *the Most Learned Woman in America*, 227 and passim.

> a perfect Idea of the Pitch of a past Sound, so as to compare with it the Pitch of a succeeding Sound, and judge truly of their Agreement or Disagreement, there may and does arise from thence a Sense of Harmony between present and past Sounds, equally pleasing with that between two present Sounds. Now the Construction of the old Scotch Tunes is this, that almost every succeeding *emphatical* Note, is a Third, a Fifth, an Octave, or in short some Note that is in Concord with the preceding Note.[34]

Franklin's letter perpetuates the notion that the Scottish tunes circulating in Britain and America were quite old. His description evokes the recitation of poetry in the ancient world: "Farther, when we consider by whom these ancient Tunes were composed, and how they were first performed, we shall see that such harmonical Succession of Sounds was natural and even necessary in their Construction. They were compos'd by the Minstrels of those days, to be plaid on the Harp accompany'd by the Voice. The Harp was strung with Wire, and had no Contrivance like that in the modern Harpsichord." Modern Scottish musicians could approximate the sounds and sentiments of these ancient bards, but they risked corruption by the modern taste for harmony. Franklin cited the Scottish cellist James Oswald as a primary proponent of the ancient musical tradition: "Whoever has heard James Oswald play them on his Violoncello, will be less inclin'd to dispute this with me. I have more than once seen Tears of Pleasure in the Eyes of his Auditors; and yet I think even his Playing those Tunes would please more, if he gave them less modern Ornament."

Graeme was still in London when Franklin wrote this letter, not yet having been called home. Franklin visited her during her stay there, and it is quite possible that they discussed the same ideas during one of these visits.[35] In any case, while Franklin's letter started as a private document, he soon published it, rendering it part of the public sphere. Similar ideas were expressed by other writers, both in America and in Britain, over the next decades, as I will discuss further below. While Franklin claimed to eschew all harmony and expressed distaste for the modern ornamental style, Graeme's salon gatherings likely included performances of the music of

34. Benjamin Franklin to Henry Home, Lord Kames, June 2, 1765. https://franklinpapers.org (accessed December 23, 2019). The letter was included in Benjamin Franklin, *Experiments and Observations on Electricity*, 467–72.

35. Stabile, "Salons and Power in the Era of Revolution," 133–35.

Handel, Corelli, Scarlatti, and other European composers, as well as adaptations and arrangements of popular music made by Bremner, Hopkinson, and others. Nevertheless, Graeme and her friends clearly shared Franklin's admiration for Scottish airs, and this repertoire likely formed part of their salon gatherings.

For the Scottish airs, too, there were ready avenues of transmission across the Atlantic. Franklin's mention of James Oswald may have been not only in recognition of his superior performance skills, but also because he was widely recognized for his enormous published collection of Scottish tunes, which included words and melodies alone, omitting accompaniment entirely. This encyclopedic collection, his *Caledonian Pocket Companion*, together with other publications, would likely have been brought to the colonies by travelers such as Graeme and Hopkinson. Moreover, Robert Bremner published volumes of Scottish airs arranged for various configurations of instruments and voices, offering another means of procuring copies of these songs.

Graeme's engagement with Scottish airs and the practice of adapting them to new poetry points to one overarching conception of music in her work and the work of others in her circle. As the literary historian Gillen D'Arcy Wood has noted, the pastoral poetry of John Milton—especially his *L'allegro* and *Il penseroso*—were foundational texts for the neoclassical school that flourished in Lichfield. In particular, the poetry of Anna Seward is infused with Milton's pastoral register, and, more specifically, the interpretation of Milton's work in George Frideric Handel's musical setting, *L'allegro, il penseroso, ed il moderato*. As Wood points out, Handel's pastoral oratorio offered Milton's poetry a sociable and performative orientation, allowing it to be proclaimed, heard, and shared in the company of friends. In England, Handel's music—especially around the 1784 centenary commemoration of his birth—served to unite a fractured public. For Seward and other "sociable poets" like her, "the arts, poetic *and* musical, [served] as vehicles of sentiment and sympathy and thus, by extension, as an instrument of social cohesion."[36] Seward's poetry reflects a self-conscious posture of communal experience—a posture that would soon come to be interpreted as forced and stilted, and that would be rendered outdated by the early nineteenth-century poetics of Romantic solitude. Graeme's poetry took its inspiration from the writings of the Lichfield circle, which imagined literature as a communal experience to be read aloud, sung, and heard.

36. Wood, "The Female Penseroso," 459.

Graeme was not alone in her literary and social circles in adopting this aesthetic of communal, audible poetry, filtered especially through the lens of Milton's neoclassical aesthetic and embrace of the pastoral. In 1757, Francis Hopkinson's adaptations of *L'allegro* and *Il penseroso* were published anonymously in the *American Magazine and Monthly Chronicle for the British Colonies*, a journal devoted primarily to promoting Philadelphia's political and economic interests but that also sought to cultivate American literature by including a space for "poetical essays."[37] Hopkinson, who had studied with the magazine's editor, William Smith, paraphrases Milton throughout. For example, where Milton observes, "Sometime walking, not unseen, / by hedgerow elms, on hillocks green, / Right against the eastern gate, / Where the great sun begins his state, / Robed in flames and amber light," Hopkinson responds, "Thus, thus! attend me whilst I stray / Wild as fancy leads the way; / Oe'r high hills by valleys bounded, / And o'er plains by woods surrounded."[38] Yet he transplants the Miltonian pastoral to America. By inserting references to the two dedicatees of his poem ("thou O S—th! My more than friend" refers to William Smith, and "the lawyer . . . Ch—w" to the jurist Benjamin Chew), Hopkinson fixes a generic pastoral landscape within his specific social circle of elite, educated men in mid-century Philadelphia. In fact, it seems that William Smith viewed imitation of Milton's poetry as a key mode of instruction in belles lettres among his students at the College of Philadelphia.[39]

Graeme, too, engaged with *L'allegro* and *Il penseroso* throughout her life. Included in the excerpt of her travel diary copied out by Milcah Martha Moore is a poem written for her physician in London, Dr. John Fothergill. Extolling the virtues of a solitary life, she seems to evoke Milton's pastoral poems in writing, "A moon light Walk indulge me on the Green, / Or when the Sun makes ev'ry Shadow seen / In Forms gigantick, let me stroll along, / To hear the Mock-bird chaunt his rural song."[40] If that poem seems only loosely to refer to Milton's work, Graeme's lengthy poem bemoan-

37. On the *American Magazine* within the context of periodicals published in Philadelphia, see Lyon N. Richardson, *A History of Early American Magazines 1741–1789* (New York: Octagon Books, Inc., 1966), 17–35; an assessment of Hopkinson's *L'Allegro* and *Il Penseroso* is on 115–16.

38. Francis Hopkinson, "L'Allegro. Il Penseroso," *American Magazine and Monthly Chronicle for the British Colonies* 1 (November 1757): 84–88.

39. Rodney Mader, "Elizabeth Graeme Fergusson's 'The Deserted Wife,'" *Pennsylvania Magazine of History and Biography* 135, no. 2 (April 2011): 153.

40. Moore, *Milcah Martha Moore's Book*, 215.

ing her unhappy, broken marriage, written between 1780 and 1782, refers to it overtly: the work is titled "Il Penseroso: or the Deserted-Wife."[41] In both cases, solitude is a theme that is shared, paradoxically, with a circle of sympathetic friends. By sending her work to Moore, Graeme mitigated the loneliness of the pastoral landscape through their friendship. And, as late as 1793, Graeme sent her "Deserted Wife" to her friend Annis Boudinot Stockton, fulfilling a request from Stockton to commemorate the story of Fergusson's desertion of his wife "at a time when many of [Graeme's] other friends refused to hear anything more about it."[42]

Milton's neoclassical aesthetic; the audible, sociable art of poetry in the Lichfield group; and the longing for a distant, mythical past in the Scottish airs—all these merge within Graeme's poetic sensibilities. The Scottish countryside and the stories situated there in the writings of Ossian become a stand-in for the poetic pastoral as a whole. And, as I will show, Graeme understood this pastoral aesthetic as encompassing a deeply spiritual, Christian aspect, reflecting her own piety. The biblical book of Psalms and the pure poetic art that it represented to her became overlaid with the pastoral poetic tropes of Milton and Ossian. In all these traditions, Graeme's sensibilities were contingent on sound: poetry was to be read or sung aloud, and the art of poetry became fully realized only when it could be heard.

Graeme's Psalm Paraphrases and Her Spiritual Understandings of Music

If the circumstances of Graeme's life, her poetic output, her musical studies, and her connection to leading musicians of colonial Philadelphia suggest that music was indeed practiced in her salon gatherings, another source of evidence, unexplored until now, is instructive in demonstrating what music actually meant to her. The source is a manuscript copy book of her poetic paraphrases of the biblical book of Psalms. She started writing these Psalm paraphrases after being called back to Philadelphia from her journey in Britain because of the death of her mother. Fearing that she would be "overwhelmed by grief" for her mother and her sister, Ann Stedman, who had also recently died, she turned to work on the Psalms as "a rational, and

41. The poem is introduced and reproduced in Mader, "Elizabeth Graeme Fergusson's 'The Deserted Wife,'" 151–90.

42. Mader, "Elizabeth Graeme Fergusson's 'The Deserted Wife,'" 153.

pious source of entertainment to a pensive mind."[43] In 1769 she presented the first copy of her Psalm paraphrases to the Reverend Richard Peters, an older family friend to whose care her parents had entrusted her during her travels abroad.[44] In addition, she created a second manuscript copy of the Psalm paraphrases, nesting them within a commonplace book that included copies of dozens of related texts—essays, poems, and letters—by theologians, poets, literary theorists, musicians, and music critics. This latter manuscript, which bears the title *Sunday Matters*, reflects on the synthesis of poetry and music in the biblical Psalms, and it forms a framework within which to understand Graeme's views on music.[45]

While men of the English church and universities engaged in adaptation and study of the poetics of the Psalms, the practice of reciting the Psalms was long associated with women. In the eighteenth century, adaptation or paraphrase of the Psalms became a practice demonstrating Christian women's devotion and spirituality.[46] Thus that heroine of the eighteenth century, Samuel Richardson's fictional character Pamela Andrews, adapts Psalm 137 to reflect her own distressing circumstances. In Richardson's novel, the reverend Mr. Williams first reads the first two stanzas of the metrical

43. Am.067, Elizabeth Graeme Fergusson Collection, Historical Society of Pennsylvania. This citation is on 1:12.

44. Ousterhout, *The Most Learned Woman in America*, 81.

45. The manuscript of the Psalm paraphrases that Graeme seems to have begun earlier is Psalms, vols. 1–2, 12716Q, Elizabeth Graeme Fergusson Papers, Library Company of Philadelphia. The manuscript containing copies of poetry, essays, and letters that will be the focus of my attention in this section is Am.067, Elizabeth Graeme Fergusson Collection, Historical Society of Pennsylvania, which bears the title *Sunday Matters*. Henceforth I will refer to this volume as Graeme, *Sunday Matters*. When Graeme and Richard Peters had departed for their trip across the Atlantic, Elizabeth was unaware that her mother was ill; Rush's account suggests that Ann had known of her own impending death and purposefully sent her daughter away: she "wished her daughter to be removed beyond the sphere of the counter attraction of her affections from the world of spirits, which her presence near her deathbed, would excite." See Rush, "An Account of the Life and Character of Mrs. Elizabeth Ferguson," 521.

46. The German Psalm translations written by Moses Mendelssohn, referred to in chapter 5 of this volume, should be understood in this context; Mendelssohn viewed the Psalms as a cross-confessional aesthetic space that could serve to unite Jews and Christians. This optimistic view was not shared by many Christians, however, and anti-Jewish sentiment was common, despite the long-standing Jewish presence in colonial America. See Hannah Callender Sansom, *The Diary of Hannah Callender Sansom: Sense and Sensibility in the Age of the American Revolution*, ed. Susan E. Klepp and Karin Wulf (Ithaca, NY, and London: Cornell University Press, 2010), 35.

translation in the *Book of Common Prayer* ("When we did sit in Babylon, / The Rivers round about; / Then in remembrance of Sion, / The Tears for Grief burst out"[47]) and then Pamela's adaptation is read aloud: "When I sad sat in B[rando]n hall, / All watched round about, / And thought of ev'ry absent Friend, / The Tears for Grief burst out."[48] Pamela's experience stood for that of many pious women. Jayne Elizabeth Lewis explains, "Psalms opened not only parallel but recursive and self-ironizing paths to sublimity for women poets of the period, who regardless of creed found in these adjustable and shareable pieces of experimental divinity the chance to reflect on their personal freedom to become visible in contemporary literary culture."[49]

In the manuscript *Sunday Matters*, Graeme included both the Psalm paraphrases themselves and over 150 pages of excerpts of writings copied from other sources on the Psalms, on biblical poetry as a whole, and, significantly, on the relationship between ancient and modern music and musical aesthetics. After all, the Psalms were another distinctly musical form of poetry, as indicated by their many allusions to performance practice, musical modes, and instruments. While the actual sounds of this ancient spiritual music were lost, eighteenth-century writers understood them as retaining a musical sensibility; this is why they would prompt Graeme to collect and reflect upon music in the context of this manuscript. The sources that she transcribes in *Sunday Matters* range from poetic treatises to sermons, historical studies to correspondence, and they form a robust interpretive apparatus for the Psalms, shedding light on how Elizabeth Graeme understood the musical art of biblical poetry. Some of these date to the period before she began working on the Psalms, and they probably shaped her project from the beginning. Others were written or published after her Psalm paraphrases were already underway or completed. Nevertheless, the whole collection elucidates how Graeme understood these poems in a distinctly musical context.

47. *The Book of Common Prayer and Administration of the Sacraments . . . According to the Church of England: Together with the Psalter or Psalms of David* (Oxford: John Baskett, 1727), Psalm 137 [n.p.].

48. Samuel Richardson, *Pamela: or Virtue Rewarded . . . In Two Volumes*, 5th ed. (London: C. Rivington; J. Osborn, 1741), 2:137–38.

49. Jayne Elizabeth Lewis, "The Eighteenth-Century Psalm," in *Oxford Handbooks Online*, January 10, 2017, https://www.oxfordhandbooks.com/view/10.1093/oxfordhb/9780199935338.001.0001/oxfordhb-9780199935338-e-150#ref_oxfordhb-9780199935338-e-150-note-69 (accessed December 26, 2019).

At the outset of the manuscript, Elizabeth Graeme reproduced a letter from her mother that explains the impetus for the project, suggesting that both mother and daughter understood engagement with the Psalms as a particular source of joy and comfort for women. In the "Extract of a letter from Mrs. Ann Graeme, to her daughter aged 15 on the Psalms of David," Ann wrote, "I have found great Pleasure and help to Devotion in the *Psalms*, and I warmly recommend you learning some that please you by heart. . . . There is no stage of Life but they are applicable to and they contain the most ardent prayers."[50] Elizabeth next included an excerpt from the letter that she had written to Reverend Peters when she gave him the original manuscript. She explained that the Psalms forged a bond between herself and her mother, especially because of the impression made by reading them aloud—by performing them: "When I was young my worthy mother frequently made me read the *Psalms* to her and I so early imbibed a fondness for them, that like all other first impressions they are like to be lasting."[51] In the same letter she mentions some of the Psalm paraphrases that had influenced her, including the metrical Psalms of Tate and Brady, which had been widely used for musical settings and church worship since their first appearance in 1696.[52] She had also derived inspiration from the theologian and critic Joseph Addison, who had published only a handful of Psalm paraphrases, but whose "elegant" writing had epitomized, respectively, Psalms in the "simple *Pastoral*" and the "sublime" styles. She is likely to have known the paraphrases of Hopkinson, which were published in 1767, while she was in the midst of her project.[53] And, later in the volume, she mentions the fictional heroine Pamela, who turned to the Psalms when she was undergoing the harshest trials.[54]

Graeme followed the examples of both Addison and Tate and Brady in using iambic tetrameter—what she called "a meter of light syllables"—for her Psalm paraphrases.[55] This regular and easy meter implies that they

50. Graeme, *Sunday Matters*, 9.

51. Graeme, *Sunday Matters*, 14.

52. Nahum Tate and Nicholas Brady, *A New Version of the Psalms of David, Fitted to the Tunes Used in Churches* (London: M. Clark, 1696).

53. Francis Hopkinson, *The Psalms of David with the Ten Commandments, Creed, Lord's Prayer, &c. in Metre. Also, the Catechism, Confession of Faith, Liturgy, &c. Translated from the Dutch. For the use of the Reformed Protestant Dutch Church of the City of New-York* (New York: James Parker, 1767).

54. Graeme, *Sunday Matters*, 183.

55. Graeme, *Sunday Matters*, see the title page, figure 7.5.

were designed with a musical realization in mind. Indeed, the title of Tate and Brady's volume indicates clearly that musical setting and musical performance was the object of the volume: they were the "Psalms of David, fitted to the tunes used in churches." In facilitating musical performance, these various poets likely thought that they were simply highlighting an important aspect of the life and character of King David, a musician, as well as the Levitic tribe of the ancient Hebrews, who served as musicians in the Temple and who used the Psalms as part of their worship.

A number of the sources in Graeme's *Sunday Matters* confirm the point that the Psalms achieved their truest realization through song. For example, she includes a long passage from Hugh Blair, the Scottish theologian who also wrote a dissertation on Ossian, who notes that "from the earliest times, Music and Poetry were cultivated among the Hebrews." While he recounts some musical episodes in the biblical days of prophets before King David, Blair asserts that "in the days of King David, Music and Poetry were carried to their greatest height. For the service of the Tabernacle, he appointed four thousand Levites, divided into twenty-four courses, and marshalled under several leaders, whose sole business it was to sing Hymns, and to perform the instrumental music in the public workshop. Asaph, Heman, and Jeduthun, were the chief directors of the music; and, from the titles of some Psalms, it would appear that they were also eminent composers of Hymns or sacred Poems."[56] Blair further explains that the unique poetic structures used in the book of Psalms were the result of the ancient Hebrews' musical performance practices. They frequently use parallel constructions in order to accommodate "alternatim" performance. Blair goes on to describe the noble effect of this manner of musical–poetic performance, showing, too, that it spread to the New Testament from the Jewish practice. And, he notes, the Psalms "bear plain marks of their being composed in order to be thus performed."[57]

Graeme's *Sunday Matters* quotes a 1718 essay in Joseph Addison's *Spectator* that was frequently reprinted throughout the eighteenth century. Here Addison affirms that "Music among those who were stiled the chosen people was a religious art. The songs of *Sion*, which we have reason to believe were in high repute among the courts of the eastern monarchs, were

56. Graeme, *Sunday Matters*, 68; copied from Hugh Blair, *Lectures on Rhetoric and Belles lettres* (Philadelphia: Robert Aitken, 1784), 384–86.

57. Graeme, *Sunday Matters*, 66; copied from Blair, *Lectures on Rhetoric and Belles lettres*, 385.

nothing else but psalms and pieces of poetry that adored or celebrated the Supreme Being."[58] Addison, too, and Graeme after him, affirmed the role that music plays in inspiring devotion: "Music, when thus applied, raises noble hints in the mind of the hearer, and fills it with great conceptions. It strengthens devotion, and advances praise into rapture, lengthens out every act of worship, and produces more lasting and permanent impressions in the mind, than those which accompany any transient form of words that are uttered in the ordinary method of religious worship." Another of the many sources that Graeme quotes is Charles Burney's *General History of Music*, which includes a detailed passage on music among the ancient Hebrews, paying special attention to the Psalms.[59]

Many of the writers whom Elizabeth Graeme quotes in *Sunday Matters* assert a link between the ancient Psalms and modern musical–poetic practice. As Blair explains, the poetic ode, a neoclassical, Miltonian genre in which Elizabeth Graeme and others in her circle frequently wrote, was the heir of biblical Psalmody; the most notable feature of this genre was its connection to music:

> Its peculiar character is, that it is intended to be sung, or accompanied with music. Its designation implies this. Ode is, in Greek, the same with Song or Hymn, and Lyric Poetry imports, that the Verses are accompanied with a lyre, or musical instrument. This distinction was not, at the first, peculiar to any one species of Poetry. For as I observed . . . Music and Poetry were coeval, and were, originally, always joined together. But after their separation took place, after Bards had begun to make Verse Compositions, which were to be recited or read, not to be sung, Poems as were designed to be still joined with Music or Song, were, by way of distinction, called Odes. In the Ode, therefore, Poetry retains its first and most antient form.[60]

Blair goes on to articulate the benefits that music offers to poetry, and *Sunday Matters* includes this passage as well: music "fills [the mind] with high enthusiastic emotions; or to soothe, and melt it into the gentle pleasurable

58. Graeme, *Sunday Matters*, 106; copied from Joseph Addison, [no title], in *The Spectator* 6 (Saturday, June 14, 1712): 43.

59. Graeme, *Sunday Matters*, 114–15; copied from Charles Burney, *A General History of Music*, 1:224.

60. Blair, *Lectures on Rhetoric and Belles lettres*, 370.

feelings. Hence, the Ode may either aspire to the former character of the sublime and noble, or it may descend to the latter of the pleasant and the gay."

In her Psalm paraphrases themselves, Graeme sometimes took an especially musical approach, foregrounding the idea of sounding performance, and sometimes altering the text so that it indicates not solo or solitary song, but communal song. Her paraphrase of Psalm 9 demonstrates this point. In the original Hebrew text, as well as the King James Version, which Graeme indicates that she used, the second stanza states only that the speaker will sing by himself: "I will be glad and rejoice in thee: I will sing praise to thy name, O thou most High"; only in verse 11 does he command, "Sing praises to the LORD, which dwelleth in Zion."[61] Similarly, Tate and Brady maintain the first-person singular in this stanza: "The thought of them shall to my soul / exalted pleasure bring; Whilst to thy Name, O thou most High, triumphant praise I sing." Graeme, by contrast, renders the singing in the second verse as a communal act:

The flowing harmony shall join
And every wish and thought combine;
The praise of Heaven's high King to sound
And echo forth to nations round.[62]

The original Hebrew of Psalm 19, as well as its counterparts in the King James Version and in Tate and Brady, makes no mention of music *per se*, instead using imagery of speech: "(1) The heavens declare the glory of God; and the firmament sheweth his handywork. (2) Day until day uttereth speech, and night unto night sheweth knowledge. (3) There is no speech nor language, where their voice is not heard." Joseph Addison's version, first published in *The Spectator*, alters the third verse slightly to include a reference to heavenly music:

I.

The spacious firmament on high,
With all the blue ethereal sky

61. I quote from *The Holy Bible, Containing the Old and New Testaments: Newly Translated Out of the Original Tongues, and with the Former Translations Diligently Compared and Revised* (Oxford: Thomas Baskett, 1760).

62. Graeme, *Sunday Matters*, 159.

And spangled heav'ns, a shining frame,
Their great original proclaim:
Th' unwearied sun, from day to day,
Does his Creator's power display
And publishes to every land
The work of an Almighty hand.

II.

Soon as the evening shades prevail,
The moon takes up the wondrous tale,
And nightly to the listning earth
Repeats the story of her birth:
Whilst all the stars that round her burn,
And all the planets in their turn,
Confirm the tidings as they rowl,
And spread the truth from pole to pole.

III.

What though, in solemn silence, all
Move round the dark terrestrial ball?
What tho' nor real voice nor sound
Amid their radiant orbs be found?
In Reason's ear they all rejoice,
And utter forth a glorious voice,
For ever singing, as they shine,
"The hand that made us is divine."[63]

Graeme's version of the third stanza borrows some of Addison's language, and, indeed, she acknowledged her debt to Addison's version in a note at the end of this paraphrase.[64] But she alters the text beyond what Addison had done to foreground heavenly music still further. Her use of the word "accord" in the second stanza points to the music emanating from heaven, and this is clarified still further in the third stanza:

63. I quote from Joseph Addison, *The Works of the Late Right Honourable Joseph Addison, Esq.*, 2nd ed. (London: Jacob Tonson, 1730), 3:534.

64. Graeme, *Sunday Matters*, 210.

I.

On high God's wondrous works are shown,
His power the firmament doth own.
The heavenly systems all combine
And in resplendent glory shine.

II.

Revolving day with night accord
To praise their all creating Lord.
They know their fixed appointed time
To veil in shades, or radiant shine.

III.

With harmony divine they roll,
And sound a voice from pole to pole,
Whirld from their great first movin[g] hand
Their cause proscribed by His command.[65]

This emphasis on music, and on communal music in particular, is a theme that runs through many of Graeme's Psalm paraphrases, and it shows a distinct interest in the communal spirituality that music afforded. This interest is confirmed by the extensive commentaries, letters, sermons, and essays that she excerpted for inclusion in *Sunday Matters*, which extend to hundreds of pages and of which I have described only a handful. That she engaged with these works and copied them into her manuscript suggests that she valued them and absorbed their messages. In the case of the Psalms, she absorbed not only the overarching message conveyed by her mother—that engagement with the Psalms would be edifying and comforting to her in times of distress—but also the broader argument, put forth in many of these sources, that biblical poetry was inherently and essentially musical. Music, in turn, served a spiritual purpose, directing the heart and mind to pious thoughts.

A hint that this purpose underpinned not only music with an overtly sacred text but also other forms of musical practice lies in Graeme's title page introducing her paraphrases of the Psalms themselves (fig. 7.5). This title

65. Graeme, *Sunday Matters*, 207.

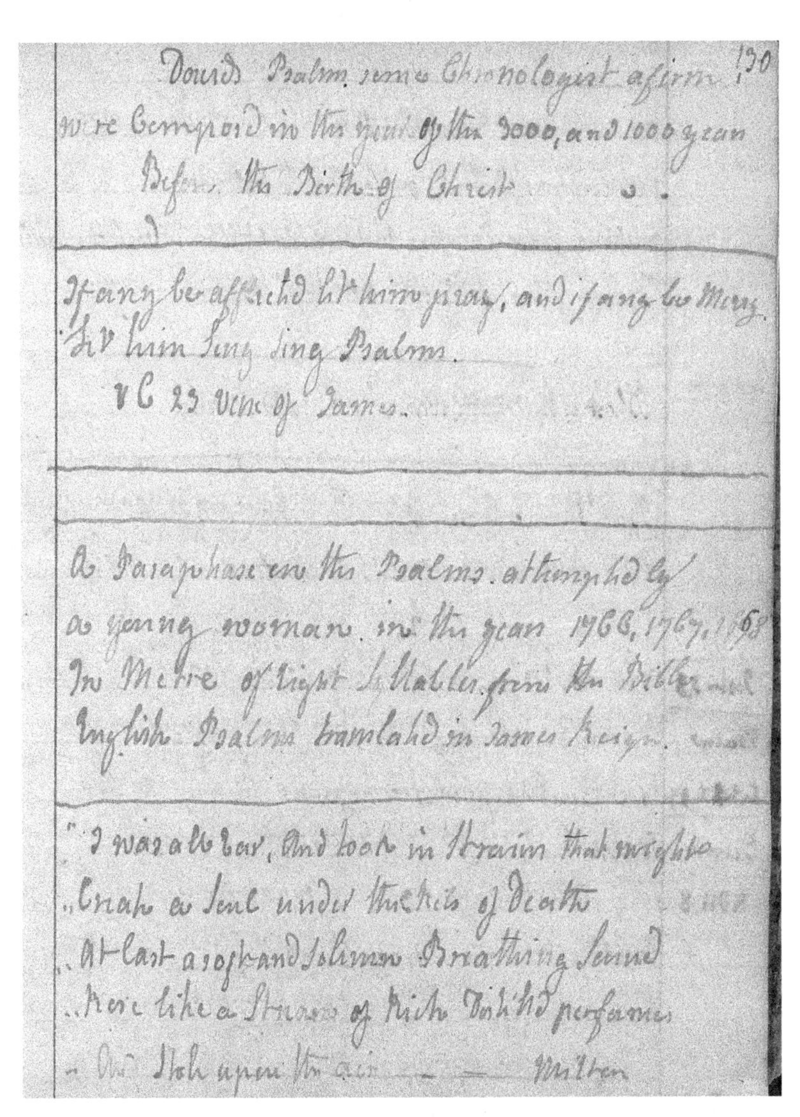
Davids Psalms some Chronologist affirm 130
were Composed in the year of the 3000, and 1000 years
Before the Birth of Christ

If any be afflicted let him pray, and if any be Merry
Let him Sing Sing Psalms.
5 C 13 verse of James.

A Paraphrase on the Psalms. attempted by
a young woman in the years 1766, 1767, 1768
In Metre of light Syllables from the Bible and
English Psalms translated in James Reign.

"I was all Ear, and took in strains that might
"Create a Soul under the ribs of Death
"At last a soft and solemn breathing sound
"Rose like a Stream of rich distill'd perfumes
"And stole upon the air — Milton

Figure 7.5 Elizabeth Graeme, title page introducing her Psalm paraphrases: "A paraphrase on the Psalms. Attempted by a young woman in the years 1766, 1767, [17]68. In meter of light syllables from the Bible. English Psalms translated in James Reign." From Graeme's manuscript titled *Sunday Matters* [Psalms commonplace book] [1760–1780s]. Elizabeth Graeme Fergusson Collection, Am.067, Volume 1, Historical Society of Pennsylvania. Reproduced with permission from the Historical Society of Pennsylvania.

page is nested deep within the manuscript, as it is preceded by 129 pages of other material. The title page includes two epigraphs. The first is from the book of James: "If any be afflicted let him pray, and if any be merry let him sing Psalms." The second is adapted from Milton:

> I was all ear, and took in strains that might
> Create a soul under the ribs of death.
> At last a soft and solemn breathing sound
> Rose like a steam of rich distill'd perfumes
> And stole upon the air.[66]

This excerpt from Milton's masque *Comus* provides a pastoral framing for the Psalms, evoking not Christian spirituality divorced from the world, but a spirituality in which sacred and the neoclassical are fused, in which nature forms the manifestation of God's presence on earth, and in which the ancient poetry of the Hebrews can be evoked (if not fully revived) through modern, musically oriented words. Indeed, this passage frames the Psalms as inherently and essentially musical—as texts for singing aloud. In a musical performance, the Psalms have the power to "create a soul under the ribs of death," to revive bodies with sounding spirituality, much as the Divine Creator initiated life through the utterance of words. In the quest to recover these ancient sounds, Elizabeth Graeme showed herself to be not just "all ear," but also a contributor to this musical–poetic tradition. The sources that she curated and collected in *Sunday Matters* frame her own creative project.

Scottish Airs, Psalmody, and Friendship in Eighteenth-Century Philadelphia

One source that Graeme included in *Sunday Matters* is significant because of its explicit juxtaposition of church music with the Scottish airs of which Graeme and her friends were so fond. While the source in question was not published until 1781, it reflects the same overarching understanding of the link between the Christian devotion in the book of Psalms and secular pas-

66. The original source is Milton's *Comus: A Mask*; an edition to which Graeme might have had access is John Milton, *Paradise Regain'd: A Poem in Four Books; to Which Is Added Samson Agonistes; and Poems Upon Several Occasions* (London: J. and R. Tonson, 1742), 256.

toral sensibilities as that conveyed by Graeme's epigraph from Milton. The passage in question comes from a treatise by the composer and theologian Reverend John Wesley, published in the *Arminian Magazine*, which argues for the supremacy of simple melodies of Scottish and Irish airs above the complex, artificial concert music heard most often in the church and concert hall. Graeme quotes Wesley's treatise as it first laments the excessive complexity of modern music—especially sacred music. Wesley draws on the centuries-long tradition of venerating the ancient Greeks, who knew how to use music to move the passions, and contrasts their art with modern musical practice, which, he claims, invariably fails to move listeners. For Wesley, only one form of modern music can succeed: "when the music has been extremely simple and inartificial, the composer having attended to melody, not harmony. Then, and only then, the natural power of music to move the passions has appeared. . . . Upon this ground it is, that so many persons are so much affected by the Scotch or Irish airs. They are composed, not according to art, but nature; they are simple in the highest degree."[67] In situating this excerpt within *Sunday Matters*, Graeme was connecting its argument to the Psalms. She must have observed a similarity between the simple musical–poetic rhetoric of the Psalms, identified by so many of the writers that she quotes, and the simplicity of the Scottish airs. In this understanding, the aesthetics of King David's Psalms merge with those of Ossian's odes; the simplicity and naturalness of the ancient past become manifest in modern-day Philadelphia.

Graeme's inclusion of Wesley's essay, together with the epigraph from Milton on the title page of her Psalm paraphrases, opens the way to an interpretation of the Psalms as connected to a wide range of pastoral poetic traditions. God the Shepherd, manifested most clearly in Psalm 23, seems, in Graeme's conception, to have reigned over the pastoral landscapes of Milton's poetry. Of course, by Graeme's lifetime there was a long tradition that overlaid a sacred interpretive framework on non-Christian pastoral mythology. And yet, that this multilayered meaning infused the musical–poetic understandings of a woman of the American Enlightenment forms another piece in a growing body of evidence that the Enlightenment was not straightforwardly a secularizing movement.[68]

67. Graeme, *Sunday Matters*, 119. Copied from John Wesley, "Thoughts on the Power of Music," *Arminian Magazine* (February 1781): 103–7.

68. See David Sorkin, *The Religious Enlightenment: Protestants, Jews, and Catholics from London to Vienna* (Princeton, NJ: Princeton University Press, 2008).

It is with this notion in mind that I return to a discussion of Graeme's practice of writing new poetry for Scottish airs—a discussion that will, in turn, lead back to consideration of Francis Hopkinson's musical–poetic elegy for James Bremner, which uses a familiar Scottish tune as its basis. The mid- to late eighteenth century saw the development of strong intellectual, cultural, social, and familial bonds between Philadelphia and Scotland, and Graeme's circle partook avidly of the vogue for Scottish culture. Her poem "Content in a Cottage," written to be sung to the same tune that Hopkinson would later use for his elegy, as well as the other poems that she wrote to suit other Scottish airs, forms just one example of this fashion for Scottish culture among the intellectual and social elite of eighteenth-century Philadelphia.

Hugh Blair, whose writings on the biblical Psalms appear in Graeme's *Sunday Matters*, also wrote praises of the poems of Ossian. Just as the Psalms of the ancient Israelites formed an epitome of sung poetry in the Hebrew language, in Ossian's work, Blair wrote, "we find the fire and the enthusiasm of the most early times, combined with an amazing degree of regularity and art. We find tenderness, and even delicacy of sentiment, greatly predominant over fierceness and barbarity. Our hearts are melted with the softest feelings, and at the same time elevated with the highest ideas of magnanimity, generosity, and true heroism."[69] Ossian's poetry was taken to represent the noble simplicity of ancient times; its beauty lay in its unadorned, seemingly natural style. Through the continual exchange of ideas and fashions across the Atlantic, Ossian achieved pride of place in the literary tastes of the American colonies.

By the time Elizabeth Graeme Fergusson created her commonplace book for Annis Boudinot Stockton, the two had a long history of friendship fostered through both lived sociability and written exchanges of letters and poetry. Scholars disagree about the dates of their earliest exchanges, but they had grown up in overlapping social circles in Philadelphia, and, using their pseudonyms—Graeme was "Laura" and Boudinot was "Emilia"—they had begun to share poetry and correspondence by the 1750s. Boudinot used the image of music in describing Graeme's accomplishments, calling Graeme's mind "the seat of harmony."[70] She wrote that the favor Graeme would bestow on her by accepting her praise could never be repaid:

69. Hugh Blair, *A Critical Dissertation on the Poems of Ossian* (London: T. Becket and P. A. De Hondt, 1763), 11.

70. Annis Boudinot Stockton, "To Laura—a card," in Stockton, *Only for the Eye of a Friend*, 79. Ousterhout dates this poem to September 1766 (Ousterhout, *The Most Learned*

On you Apollo shines with brightest beam,
Which makes your praise alone an equal theme,
For numbers such as your's inspir'd by him,
But tho' I cannot sing with tuneful skill
Of the soft theme, I all its power can feel:
And do, my friend with sympathetic heart,
In all your sorrows, bear a tender part.[71]

While this poem indicates that Boudinot was not musically inclined herself ("I cannot sing with tuneful skill"), there is reason to think that she participated in the custom of writing new poetry to be sung to Scottish airs. In the second stanza of a poem that Boudinot wrote in 1762, titled "Doubt a pastoral ballad," she seems to allude to this practice:

When I take up my harp tis to sooth him to rest
I set it to strains that I know he admires
My only ambitions to live in his breast
And his smile of applause—the muse that inspires.

While the phrase "the strains that I know he admires" may refer only to the euphonious tuning of the harp, it seems more likely that it indicates the *songs* that her beloved admires. In fact, the meter of this poem and its organization into four-line stanzas means that it can easily be fitted to one of many popular Scottish airs. (That Boudinot partook of the vogue for Scottish culture is clear from the fact that she and her husband, Richard Stockton, named their estate in Princeton, New Jersey, "Morven" after the kingdom known by that name in Ossian.) One such air was "The Birks of Endermay," printed in numerous music collections that circulated in the American colonies; figure 7.6 shows the version printed in Robert Bremner's *Thirty Scots Songs*. Elizabeth Graeme wrote poetry to be sung to this tune at least twice. One version remained in manuscript:

Woman in America, 121), but Mulford's date of ca. May 1757 appears more plausible. One of Boudinot's poems for Graeme bears a date of 1759 in the title, so they were certainly exchanging poetry and correspondence by then (Stockton, "An Epistle to a friend who urg'd to have some poetry sent her in the year 1759, in the winter," in *Only for the Eye of a Friend*, 85).

71. Annis Boudinot Stockton, "To Laura," in *Only for the Eye of a Friend*, 80.

Air of the hymn Birks of Invermay

In awful gloom where sorrow reigns
And no mild sun the eye details,
God bears an universal sway,
As in the brighter realms of day.
No spot so distant or obscure,
But must his piercing glance ensure,
No folds of dark *Egyptian night*
Can dare elude the Lord of Light.[72]

The other was printed under the name "Laura" in a 1791 periodical:

A HYMN to the beauties of Creation. Air, the birks of Invermay.

The glorious sun, with lustre bright;
And sparkling stars, a dazzling sight,
As through their azure fields they roll,
The wondrous works of God extol.
The *silver moon*, who moves serene,
And gilds with beams the midnight scene,
In silent majesty declares,
That she transcendent beauty shares![73]

In both cases, Graeme's poetry takes on a Christian spiritual aspect that recalls her Psalm paraphrases, as shown below. These poems underscore the link, in Graeme's conception, between Scottish airs and Christian Psalmody; both repertoires achieve their truest realization in music. Example 7.1 presents a transcription of Bremner's setting of "The Birks of Invermay," underlaid with both a stanza from Boudinot's "Doubt a pastoral ballad" and a stanza from Graeme's "Hymn to the beauties of Creation. Air, the birks of Invermay" (both can be heard in audio ex. 7.1 ♫).

The commonplace book that Elizabeth Graeme Fergusson created for Annis Boudinot Stockton in 1787 contains some 47 items, ranging from

72. Elizabeth Graeme, "Air of the hymn Birks of Invermay." Elizabeth Graeme Fergusson Collection, Am.067, Historical Society of Pennsylvania.

73. Elizabeth Graeme, "A hymn to the beauties of Creation. Air, the birks of Invermay," *The Universal Asylum, and Columbian Magazine* 1 (April 1791): 256.

Figure 7.6 "The Birks of Endermay" and "Bessy Bell & Mary Gray," from Robert Bremner, *Thirty Scots Songs Adapted for a Voice and Harpsichord by Robert Bremner. The Words by Allen Ramsey* (London: Robert Bremner, 1770), 5.

Example 7.1A Music from "The Birks of Endermay," from Robert Bremner, *Thirty Scots Songs Adapted for a Voice and Harpsichord by Robert Bremner. The Words by Allen Ramsey* (London: Robert Bremner, 1770), 5. The first text is from Annis Boudinot, "Doubt a pastoral ballad." The second text is from Elizabeth Graeme, "Hymn to the beauties of Creation. Air, the birks of Invermay."

short odes and elegies in a neoclassical style, to long excerpts of correspondence with friends, to poetic adaptations of Milton. In keeping with the purpose of commonplacing as a whole, the themes of time and memory recur throughout the manuscript. When Elizabeth copied Francis Hopkinson's elegy for James Bremner into this commonplace book, she drew on a wide network of associations: the spiritual dimension of the Psalms, the simple nobility of Ossian, the fostering of a vibrant artistic world in the "Athens of North America," and memories of her salon gatherings among friends in the 1760s.

Graeme must have copied her poem from a published version which I have not identified, for she precedes the poem with a note to the editor: "Sir Mr Bremner was known to many of your Readers, by whom the following Lines will doubtless be recvd with pleasure, not only on account of their political Merit but because the author is far from having overated the Merit of His deceased Friend, who will be long rememberd with Regret by the Lovers of harmony and with affectionate esteem by all the acquaintances." At the end of the song text, Elizabeth's manuscript indicates the poem "sett to the music of the Lass of Patys Mill which Mr. Bremner was particularly fond of." Hopkinson's music is predictably simple, in keeping with the aesthetics of Scottish airs.

Hopkinson's poem evokes music's connection to the natural world, but it emphasizes Bremner's role in shaping and harnessing nature to cultivate artistry. The text is divided into two sections—an introductory stanza followed by a set of three stanzas—by virtue of a change in poetic meter:

Sing to his shade a solemn strain,
Let music's sweetest notes complain!
Let Echo tell from shore to shore:
The Swan of Schuylkill is no more.
From Scotia's land he came;
And brought the pleasing art;
To raise the sacred flame:
And warm a feeling heart.
The magic powers of sound!
Obeyed at his command,
And breathd delight around,
Wak'd by the skillful hand.
Oh, sanctify the ground,
The ground where he is laid,

Plant roses all around,
Let not those roses fade.
Let none his tomb pass by!
Without a generous tear,
Or sigh—and let that sigh
Be like himself sincere.

In the musical setting, transcribed in example 7.2 and recreated in audio example 7.2, Hopkinson provides a mournful introduction, newly composed, to complement his original poetry. ♫ In the second part, Hopkinson indeed set his original text to "The Lass of Peatty's Mill." In an age when the simple and touching melodies of Scottish songs were in vogue on both sides of the Atlantic, it was appropriate that Bremner, a native of Scotland, should be memorialized through the music of his country. Its ancient, spiritual, almost mystical associations through Ossian, as well as through the Judeo-Christian tradition of elegiac Psalmody, likewise resonate through the music.

Another layer of meaning lies in the fact that Hopkinson clearly copied the music for the air from Robert Bremner's *Thirty Scots Songs Adapted for a Voice and Harpsichord* (see fig. 7.7). Hopkinson notates almost every detail in this edition, including the articulation markings, distinctive ornaments, and bass figures. In performance, the Scottish tune emerges from Hopkinson's doleful introduction as an old friend—a sonic avatar, perhaps, for James Bremner himself—and the familiarity of the tune would have enabled anyone to join in the singing. The music, like the poem, offers a means of personal and communal remembrance. James Bremner's status as a Scottish immigrant added to the air of authenticity that was inherent in the Scottish tunes as a whole. As with figures such as James Oswald, the Earl of Kelly, and Lord Kames, Bremner's link to the idyllic land of Scotland, with its purportedly ancient musical tradition, would have lent special meaning to the performance of Scottish airs in Graeme's salon, and the elegy is designed to recall that meaning. Because of Bremner, Scotland was not just a thing of the imagination, a distant land removed from their everyday lives, but, rather, a palpable and sounding reality.

The first page of Elizabeth Graeme Fergusson's commonplace book for Annis Boudinot Stockton bears an epigraph from Addison and Steele's *The Tatler* that asserts the importance of poetry in moral education: "I have always been of the opinion that virtue sinks deepest into the heart of man

Example 7.2A Transcription of Francis Hopkinson, "Sing to His Shade a Solemn Strain," from Hopkinson's manuscript *Duets / Songs*, Marian S. Carson Collection, Library of Congress ML96 .H83 no. 2, Washington, DC, USA (see fig. 7.1).

16
tr
shore__ to shore, The Swan of__ Schuyl-kill____ is no__more.
6 6 6 6♮ 6 9 8 6 5
5 5 4 4 3
3
19
6♮ 6 6 6 5
4 5 4 3
3
Moderato
From Sco-tia's_ land_he came;____ and brought the__ plea - sing
Oh,__ sanc-t - fy__the ground,____ The ground_ where he____ was
6 6
24
art; To__ raise the__ sa-cred flame:____ And warm__ a feel - ing
laid, Plant ro-ses__ all__ a- round,____ Let not__those ro - ses
6 5 6
4 3
28
29
Heart. The ma gic_powers of__ sound!____ O - beyed__ at his____com
fade. Let none his_tomb pass by!____ With- out__ a gene - rous
6 6 4 6 6
5 2

Example 7.2B

Example 7.2c

when it comes recommended by the powerful charms of poetry."[74] While reading is undoubtedly the central theme of this manuscript, music figures prominently as well. In addition to the elegy for Bremner, Graeme includes other poems set to Scottish airs—"Lovely Nancy," "Farewell to Lochaber," "A Dawning Hope," and "Bush Above Fragrances." In addition to these poems designed for singing, Graeme's manuscript is filled with references to song. In copying a poem that she had written in 1775 to mark the third wedding anniversary of her niece Anna Young, Graeme evoked the musical sociability that she and Stockton had both enjoyed in years past:

> How does my gratfull heart with Joy oer flow
> That we together are again ristord;
> Where heartfelt Joy and guiltless mirth resound
> While friends and dear [ones] smile around
> For this my *music* shall raise the gratfull song
> And pray that heaven these happy hours prolong.

This and other works in the commonplace book suggest a sense of nostalgia for the salon that Graeme had hosted in the 1760s and early 1770s.

74. The text can be found in Joseph Addison and Richard Steele, *The Tatler, with Notes, and a General Index Complete in One Volume* (Philadelphia: J. J. Woodward, 1831), 199.

Figure 7.7 "Peatie's Mill" and "See him Father," from Robert Bremner, *Thirty Scots Songs Adapted for a Voice and Harpsichord by Robert Bremner. The Words by Allen Ramsey* (London: Robert Bremner, 1770), 6.

Out of the public eye, she had welcomed the leading intellectuals, statesmen, philosophers, and socialites of colonial Philadelphia and its environs, helping to plant the seeds of a flourishing artistic community there. Her engagement with poetry and music, with the ideals of simplicity in the Scottish airs and the spirituality of the biblical Psalms, helped shape this artistic environment. Hopkinson's lament for Bremner, and Elizabeth Graeme Fergusson's manuscript copy of it, attest to the significance of poetry and music in expressions of sentiment, friendship, and memory in early America. And, significantly, it points to Elizabeth Graeme's salon, with its musical–poetic aesthetics, as a site of cultural formation through friendship and artistry.

*

Conclusion

In this book I have offered a picture of musical salons in Europe and America between approximately 1760 and 1800. The stories of some of these salons are more complete than others: in some cases, the evidence is fragmentary, and the sounds and practices of musical salons remain obscured behind a veil of privacy. As I have suggested, this air of privacy was part of the allure of salons: situated between the public and private spheres, musical salons were both inviting and exclusive. Opening themselves to guests from the middle classes and aristocracy as well as the class of professional musicians, artists, and writers, musical salons nevertheless remained obscured from public view and widespread participation. It was precisely because of their veneer of domesticity—their situation within the home—that the women who hosted them could use them as platforms for exercising agency in the definition and shaping of their musical environments.

In our own age, musical salons can be seen as problematic precisely because they were exclusive. The *salonnières* who hosted them often subscribed to ideas of class distinctions that grate on modern sensibilities of equity and inclusion. Indeed, in the eighteenth century, musical education as a whole—especially among women—became a marker of status associated with practices of leisure. Hosting musical salons, along with the patronage and collecting that they required, demanded even more financial expense than simply taking music lessons and sharing one's talents among friends. And yet, the practice of hosting musical salons became more widespread as the century progressed, with professional-class women engaging in the practice with increasing frequency.

Moreover, understanding the institution of the musical salon helps elucidate aspects of the history of women in music that have, with some notable exceptions, been largely overlooked up until this point. By highlighting the institution of the musical salon, I have shown connections among figures in musical history that might otherwise go unnoticed. Whether they engaged in the art of composition or not, whether music was their primary art or took a secondary place to painting or poetry, the women at the center of this book were linked by their shared cultural practices. Viewing eighteenth-century musical history through the institution of the salon enables us to expand our understanding of women's authorship and women's exercise of musical agency. Marianna Martines might be understood to stand on one end of this spectrum, since she engaged in composition in the conventional sense; yet she used the institution of the musical salon to mitigate some of the social risks associated with composition. Madame Brillon composed, too—but her unstudied approach to the act of composition was quite different from that of Martines. As shown by the case of Boccherini's violin sonatas dedicated to Brillon, the act of patronage and engagement with salon sociability could themselves lead to a form of authorship.

Other women such as Sara Levy apparently never composed at all, meaning that their agency in the shaping of musical culture must be sought out elsewhere. The field of performance studies helps us recognize Levy's agency in the acts of collecting and performing—in cultivating what Diana Taylor has called "the archive and the repertoire," as discussed in chapter 5. For Elizabeth Graeme and Angelica Kauffman, the arts of writing and painting, respectively, held pride of place in their salons. Still, thinking through the lens of the musical salon reveals significant aspects of their creative lives. The stories of numerous other musical *salonnières* of the eighteenth century await explication.

The history of musical salons in the Enlightenment can be seen as a manifestation of that key aesthetic principle of the age: "unity in diversity." If the women who hosted musical salons and played music in them can be understood to have participated in a single set of practices, these practices assumed various forms, in line with the tastes, interests, and talents of the *salonnière*. As I argued in chapter 2, while many genres of musical composition can be understood as expressions of salon sociability, thinking through the act of performance suggests that virtually any composition can be rendered "sociable" within the environment of the salon. The salon shaped interpretations of music by virtue of its social framing. Of key importance were bonds of family and friendship, competition and romantic encounters, as well as games, theatricals, and, above all, the art of conversation. Thus the highly cultivated and virtuosic Italian cantatas of Martines can be understood as linked with the ephemeral art of the Italian *improvvisatrici*; the light, simple keyboard duets of Maria Cosway or Madame Brillon were connected to the performance practices of music in the Prussian tradition cultivated by Sara Levy and her sisters; the Scottish airs sung in the salon of Elizabeth Graeme resonated with the strains of the glass armonica across Europe; the Handel arias performed in the salon of Anna Seward were linked to the array of Spanish and central European instrumental and vocal music performed in the salon of María Josefa Pimentel in Madrid; novel instruments such as the glass armonica, *vis-à-vis* double-keyboard instruments, and pianos, harps, and harpsichords of all sorts were collected alongside scores of music that documented an interest in the musical past, present, and future. Musical salons form a thread that connects the priorities and practices of women across Europe and America, even as it articulates their differences and individuality.

Bibliography

ARCHIVES AND SPECIAL COLLECTIONS

American Philosophical Society (US-PHps)
Civico Museo Bibliografico Musicale, Bologna (I-Bc)
Conservatorio di musica San Pietro a Majella (I-Nc)
Cornell University, Division of Rare and Manuscript Collections, Kroch Library (US-I)
Historical Society of Pennsylvania (US-PHhs)
Istituto Nazionale per la Storia del Movimento di Liberazione in Italia, Istituto storico nazionale Parri, Milan (Parri)
Leipzig University Library, Biblioteca Albertina (D-LEu)
Library Company of Philadelphia (US-PHlc)
Library of Congress, Washington, DC (US-Wc)
Newberry Library, Chicago (US-Cn)
Österreichisches Nationalbibliothek (A-Wn)
Pennsylvania Historical and Museum Commission, Pennsylvania State Archives (US-HG)
Sing-Akademie zu Berlin, housed in the Staatsbibliothek zu Berlin (D-Bsa)
Staatsbibliothek zu Berlin (D-B)

MANUSCRIPTS CITED

Bach, Carl Philipp Emanuel. Concerto for harpsichord, fortepiano, and orchestra, Wq. 47. Autograph manuscript, probably owned by Sara Levy. D-B N. Mus. SA 4.

———. Quartet for flute, viola, and keyboard in D major, Wq. 95. Autograph manuscript, probably owned by Sara Levy. D-Bsa SA 3328.

———. Sonatina for cembalo and orchestra, Wq. 110 / H. 459. Autograph manuscript owned by Sara Levy. D-Bsa SA 4835.

Bach, Johann Sebastian [?]. Sonata in E-flat major for flute and cembalo. Manuscript copy owned by Sara Levy. D-Bsa SA 3587.

Bach, Johann Sebastian. B-major fugue from book two of *The Well-Tempered Clavier.* Manuscript copy owned by Sara Levy. US-Cn, Case MS 6A 72.

———. Organ Trio, BWV 526 in the arrangement for two keyboards. Manuscript copy owned by Fanny von Arnstein. A-Wn Mus.Hs.5008.

Bach, Wilhelm Friedemann. Duets for two violas, Fk. 60–62. Manuscripts owned by Sara Levy. D-Bsa SA 3912, 3913, 3914, and 3921.

Brillon de Jouy, Anne-Louise Boyvin d'Hardancourt. Duets for harpsichord and forte-piano; trios for harpsichord, English piano, and German piano. US-PHps.

———. "Marche des insurgents." US-PHps.

———. *Troisieme recueil de sonates pour le piano forte avec accompag.t par Madame Brillon* (ad libitum violin part lost). US-PHps.

———. *Romances.* US-PHps.

Catalogue de la musique de Madame la Comtesse de Rumford. US-I, Lavoisier 4712 Bd. Ms.11.

Catalogue des livres de la bibliothèque de Madame la Comtesse de Rumford. US-I, Lavoisier 4712 Bd. Ms. 44++.

Fergusson, Elizabeth Graeme. "Air of the hymn Birks of Invermay." Elizabeth Graeme Fergusson Collection, US-PHhs, Am.067.

———. "Content in a Cottage." Library Company of Philadelphia, MS *Poemata Juvenalia*, vol. 2. no. 85. US-PHlc, 13494.Q.

———. Elizabeth Graeme to [Mary] Campbell, January 10, 1764. US-HG, Manuscript Group 8, Pennsylvania Collection (Miscellaneous).

———. Psalms, vols. 1–2. 1766–1767. Elizabeth Graeme Fergusson Papers. US-PHlc, 12716Q, vols. 3–4.

———. *Sunday Matters* [Psalms commonplace book] [1760–1780s]. Elizabeth Graeme Fergusson Collection, US-PHhs, Am.067, vol. 1.

Hasse, Johann Adolf. *Artaserse* (1760 Naples revival). D-LEu N.I.10286a.

Hopkinson, Francis. Francis Hopkinson to Elizabeth Graeme, February 21, 1767. Hopkinson Papers, US-PHps.

———. "Sing to His Shade a Solemn Strain," in *Songs.* US-Wc ML96 .H83 no. 2.

Martines, Marianna. *La tempesta.* A-Wn, Mus. Hs. 16569.

———. *L'inverno.* I-Bc, GG 157.

———. *Scelta d'arie composte per suo diletto.* I-Nc, 33–327/8.

Nicolini, Nicola. *Musiche per poesie estemporanee ad uso di Nicola Nicolini.* Parri, Fondo Malvezzi, b. 12, fasc. 43/17.

Reimarus, Elise. Letters of Elise Reimarus to Sara Levy. D-B, Nachlass 434 (Familie Cauer), case 3.

Schobert, Johann. "Sonatina a quatuor," op. 7 no. 1. Manuscript owned by Sara Levy. D-Bsa SA 4858.

PRINTED SOURCES

Abbate, Carolyn. "Music—Drastic or Gnostic?" *Critical Inquiry* 30, no. 3 (Spring 2004): 505–36.

Abravanel, Don Isaac. *Perush Abravanel 'al Ha-Torah* [Abravanel's commentary on the Torah]. 5 vols. Jerusalem: Ḥoreb, 5757 [=1996–1997].

Adams, Abigail. Abigail Adams the Younger to John Quincy Adams, August 26, 1785. *Founders Online*. National Archives, last modified June 13, 2018. http://founders.archives.gov/documents/Adams/04-06-02-0096. Accessed September 3, 2020.

Adams, William Howard. *The Paris Years of Thomas Jefferson*. New Haven, CT, and London: Yale University Press, 1997.

Addison, Joseph. [No title]. *The Spectator* 6 (June 14, 1712): 41–44.

———. *The Works of the Late Right Honourable Joseph Addison, Esq*. 2nd ed. 4 vols. London: Jacob Tonson, 1730.

Addison, Joseph, and Richard Steele. *The Tatler, with Notes, and a General Index Complete in One Volume*. Philadelphia: J. J. Woodward, 1831.

Adunanza tenuta dagli Arcadi per la coronazione della celebre Pastorella Corilla Olimpica. Rome: Dalle Stampe del Salmoni, 1775.

Agnew, Vanessa. *Enlightenment Orpheus: The Power of Music in Other Worlds*. Oxford: Oxford University Press, 2008.

———. "History's Affective Turn: Historical Reenactment and Its Work in the Present." *Rethinking History* 11, no. 3 (September 2007): 299–312.

Alberti, Leon Battista. *On Painting and On Sculpture: The Latin Texts of "De pictura" and "De statua."* Edited and translated with notes by Cecil Grayson. London: Phaidon, 1972.

Altmann, Alexander. *Moses Mendelssohn: A Biographical Study*. Tuscaloosa: University of Alabama Press, 1973.

Ankersmit, Frank R. *Meaning, Truth, and Reference in Historical Representation*. Ithaca, NY: Cornell University Press, 2012.

Applegate, Celia. *Bach in Berlin: Nation and Culture in Mendelssohn's Revival of the "St. Matthew Passion."* Ithaca, NY: Cornell University Press, 2005.

Bach, Johann Christian. *Six sonates pour le clavecin accompagnées d'un violon ou flute traversière et d'un violoncello*, op. 2. London: Author, 1770.

[Bandettini, Teresa] Amarilli Estrusca. *Rime estemporanee di Amarilli Etrusca conservate in varie città*. Lucca: Presso Francesco Bertini, 1807.

Basedow, Johann Bernhard. *Das Elementarwerk für die Jugend und ihre Freunde*. Berlin and Dessau: Basedow, 1774.

Beghin, Tom. *The Virtual Haydn: Paradox of a Twenty-First-Century Keyboardist*. Chicago and London: University of Chicago Press, 2015.

Bertucci, Paola. *Artisanal Enlightenment: Science and the Mechanical Arts in Old Regime France*. New Haven, CT, and London: Yale University Press, 2017.

Bettinelli, Saverio. *Dell'entusiasmo delle belle arti*. Milan: Galeazzi, 1769.

Blair, Hugh. *A Critical Dissertation on the Poems of Ossian*. London: T. Becket and P. A. De Hondt, 1763.

———. *Lectures on Rhetoric and Belles lettres*. Philadelphia: Robert Aitken, 1784.

Boccherini, Luigi. *Sei sonate di cembalo e violino obbligato dedicate, a Madama Brillon de Jouy . . . opera V*. Paris: Veuve Leclair, 1768. Modern edition: Luigi Boccherini, *6 sonate per tastiera e violino*. Edited by Rudolf Rasch. Bologna: Ut Orpheus Edizioni, 2009.

Bodoni, Giambattista, Domenico Cagnoni, and Evangelista Ferrari. *Atti della solenne coronazione fatta in campidoglio della insigne poetessa D.na Maria Maddalena Morelli Fernandez Pistoiese tra gli Arcadi Corilla Olimpica*. Parma: Impresso nella Stamperia reale di Parma, 1779.

Bonds, Mark Evan. *Music as Thought: Listening to the Symphony in the Age of Beethoven*. Princeton, NJ, and Oxford: Princeton University Press, 2006.

The Book of Common Prayer and Administration of the Sacraments . . . According to the Church of England: Together with the Psalter or Psalms of David. Oxford: John Baskett, 1727.

Borgias, Adriane P. "Marie Anne Pierrette Paulze Lavoisier (1758–1836)." In *Women in Chemistry and Physics: A Biobibliographic Sourcebook*, edited by Louise S. Grinstein, Rose K. Rose, and Miriam H. Rafailovich, 314–19. Westport, CT: Greenwood Press, 1993.

Botstein, Leon. "The Aesthetics of Assimilation and Affirmation: Reconstructing the Career of Felix Mendelssohn." In *Mendelssohn and His World*, edited by R. Larry Todd, 5–42. Princeton, NJ: Princeton University Press, 2012.

Boyer, Abel. *The Royal Dictionary, French and English, and English and French: Extracted from the Writings of the Best Authors in Both Languages*. London: T. Osborne et al., 1764.

Bremner, Robert. *Thirty Scots Songs Adapted for a Voice and Harpsichord by Robert Bremner. The Words by Allen Ramsey*. London: Robert Bremner, 1770.

Brillon de Jouy, Anne-Louise Boyvin d'Hardancourt. Anne-Louise Boyvin d'Hardancourt Brillon de Jouy to Benjamin Franklin, after November 14, 1780. French text at https://franklinpapers.org. Accessed July 14, 2019.

———. Anne-Louise Boyvin d'Hardancourt Brillon de Jouy to Benjamin Franklin, March 6, 1789. https://franklinpapers.org. Accessed July 31, 2019.

Britton, Jeanne. "Translating Sympathy by the Letter: Henry Mackenzie, Sophie de Condorcet, and Adam Smith." *Eighteenth-Century Fiction* 22, no. 1 (Fall 2009): 71–98.

Brown, A. Peter. "Marianna Martines' Autobiography as a New Source for Haydn's Biography during the 1750's." *Haydn-Studien* 6, no. 1 (1986): 68–70.

Brun, Friederike. *Tagebuch über Rom 1795–1796*. 2 vols. Zurich: Orell, Füssli, and Company, 1800.

Bunzel, Anja, and Natasha Loges, eds. *Musical Salon Culture in the Long Nineteenth Century*. Woodbridge, UK: Boydell Press, 2019.

Burden, Michael. *Regina Mingotti: Diva and Impresario at the King's Theatre, London*. London and New York: Routledge, 2017.

Burney, Charles. *A General History of Music from the Earliest Ages to the Present Period*. 4 vols. London: Printed for the author and sold by Payne and Son, 1776–1789.

———. *Dr. Burney's Musical Tours in Europe*. Edited by Percy Alfred Scholes. 2 vols. Oxford: Oxford University Press, 1959.

———. *Memoirs of the Life and Writings of the Abate Metastasio: In Which Are Incorporated, Translations of His Principal Letters*. 3 vols. London: G. G. and J. Robinson, 1796.

———. *Music, Men, and Manners in France and Italy*. Edited by H. Edmund Poole. London: Folio Society, 1969.

———. Preface to *Four Sonatas or Duets for Two Performers on One Piano-forte or Harpsichord*. London: Printed for the Author, 1777.

———. *The Present State of Music in France and Italy: Or, The Journal of a Tour through Those Countries, Undertaken to Collect Materials for a General History of Music.* 2nd ed. London: T. Becket and Co., J. Robson, and G. Robinson, 1773.

———. *The Present State of Music in Germany, the Netherlands, and United Provinces.* Vol. 1. London: T. Becket, 1773.

Burstein, L. Poundie. "'*Zierlichkeit und Genie*': Grace and Genius in Marianna Martines's Sonata in A Major." In *Analytical Essays on Music by Women Composers: Secular & Sacred Music to 1900*, edited by Laurel Parsons and Brenda Ravenscroft, 131–45. Oxford: Oxford University Press, 2018.

Butt, John. *Playing with History: The Historical Approach to Musical Performance.* Musical Performance and Reception. Cambridge and New York: Cambridge University Press, 2002.

Caruso, Marie. "Ten Fugues Shed Light on an Old Debate." *Il saggiatore musicale: Rivista semestrale di musicologia* 21, no. 1 (2014): 5–43.

Cauchie, Maurice. "La version authentique de la romance 'Plaisir d'amour.'" *Revue de Musicologie* 18, no. 61 (1937): 12–14.

Cavazza, Marta. "Between Modesty and Spectacle: Women and Science in Eighteenth-Century Italy." In *Italy's Eighteenth Century: Gender and Culture in the Age of the Grand Tour*, edited by Paula Findlen, Wendy Wassyng Roworth, and Catherine M. Sama, 275–302. Stanford, CA: Stanford University Press, 2009.

Chinard, Gilbert. "Random Notes on Two 'Bagatelles.'" *Proceedings of the American Philosophical Society* 103, no. 6 (December 1959): 727–60.

Christensen, Thomas. "Four-Hand Piano Transcription and Geographies of Nineteenth-Century Musical Reception." *Journal of the American Musicological Society* 52, no. 2 (Summer 1999): 255–98.

Cianfogni, Domenico. Introduction to Bernardino Perfetti, *Saggi di poesie parte dette all'improvviso, e parte scritte.* Florence: Nella Stamperia Bonducciana, 1774.

Cillerai, Chiara. "Scribal Publication of Elizabeth Graeme Fergusson's Commonplace Books." *Studies in Eighteenth-Century Culture* 48, no. 1 (2019): 75–87.

Clark, Anthony M. "Roma mi è sempre in pensiero." In *Studies in Roman Eighteenth-Century Painting*, edited by Edgar Peters Bowron, 125–38. Art History Series 4. Washington, DC: Decatur House Press, 1981.

Clark, Peter. *British Clubs and Societies 1580–1800: The Origins of an Associational World.* Oxford Studies in Social History. Oxford: Oxford University Press, 2000.

Coccia, Maria Rosa, et al. *Esperimento estemporaneo fatto dalla Signora Maria Rosa Coccia romana nell'esame da essa sostenuto avanti i quattro sig. maestri di cappella esaminatori della congregazione de' signori musici di Santa Cecilia di Roma . . . coll'aggiunta di vari poeticii componmenti, che in quell'occasione furono al di lei merito dedicati.* Rome: nella stamperia di San Michele a Ripa, presso Paolo Giunchi, 1775.

Cohn, Ellen R. "The Printer at Passy." In *Benjamin Franklin: In Search of a Better World*, edited by Page Talbott, 241–45. New Haven, CT: Yale University Press, 2005.

Cole, Michael. *The Pianoforte in the Classical Era.* Oxford: Clarendon Press, 1998.

Cone, Edward T. *The Composer's Voice.* Ernest Bloch Lectures. Berkeley: University of California Press, 1974.

Conway, David. *Jewry in Music: Entry to the Profession from the Enlightenment to Richard Wagner*. Cambridge: Cambridge University Press, 2012.

Cosway, Maria. *Deux sonates pour le clavecin, avec un violon . . . arrangées pour deux. Harpe et clavecin, piano-forté, ou l'orgue par P. J. Meyer*. London: Chez Messrs. Birchall & Andrews, [1785].

Couperin, François. *Concert instrumental sous le titre d'Apotheose: composé à la mémoire immortelle de l'incomparable Monsieur de Lully*. Paris: L'auteur and Le Sieur Boivin, 1725.

Craveri, Benedetta. *The Age of Conversation*. Translated by Teresa Waugh. New York: New York Review Books, 2005.

Croce, Benedetto. "Gl'improvvisatori." *Quaderni della critica* 6 (November 1946): 38–56.

———. "L'Arcadia e la poesia del settecento." *Quaderni della critica* 6 (1946): 1–10.

Cusick, Suzanne. "Gender and the Cultural Work of a Classical Music Performance." *repercussions* 3, no. 1 (Spring 1994): 77–110.

Cypess, Rebecca. "Ancient Poetry, Modern Music, and the *Wechselgesang der Mirjam und Debora*: The Meanings of Song in the Itzig Circle." *Bach: Journal of the Riemenschneider Bach Institute* 47, no. 1 (2016): 21–65.

———. "Arrangement Practices in the Bach Tradition, Then and Now: Historical Precedent for Modern Practice." *Journal of Musicological Research* 39, nos. 2–3 (2020): 187–212.

———. "At the Crossroads of Musical Practice and Jewish Identity: Meanings of the Keyboard Duo in the Circle of Sara Levy." In *Sara Levy's World: Gender, Judaism, and the Bach Tradition in Enlightenment Berlin*, edited by Rebecca Cypess and Nancy Sinkoff, 181–204. Eastman Studies in Music 145. Rochester, NY: University of Rochester Press, 2018.

———. "Fortepiano–Harpsichord Duos in Two Late Eighteenth-Century Salons." *Harpsichord and Fortepiano Magazine* (Spring 2018): 20–26.

———. "How Thorough Was Bach's Thoroughbass? A Reconsideration of the Trio Texture." *Early Music* 47, no. 1 (2019): 83–97.

———. "Keyboard-Duo Arrangements in Eighteenth-Century Musical Life." *Eighteenth-Century Music* 14, no. 2 (September 2017): 183–214.

———. "Madame Lavoisier's Music Collection: Lessons from a Private Library of the Nineteenth Century." *Notes: The Quarterly Journal of the Music Library Association* 77, no. 2 (2020): 224–52.

———. "Music Historicism: Sara Levy and the Jewish Enlightenment." In *Bach Perspectives 12: Bach and the Counterpoint of Religion*, edited by Robin A. Leaver, 129–52. Springfield: University of Illinois Press, 2018.

———. "Timbre, Expression, and Combination Keyboard Instruments: Milchmeyer's Art of *Veränderung*." *Keyboard Perspectives* 8 (2015): 43–69.

Cypess, Rebecca, and Lynette Bowring. "Orality and Literacy in the Worlds of Salamone Rossi." In *Music and Jewish Culture in Early Modern Italy: New Perspectives*, edited by Lynette Bowring, Rebecca Cypess, and Liza Malamut, 197–232. Bloomington: Indiana University Press, 2022.

Cypess, Rebecca, and Nancy Sinkoff, eds. *Sara Levy's World: Gender, Judaism, and the Bach Tradition in Enlightenment Berlin*. Eastman Studies in Music 145. Rochester, NY: University of Rochester Press, 2018.

Dabakis, Melissa. "Angelika Kauffmann, Goethe, and the Arcadian Academy in Rome." In *The Enlightened Eye: Goethe and Visual Culture*, edited by Evelyn K. Moore and Patricia Anne Simpson, 23–40. Amsterdam and New York: Rodopi, 2007.

Darling, James S. "Preface." In Robert Bremner, *Harpsichord or Spinnet Miscellany: A Facsimile Reproduction of the Original Edition of About 1765, from a Copy Belonging to Colonial Williamsburg*. Williamsburg, VA: Colonial Williamsburg Foundation, 1972.

Daube, Johann Friedrich. *The Musical Dilettante: A Treatise on Composition by J. F. Daube*. Translated by Susan P. Snook-Luther. Cambridge Studies in Music Theory and Analysis 3. Cambridge: Cambridge University Press, 1992.

———. *Der musikalische Dilettant: eine Abhandlung der Komposition*. Vienna: Johann Thomas Edlen von Trattnern, 1773.

David, Hans T., and Arthur Mendel, eds. *The New Bach Reader: A Life of Johann Sebastian Bach in Letters and Documents*. Revised and Enlarged by Christoph Wolff. New York London: W. W. Norton, 1999.

Davidson, Wolf. *Ueber die bürgerliche Verbesserung der Juden*. Berlin: Ernst Felisch, 1798.

Dawson, Ruth. "'Lights Out! Lights Out!' Women and the Enlightenment." In *Gender in Transition: Discourse and Practice in German-Speaking Europe, 1750–1830*, edited by Ulrike Gleixner and Marion W. Gray, 218–45. Social History, Popular Culture, and Politics in Germany. Ann Arbor: University of Michigan Press, 2009.

Day-O'Connell, Sarah. "The Composer, the Surgeon, His Wife and Her Poems: Haydn and the Anatomy of the English Canzonetta." *Eighteenth Century Music* 6, no. 1 (2009): 77–112.

Delany, Mary. *The Autobiography and Correspondence of Mary Granville, Mrs Delany*. Edited by Augusta Hall, Baroness Llanover. 3 vols. London: Richard Bentley, 1861.

De Rossi, Giovanni Gherardo. *Vita di Angelica Kauffmann, pittrice*. Florence: A Spese di Molini, Landi, e Comp., 1810.

De Staël, Germaine. *Corinne, or Italy*. Translated by Sylvia Raphael. Introduction by John Isbell. Oxford and New York: Oxford University Press, 1998.

Diderot, Denis. "Bien, (*homme de*) *homme d'honneur, honnête homme*." In *Encyclopédie, ou dictionnaire raisonné des sciences, des arts et des métiers, etc.*, edited by Denis Diderot and Jean le Rond d'Alembert, 2:244. University of Chicago: ARTFL Encyclopédie Project (Autumn 2017 ed.), ed. Robert Morrissey and Glenn Roe. http://encyclopedie.uchicago.edu. Accessed August 5, 2019.

——— [?]. "Romance." In *Encyclopédie, ou dictionnaire raisonné des sciences, des arts et des métiers, etc.*, edited by Denis Diderot and Jean le Rond d'Alembert, 14:344. University of Chicago: ARTFL Encyclopédie Project (Autumn 2017 ed.), ed. Robert Morrissey and Glenn Roe. http://encyclopedie.uchicago.edu. Accessed August 5, 2019.

Di Ricco, Alessandra. *L'inutile e maraviglioso mestiere: poeti improvvisatori di fine Settecento*. Collana Letteratura 10. Milan: Franco Angeli, 1990.

———. "Poeti improvvisatori aulici in età moderna." In *Cantar ottave: per una storia culturale dell'intonazione cantata in ottava rima*, edited by Maurizio Agamennone, 113–34. Lucca: Libreria Musicale Italiana, 2017.

Dolan, Emily I. *The Orchestral Revolution: Haydn and the Technologies of Timbre*. Cambridge: Cambridge University Press, 2013.

Donato, Maria Pia. "The Temple of Female Glory: Female Self-Affirmation in the Roman Salon of the Grand Tour." In *Italy's Eighteenth Century: Gender and Culture in the Age of the Grand Tour*, edited by Paula Findlen, Wendy Wassyng Roworth, and Catherine M. Sama, 59–78. Stanford, CA: Stanford University Press, 2009.

Dupuy-Vachey, Marie-Anne. Review of Melissa Percival, *Fragonard and the Fantasy Figure: Painting the Imagination*. *The Art Tribune* (July 20, 2012). http://www.thearttribune.com/Fragonard-and-the-Fantasy-Figure.html. Accessed August 6, 2019.

Duveen, Denis I. "Madame Lavoisier 1758–1836." *Chymia* 4 (1953): 13–29.

Dwyer, John. *Virtuous Discourse: Sensibility and Community in Late Eighteenth-Century Scotland*. Edinburgh: John Donald, 1987.

Eger, Elizabeth. "Representing Culture: 'The Nine Living Muses of Great Britain' (1779)." In *Women, Writing and the Public Sphere, 1700–1830*, edited by Elizabeth Eger, Charlotte Grant, Clíona Ó Gallchoir, and Penny Warburton, 104–32. Cambridge: Cambridge University Press, 2001.

Esse, Melina. "Encountering the *Improvvisatrice* in Italian Opera." *Journal of the American Musicological Society* 66, no. 3 (Fall 2013): 709–70.

Fantastici, Fortunata Sulgher. *Poesie*. Florence: Nella Stamperia Granducale, 1796.

———. *Poesie*. Livorno: Nella Stamperia di Tommaso Masi e Comp., 1794.

Feiner, Shmuel. *Haskalah and History: The Emergence of a Modern Jewish Historical Consciousness*. Translated by Chaya Naor and Sondra Silverston. Oxford and Portland, OR: Littman Library of Jewish Civilization, 2002.

Felici, Candida. *Maria Rosa Coccia: maestra compositora romana*. Memorie romane. Rome: Colombo Duemila, 2004.

Fernández-Cortés, Juan Pablo. *La música en las Casas de Osuna y Benavente (1733–1882): un estudio sobre el mecenazgo musical de la alta nobleza española*. Madrid: Sociedad Española de Musicología, 2007.

Fernow, Carl Ludwig. "Über die Improvisatoren." *Römische Studien* 2 (1806): 303–416.

Ford, Ann. *Instructions for Playing on the Musical Glasses: So That Any Person, Who Has the Least Knowledge of Music, or a Good Ear, May Be Able to Perform in a Few Days, If Not in a Few Hours: With Clear and Proper Directions How to Provide a Compleat Set of Well-Tuned Glasses at a Very Moderate Expense*. [London]: s.n., 1761.

———. *Lessons and Instructions for Playing on the Guitar*. [London]: Author, [1761].

Forget, Evelyn L. "Cultivating Sympathy: Sophie Condorcet's Letters on Sympathy." *Journal of the History of Economic Thought* 23, no. 3 (2001): 319–37.

Forkel, Johann Nikolaus. *Allgemeine Geschichte der Musik*. 2 vols. Leipzig: im Schwickertschen Verlage, 1788.

———. *Vier und zwanzig Veränderungen fürs Clavichord oder Fortepiano auf das englische Volkslied: God Save the King*. Göttingen: beym Autor, und in der Vandenhoek-Ruprechtischen Buchhandlung, 1791.

Franceschi, Francesco. "A chi leggerà," introduction to Amarilli Etrusca [Teresa Bandettini], *Rime estemporanee*. Lucca: Francesco Bertini, 1807.

Franklin, Benjamin. *The Bagatelles from Passy: Text and Facsimile*. New York: Eakins Press, 1967.

———. Benjamin Franklin to Anne-Louise Boyvin d'Hardancourt Brillon de Jouy, "The Ephemera," September 20, 1778. *Founders Online*. https://founders.archives.gov/documents/Franklin/01-27-02-0408. Accessed November 23, 2021.

———. Benjamin Franklin to Anne-Louise Brillon de Jouy, after December 10, 1778? https://franklinpapers.org. Accessed August 4, 2019.

———. Benjamin Franklin to William Carmichael, June 17, 1780. https://franklinpapers.org. Accessed August 2, 2019.

———. Benjamin Franklin to Louis-Guillaume Le Veillard, December 10, 1788. https://franklinpapers.org. Accessed July 31, 2019.

———. *Experiments and Observations on Electricity: Made at Philadelphia in America: To Which Are Added, Letters and Papers on Philosophical Subjects*. London: David Henry, 1769.

———. "The Morals of Chess." *The Columbian Magazine*, The Papers of Benjamin Franklin, 1 (December 1786): 159–61.

———. "Song for a Brillon Party," [ca. April 10, 1778?]. https://franklinpapers.org. Accessed June 4, 2021.

Fuchs, Ingrid. "'. . . spielt das Fortepiano mit vieler Empfindung und Präzision': Damen im musikalischen Salon rund um Joseph Haydn." In *Phänomen Haydn 1732–1809: prachtliebend, bürgerlich, gottbefohlen, crossover*, edited by Theresia Gabriel, 144–53. Eisenstadt: Schloss Esterházy, 2009.

Fuller, David. "Of Portraits, 'Sapho' and Couperin: Titles and Characters in French Instrumental Music of the High Baroque." *Music and Letters* 78, no. 2 (May 1997): 149–74.

Gambassi, Osvaldo. *L'Accademia filarmonica di Bologna: fondazione, statuti e aggregazioni*. Programma di studi e ricerche sulla cultura e la vita civile del Settecento in Emilia-Romagna promosso dalla Regione 4. Florence: Olschki, 1992.

Genlis, Stéphanie Félicité Ducrest de Saint-Aubin, Comtesse de. *Lessons of a Governess to Her Pupils*. Translated by Anonymous. Dublin: P. Wogan et al., 1792.

———. *Mémoires inédits sur le dix-huitième siècle et la Révolution Française, depuis 1756 jusqu'à nos jours*. 10 vols. Paris: Chez Ladvocat, 1825.

———. *Nouvelle méthode pour apprendre à jouer de la harpe en moins de six mois de leçons*. Paris: Chez Mme. Duhan et compagnie, 1800.

Gerber, Ludwig. *Historisch–Biographisches Lexicon der Tonkünstler: welches Nachrichten von dem Leben und Werken musikalischer Schriftsteller, beruhmter Compositionen, Sänger, Meister auf Instrumenten, Dilettanten, Orgel- und Instrumentenmacher, enthält*. 2 vols. Leipzig: Johann Gottlob Immanuel Breitkopf, 1790.

Ghirardini, Cristina. "*L'improvvisatore* in Genre Scenes by Foreign and Italian Artists in the 19th Century." *L'Idomeneo* 21 (2016): 37–62.

Gidal, Eric. *Ossianic Unconformities: Bardic Poetry in the Industrial Age*. Under the Sign of Nature: Explorations in Ecocriticism. Charlottesville: University of Virginia Press, 2015.

Gillman, Abigail E. "Between Religion and Culture: Mendelssohn, Buber, Rosenzweig and the Enterprise of Biblical Translation." In *Biblical Translation in Context*, edited by Frederick W. Knobloch, 93–114. Studies and Texts in Jewish History and Culture 10. Bethesda: University Press of Maryland, 2002.

Giuli, Paola. "Women Poets and Improvisers: Cultural Assumptions and Literary Values in Arcadia." *Studies in Eighteenth-Century Culture* 32, no. 1 (2003): 69–92.

"Glass Armonica." The Bakken Library and Museum website. https://web.archive.org/web/20070405115543/http://www.thebakken.org/exhibits/mesmer/glass-armonica.htm. Accessed August 1, 2019.

Glover, Jane. *Mozart's Women: His Family, His Friends, His Music*. Oxford: Macmillan, 2005.

Godt, Irving. *Marianna Martines: A Woman Composer in the Vienna of Mozart and Haydn*. Edited by John A. Rice. Eastman Studies in Music. Rochester, NY: University of Rochester Press, 2010.

Goehr, Lydia. *The Imaginary Museum of Musical Works: An Essay in the Philosophy of Music*. Oxford: Oxford University Press, 1992.

Goldsmith, Elizabeth C. *Exclusive Conversations: The Art of Interaction in Seventeenth-Century France*. Philadelphia: University of Pennsylvania Press, 1988.

Goncourt, Edmond de, and Jules de Goncourt. *The Woman of the Eighteenth Century: Her Life, from Birth to Death, Her Love and Her Philosophy in the Worlds of Salon, Shop and Street*. Translated by Jacques Le Clerq and Ralph Roeder. New York: Routledge, 2013 (reprint).

Goodman, Dena. *Becoming a Woman in the Age of Letters*. Ithaca, NY, and London: Cornell University Press, 2009.

———. *The Republic of Letters: A Cultural History of the French Enlightenment*. Cornell Paperbacks. Ithaca, NY: Cornell University Press, 1994.

Goodman, Glenda. *Cultivated by Hand: Amateur Musicians in the New American Republic*. The New Cultural History of Music Series. New York and Oxford: Oxford University Press, 2020.

Goozé, Marjanne E. "What Was the Berlin Jewish Salon Around 1800?" In *Sara Levy's World: Gender, Judaism, and the Bach Tradition in Enlightenment Berlin*, edited by Rebecca Cypess and Nancy Sinkoff, 21–38. Eastman Studies in Music 145. Rochester, NY: University of Rochester Press, 2018.

Gordon, Bonnie. "What Mr. Jefferson Didn't Hear." In *Rethinking Difference in Music Scholarship*, edited by Olivia Bloechl, Melanie Lowe, and Jeffrey Kallberg, 108–32. Cambridge: Cambridge University Press, 2014.

Gordon, Daniel. *Citizens Without Sovereignty: Equality and Sociability in French Thought, 1670–1789*. Princeton, NJ: Princeton University Press, 2017.

Gordon-Seifert, Catherine Elizabeth. *Music and the Language of Love: Seventeenth-Century French Airs*. Music and the Early Modern Imagination. Bloomington: Indiana University Press, 2011.

Graeme, Elizabeth. "A Hymn to the Beauties of Creation. Air, the Birks of Invermay." *The Universal Asylum, and Columbian Magazine* 1 (April 1791): 256.

Green, Emily. *Dedicating Music, 1785–1850*. Eastman Studies in Music, vol. 155. Rochester, NY: University of Rochester Press, 2019.

Grouchy, Sophie de. *Letters on Sympathy (1798): A Critical Edition.* Edited by Karin Brown. Translated by James E. McClellan III. Transactions of the American Philosophical Society Held at Philadelphia for Promoting Useful Knowledge, vol. 98, pt. 4. Philadelphia: American Philosophical Society, 2008.

Gustafson, Bruce. "Madame Brillon et son salon." *Revue de musicologie* 85, no. 2 (1999): 297–332.

———. "The Music of Madame Brillon: A Unified Manuscript Collection from Benjamin Franklin's Circle." *Notes* 43, no. 3 (March 1987): 522–43.

Habermas, Jürgen. *The Structural Transformation of the Public Sphere: An Inquiry into a Category of Bourgeois Society.* Translated by Thomas Burger with the assistance of Frederick Lawrence. Studies in Contemporary German Social Thought. Cambridge, MA: MIT Press, 1991 (reprint).

HaCohen, Ruth. *The Music Libel against the Jews.* New Haven, CT: Yale University Press, 2011.

Hadlock, Heather. "Sonorous Bodies: Women and the Glass Harmonica." *Journal of the American Musicological Society* 53, no. 3 (Autumn 2000): 507–42.

Handel, George Frideric. *Handel's Songs Selected from His Oratorios for the Harpsichord, Voice, Hoboy or German Flute.* London: John Walsh, ca. 1765(?).

Hanning, Barbara Russano. "Conversation and Musical Style in the Late Eighteenth-Century Parisian Salon." *Eighteenth-Century Studies* 22, no. 4 (1989): 512–28.

Harer, Ingeborg. "Alte Musik in Wien um 1800: Neue Erkenntnisse zu Marianne Martines (1744–1812)—Ein Beitrag zur Erinnerung an den 200. Todestag der Musikerin, Sängerin und Komponistin." *Musicologica austriaca* 30 (2011): 27–42.

Hayes, Deborah. "Marie-Emmanuelle Bayon, Later Madame Louis, and Music in Late Eighteenth-Century France." *College Music Symposium* 30, no. 1 (Spring 1990): 14–33.

Haynes, Bruce. *The End of Early Music: A Period Performer's History of Music for the Twenty-First Century.* Oxford and New York: Oxford University Press, 2007.

Head, Matthew. "Rethinking Authorship through Women Composers: *Women Writing Opera: Creativity and Controversy in the Age of the French Revolution*, by Jacqueline Letzter and Robert Adelson." *Women and Music: A Journal of Gender and Culture* 6 (2002): 36–50.

———. *Sovereign Feminine: Music and Gender in Eighteenth-Century Germany.* Berkeley, Los Angeles, and London: University of California Press, 2013.

Heartz, Daniel. "The Beginnings of the Operatic Romance: Rousseau, Sedaine, and Monsigny." *Eighteenth-Century Studies* 15, no. 2 (Winter 1981–1982): 149–78.

———. *Music in European Capitals: The Galant Style, 1720–1780.* New York and London: Norton, 2003.

Hedges, Stephen A. "Dice Music in the Eighteenth Century." *Music and Letters* 59, no. 2 (April 1978): 180–87.

Helfer, Martha B. *The Word Unheard: Legacies of Anti-Semitism in German Literature and Culture.* Evanston, IL: Northwestern University Press, 2011.

Helyard, Erin. "'To Prevent the Abuse of the Open Pedal': Meticulous Pedal Markings from Madame Du Brillon to Moscheles." *Keyboard Perspectives* 9 (2016): 95–118.

Herder, Johann Gottfried. *The Spirit of Hebrew Poetry*. Translated by J. Marsh. Burlington, VT: Edward Smith, 1833.

———. *Vom Geist der Ebräischen Poesie: Eine Anleitung für Liebhaber derselben und der ältesten Geschichte des menschlichen Geistes*. Vol. 2. Dessau: Buchhandlung der Gelehrten, 1783.

Hertz, Deborah. *Jewish High Society in Old Regime Berlin*. New Haven, CT: Yale University Press, 1988.

Heyden-Rynsch, Verena von der. *Europäische Salons: Höhepunkte einer versunkenen weiblichen Kultur*. Munich: Artemis & Winkler, 1992.

Höcker, Karla. *Hauskonzerte in Berlin*. Berlin: Rembrandt Verlag, 1970.

Hoffmann-Erbrecht, Lothar. "Der Nürnberger Musikverleger Johann Ulrich Haffner." *Acta musicologica* 26, no. 3–4 (August–December 1954): 114–26.

Holman, Peter. "Ann Ford Revisited." *Eighteenth-Century Music* 1, no. 2 (2004): 157–81.

———. *Life after Death: The Viola Da Gamba in Britain from Purcell to Dolmetsch*. Woodbridge, UK: Boydell Press, 2010.

The Holy Bible, Containing the Old and New Testaments: Newly Translated Out of the Original Tongues, and with the Former Translations Diligently Compared and Revised. Oxford: Thomas Baskett, 1760.

Hopkinson, Francis. Francis Hopkinson to Robert Bremner, November 28, 1783. https://founders.archives.gov/documents/Jefferson/01-06-02-0285. Accessed July 22, 2020.

———. "L'Allegro. Il Penseroso." *American Magazine and Monthly Chronicle for the British Colonies* 1 (November 1757): 84–88.

———. *The Psalms of David with the Ten Commandments, Creed, Lord's Prayer, &c. in Metre. Also, the Catechism, Confession of Faith, Liturgy, &c. Translated from the Dutch. For the Use of the Reformed Protestant Dutch Church of the City of New-York*. New York: James Parker, 1767.

———. *Seven [Eight] Songs for the Harpsichord or Forte Piano*. Philadelphia: Laitken, 1788.

Hume, David. "Of Luxury." In *Essays and Treatises on Several Subjects*. Vol. 4, *Political Discourses*, 3rd ed. with additions and corrections, 20–35. London: A. Millard; Edinburgh: A. Kincaid and A. Donaldson, 1754.

Irving, David R. M. "Ancient Greeks, World Music, and Early Modern Constructions of Western European Identity." In *Studies on a Global History of Music: A Balzan Musicology Project, 2013–2015*, edited by Reinhard Strohm, 21–41. Abingdon: Routledge, 2018.

Jackson, Barbara Garvey. *"Say You Can Deny Me": A Guide to Surviving Music by Women from the 16th Through the 18th Centuries*. Fayetteville: University of Arkansas Press, 1994.

Jameson, Anna Brownell. *The Diary of an Ennuyée: A New Edition*. Paris: Baudry's European Library, 1836.

Jones, Catherine. *Literature and Music in the Atlantic World, 1767–1867*. Edinburgh Studies in Transatlantic Literatures. Edinburgh: Edinburgh University Press, 2014.

Jones, Jennifer M. "Repackaging Rousseau: Femininity and Fashion in Old Regime France." *French Historical Studies* 18, no. 4 (Autumn 1994): 939–67.

Jones, Richard D. P. "The Keyboard Works: Bach as Teacher and Virtuoso." In *The Cambridge Companion to Bach*, edited by John Butt, 136–53. Cambridge: Cambridge University Press, 1997.

Kale, Steven. *French Salons: High Society and Political Sociability from the Old Regime to the Revolution of 1848*. Baltimore: Johns Hopkins University Press, 2004.

Kauffman, Angelica. *"Mir träumte vor ein paar Nächten, ich hätte Briefe von Ihnen empfangen": Gesammelte Briefe in den Originalsprachen*. Edited by Waltrud Maierhofer. Lengwil am Bodensee: Libelle Verlag, 2001.

Kelly, Michael [and Theodore Hook]. *Reminiscences of Michael Kelly of the King's Theatre, and Theatre Royal, Drury Lane, Including a Period of Nearly Half a Century; with Original Anecdotes of Many Distinguished Persons, Political, Literary, and Musical*. 2 vols. London: Henry Colburn, 1826.

Kerber, Linda K. *Women of the Republic: Intellect and Ideology in Revolutionary America*. Chapel Hill: University of North Carolina Press, 2014.

Keuck, Thekla. *Hofjuden und Kulturbürger: Die Geschichte der Familie Itzig in Berlin*. Jüdische Religion, Geschichte und Kultur, Bd. 12. Göttingen: Vandenhoeck & Ruprecht, 2011.

Kierner, Cynthia A. *Martha Jefferson Randolph, Daughter of Monticello: Her Life and Times*. Chapel Hill: University of North Carolina Press, 2012.

Kirnberger, Johann Philipp. *Oden mit Melodien*. Danzig: Jobst Hermann Flörcke, 1773.

Klorman, Edward. *Mozart's Music of Friends: Social Interplay in the Chamber Works*. Cambridge: Cambridge University Press, 2016.

Kornemann, Matthias. "Zelter's Archive: Portrait of a Collector/Zelters Archiv: Porträt Eines Sammlers." In *The Archive of the Sing-Akademie zu Berlin: Catalogue/Das Archiv der Sing-Akademie Zu Berlin: Katalog*, edited by Axel Fischer and Matthias Kornemann, 19–25. Berlin and New York: De Gruyter, 2010.

Krauss, Anne McClenny. "James Bremner, Alexander Reinagle and the Influence of the Edinburgh Musical Society on Philadelphia." In *Scotland and America in the Age of the Enlightenment*, edited by Richard B. Sher and Jeffrey R. Smitten, 259–74. Edinburgh: Edinburgh University Press, 1990.

Kuijken, Barthold. *The Notation Is Not the Music: Reflections on Early Music Practice and Performance*. Publications of the Early Music Institute. Bloomington and Indianapolis: Indiana University Press, 2013.

Lamb, Jonathan. *The Evolution of Sympathy in the Long Eighteenth Century*. New York: Routledge, 2016.

Landes, Joan B. "Public and Private: Public and Private Lives in Eighteenth-Century France." In *A Cultural History of Women*, edited by Ellen Pollak, vol. 4, *A Cultural History of Women in the Age of Enlightenment*, general editor Linda Kalof, 121–41. London and New York: Bloomsbury Academic, 2013.

———. *Women and the Public Sphere in the Age of the French Revolution*. Ithaca, NY, and London: Cornell University Press, 1988.

Latcham, Michael. "The Apotheosis of Merlin." In *Musique ancienne: Instruments et imagination. Actes des rencontres internationales "harmoniques," Lausanne 2004 / Music of the Past: Instruments and Imagination. Proceedings of the "Harmoniques" International Congress, Lausanne 2004*, edited by Michael Latcham, 271–98. Bern: Peter Lang, 2006.

———. "The Combination of the Piano and the Harpsichord Throughout the Eighteenth Century." In *Instruments à claviers—Expressivité et flexibilité sonore / Keyboard Instruments—Flexibility of Sound and Expression: Actes des rencontres internationales harmoniques / Proceedings of the Harmoniques International Congress, Lausanne 2002*, edited by Thomas Steiner, 113–52. Bern: Peter Lang, 2004.

———. "Swirling from One Level of the Affects to Another: The Expressive *Clavier* in Mozart's Time." *Early Music* 30, no. 4 (November 2002): 502–20.

Lavoisier, Antoine-Laurent, and Marie-Anne Pierrette Paulze Lavoisier to Benjamin Franklin, January 24, 1783. Transcribed at https://franklinpapers.org. Accessed July 14, 2019.

———. *Traité élémentaire de chimie, présenté dans un ordre nouveau et d'après les découvertes modernes par M. Lavoisier . . . avec figures & tableaux*. Paris: chez Cuchet, 1789.

Le Guin, Elisabeth. *Boccherini's Body: An Essay in Carnal Musicology*. Berkeley, Los Angeles, and London: University of California Press, 2006.

———. "A Visit to the Salon de Parnasse." In *Haydn and the Performance of Rhetoric*, edited by Tom Beghin and Sander M. Goldberg, 14–35. Chicago and London: University of Chicago Press, 2007.

Le Veillard, Louis-Guillaume. Louis-Guillaume Le Veillard to Benjamin Franklin, February 21, 1789. https://franklinpapers.org. Accessed July 31, 2019.

Lee, Rensselaer W. "*Ut pictura poesis*: The Humanistic Theory of Painting." *Art Bulletin* 22, no. 4 (December 1940): 197–269.

Leppert, Richard. *Music and Image: Domesticity, Ideology, and Socio-Cultural Formation in Eighteenth-Century England*. Cambridge: Cambridge University Press, 1988.

Lewis, Jayne Elizabeth. "The Eighteenth-Century Psalm." *Oxford Handbooks Online*. http://oxfordhandbooks.com/view/10.1093/oxfordhb/9780199935338.001.0001/oxfordhb-9780199935338-e-150. Accessed August 1, 2020.

L'Hardy, Louis-Eusébe-Henri Gaullieur. *Porte-feuille ichnographique précédé d'une notice architectonographique sur le grand-théâtre de Bordeaux, rédigée d'après des documens authentiques*. Paris: Chez Carilian-Goery, 1828.

Lilti, Antoine. *Le monde des salons: Sociabilité et mondanité à Paris au XVIIIe siècle*. Paris: Fayard, 2005.

———. "Private Lives, Public Space: A New Social History of the Enlightenment." In *The Cambridge Companion to the French Enlightenment*, edited by Daniel Brewer, 14–28. Cambridge: Cambridge University Press, 2014.

———. *The World of the Salons: Sociability and Worldliness in Eighteenth-Century Paris*. Translated by Lydia G. Cochrane. Oxford: Oxford University Press, 2015.

Link, Dorothea. "Vienna's Private Theatrical and Musical Life, 1783–92, as Reported by Count Karl Zinzendorf." *Journal of the Royal Musical Association* 122, no. 2 (1997): 205–57.

Lomazzo, Giovanni Paolo. *Trattato dell'arte della pittura, scoltura, et architettura . . . diviso in sette libri*. Milan: Paolo Gottardo Pontio for Pietro Tini, 1585.

Lopez, Claude-Anne. *Mon cher papa: Franklin and the Ladies of Paris*. New Haven, CT: Yale University Press, 1990.

Lorenz, Michael. "Martines, Maron and a Latin Inscription." October 12, 2012. http://michaelorenz.blogspot.com/2012/10/martines-maron-and-latin-inscription.html. Accessed July 15, 2020.

Loughridge, Deirdre. *Haydn's Sunrise, Beethoven's Shadow: Audiovisual Culture and the Emergence of Musical Romanticism*. Chicago and London: University of Chicago Press, 2016.

———. "Timbre Before Timbre: Listening to the Effects of Organ Stops, Violin Mutes, and Piano Pedals, ca. 1650–1800." In *The Oxford Handbook of Timbre*, edited by Emily I. Dolan and Alexander Rehding, 269–90. New York: Oxford University Press, 2021.

Löwe, Joel Bril. Introduction to Moses Mendelssohn, *Sefer zemirot Yisra'el: hu sefer Tehilim 'im targum Ashkenazi me-ha-rav Rabenu Moshe Ben Menaḥem* [Book of the Songs of Israel: That is, Book of Psalms with a German Translation by the rabbi, our teacher Moses son of Menaḥem]. Edited with introduction by Joel Bril Löwe. Berlin: Shoḥarei ha-tov ve-ha-tushiyah, 1791.

M. D. L. [Charles de Lusse]. *Recueil de romances historiques, tendres, et burlesques, tant anciennes que modernes, avec les airs notés*. s.l.: Par de Lusse d'après Barbier, 1767.

———. *Recueil de romances. Tome second*. s.l.: Par de Lusse d'après Barbier, 1774.

Lütteken, Laurenz. "Zwischen Ohr und Verstand: Moses Mendelssohn, Johann Philipp Kirnberger und die Begründung des 'reinen Satzes' in der Musik." In *Musik und Ästhetik im Berlin Moses Mendelssohns*, edited by Anselm Gerhard, 135–63. Wolfenbütteler Studien zur Aufklärung, Bd. 25. Tübingen: Max Niemeyer Verlag, 1999.

Lutzow, Carl von. "Das Testament der Angelica Kauffmann." *Zeitschrift für bildende Kunst* 24 (1889): 294–300.

Macaulay, Catharine. *Letters on Education; with Observations on Religious and Metaphysical Subjects*. Dublin: H. Chamberlaine et al., 1790.

MacLeod, Jennifer. "The Edinburgh Musical Society: Its Membership and Repertoire, 1728–1797." PhD dissertation, University of Edinburgh, 2001.

Mader, Rodney. "Elizabeth Graeme Fergusson's 'The Deserted Wife.'" *Pennsylvania Magazine of History and Biography* 135, no. 2 (April 2011): 151–90.

Madia, Giuseppe. Introduction to Nicola Nicolini, *Quistioni di dritto, novella edizione*. Naples: Nicola Jovene and C. Pedone Lauriel, 1870.

Mallio, Michele, et al. *Elogio storico della signora Maria Rosa Coccia romana*. Rome: Cannetti, 1780.

Mancini, Giambattista. *Riflessioni pratiche sul canto figurato*. 3rd ed. Milan: Giuseppe Galeazzi, 1777.

Mandeville, Bernard. *The Fable of the Bees, or, Private Vices, Publick Benefits*. London: J. Tonson, 1724.

Manners, Victoria, and George C. Williamson. *Angelica Kauffman, R. A., Her Life and Her Works*. New York: Brentano's, s.d.

Marionneau, Charles. *Victor Louis, architecte du Théâtre de Bordeaux: sa vie, ses travaux et sa correspondance, 1731–1800*. Bordeaux: Imprimerie G. Gounouilhou, 1881.

Marissen, Michael. *Bach & God*. New York and Oxford: Oxford University Press, 2016.

———. *Lutheranism, Anti-Judaism, and Bach's* St. John Passion*: With an Annotated Literal Translation of the Libretto*. New York and Oxford: Oxford University Press, 1998.

Marshall, David. "Adam Smith and the Theatricality of Moral Sentiments." *Critical Inquiry* 10, no. 4 (June 1984): 592–613.

Martini, [Jean-Paul-Gilles]. *Airs du Droit du seigneur et trois romances nouvelles avec accompagnement de harpe ou forté piano*. Paris: Chez le portier de Mr Lenormant d'Etiolles, ca. 1784.

Martindale, Meredith, and Toby Molenaar. *Benjamin Franklin: Citizen of Two Worlds*. Produced by Stanley Cohen and Olivier Frapier. New York: Phoenix/BFA Films & Video, 1979.

Matthison, Friedrich von. *Schriften*. 8 vols. Zurich: Orell and Füssli, 1835.

McVeigh, Simon. *Concert Life in London from Mozart to Haydn*. Cambridge: Cambridge University Press, 1993.

Melton, James Van Horn. *The Rise of the Public in Enlightenment Europe*. New Approaches to European History 22. Cambridge: Cambridge University Press, 2001.

———. "School, Stage, Salon: Musical Cultures in Haydn's Vienna." *Journal of Modern History* 76, no. 2 (June 2004): 251–79.

Mendelssohn, Moses. *Gesammelte Schriften: Jubiläumsausgabe*. 24 vols. Edited by Fritz Bamberger et al. Stuttgart-Bad Canstatt: Frommann, 1971.

———. *Moses Mendelssohn: Writings on Judaism, Christianity, & the Bible*. Edited by Michah Gottlieb. Translated by Curtis Bowman, Elias Sacks, and Allan Arkush. Tauber Institute Series for the Study of European Jewry. Waltham, MA: Brandeis University Press, 2011.

———. "On the Main Principles of the Fine Arts and Sciences." In *Philosophical Writings*, translated by David O. Dahlstrom, 169–91. Cambridge Texts in the History of Philosophy. Cambridge: Cambridge University Press, 1997.

———. Review of *Robert Lowths Akademische Vorlesungen von der heiligen Dichtkunst der Hebräer; nebst einer kurtzen Widerlegung des harianischen Systems von der Prosodie der Hebräer*. *Bibliothek der schönen Wissenschaften und der freyen Künste* 1, no. 1–2 (1757): 122–52, 269–97.

———. *Sefer zemirot Yisra'el: hu sefer Tehilim 'im targum Ashkenazi me-ha-rav Rabenu Moshe Ben Menaḥem* [Book of the Songs of Israel: That is, Book of Psalms with a German Translation by the rabbi, our teacher Moses son of Menaḥem]. Edited with introduction by Joel Bril Löwe. Berlin: Shoḥarei ha-tov ve-ha-tushiyah, 1791.

Metastasio, Pietro. *Lettere del signor Abate Pietro Metastasio*. 5 vols. Nizza: Presso la Società Tipografica, 1786.

———. *Tutte le opere di Pietro Metastasio*. Edited by Bruno Brunelli. Vol. 5, *Lettere*. Milan: A. Mondadori, 1954.

Millot, Claude François Xavier. *Élémens d'histoire generale*. 4 vols. Paris: Durand, 1778.

Milton, John. *Paradise Regain'd: A Poem in Four Books; to Which Is Added Samson Agonistes; and Poems Upon Several Occasions*. London: J. and R. Tonson, 1742.

Moncrif, François-Augustin Paradis de. *Choix de chansons, à commencer de celles du Comte de Champagne*. Paris: s.n., 1755.

———. *Les constantes amours d'Alix et d'Alexis, romance*. s.l.: s.n., 1738.

Moore, Milcah Martha. *Milcah Martha Moore's Book: A Commonplace Book from Revolutionary America*. Edited by Catherine La Couyerre Blecki and Karin A. Wulf. University Park: Pennsylvania State University Press, 1997.

More, Hannah. *Strictures on the Modern System of Female Education*. 2 vols. London: Printed for T. Cadell Jr. and W. Davies, 1799.

Morgan, Elizabeth. "The Accompanied Sonata and the Domestic Novel in Britain at the Turn of the Nineteenth Century." *19th-Century Music* 36, no. 2 (Fall 2012): 88–100.

Morrow, Mary Sue. *Concert Life in Haydn's Vienna: Aspects of a Developing Musical and Social Institution*. Sociology of Music, no. 7. Stuyvesant, NY: Pendragon Press, 1989.

Moseley, Roger. *Keys to Play: Music as a Ludic Medium from Apollo to Nintendo*. Oakland: University of California Press, 2016.

Mozart, Leopold. *Versuch einer gründlichen Violinschule*. Augsburg: Johann Jacob Lotter, 1756.

Naimark-Goldberg, Natalie. "Entrepreneurs in the Library of the Haskalah: Editors and the Production of Maskilic Books" (Hebrew). In *The Library of the Haskalah: The Creation of a Modern Republic of Letters in Jewish Society in the German-Speaking Sphere*, edited by Schmuel Feiner, Zohar Shavit, Natalie Naimark-Goldberg, and Tal Kogman, 112–16. Tel Aviv: Am Oved Publishers, Ltd., 2014.

———. *Jewish Women in Enlightenment Berlin*. Portland, OR: Littman Library of Jewish Civilization, 2013.

Necker, Suzanne. *Mélanges extraits des manuscrits de Mme. Necker*. 3 vols. Paris: Charles Pougens, 1798.

Neve, Richard. *Arts Improvement: Or, Choice Experiments and Observations in Building, Husbandry, Gardening, Mechanicks, Chimistry, Painting, Japaning, Varnishing, Guilding, Inlaying, Embossing, Carving, Preserving Several Things in Their Natural Shape and Colour and in Other Arts and Sciences Profitable and Pleasant*. London: D. Brown, 1703.

November, Nancy. *Cultivating String Quartets in Beethoven's Vienna*. Woodbridge, UK: Boydell Press, 2017.

Offen, Karen. *The Woman Question in France, 1400–1870*. Cambridge and New York: Cambridge University Press, 2017.

Oleskiewicz, Mary. "Quantz's *Quatuors* and Other Works Newly Discovered." *Early Music* 31, no. 4 (November 2003): 484–505.

Ortega, Judith. "Repertorio musical en la casa de Benavente-Osuna: El Yndice de música de la condesa-duquesa de Benavente de 1824." *Revista de Musicología* 28, no. 1 (2005): 366–91.

Ousterhout, Anne M. *The Most Learned Woman in America: A Life of Elizabeth Graeme Fergusson*. Introduction by Susan Stabile. University Park: Pennsylvania State University Press, 2004.

Painter, Karen. "Mozart at Work: Biography and a Musical Aesthetic for the Emerging German Bourgeoisie." *Musical Quarterly* 86, no. 1 (Spring 2002): 186–235.

Pas, Christine de. *Madame Brillon de Jouy et son salon: une musicienne des Lumières, intime de Benjamin Franklin*. Pantin: Petit page, 2014.

Pasquini, Elisabetta. *L'esemplare, o sia, saggio fondamentale pratico di contrappunto: Padre Martini teorico e didatta della musica*. Historiae Musicae Cultores 103. Florence: Olschki, 2004.

Pellettiere, Kelsa. "Friendship and Sociability: A Reexamination of Benjamin Franklin's Friendship with Madame Brillon de Jouy." *Age of Revolutions*, January 12, 2021. https://ageofrevolutions.com/2021/01/12/friendship-and-sociability-a-reexamination-of-benjamin-franklins-friendship-with-madame-brillon-de-jouy/. Accessed June 1, 2021.

Percival, Melissa. "Sentimental Poses in the *Souvenirs* of Élisabeth Vigée Le Brun." *French Studies* 57, no. 2 (2003): 149–65.

Piozzi, Hester Lynch [Thrale]. *Observations and Reflections Made in the Course of a Journey, through France, Italy, and Germany*. 2 vols. London: A. Strahan and T. Cadell, 1789.

———. Hester Lynch Piozzi [formerly Mrs. Thrale; née Salusbury] to Hester Maria Elphinstone, Viscountess Keith [née Thrale], Tuesday, 26 July 1785. *Electronic Enlightenment*, http://www.e-enlightenment.com/item/piozheUD0010156b1c/?letters=corr&s=piozzheste005720&r=58. Accessed August 14, 2018.

Poirier, Jean-Pierre. *La science et l'amour: Madame Lavoisier*. Paris: Pygmalion, 2004.

Potelet, Constant. *Catalogue de livres faisant partie de la bibliothèque de feu Madame Lavoisier, comtesse de Rumford*. Paris: Galliot, 1836.

Prendergast, Amy. *Literary Salons across Britain and Ireland in the Long Eighteenth Century*. Palgrave Studies in the Enlightenment, Romanticism and the Cultures of Print. London: Palgrave Macmillan, 2015.

Raritan Players, directed by Rebecca Cypess. *In Sara Levy's Salon*. Acis Productions, B06ZYP8SRN, 2017.

———. *In the Salon of Madame Brillon: Music and Friendship in Benjamin Franklin's Paris*. Acis Productions, B08ZBJFHSB, 2021.

———. *Sisters, Face to Face: The Bach Legacy in Women's Hands*. Acis Productions, B07QFF618L, 2019.

Rasch, Rudolf. "Introduction" and "Description of the Sources." In Luigi Boccherini, *Sei sonate per tastiera e violino*. Edited by Rudolf Rasch. Bologna: Ut Orpheus Edizioni, 2009.

Redekop, Benjamin W. *Enlightenment and Community: Lessing, Abbt, Herder, and the Quest for a German Public*. Montreal and Kingston: McGill-Queen's University Press, 2000.

Rellstab, Ludwig. *Aus meinem Leben*. 2 vols. s.l.: J. Guttentag, 1861.

Rheinische Kantorei, directed by Hermann Max. *Johann Hermann Schein: Fontana d'Israel, "Israelis Brünnlein 1623."* Capriccio 10 290/91, 1990.

Rice, John A. "Marianna's Weekly Conversazione: An Account by an Italian Visitor

ıttps://sites.google.com/site/johnaricecv/marianna-s-weekly
essed July 19, 2020.
Free Fantasia and the Musical Picturesque. New Perspectives in
:riticism. Cambridge: Cambridge University Press, 2000.
or the Otherworldly Voice of the Glass Armonica." *Keyboard*
1–42.
History of Early American Magazines 1741–1789. New York: Octagon Books Inc., 1966.

Richardson, Samuel. *Pamela: Or Virtue Rewarded . . . In Two Volumes*. 5th ed. London: C. Rivington; J. Osborn, 1741.

Richelet, Pierre. *Dictionnaire de la langue françoise ancienne et moderne . . . nouvelle édition corrigée & augmentée d'un grand nombre d'articles*. 3 vols. Basel: Chez Jean Brandmuller, 1735.

Rigel, Henri-Joseph. *Duo pour piano-forte et clavecin, op. 14 no. 1 [2, and 3]*. Versailles: Éditions du Centre de Musique Baroque de Versailles, 2008.

———. *Sonates en quatuor pour le clavecin avec accompagnement de deux violons, deux cors et violoncelle ad libitum . . . Oeuvre VII*. Paris: l'Auteur, ca. 1772.

———. *Trois duo pour le forte-piano et clavecin . . . oeuvre XIV. On peut exécuter ces duo en quatuor sur le piano-forté avec deux violons et violoncelle qui sont gravés séparément, et qui se vendent en place du clavecin pour le même prix*. Paris: L'auteur, 1778.

Riley, Matthew. *Musical Listening in the German Enlightenment: Attention, Wonder and Astonishment*. Aldershot: Ashgate, 2004.

Riskin, Jessica. *Science in the Age of Sensibility: The Sentimental Empiricists of the French Enlightenment*. Chicago: University of Chicago Press, 2002.

Ritchie, Leslie. *Women Writing Music in Late Eighteenth-Century England: Social Harmony in Literature and Performance*. Performance in the Long Eighteenth Century: Studies in Theatre, Music, Dance. Aldershot, UK, and Burlington, VT: Ashgate, 2008.

Roberts, Meghan K. *Sentimental Savants: Philosophical Families in Enlightenment France*. Chicago: University of Chicago Press, 2016.

Rosand, David. "The Portrait, the Courtier, and Death." In *Castiglione: The Ideal and the Real in Renaissance Culture*, edited by Robert W. Hanning and David Rosand, 91–129. New Haven, CT: Yale University Press, 1983.

Rose, Stephen. *Musical Authorship from Schütz to Bach*. Cambridge: Cambridge University Press, 2019.

Rosenthal, Angela. *Angelica Kauffman: Art and Sensibility*. New Haven, CT: Published for the Paul Mellon Centre for Studies in British Art by Yale University Press, 2006.

Rosman, Moshe. *How Jewish Is Jewish History?* Oxford and Portland, OR: Littman Library of Jewish Civilization, 2007.

Rousseau, Jean-Jacques. *Dictionnaire de musique*. Paris: Veuve Duchesne, 1768.

———. "Lettre à M. d'Alembert." In *Collection complète des oeuvres*, vol. 6. Geneva, 1780. Transcribed at https://www.rousseauonline.ch/pdf/rousseauonline-0029.pdf. Accessed August 3, 2020.

———. *Politics and the Arts: Letter to M. D'Alembert on the Theatre*. Translat
and an introduction by Allan Bloom. Ithaca, NY: Cornell University Press, 19

Roworth, Wendy Wassyng. "Anatomy Is Destiny: Regarding the Body in the Art of Angelica Kauffman." In *Femininity and Masculinity in Eighteenth-Century Art and Culture*, edited by Gill Perry and Michael Rosington, 41–62. New York: Manchester University Press, 1994.

———. "Angelica Kauffman's 'Memorandum of Paintings.'" *The Burlington Magazine* 126, no. 979 (October 1984): 627–30.

———. "Kauffman and the Art of Painting in England." In *Angelica Kauffman: A Continental Artist in Georgian England*, edited by Wendy Wassyng Roworth and David Alexander, 11–95. London: Reaktion Books, 1992.

———. "'The Residence of the Arts': Angelica Kauffman's Place in Rome." In *Italy's Eighteenth Century: Gender and Culture in the Age of the Grand Tour*, edited by Paula Findlen, Wendy Wassyng Roworth, and Catherine M. Sama, 151–71. Stanford, CA: Stanford University Press, 2009.

Ruelland, Jacques. "Marie-Anne Pierrette Paulze-Lavoisier, comtesse de Rumford (1758–1836): Lumière surgie de l'ombre." *Dix-huitième Siècle* 36, no. 1 (2004): 99–112.

Rush, Benjamin. "An Account of the Life and Character of Mrs. Elizabeth Ferguson." *The Port Folio* 1 (1809): 520–27.

———. *Essays, Literary, Moral and Philosophical*. 2nd ed. Philadelphia: Thomas and William Bradford, 1806.

Russell, Gillian, and Clara Tuite. "Introducing Romantic Sociability." In *Romantic Sociability: Social Networks and Literary Culture in Britain, 1770–1840*, edited by Gillian Russell and Clara Tuite, 1–23. Cambridge: Cambridge University Press, 2002.

Ryerson, Richard Alan, ed. *The Adams Papers*, Adams Family Correspondence, vol. 6, *December 1784–December 1785*: 299–312. Cambridge, MA: Harvard University Press, 1993.

Sacks, Elias. *Moses Mendelssohn's Living Script: Philosophy, Practice, History, Judaism*. Bloomington: Indiana University Press, 2017.

Sage, Jack, Susana Friedmann, and Roger Hickman. "Romance." *Grove Music Online*, 2001. https://www.oxfordmusiconline.com. Accessed July 18, 2019.

Sansom, Hannah Callender. *The Diary of Hannah Callender Sansom: Sense and Sensibility in the Age of the American Revolution*. Edited by Susan E. Klepp and Karin A. Wulf. Cornell Paperbacks. Ithaca, NY, and London: Cornell University Press, 2010.

Schobert, Johann. *Ein sonderbares musicalisches Stuck; welches auf dem Clavier, der Violin und dem Bass, und zwar auf verschiedene Arten, kan gespielet werden*. Nürnberg: Winterschmidt, n.d.

———. *Sonates en trio pour le clavecin avec accompagnement de violon et basse ad libitum dédiées a Madame Brillon de Joüy*. Paris: Vendôme, 1765.

Schönfeld, Johann Ferdinand von. *Jahrbuch der Tonkunst von Wien und Prag*. s.l.: im von Schönfeldischen Verlag, 1796.

Schulenberg, David. *The Music of Wilhelm Friedemann Bach*. Eastman Studies in Music 79. Rochester, NY: University of Rochester Press, 2010.

Schulze, Hans-Joachim, ed. *Bach-Dokumente III: Dokumente zum Nachwirken Johann Sebastian Bachs, 1750–1800*. Kassel: Bärenreiter, 1984.

Scurr, Ruth. "Inequality and Political Stability from Ancien Régime to Revolution: The Reception of Adam Smith's *Theory of Moral Sentiments* in France." *History of European Ideas* 35, no. 4 (2009): 441–49.

Ségur, Pierre Marie Maurice Henri, Marquis de. *Le royaume de la rue Saint-Honoré: Madame Geoffrin et sa fille*. Paris: Calmann Lévy, 1897.

Sela, Yael. "Longing for the Sublime: Music and Jewish Self-Consciousness at Bach's *St. Matthew Passion* in Biedermeier Berlin." In *Sara Levy's World: Gender, Judaism, and the Bach Tradition in Enlightenment Berlin*, edited by Rebecca Cypess and Nancy Sinkoff, 147–80. Eastman Studies in Music 145. Rochester, NY: University of Rochester Press, 2018.

———. "Songs of the Nation: The Book of Psalms in Late Eighteenth-Century Jewish Enlightenment." *Musical Quarterly* 101, no. 4 (Winter 2018): 331–62.

———. "The Voice of the Psalmist: On the Performative Role of Psalms in Moses Mendelssohn's *Jerusalem*." In *Psalms In/On Jerusalem*, edited by Ilana Pardes and Ophir Münz-Manor, 109–34. Perspectives on Jewish Texts and Contexts, vol. 9. Berlin: De Gruyter, 2019.

Sela-Teichler, Yael. "Music, Acculturation, and Haskalah between Berlin and Königsberg in the 1780s." *Jewish Quarterly Review* 103, no. 3 (2013): 352–84.

Seward, Anna. *The Poetical Works of Anna Seward: With Extracts from Her Literary Correspondence . . . in Three Volumes*. Edited by Walter Scott. 3 vols. Edinburgh: James Balllantyne and Co., 1810.

Seydelmann, Franz. *Sechs Sonaten für zwo Personen auf einem Clavier*. Leipzig: Gottlob Immanuel Breitkopf, 1781.

"Sketches of Portraits: The Fantasy Figures Identified." National Gallery of Art website. https://www.nga.gov/features/fantasy-figures-identified.html. Accessed August 6, 2019.

Slotten, Martha C. "Elizabeth Graeme Ferguson: A Poet in 'The Athens of North America.'" *Pennsylvania Magazine of History and Biography* 108, no. 3 (July 1984): 259–88.

Small, Christopher. *Musicking: The Meanings of Performing and Listening*. Middletown, CT: Wesleyan University Press, 1998.

Smith, Adam. *The Theory of Moral Sentiments*. 2nd ed. London: Millar, 1769.

Solie, Ruth. "Whose Life? The Gendered Self in Schumann's *Frauenliebe* Songs." In *Music and Text: Critical Inquiries*, edited by Steven P. Scher, 219–40. Cambridge: Cambridge University Press, 1992.

Sonneck, Oscar G. *Francis Hopkinson, the First American Poet–Composer, 1737–1791 and James Lyon, Patrior, Preacher, Psalmodist, 1735–1794*. New York: Da Capo Press, 1967.

Sorkin, David. *Moses Mendelssohn and the Religious Enlightenment*. London: Peter Halban, 2012.

———. *The Religious Enlightenment: Protestants, Jews, and Catholics from London to Vienna*. Jews, Christians, and Muslims from the Ancient to the Modern World. Princeton, NJ: Princeton University Press, 2008.

Spiel, Hilde. *Fanny von Arnstein: Daughter of the Enlightenment*. Translated by Christine Shuttleworth. Introduction by Michael Z. Wise. New York: New Vessel Press, 2013.

Sposato, Jeffrey S. *The Price of Assimilation: Felix Mendelssohn and the Nineteenth-Century Anti-Semitic Tradition*. Oxford: Oxford University Press, 2006.

Stabile, Susan. "Introduction: Elizabeth Fergusson and British–American Literary History." In Anne M. Ousterhout, *The Most Learned Woman in America: A Life of Elizabeth Graeme Fergusson*, 1–28. University Park: Pennsylvania State University Press, 2004.

———. *Memory's Daughters: The Material Culture of Remembrance in Eighteenth-Century America*. Ithaca, NY, and London: Cornell University Press, 2004.

———. "Salons and Power in the Era of Revolution: From Literary Coteries to Epistolary Enlightenment." In *Benjamin Franklin and Women*, edited by Larry E. Tise, 129–48. University Park: Pennsylvania State University Press, 2000.

Staves, Susan. "The Learned Female Soprano." In *Bluestockings Displayed: Portraiture, Performance and Patronage, 1730–1830*, edited by Elizabeth Eger, 141–63. Cambridge: Cambridge University Press, 2013.

Steele, Brian. *Thomas Jefferson and American Nationhood*. Cambridge Studies on the American South. Cambridge: Cambridge University Press, 2012.

Stockton, Annis Boudinot. *Only for the Eye of a Friend: The Poems of Annis Boudinot Stockton*. Edited by Carla Mulford. Charlottesville and London: University Press of Virginia, 1995.

Stras, Laurie. *Women and Music in Sixteenth-Century Ferrara*. New Perspectives in Music History and Criticism. Cambridge: Cambridge University Press, 2018.

Strobel, Heidi A. "Royal 'Matronage' of Women Artists in the Late-18th Century." *Woman's Art Journal* 26, no. 2 (Autumn 2005–Winter 2006): 3–9.

"Studying the Lied: Hermeneutic Traditions and the Challenge of Performance. Convened by Jennifer Ronyak." *Journal of the American Musicological Society* 67, no. 2 (2014): 543–81.

Sturz, Peter Helfrich. *Schriften*. Leipzig: Weidmanns Erben und Reich, 1786.

Sutcliffe, W. Dean. *Instrumental Music in an Age of Sociability: Haydn, Mozart and Friends*. Cambridge: Cambridge University Press, 2020.

———. "The Shapes of Sociability in the Instrumental Music of the Later Eighteenth Century." *Journal of the Royal Musical Association* 138, no. 1 (2013): 1–45.

Swack, Jeanne. "Quantz and the Sonata in E-flat Major for Flute and Cembalo, BWV 1031." *Early Music* 23, no. 1 (1995): 31–53.

Tapray, Jean-François. *Four* Symphonies concertantes *for Harpsichord and Piano with Orchestra* Ad libitum. Edited by Bruce Gustafson. Recent Researches in the Music of the Classical Era 44. Madison, WI: A-R Editions, 1995.

Taruskin, Richard. "On Letting the Music Speak for Itself." In *Text and Act: Essays on Music and Performance*, 51–66. New York and Oxford: Oxford University Press, 1995.

Tasso, Torquato. *Jerusalem Delivered (Gerusalemme Liberata)*. Edited and translated by Anthony M. Esolen. Baltimore and London: Johns Hopkins University Press, 2000.

Tate, Nahum, and Nicholas Brady. *A New Version of the Psalms of David, Fitted to the Tunes Used in Churches*. London: M. Clark, 1696.

Taylor, Diana. *The Archive and the Repertoire: Performing Cultural Memory in the Americas*. Durham, NC, and London: Duke University Press, 2003.

Thormählen, Wiebke. "Playing with Art: Musical Arrangements as Educational Tools in van Swieten's Vienna." *Journal of Musicology* 27, no. 3 (Summer 2010): 342–76.

Tillman, Kacy Dowd. "Women Left Behind: Female Loyalism, Coverture, and Grace Growden Galloway's Empire of Self." In *Women's Narratives of the Early Americas and the Formation of Empire*, edited by Mary McAleer Balkun and Susan C. Imbarrato, 141–55. New York: Palgrave Macmillan, 2016.

Todd, R. Larry. *Mendelssohn: A Life in Music*. New York and Oxford: Oxford University Press, 2003.

———. *Mendelssohn Essays*. New York: Routledge, 2008.

Tomaselli, Sylvana. "The Enlightenment Debate on Women." *History Workshop* 20 (Autumn 1985): 101–24.

Trouflaut, Gilbert. "Lettre aux auteurs de ce journal, sur les clavecins en peau de buffle, inventés par Mr. Pascal." *Journal de musique* 5 (December 1773): 10–19.

Varnhagen, Rahel Levin. *Edition Rahel Levin Varnhagen*. Edited by Barbara Hahn and Ursula Isselstein. Munich: Beck Verlag, 1997–.

Varnhagen, Rahel. *Rahel: ein Buch des Andenkens für ihre Freunde*. Edited by Barbara Hahn. 6 vols. Göttingen: Wallstein Verlag, 2011.

Vidal, Mary. "David among the Moderns: Art, Science, and the Lavoisiers." *Journal of the History of Ideas* 56, no. 4 (October 1995): 595–623.

Vigée Le Brun, Louise-Élisabeth. *Souvenirs: notes et portraits 1755–1789*. Paris: Arthème Fayard, [1909].

Vocal Concert Dresden, directed by Peter Kopp. *Bachs Schüler: Motetten*. Carus 83.263, 2008.

Voskuhl, Adelheid. *Androids in the Enlightenment: Mechanics, Artisans, and Cultures of the Self*. Chicago and London: University of Chicago Press, 2013.

Waltz, Sarah Clemmens. Introduction. In *German Settings of Ossianic Texts, 1770–1815*, edited by Sarah Clemmens Waltz, ix–xxxiv. Middleton, WI: A-R Editions, 2016.

Weckel, Ulrike. "A Lost Paradise of a Female Culture? Some Critical Questions Regarding the Scholarship on Late Eighteenth- and Early Nineteenth-Century German Salons." *German History* 18, no. 3 (2000): 310–36.

Wesley, John. "Thoughts on the Power of Music." *Arminian Magazine* (February 1781): 103–7.

Wessely, Naphtali Herz, ed. *Divrei Shalom Ve-Emet*. Berlin: Ḥevrat Ḥinuch Ne'arim, 1782.

Wharton, Anne Hollingsworth. *Salons Colonial and Republican*. Philadelphia and London: J. B. Lippincott Company, 1900.

White, Harry. "'If It's Baroque, Don't Fix It': Reflections on Lydia Goehr's 'Work-Concept' and the Historical Integrity of Musical Composition." *Acta Musicologica* 69, no. 1 (1997): 94–104.

Wilmot, Catherine. *An Irish Peer on the Continent (1801–1803). Being a Narrative of the Tour of Stephen, 2nd Earl Mount Cashell, Through France, Italy, Etc., as Related by*

Catherine Wilmot. Edited by Thomas U. Sadleir. London: Williams and Norgate, 1920.

Winckelmann, Johann Joachim. Letter of August 18, 1764. In Johann Winckelmann, *Johann Winckelmanns sämtliche Werke. Einzige vollständige Ausgabe*, edited by Joseph Eiselein, 96–97. Donauöschingen: im Verlag deutscher Classiker, 1825.

Winter, Susanne. "Performatività e improvvisazione: L'artista Teresa Bandettini Landucci." *Italica Wratislaviensia* 10, no. 2 (2019): 161–74.

Wolff, Christoph. "A Bach Cult in Late-Eighteenth-Century Berlin: Sara Levy's Musical Salon." *Bulletin of the American Academy of Arts and Sciences* 58, no. 3 (Spring 2005): 26–31.

———. "Recovered in Kiev: Bach et al. A Preliminary Report on the Music Archive of the Berlin Sing-Akademie." *Notes*, 2nd series, 58, no. 2 (December 2001): 259–71.

———. "Sara Levy's Musical Salon and Her Bach Collection." In *Sara Levy's World: Gender, Judaism, and the Bach Tradition in Enlightenment Berlin*, edited by Rebecca Cypess and Nancy Sinkoff, 39–51. Eastman Studies in Music 145. Rochester, NY: University of Rochester Press, 2018.

Wolff, Sabatia Joseph. *Maimoniana: oder Rhapsodien zur Charakteristik Salomon Maimon's aus seinem Privatleben gesammelt*. Berlin: G. Hayn, 1813.

Wollny, Peter. "Anmerkungen zur Bach-Pflege im Umfeld Sara Levys." In *"Zu groß, zu unerreichbar": Bach-Rezeption im Zeitalter Mendelssohns und Schumanns*, edited by Anselm Hartinger, Christoph Wolff, and Peter Wollny, 39–50. Wiesbaden, Leipzig, and Paris: Breitkopf & Härtel, 2007.

———. "'Ein förmlicher Sebastian und Philipp Emanuel Bach-Kultus': Sara Levi, geb. Itzig, und ihr musikalisch-literarischer Salon." In *Musik und Ästhetik im Berlin Moses Mendelssohns*, edited by Anselm Gerhard, 217–55. Wolfenbütteler Studien zur Aufklärung. Tübingen: Max Niemeyer, 1999.

———. *"Ein förmlicher Sebastian und Philipp Emanuel Bach-Kultus": Sara Levy und ihr musikalisches Wirken, mit einer Dokumentensammlung zur musikalischen Familiengeschichte der Vorfahren von Felix Mendelssohn Bartholdy*. Beiträge zur Geschichte der Bach-Rezeption, Bd. 2. Wiesbaden: Breitkopf & Härtel, 2010.

———. "Sara Levy and the Making of Musical Taste in Berlin." *Musical Quarterly* 77, no. 4 (Winter 1993): 651–88.

Wollstonecraft, Mary. *Thoughts on the Education of Daughters, with Reflections on Female Conduct in the More Important Duties of Life*. London: J. Johnson, 1787.

Wood, Gillen D'Arcy. "The Female Penseroso: Anna Seward, Sociable Poetry, and the Handelian Consensus." *Modern Language Quarterly* 67, no. 4 (December 2006): 451–77.

———. "'Have You Met Miss Ford?' Or, Accomplishment Revisited." *European Romantic Review* 23, no. 3 (2012): 283–91.

Wyngaard, Amy S. *From Savage to Citizen: The Invention of the Peasant in the French Enlightenment*. Newark: University of Delaware Press, 2004.

Yearsley, David. *Bach and the Meanings of Counterpoint*. New Perspectives in Music History and Criticism. Cambridge: Cambridge University Press, 2002.

———. "'Nothing More to Conquer: Müthel's *Duetto* in the Burney Drawing Room and Beyond." *Keyboard Perspectives* 9 (2016): 1–31.

Young, Arthur. *Travels during the Years 1787, 1788, and 1789*. London: W. Richardson, 1792.

Zohn, Steven. "The Sociability of Salon Culture and Carl Philipp Emanuel Bach's Quartets." In *Sara Levy's World: Gender, Judaism, and the Bach Tradition in Enlightenment Berlin*, edited by Rebecca Cypess and Nancy Sinkoff, 205–42. Eastman Studies in Music 145. Rochester, NY: University of Rochester Press, 2018.

*

Index

Page numbers in italics refer to figures.